ALASKA ATLAS
& GAZETTEER™

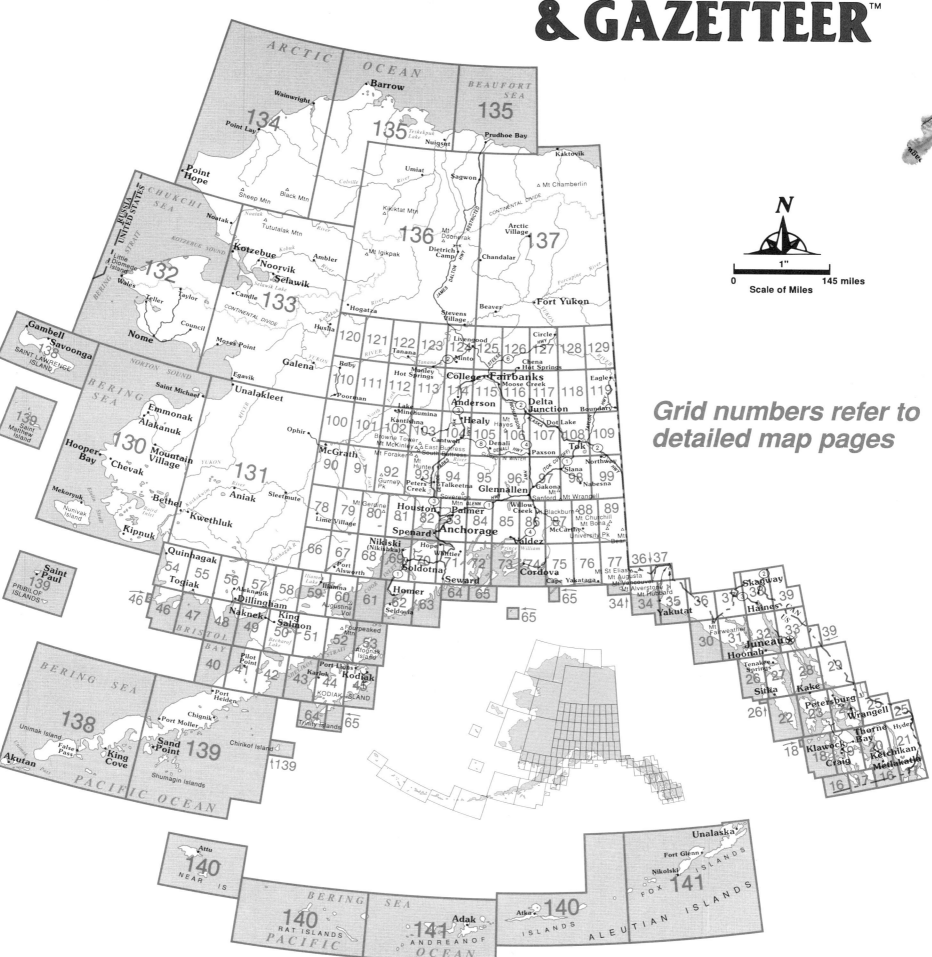

Grid numbers refer to detailed map pages

Nothing in this publication implies the right to use private property. There may be private inholdings within the boundaries of public reservations. Landowner restrictions must be respected.

Many roads are closed in winter. For more information, contact the Alaska Department of Transportation at 1-800-478-7675.

This Atlas is not intended for marine or aeronautical navigation. Source for landing area information: FAA Sectional Aeronautical Charts.

Listings may be seasonal and may have admission fees. Please be sure to confirm this information when making plans.

FIRST EDITION
Copyright © 1992 DeLorme Mapping
P.O. Box 298, Freeport, Maine 04032   (207) 865-4171
All rights reserved.
ISBN 0-89933-201-3

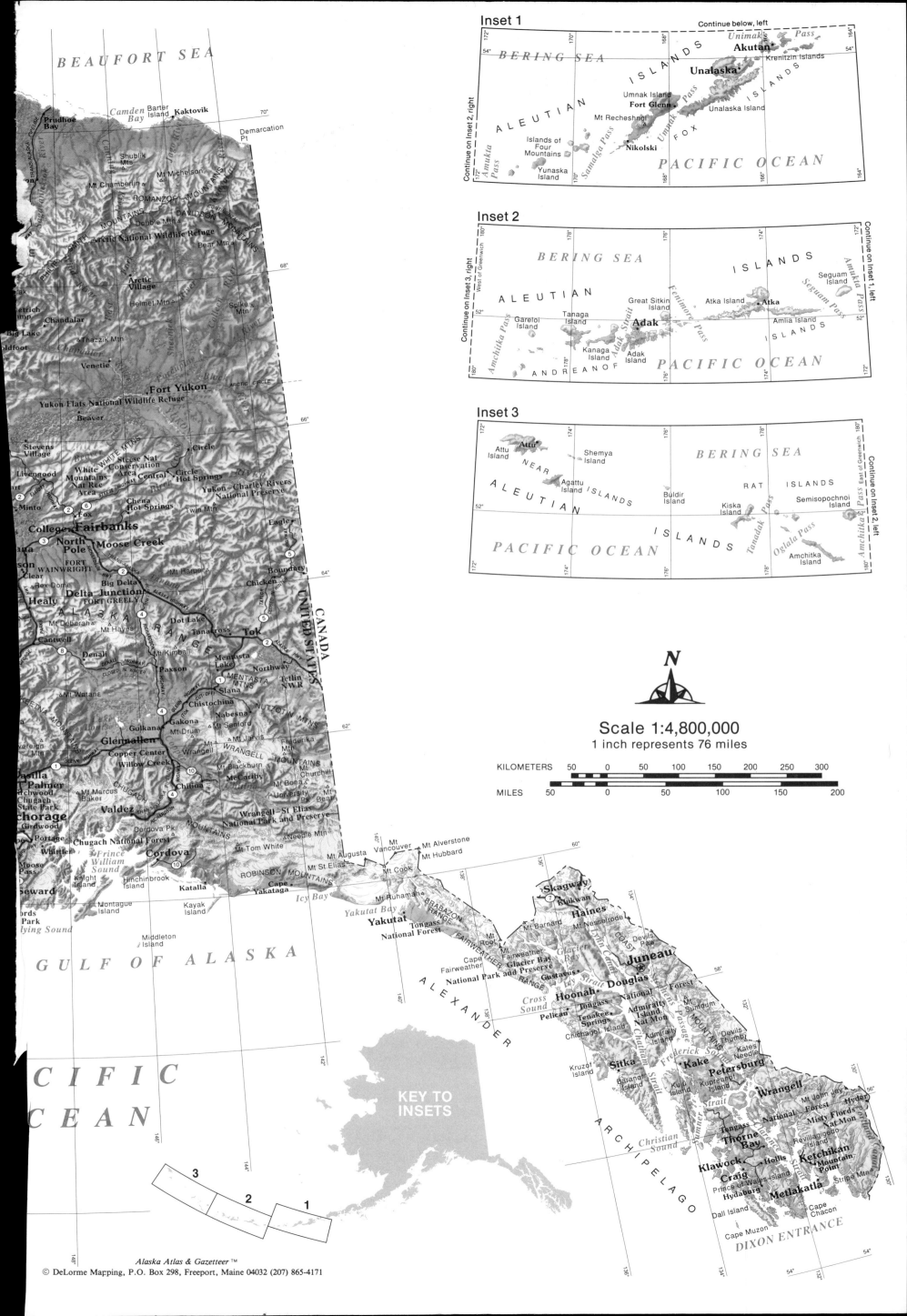

ALASKA
PHYSICAL RELIEF

ARCTIC OCEAN

Barrow · Point Barrow
Dease Inlet
Peard Bay · Smith Bay
Wainwright
Icy Cape
Alaktak
Harrison Bay
Point Lay
National Petroleum Reserve in Alaska
Nuiqsut
Howard Hill
Umiat

CHUKCHI SEA

Cape Lisburne · Wevok
Point Hope
ISBURNE PENINSULA
Alaska Maritime National Wildlife Refuge
DE LONG MOUNTAINS
Meat Mtn · LOOKOUT RIDGE · Anaku River · Colville River
Black Mtn
Sheep Mtn
BROOKS
Imnavait M.
RANGE
Kivalina
MULGRAVE HILLS · Noatak
Tututalak Mtn · Mishaguk Mtn · Noatak National Preserve
Kikiktat Mtn
ARCTIC CIRCLE
Cape Krusenstern National Monument
Noatak
BAIRD MOUNTAINS
Gates of the Arctic National Park and Preserve
ENDICOTT MOUNTAINS
Anaktuvuk Pass
IGICHUK HILLS
Kobuk Valley National Park
Mt Igikpak
Silvasheen Mtn
Matthews Dome
Wiseman

RUSSIA
UNITED STATES

Kotzebue
Shishmaref
KOTZEBUE SOUND
Cape Espenberg
Kiana
Ambler
WARING MOUNTAINS
ALATNA HILLS
Bettles · Evansville
Noorvik
Selawik National Wildlife Refuge
Anguikada Pk
Allakaket · Kanuti National Wildlife Refuge
Selawik
SELAWIK HILLS
PURCELL MOUNTAINS
Hogatza
BERING STRAIT
Big Diomede Island · Little Diomede Island
Bering Land Bridge National Preserve
Deering
SELAWIK HILLS
Hughes
Huslia
Wales · Cape Prince of Wales
CONTINENTAL DIVIDE
Candle
Buckland
Koyukuk National Wildlife Refuge
BAY MOUNTAINS
Mt Tozi

Prince of Wales
King Island
Cape Douglas
YORK MTNS
Taylor
Teller
SEWARD PENINSULA
Council
Koyukuk
Wolf Mtn
Tanana
Tofty
Eureka
Ramp

Gambell
KIGLUAIK MTNS · Mt Osborn
BENDELEBEN MTNS
DARBY MTNS
Moses Point
Nulato
Innoko NWR
Galena · Ruby
Nowitna National Wildlife Refuge
Mooseheart Mtn
Manley Hot Springs

Savoonga · Atuk Mtn
SAINT LAWRENCE ISLAND
Nome · Cape Nome
Norton Bay
Debauch Mtn
Long
Poorman
Nen
Ander

BERING SEA

NORTON SOUND
Unalakleet
Egavik
Khotol Mtn
Innoko National Wildlife Refuge
Ophir
Lake Minchumina
Kantishna

Stuart Island
Stebbins
Saint Michael
Pastol Bay
Mt McDonald
Shageluk
Iditarod
McGrath
Sterling Landing
Denali National Park and Preserve
Mt McKinley · East Buttress
Mt Foraker · South Buttress
Mt Hunter

Saint Matthew Island
Emmonak
Alakanuk
Kotlik
Saint Marys
Wolf Creek Mtn
Holy Cross
Flat
Browne Tower
Peters Creek
Kosnat Pk
Talkeetna
Trapper Creek

Mountain Village
Scammon Bay
Pilot Station
Marshall
Russian Mission
KUSKOKWIM RIVER
Sleetmute
Mt Hesperus
Mt Gerdine
Willow
Houston

Cape Romanzof
Hooper Bay
Chevak
Yukon Delta National Wildlife Refuge
Lower Kalskag
Aniak
Lime Village
Cairn Mtn
Mt Torbert
Eagle River
Spenard · An

Hazen Bay
Nelson Island
Mekoryuk
Nunivak Island
Etolin Strait
Yukon Delta NWR
Kasigluk
Toksook Bay
Tuntutuliak
Bethel · Kwethluk
Taluksak
KILBUCK MOUNTAINS
TAYLOR MOUNTAINS
COOK INLET
Nikiski (Nikishka) · Sterling
Kenai
Soldotna
Kenai Cooper Landing
Kasilof

Kipnuk
Chefornak
Eek
Glenuk Mtn
Wood-Tikchik State Park
Redoubt Vol
Lake Clark National Park and Preserve
Clam Gulch
Kenai NWR
Ninilchik
Happy Valley
Kachemak · Kenai National

Quinhagak
KUSKOKWIM BAY
Kanektok River
ARIKON
Goodnews Bay
Togiak National Wildlife Refuge
MOUNTAINS
Aleknagik
New Stuyahok
Iliamna
Newhalen
Iliamna Lake
Port Alsworth
Iliamna Vol
Anchor Point
Homer
Seldovia
Kachemak Bay State Park
KENAI MTNS

Togiak
Togiak Bay
Manokotak
Dillingham
Naknek
Augustine Vol
Kennedy Entrance
Barren Islands

Platinum
Cape Newenham
Hagemeister Island
Cape Constantine
King Salmon
Katmai National Park and Preserve
Fourpeaked Mtn
Stevenson Entrance
Shuyak Island
Afognak Island

Saint Paul Island
Saint Paul
BRISTOL BAY
Kvichak Bay
Egegik
Becharof NWR
SHELIKOF STRAIT
Port Lions
Kodiak
KODIAK ISLAND
Karluk
Koniag Pk

PRIBILOF ISLANDS
Saint George
Saint George Island
Pilot Point
Ugashik
ALASKA PENINSULA
Alaska Peninsula NWR
Wide Bay
ALEUTIAN
Kodiak National Wildlife Refuge
Karluk
PA

Port Heiden
Aniakchak National Monument and Preserve
Sutwik Island
Sitkinak Strait
Trinity Islands
Chirikof Island

Herendeen Bay
Mt Veniaminof
Chignik
Chignik Bay
Refuge
Semidi Islands

Izembek National Wildlife Refuge
Cold Bay
Pavlof Vol
Port Moller
ALASKA PENINSULA
Perryville
Stepovak Bay

Unimak Island
False Pass
Shishaldin Vol
Ikatan Bay
King Cove
Deer Island
Alaska Peninsula National
Unga I
Sand Point
Nagai I
Shumagin Islands
Sanak Islands

Continue on Inset 1, top
Unimak Pass

ALASKA
PERSPECTIVES

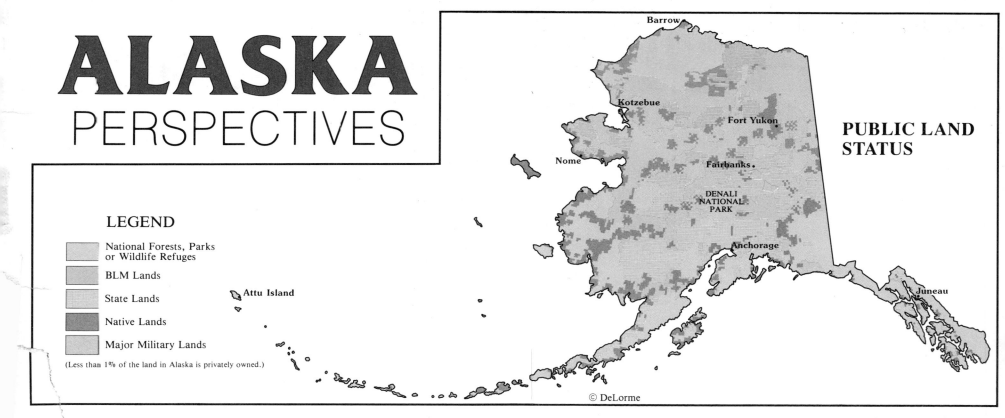

PUBLIC LAND STATUS

LEGEND

- National Forests, Parks or Wildlife Refuges
- BLM Lands
- State Lands
- Native Lands
- Major Military Lands

(Less than 1% of the land in Alaska is privately owned.)

© DeLorme

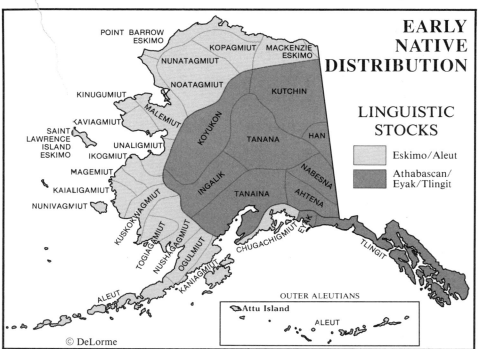

EARLY NATIVE DISTRIBUTION

LINGUISTIC STOCKS

- Eskimo/Aleut
- Athabascan/ Eyak/Tlingit

© DeLorme

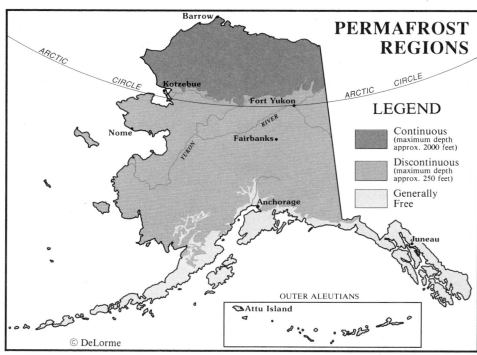

PERMAFROST REGIONS

LEGEND

- Continuous (maximum depth approx. 2000 feet)
- Discontinuous (maximum depth approx. 250 feet)
- Generally Free

© DeLorme

TEMPERATURE/PRECIPITATION/DAYLIGHT HOURS
average minimum/maximum temperatures (Fahrenheit); precipitation in inches

		Anchorage	Barrow	Bethel	Fairbanks	Juneau	Ketchikan	Kodiak	Nome		
January	Temperature	8/25	−20/−14	−5/13	−17/−1	22/29	26/38	24/33	−4/13	Temperature	January
	Precipitation	0.80	0.20	0.81	0.55	3.98	14.01	9.52	0.88	Precipitation	
	Daylight Hours	6:25	0	6:31	5:07	7:07	7:43	7:16	5:16	Daylight Hours	
February	Temperature	13/27	−24/−20	−2/20	−17/7	25/36	30/40	24/37	−8/10	Temperature	February
	Precipitation	0.86	0.18	0.71	0.41	3.66	12.36	5.67	0.56	Precipitation	
	Daylight Hours	9:04	6:58	9:07	8:31	9:23	9:41	9:28	8:34	Daylight Hours	
March	Temperature	12/35	−30/−15	4/26	−5/23	30/40	31/44	27/39	−4/14	Temperature	March
	Precipitation	0.65	0.15	0.80	0.37	3.24	12.22	5.16	0.63	Precipitation	
	Daylight Hours	11:44	11:32	11:41	11:41	11:46	11:48	11:46	11:41	Daylight Hours	
April	Temperature	26/45	−8/3	14/36	18/41	37/49	36/49	30/40	7/25	Temperature	April
	Precipitation	0.63	0.20	0.65	0.28	2.83	11.93	4.47	0.67	Precipitation	
	Daylight Hours	14:42	16:31	14:39	15:10	14:24	14:08	14:21	15:08	Daylight Hours	
May	Temperature	36/55	14/24	32/51	35/60	38/55	40/59	36/52	26/40	Temperature	May
	Precipitation	0.63	0.16	0.83	0.57	3.46	9.06	6.65	0.58	Precipitation	
	Daylight Hours	17:27	24:00	17:21	18:39	16:47	16:12	16:39	18:29	Daylight Hours	
June	Temperature	46/62	28/39	42/61	46/68	43/63	46/63	41/56	38/54	Temperature	June
	Precipitation	1.02	0.36	1.29	1.29	3.02	7.36	5.72	1.14	Precipitation	
	Daylight Hours	19:18	24:00	19:07	21:39	18:15	17:26	18:04	21:21	Daylight Hours	
July	Temperature	51/65	34/45	45/66	50/72	48/65	50/64	48/60	45/57	Temperature	July
	Precipitation	1.96	0.87	2.18	1.84	4.09	7.80	3.80	2.18	Precipitation	
	Daylight Hours	18:27	24:00	18:21	20:11	17:36	16:54	17:26	20:00	Daylight Hours	
August	Temperature	45/64	34/44	46/61	45/67	48/65	51/66	49/60	45/56	Temperature	August
	Precipitation	2.31	0.97	3.65	1.82	5.10	10.60	4.03	3.20	Precipitation	
	Daylight Hours	15:51	19:03	15:47	16:35	15:25	15:02	15:20	16:31	Daylight Hours	
September	Temperature	40/55	28/35	38/53	35/55	44/58	45/59	45/55	35/47	Temperature	September
	Precipitation	2.51	0.64	2.58	1.02	6.25	13.61	7.18	2.59	Precipitation	
	Daylight Hours	12:57	13:31	12:56	13:06	12:51	12:46	12:50	13:05	Daylight Hours	
October	Temperature	26/42	9/19	24/38	16/31	38/49	41/51	35/49	23/33	Temperature	October
	Precipitation	1.86	0.51	1.48	0.81	7.64	22.55	7.85	1.38	Precipitation	
	Daylight Hours	10:07	8:51	10:09	9:47	10:20	10:31	10:22	9:48	Daylight Hours	
November	Temperature	15/28	−7/4	11/30	−7/11	30/38	35/45	30/43	10/20	Temperature	November
	Precipitation	1.08	0.27	0.98	0.67	5.13	17.90	6.89	1.02	Precipitation	
	Daylight Hours	7:18	2:37	7:23	6:19	7:52	8:22	7:59	6:25	Daylight Hours	
December	Temperature	6/21	−19/−12	−2/19	−15/0	25/33	31/39	25/35	−4/11	Temperature	December
	Precipitation	1.06	0.17	0.95	0.73	4.48	15.82	7.39	0.82	Precipitation	
	Daylight Hours	5:32	0	5:41	3:49	6:25	7:08	6:35	4:00	Daylight Hours	

SIZE COMPARISON

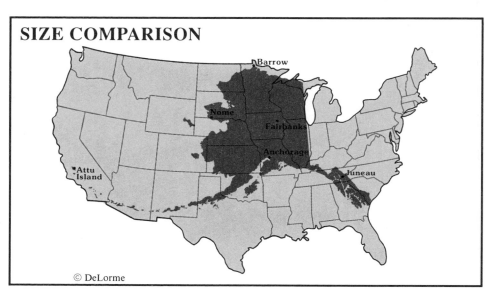

© DeLorme

POLAR VIEW
(air distances in miles)

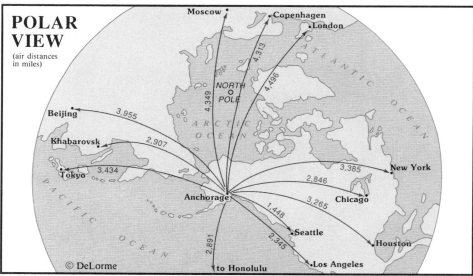

© DeLorme

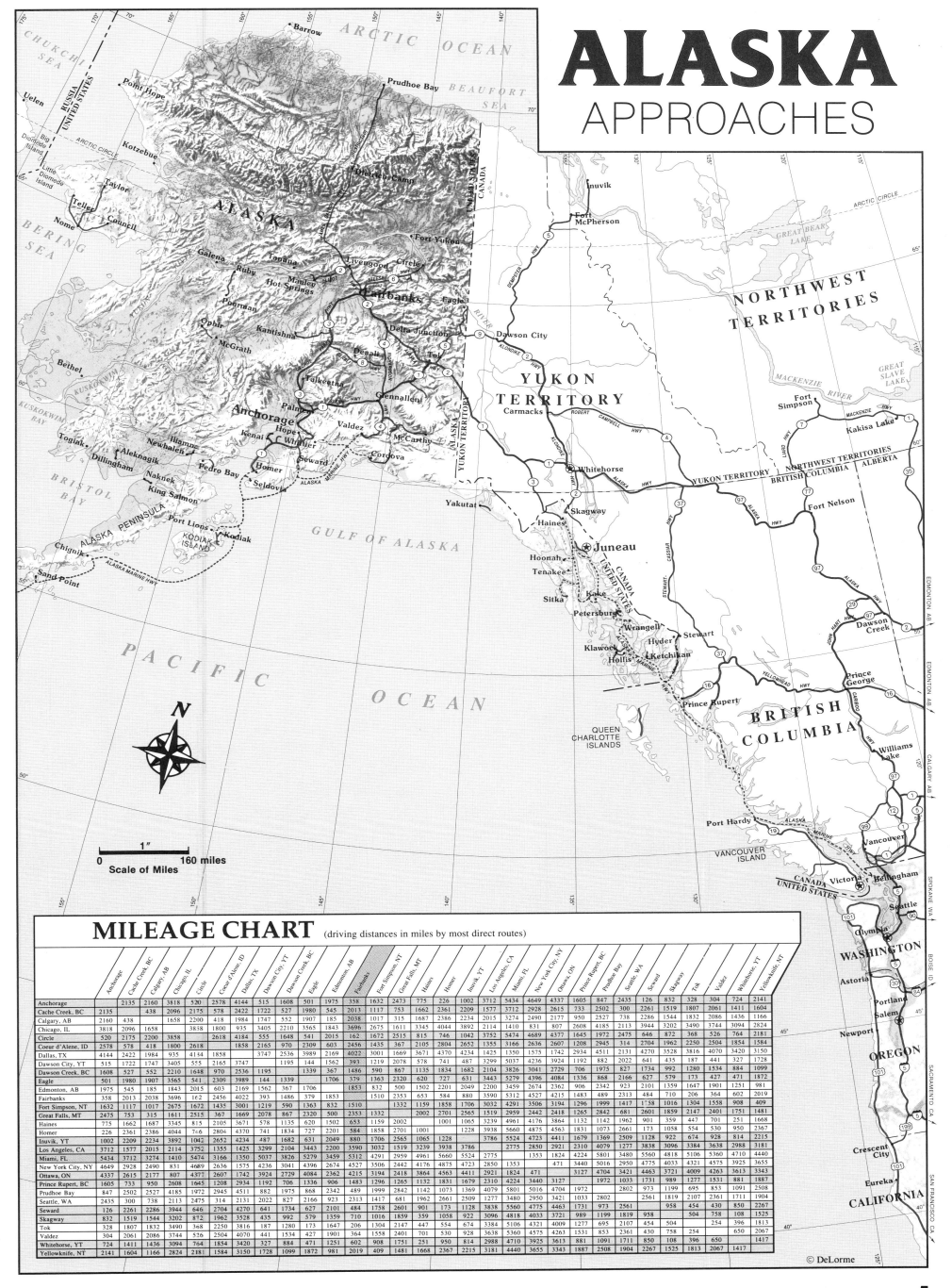

ALASKA
APPROACHES

Scale of Miles — 1″ = 160 miles

N (compass rose)

© DeLorme

MILEAGE CHART (driving distances in miles by most direct routes)

	Anchorage	Cache Creek, BC	Calgary, AB	Chicago, IL	Circle	Coeur d'Alene, ID	Dallas, TX	Dawson City, YT	Dawson Creek, BC	Eagle	Edmonton, AB	Fairbanks	Fort Simpson, NT	Great Falls, MT	Haines	Homer	Inuvik, YT	Los Angeles, CA	Miami, FL	New York City, NY	Ottawa, ON	Prince Rupert, BC	Prudhoe Bay	Seattle, WA	Seward	Skagway	Tok	Valdez	Whitehorse, YT	Yellowknife, NT
Anchorage		2135	2160	3818	520	2578	4144	515	1608	501	1975	358	1632	2473	775	226	1002	3712	5434	4649	4337	1605	847	2435	126	832	328	304	724	2141
Cache Creek, BC	2135		438	2096	2175	578	2422	1722	527	1980	545	2013	1117	753	1662	2361	2209	1577	3712	2928	2615	733	2502	300	2261	1519	1807	2061	1411	1604
Calgary, AB	2160	438		1658	2200	418	1984	1747	552	1907	185	2038	1017	315	1687	2386	2234	2015	3274	2490	2177	950	2527	738	2286	1544	1832	2086	1436	1166
Chicago, IL	3818	2096	1658		3858	1800	935	3405	2210	3565	1843	3696	2675	1611	3345	4044	3892	2114	1410	831	746	2608	3752	2113	4377	3202	3490	3744	3094	2824
Circle	520	2175	2200	3858		2618	4184	555	1648	541	2015	162	1672	2515	815	746	1042	3752	5474	4689	4377	1645	882	2475	872	872	368	526	764	2181
Coeur d'Alene, ID	2578	578	418	1800	2618		1858	2536	970	2309	603	2456	1435	367	2105	2804	2652	1355	3166	2636	2607	1208	2945	314	2704	1962	2250	2504	1854	1584
Dallas, TX	4144	2422	1984	935	4184	1858		3747	2309	3989	2169	4022	3001	1669	4329	4370	4234	1425	1350	1575	1742	2934	4511	2131	4270	3528	3816	4070	3420	3150
Dawson City, YT	515	1722	1747	3405	555	2536	3747		1195	367	1562	393	590	2078	1135	741	487	3299	3826	3041	2729	706	579	827	435	435	173	441	327	1728
Dawson Creek, BC	1608	527	552	2210	1648	970	2309	1195		1706	367	1486	867	590	1834	1219	1682	2104	3459	2729	2342	1336	1975	2166	2101	1359	1280	1534	884	1099
Eagle	501	1980	1907	3565	541	2309	3989	367	1706		1706	379	1502	2320	620	727	620	3443	4084	4396	4084	906	627	923	579	710	206	427	471	1872
Edmonton, AB	1975	545	185	1843	2015	603	2169	1562	367	1706		1853	832	500	1502	2201	2049	2200	2362	2674	2215	1483	2489	2313	2463	1524	1647	1901	1251	981
Fairbanks	358	2013	2038	3696	162	2456	4022	393	1486	379	1853		1510	2353	653	584	880	3590	4291	4527	4215	1296	631	1417	727	908	206	364	908	2019
Fort Simpson, NT	1632	1117	1017	2675	1672	1435	3001	590	867	1502	832	1510		1332	1159	1858	1706	3032	2959	3506	3194	1265	1142	2959	1819	1016	1359	1558	1751	409
Great Falls, MT	2475	753	315	1611	2515	367	1669	2078	590	2320	500	2353	1332		2002	2701	2565	1519	1824	1831	1824	1132	2661	880	2107	2401	2401	2401	1751	1481
Haines	775	1662	1687	3345	815	2105	4329	1135	1834	620	1502	653	1159	2002		1001	1228	3239	4563	4176	3864	1831	1336	681	1058	359	359	530	251	1668
Homer	226	2361	2386	4044	746	2804	4370	741	1219	727	2201	584	1858	2701	1001		1228	3938	5524	4875	4563	1679	868	1962	922	1058	922	928	850	2367
Inuvik, YT	1002	2209	2234	3892	1042	2652	4234	487	1682	620	2049	880	1706	2565	1228	1228		3786	4723	4723	4176	1679	173	2509	1369	989	673	928	814	2215
Los Angeles, CA	3712	1577	2015	2114	3752	1355	1425	3299	2104	3443	2200	3590	3032	1519	3239	3938	3786		2775	2850	3127	2310	4079	1277	3838	4818	3384	3638	4710	3181
Miami, FL	5434	3712	3274	1410	5474	3166	1350	3826	3459	4084	2362	4291	2959	1824	4563	5524	4723	2775		1353	1353	4224	5801	3480	5524	4818	5106	5360	3925	4440
New York City, NY	4649	2928	2490	831	4689	2636	1575	3041	2729	4396	2674	4527	3506	1831	4176	4875	4723	2850	1353		471	3440	5016	2950	4775	3721	4463	4575	3613	3655
Ottawa, ON	4337	2615	2177	746	4377	2607	1742	2729	2342	4084	2215	4215	3194	1824	3864	4563	4176	3127	1353	471		3127	4710	3421	4463	3127	4009	4263	881	3343
Prince Rupert, BC	1605	733	950	2608	1645	1208	2934	706	1336	906	1483	1296	1265	1132	1831	1679	1679	2310	4224	3440	3127		1972	1033	1279	989	695	853	1091	1887
Prudhoe Bay	847	2502	2527	3752	882	2945	4511	579	1975	627	2489	631	1142	2661	1336	868	173	4079	5801	5016	4710	1972		2802	2561	1819	1277	1531	1711	2508
Seattle, WA	2435	300	738	2113	2475	314	2131	827	2166	923	2313	1417	2959	880	681	1962	2509	1277	3480	2950	3421	1033	2802		2561	1731	2401	2361	850	2267
Seward	126	2261	2286	4377	872	2704	4270	435	2101	579	2463	727	1819	2107	1058	922	1369	3838	5524	4775	4463	1279	2561	2561		958	454	430	950	2267
Skagway	832	1519	1544	3202	872	1962	3528	435	1359	710	1524	908	1016	2401	359	1058	989	4818	4818	3721	3127	989	1819	1731	958		504	758	108	1525
Tok	328	1807	1832	3490	368	2250	3816	173	1280	206	1647	206	1359	2401	359	922	673	3384	5106	4463	4009	695	1277	2401	454	504		396	396	2067
Valdez	304	2061	2086	3744	526	2504	4070	441	1534	427	1901	364	1558	2401	530	928	928	3638	5360	4575	4263	853	1531	2361	430	758	396		650	2067
Whitehorse, YT	724	1411	1436	3094	764	1854	3420	327	884	471	1251	908	1751	1751	251	850	814	4710	3925	3613	881	1091	1711	850	950	108	396	650		1417
Yellowknife, NT	2141	1604	1166	2824	2181	1584	3150	1728	1099	1872	981	2019	409	1481	1668	2367	2215	3181	4440	3655	3343	1887	2508	2267	2267	1525	2067	2067	1417	

Visitor Information Centers

There are numerous local, regional and state visitor information centers throughout Alaska, found in most major cities and towns and along principal highways. To locate these in the Atlas, look on the maps for the appropriate symbol.

General information is available from the Alaska Division of Tourism, Ninth Floor, State Office Building, Juneau, AK 99811, (907) 465-2010.

For information on all matters relating to public lands, including parks, forests and wildlife refuges, contact one of the Public Lands Information Centers listed here. These offices represent all federal and state land managing agencies, including Alaska Department of Fish and Game, Alaska Department of Natural Resources, National Park Service, US Fish & Wildlife Service, USDA Forest Service, Bureau of Land Management and US Geological Survey.

PUBLIC LANDS INFORMATION CENTERS

605 West Fourth Avenue, Suite 105, Anchorage, AK 99501, (907) 271-2737 .... Page 82 D3
250 Cushman Street, Suite 1A, Fairbanks, AK 99701, (907) 451-7352 .... Page 115 A5
P.O. Box 359, Tok, AK 99780, (907) 883-5667 .... Page 108 C3

Campgrounds

This chart includes a selected list of private campgrounds in Alaska. To locate these campgrounds in the Atlas, look on the appropriate map for the campground symbol and corresponding four-digit number. For more information contact the Alaska Campground Owners Association, P.O. Box 84884, Fairbanks, AK 99708, (907) 883-5877 or the Alaska Division of Tourism, Ninth Floor, State Office Building, Juneau, AK 99811, (907) 465-2010.

Public campgrounds, shelters and cabins, located on state and federal land, can be identified by the symbols indicated in the Legend. Undeveloped or primitive camping is permitted on many public tracts. Contact the proper land managing agency for more information.

NAME, LOCATION	TENT SITES	RV SITES	PAGE & GRID
1000 Auke Bay RV Park, Auke Bay		50	33 C3
1005 Best View RV Park, Wasilla	20	64	83 B4
1010 Bing Brown's, Sterling	15	30	70 B1
1020 The Bull Shooter RV Park, Tok	6	49	108 C3
1030 Centennial Park Campgrounds, Soldotna	160	160	69 C5
1040 Chandalar RV Park, Willow	25	58	93 D6
1050 Clover Pass Resort, Ketchikan		32	20 C1
1060 Cripple Creek Resort, Ester		16	115 A4
1070 Crooked Creek RV Park, Kasilof	21	41	69 C5
1080 Crow Creek Gold Mine, Girdwood	10	20	71 A4
1090 Denali Grizzly Bear Campground, McKinley Village	30	30	104 B3
1100 Eagle Claw RV, Valdez	20	175	85 D5
1110 Funny River Fish Camp, Soldotna	6	5	70 C1
1120 Green Ridge Camper Park, Wasilla	50	37	83 B4
1130 H & H Lakeview Campground, Sunshine	40	20	93 D6
1140 Haines Hitch-Up RV Park, Haines		92	38 D2
1150 Harris River Wilderness Cabins, Hollis	10	3	19 C4
1160 Hillside Motel & RV Park, Anchorage		60	82 D3
1170 The Homestead RV Park, Palmer	7	60	83 B4
1180 Hylen's Camper Park, Ninilchik		75	69 D4
1190 Kenai Princess RV Park, Cooper Landing		37	70 C3
1200 Kenai Riverbend Campground, Soldotna	50	250	69 B5
1210 Kyllonen's RV Park, Anchor Point	20	30	62 A1
1220 Last Resort, Nenana	4	8	114 B2
1230 Log Cabin Resort & RV Park, Klawock	8	12	19 B3
1240 Lynx Creek Campground, McKinley Park	15	20	104 A3
1250 McKinley KOA, Healy	12	78	104 A2
1260 Mountain Point RV Park, Ketchikan		20	20 C1
1270 Nancy Lake Marina Resort, Willow	20	50	82 B3
1280 Norlite, Fairbanks	75	175	115 A5
1290 Oceanside RV Park, Haines		22	38 D2
1300 Oceanview RV Park, Homer	5	85	62 B1
1310 Petracach, Trapper Creek	5	32	93 C6
1320 Port Chilkoot Camper Park, Haines	20	50	38 D2
1330 Rita's Campground, Tok	12	20	108 C2
1340 Sheep Mountain Lodge, Palmer	6	10	84 A3
1350 Sourdough Campground & RV Park, Tok	15	60	108 C2
1360 Sunrise Inn, Cooper Landing	12	12	71 C3
1370 Swiftwater Park Campground, Soldotna	50	50	69 C5
1380 Tanana Valley Campgrounds, Fairbanks	15	20	115 A5
1390 Tatlanika Trading Co. & Museum, Clear	15	11	114 D2
1400 Tok RV Village, Tok	11	84	108 C3
1410 Tolsona Wilderness Campground, Glennallen	30	26	96 D3
1420 Twin Creek RV Park, Petersburg		30	24 B1
1440 Willow Island Resort, Willow	50	50	82 A2

National Parklands

The federally owned lands listed in this chart cover almost 81 million acres. Most of this land is managed by the Bureau of Land Management, National Park Service or USDA Forest Service. Undeveloped or primitive camping and backcountry hiking are possible in most areas. Check with the proper authorities for hunting and fishing rules, regulations and restrictions.

For more information on any area, contact one of the Public Lands Information Centers listed in Visitor Information Centers *above.*

ACCESS ABBREVIATIONS
A–air L–land W–water

NAME, LOCATION	ACCESS	ACREAGE	CAMPSITES	CABINS/SHELTERS	BOATING	HIKING	FISHING	HUNTING	COMMENTS	PAGE & GRID
Admiralty Island National Monument–Kootznoowoo Wilderness, Tongass National Forest	AW	955,921		●	●		●	●	Called Kootznoowoo ("Fortress of the Bears") by Tlingit Indians because of large brown bear population. Largest concentration of nesting bald eagles in world.	27 B4
Aniakchak National Monument and Preserve, King Salmon	A	600,000		●	●		●	●	Very remote, extensive volcanic area. Central feature, Aniakchak Caldera *(see Float Trips and Unique Natural Features)*.	139 B5
Bering Land Bridge National Preserve, Nome	A	2,700,000			●		●		Remnant of land bridge that connected Asia and North America. Neighboring Eskimo villages. Hot springs.	132 B3
Cape Krusenstern National Monument, Kotzebue	AW	660,000			●		●		114 beach ridges along arctic coastal plain record changing shorelines of Chukchi Sea and 6,000 years of prehistoric human use *(see Historic Sites/Museums)*.	132 A4
Chena River Lakes Project, Fairbanks	L	19,710	●		●	●	●		Northernmost US flood control project. Multiuse recreation area including 250-acre lake with swimming beach.	115 A6
Chuck River Wilderness, Tongass National Forest	AW	74,298			●		●	●	Steep terrain. Fiords popular for kayaking.	28 B3
Chugach National Forest, Anchorage	ALW	5,900,000	●	●	●	●	●	●	Second largest forest in US. Portage and Columbia Glaciers and Copper River Delta *(see Unique Natural Features and Wildlife Refuges)*. 200 miles of hiking trails *(see Hiking)*.	71 A4
Coronation Island Wilderness, Tongass National Forest	AW	19,232			●		●	●	Undeveloped island with windswept beaches, cliffs and rocky shoreline. Peaks rising to nearly 2,000 feet. Access difficult.	18 A1
Denali National Park and Preserve, McKinley Park	AL	6,000,000	●			●	●	●	Spectacular subarctic wilderness with massive Mt. McKinley as towering centerpiece. Short loop trails and backcountry hiking. Mountaineering. 91-mile McKinley Park Road. Barren-ground caribou, grizzly bears, moose, wolves and Dall sheep. Includes 1.9-million-acre Wilderness.	104 B2
Endicott River Wilderness, Tongass National Forest	AW	98,729			●		●	●	Endicott River flows through glacially carved canyon. Terrain from spruce–hemlock rainforest, brush and small trees to glacial alpine areas over 5,000 feet high.	32 A2
Gates of the Arctic National Park and Preserve, Anaktuvuk Pass	A	8,400,000			●		●	●	Vast arctic tundra and scenic headland of Brooks Range. Inhabited by Nunamiut Eskimo and Athabascan peoples. Major barren-ground caribou range. Includes 7-million-acre Wilderness.	136 C3
Glacier Bay National Park and Preserve, Gustavus	AW	3,300,000	●		●	●	●	●	16 tidewater glaciers. Humpback, minke and orca whales; porpoises and seals. Peaks over 10,000 feet, including Mt. Fairweather (15,300 feet). Glacier tour boats. Includes 2.8-million-acre Wilderness. *(See Unique Natural Features.)*	32 C1
Karta River Wilderness, Tongass National Forest	AW	39,889		●	●	●	●	●	Located on western side of Prince of Wales Island. Karta River, Salmon and Karta Lakes. Five-mile hiking trail along river. Four cabins.	19 B4
Katmai National Park and Preserve, King Salmon	AW	4,000,000	●		●	●	●	●	Rich volcanic history with 15 active volcanoes. Critical brown bear habitat. Valley of 10,000 Smokes *(see Unique Natural Features)*. Backcountry hiking. Includes 3.5-million-acre Wilderness. *(See Unique Natural Features.)*	50 B3
Kenai Fjords National Park, Seward	ALW	669,000	●	●	●	●	●		Glacially carved coastal mountain fiords. Exit Glacier *(see Unique Natural Features)*. Mountain goats, moose, bald eagles, sea lions and seals.	71 D3
Klondike Gold Rush National Historical Park, Skagway	ALW	13,000		●		●	●		Historic center of Klondike Gold Rush surrounded by spectacular wilderness. Chilkoot and White Pass Trails. Visitor center. Museum. *(See Hiking and Historic Sites/Museums.)*	38 C2
Kobuk Valley National Park, Kotzebue	AW	1,700,000			●		●		Arctic area surrounded by Baird and Waring Mountains. Great Kobuk Sand Dunes *(see Unique Natural Features)*. Caribou herds. Includes 190,000-acre Wilderness.	133 A6
Kuiu Wilderness, Tongass National Forest	AW	60,581			●	●	●	●	On southern part of Kuiu Island, encompasses many bays and islands. Scenic portage trail from Affleck Canal to Petrof Bay.	23 C3
Lake Clark National Park and Preserve, Anchorage	A	4,000,000			●		●	●	"Alaskan Alps" where Alaska and Aleutian Ranges meet. Iliamna and Redoubt Volcanoes *(see Unique Natural Features)*. 50-mile-long Lake Clark. River running. Includes 2.5-million-acre Wilderness.	67 D4
Maurelle Islands Wilderness, Tongass National Forest	AW	4,937			●		●	●	Group of nearly 30 islands rising to 400 feet above sea level. Rocky shoals and windformed trees.	18 B2
Misty Fiords National Monument Wilderness, Tongass National Forest	AW	2,142,243		●	●	●	●	●	Steep-walled canyons, glaciers and long, narrow fiords. Diverse wildlife. Annual precipitation 150 inches.	21 B3
Noatak National Preserve, Kotzebue	A	6,500,000			●		●	●	Large arctic river basin ringed by mountains of Brooks Range. Excellent canoeing and kayaking on gentle, slow-moving Noatak River *(see Float Trips)*. Includes 5.8-million-acre Wilderness.	133 A4
Petersburg Creek–Duncan Salt Chuck Wilderness, Tongass National Forest	AW	46,777		●	●	●	●	●	Popular recreation area located on Kupreanof Island.	24 A1
Pleasant–Lemesurier–Inian Islands Wilderness, Tongass National Forest	W	23,096			●			●	Several islands in Icy Strait near Gustavus. Wildlife includes whales, sea otters and cliff-nesting shorebirds.	32 C1
Russell Fiord Wilderness, Tongass National Forest	ALW	348,701		●	●	●	●	●	Russell and Nunatak Fiords, tidewater glaciers, icebergs. Snow-capped mountain peaks to 8,460 feet.	35 B4
Sitka National Historical Park, Sitka	AW	106				●			Park commemorates 1804 Battle of Sitka. Town important hub of 19th-century Russian America. *(See Historic Sites/Museums.)*	27 D3
South Baranof Wilderness, Tongass National Forest	AW	319,568		●	●	●	●	●	Dense coastal rainforest on southern Baranof Island. Annual precipitation over 200 inches. 4,000-foot mountains and numerous glaciers.	22 B2
South Etolin Island Wilderness, Tongass National Forest	W	83,371			●		●	●	Located on south end of Etolin Island. Numerous passages and small islands.	24 D2
South Prince of Wales Wilderness, Tongass National Forest	AW	90,996		●	●		●	●	Southern tip of Prince of Wales Island. Low tidal wetlands to 2,000-foot rock walls. Klinkwan, 19th-century deserted Indian village. Includes 75 smaller islands.	17 A4
Steese National Conservation Area, Chena Hot Springs	L	1,200,000			●	●	●	●	Primary attractions Birch Creek National Wild River *(see Float Trips)* and Pinnell Mountain National Recreation Trail *(see Hiking)*.	126 C3
Stikine–LeConte Wilderness, Tongass National Forest	AW	448,926		●	●		●	●	Stikine River surrounded by rugged, glaciated peaks. LeConte Glacier *(see Unique Natural Features)*. Popular recreation area. Hot springs.	24 B2
Tebenkof Bay Wilderness, Tongass National Forest	AW	66,839			●	●	●	●	Located on west side of Kuiu Island. Dense rainforest, small islands, coves; alpine terrain above 2,000 feet. Kayaking in Tebenkof Bay.	23 B3
Tongass National Forest, Juneau	AW	16,500,000	●	●	●	●	●	●	Largest US national forest. 19 wilderness areas *(see this section)*. Islands, glaciers, rainforest, fiords. Mendenhall Glacier *(see Unique Natural Features)*. Over 400 miles of trails *(see Hiking)*.	32 B3
Tracy Arm–Fords Terror Wilderness, Tongass National Forest	AW	653,179			●		●	●	Two long, narrow fiords with tidewater glaciers continually calving icebergs. Rugged mountains, valleys and high waterfalls.	28 B3
Trans-Alaska Pipeline Utility Corridor, Fairbanks	LW	2,780,000			●		●	●	Scenic terrain paralleling pipeline from Yukon River to Prudhoe Bay. Fully traversed by Dalton Highway *(see Scenic Drives)*.	124 A1
Warren Island Wilderness, Tongass National Forest	AW	11,181			●		●	●	Windswept beaches, cliffs, rocky shoreline. Peaks over 2,000 feet, including Warren Peak at 2,329 feet. Access very difficult.	18 A2
West Chichagof–Yakobi Wilderness, Tongass National Forest	AW	264,747		●	●	●	●	●	Rugged mountain terrain on two islands. 65 miles of Pacific Ocean coastline.	26 C2
White Mountains National Recreation Area, Fairbanks	L	1,000,000		●	●	●	●	●	Unusual limestone cliffs. Beaver Creek National Wild River. Summer hiking and extensive winter trails. *(See Float Trips, Hiking and Unique Natural Features.)*	125 D4
Wrangell–St. Elias National Park and Preserve, Glennallen	AL	13,000,000			●		●	●	Largest US national park. Massive mountains, canyons, glaciers and icefields. Three mountain ranges. Mt. St. Elias and Malaspina Glacier *(see Unique Natural Features)*. Includes 8.7-million-acre Wilderness.	97 D4
Yukon–Charley Rivers National Preserve, Eagle	AL	2,500,000			●		●	●	130 miles of Yukon River *(see Unique Natural Features)* and entire 106-mile Charley River *(see Float Trips)*. Area untouched by glaciers. Remnants of gold mining era. Prime habitat for endangered peregrine falcon.	129 D6

State Parklands

For more information on state parklands, contact one of the Public Lands Information Centers listed in Visitor Information Centers *on page 6.*

ACCESS ABBREVIATIONS
A–air L–land W–water

NAME, NEAREST COMMUNITY	ACCESS	ACREAGE	CAMPSITES	PICNIC AREA	TOILETS	WATER	HIKING	BOAT LAUNCH	FISHING	COMMENTS	PAGE & GRID
Anchor River State Recreation Area, Homer	L	213	38		●	●			●	Located at most westerly point of US highway system. Popular fishing and camping area.	62 A1
Anchor River State Recreation Site, Homer	L	53	9		●	●			●	Campsites among large spruce trees bordering river. Fishing for Dolly Varden.	62 B1
Beecher Pass State Marine Park, Wrangell	AW	660							●	Located on Mitkof Island. Undeveloped.	24 B1
Bernice Lake State Recreation Site, Kenai	L	152	11	●	●	●		●		Quiet, peaceful wayside on small lake.	69 B5
Bettles Bay State Marine Park, Whittier	AW	680							●	Well-protected boat anchorage. Views of Bettles Glacier. Undeveloped.	72 A1
Big Bear/Baby Bear Bays State Marine Park, Sitka	AW	1,023							●	Located in Peril Strait. Undeveloped.	27 B2
Big Delta State Historical Park, Delta Junction	L	10			●	●	●			Historic crossroad. Rika's Roadhouse. Museum. *(See Historic Sites/Museums.)*	116 D3
Big Lake North State Recreation Site, Big Lake	L	19	60	●	●	●		●	●	Swimming, boating, waterskiing and sailing. Ice fishing and skating.	82 B3
Big Lake South State Recreation Site, Big Lake	L	16	20	●	●	●		●	●	Same recreational activities as northern unit *(see above)*.	82 B3
Birch Lake State Recreation Site, Delta Junction	L	191	10		●			●	●	Lake stocked with rainbow trout and silver salmon.	116 C1
Blueberry Lake State Recreation Site, Valdez	L	192	15	●	●		●		●	Panoramic views of Chugach Range, glaciers and Keystone Canyon area.	86 D1
Bonnie Lake State Recreation Site, Palmer	L	129	8		●			●	●	One-mile-long lake. Boating and canoeing. Fishing for trout, salmon and grayling.	84 A1
Boswell Bay State Marine Park, Cordova	AW	799							●	Located on Hinchinbrook Island. Beachcombing and hunting. Undeveloped.	73 C5
Buskin River State Recreation Site, Kodiak	ALW	196	18	●	●	●	●		●	Popular fishing spot. Sandy ocean beach. WWII military remnants.	45 A5
Caines Head State Recreation Area, Seward	LW	5,961	4	●	●		●		●	Beaches, alpine meadows, jagged peaks. Sweeping ocean views. Abandoned WWII fort. Coastal Trail *(see Hiking)*.	71 D4
Canoe Passage State Marine Park, Cordova	AW	2,735							●	Located on Hawkins Island. Undeveloped.	73 B5
Captain Cook State Recreation Area, Kenai	L	3,466	65	●	●	●	●	●	●	Forests, lakes, streams, saltwater beaches on Cook Inlet. Swimming. Remains of Tanaina Indian barabaras (housepits).	69 A5
Chena River State Recreation Area, Fairbanks	L	254,080	61	●	●	●	●		●	Multiuse area along winding stretch of Chena River. Ten separate recreation sites. Three hiking trails. Cross-country ski trails.	116 A1
Chena River State Recreation Site, Fairbanks	L	27	59	●	●	●		●	●	Located along river in Fairbanks.	115 A5
Chilkat Islands State Marine Park, Haines	AW	6,560							●	Located in Lynn Canal. Undeveloped.	38 D2
Chilkat State Park, Haines	LW	6,045	15	●	●	●	●	●	●	Spectacular glacier views across Chilkat Inlet. Coastline trail.	38 D2
Chilkoot Lake State Recreation Site, Haines	L	80	32	●	●	●		●	●	Campsites along scenic lakeshore.	38 C1
Chugach State Park, Anchorage	ALW	495,204	125	●	●	●	●		●	Accessible, pristine wilderness in Anchorage backyard. Spectacular alpine scenery. Tidal bore *(see Unique Natural Features)*.	83 D4
Clam Gulch State Recreation Area, Soldotna	L	129	116	●	●	●			●	Panoramic views of Aleutian Mountain Range. Popular razor clamming area.	69 D5
Clearwater State Recreation Site, Delta Junction	L	27	18		●	●		●	●	Grayling fishing. Access to Tanana and Goodpaster Rivers. Migrating sandhill cranes.	117 D4
Crooked Creek State Recreation Site, Soldotna	L	49	75	●	●	●	●		●	Bank fishing for king and silver salmon and steelhead.	69 C5
Dall Bay State Marine Park, Ketchikan	AW	585							●	Located on Gravina Island. Undeveloped.	20 D1
Decision Point State Marine Park, Whittier	AW	460	2						●	Good for kayaks and small boats. Camping beaches. Located in Passage Canal. Undeveloped.	72 A1
Deep Creek State Recreation Area, Ninilchik	L	155	300		●	●		●	●	Fishing for halibut and king salmon. Razor clamming and beachcombing. Bald eagles.	69 D4
Delta State Recreation Site, Delta Junction	AL	7	22	●	●	●				Stopping point for camping between Tok and Fairbanks.	116 D3
Denali State Park, Talkeetna	L	324,240	86	●	●	●	●	●	●	Outstanding views of Mt. McKinley *(see Unique Natural Features)* from highway and Kesugi Ridge.	93 B6
Donnelly Creek State Recreation Site, Delta Junction	L	42	12		●	●				Scenic campground with views of Alaska Range. Delta Junction Bison Range *(see Wildlife Refuges)*.	106 B3
Driftwood Bay State Marine Park, Seward	AW	1,480							●	Located in Day Harbor. Popular boat anchorage. Mountain views. Undeveloped.	64 A1
Dry Creek State Recreation Site, Glennallen	L	372	58	●	●	●	●		●	Area heavily timbered with birch and spruce.	97 D4
Eagle Trail State Recreation Site, Tok	L	640	40	●	●	●	●			Scenic setting against Alaska Range. Alpine hiking and wildlife viewing. Dall sheep. Valdez-to-Eagle Trail.	108 D2
Entry Cove State Marine Park, Whittier	AW	370	1						●	Boat anchorage. Views of Tebenkof Glacier. Located at Point Pigot. Undeveloped.	72 A1
Fielding Lake State Recreation Site, Delta Junction	L	300	7		●			●	●	Scenic campground at 2,973-foot elevation in Alaska Range.	106 D3
Finger Lake State Recreation Site, Palmer	L	47	41	●	●	●	●	●	●	Water recreation area. Swimming, boating, canoeing and sailing.	83 B4
Ft. Abercrombie State Historical Park, Kodiak	ALW	183	14	●	●	●	●		●	Remains of WWII fort *(see Historic Sites/Museums)*. Trails through stands of Sitka spruce. Whale/puffin watching. Tide pools.	45 A5
Funter Bay State Marine Park, Juneau	AW	162							●	Located on Admiralty Island. Boat dock. Undeveloped.	32 C3
Granite Bay State Marine Park, Whittier	AW	2,105							●	Anchorages in two bays. Located on Esther Island. Undeveloped.	72 A1
Gruening State Historical Park, Juneau	AW	12							●	Home and grounds of last Alaska territorial governor and first US Senator, Ernest Gruening. Good fishing access.	32 C3
Haines State Forest and Resource Mgmt Area, Haines	LW	250,600					●		●	Undeveloped, multiple-use forest with diverse terrain and habitats. 35 miles of logging roads for recreational use. Hunting.	38 C1
Halibut Point State Recreation Site, Sitka	AW	22		●	●	●	●		●	Day-use area. Forest trails. Salmon stream. Rain shelters.	27 D3
Harding Lake State Recreation Area, Delta Junction	L	169	89	●	●	●	●	●	●	One of few road-accessible recreation lakes in interior Alaska.	116 C1
Horseshoe Bay State Marine Park, Seward	AW	970							●	Located on Latouche Island. Boat anchorage. Undeveloped.	72 D2
Independence Mine State Historical Park, Palmer	L	761			●	●	●			Historic gold mine located in rugged Talkeetna Mountains *(see Historic Sites/Museums)*.	83 A4
Jack Bay State Marine Park, Valdez	AW	811	5						●	Located in Valdez Arm. Fair-weather anchorage. Undeveloped.	85 D4
Joe Mace Island State Marine Park, Wrangell	AW	62							●	Located in Sumner Strait. Undeveloped.	23 C4
Johnson Creek State Recreation Site, Juneau	AW	65								Undeveloped area.	33 C3
Johnson Lake State Recreation Area, Soldotna	L	324	50	●	●	●		●	●	Campground with lake views. Swimming and canoeing. Year-round rainbow trout and kokanee fishing.	69 C5
Juneau Trail System State Trail, Juneau	LW	15					●		●	Five trails totaling 14.7 miles, including Mt. Juneau and Perseverance *(see Hiking)*.	33 C4
Kachemak Bay State Park and Wilderness Park, Homer	AW	368,290	8	●	●		●		●	Scenic, high mountain terrain. Fiords, coves and vast glacier fields. Beachcombing. Numerous hiking trails.	62 B2
Kasilof River State Recreation Site, Soldotna	L	50	16		●	●	●		●	Campground located on Kasilof River.	69 C5
Kayak Island State Marine Park, Cordova	AW	1,437							●	Island located in Gulf of Alaska. Landing site of 1741 Bering Expedition. Undeveloped.	65 B5
Kenai River Special Management Area, Sterling	LW	2,170	138	●	●	●	●	●	●	More than 105 miles of rivers and lakes. Prime area for fishing, boating, camping and wildlife viewing.	70 C2
Kepler–Bradley Lakes State Recreation Area, Palmer	L	344		●	●	●	●	●	●	Day-use area. Seven lakes stocked with grayling, rainbow trout and silver salmon. Equestrian trails.	83 B4
King Mountain State Recreation Site, Palmer	L	20	22	●	●	●				Views of King Mountain and glacier-fed Matanuska River.	84 A1
Lake Louise State Recreation Area, Glennallen	L	90	36	●	●	●		●	●	20-mile-long chain of lakes. Fishing for lake trout and grayling. Berry picking.	96 C1
Liberty Falls State Recreation Site, Chitina	L	10	8		●		●			Scenic waterfalls.	87 B3
Little Nelchina State Recreation Site, Glennallen	L	22	11		●		●	●	●	Convenient rest area and overnight stop for travelers. Access point for hunters.	85 A4
Little Susitna River Public Use Facility, Wasilla	L	38	145	●	●	●	●	●	●	Located within Susitna Flats State Game Refuge *(see Wildlife Refuges)*.	82 C2
Little Tonsina State Recreation Site, Copper Center	L	103	8		●	●			●	Overnight stop near Trans-Alaska Pipeline. Fishing for grayling.	86 C2
Long Lake State Recreation Site, Palmer	L	480	9		●	●		●	●	Located in valley at edge of Talkeetna Mountains. Deep, mile-long lake. Fishing for grayling.	84 A1
Lower Chatanika State Recreation Area, Fairbanks	L	570	65	●	●	●		●	●	Large pond for swimming, non-motorized boating and fishing.	125 D5
Magoun Islands State Marine Park, Sitka	AW	1,130							●	Located in Krestof Sound. Undeveloped.	27 D2
Matanuska Glacier State Recreation Site, Palmer	L	229	12		●	●	●			Panoramic views of Matanuska Glacier *(see Unique Natural Features)* and Chugach Mountains.	84 A2
Montana Creek State Recreation Site, Talkeetna	L	82	89	●	●	●	●		●	Salmon fishing.	93 D6
Moon Lake State Recreation Site, Tok	L	22	15		●	●		●		Scenic location between Tanana River and Alaska Range.	108 C1
Moose Creek State Recreation Site, Palmer	L	40	12	●	●	●	●		●	Convenient base camp while touring Matanuska Valley.	83 B4
Mosquito Lake State Recreation Site, Haines	L	5	10		●	●		●	●	Small, quiet lake with fishing for cutthroat trout and Dolly Varden.	37 C5
Nancy Lake State Recreation Area, Willow	L	22,685	98	●	●	●	●	●	●	Extensive lake-studded area. Canoe trail system *(see Float Trips)*. 12 public-use cabins.	82 B2
Nancy Lake State Recreation Site, Willow	L	36	30	●	●	●		●	●	Swimming, waterskiing and sailing. Fishing for red salmon and rainbow trout.	82 B2
Ninilchik State Recreation Area, Ninilchik	L	97	165	●	●	●			●	Popular beach for razor clamming. Forest and beach campgrounds.	69 D4
Old Sitka State Historical Park, Sitka	AW	51			●		●	●	●	Historic settlement *(see Historic Sites/Museums)*. Fish migration observation area.	27 D3
Oliver Inlet State Marine Park, Juneau	AW	560			●		●	●	●	Located on Admiralty Island. Public-use cabin.	33 D4
Pasagshak State Recreation Site, Kodiak	ALW	20	10		●	●			●	Scenic Pasagshak Bay. Reversing river. King and silver salmon.	45 C5
Pioneer Park State Recreation Site, Sitka	LW	3		●	●	●	●			Day-use picnic area. Short trail along ocean.	27 D3
Point Bridget State Park, Juneau	AW	2,850					●		●	Forested mountains. Wildflower meadows. Rocky ocean beach. Spectacular views. Marine mammals.	32 B3
Porcupine Creek State Recreation Site, Tok	L	240	12		●	●	●		●	Rest area and overnight stop. Fishing for grayling.	98 B1
Portage Cove State Recreation Site, Haines	ALW	7	9	●	●	●			●	Located on bluff with panoramic views of Chilkoot Inlet and mountain ranges.	38 D2
Quartz Lake State Recreation Area, Delta Junction	L	600	16	●	●	●	●	●	●	Fishing for rainbow trout and silver salmon. Trans-Alaska Pipeline *(see Historic Sites/Museums)*.	116 D3
Refuge Cove State Recreation Site, Ketchikan	AW	13		●	●				●	Day-use picnic area located along Tongass Narrows.	20 C1
Rocky Lake State Recreation Site, Big Lake	L	48	10		●	●		●	●	Boating and waterskiing.	82 B3
Safety Cove State Marine Park, Seward	AW	960							●	Located in Day Harbor. Boat anchorage. Beach camping. Views of Ellsworth Glacier. Undeveloped.	64 A1
Salcha River State Recreation Site, Delta Junction	L	61	25	●	●	●		●	●	Fishing for grayling and king and chum salmon. Moose and bear hunting.	116 C1
Sandspit Point State Marine Park, Seward	AW	600							●	Spectacular views of Resurrection Bay and Eldorado Narrows. Beach camping. Tide pools. Undeveloped.	64 A1
Sawmill Bay State Marine Park, Valdez	AW	2,320							●	Located in Valdez Arm. Popular anchorage surrounded by 4,000-foot peaks. Undeveloped.	85 D4
Security Bay State Marine Park, Petersburg	AW	500							●	Located in Chatham Strait. Undeveloped.	23 A3
Settlers Cove State Recreation Site, Ketchikan	AW	38	12	●	●	●	●		●	Scenic swimming beach. Scuba diving. Heavily used picnic area.	20 B1
Shelter Island State Marine Park, Juneau	AW	3,560	1	●	●		●		●	Located in Lynn Canal.	32 C3
Shoup Bay State Marine Park, Valdez	AW	4,560	3						●	Located in Valdez Arm. Boat anchorage. Shoup Glacier. Kittiwake rookery. Undeveloped.	85 D4
Shuyak Island State Park, Kodiak	AW	11,000			●		●		●	Remote, rugged coastal wilderness. Popular hunting and fishing spot. Four public-use cabins.	53 B4
South Esther Island State Marine Park, Whittier	AW	3,360							●	Protected anchorage. Scenic overlooks. Fish hatchery. Located on Esther Island. Undeveloped.	72 A1
Squirrel Creek State Recreation Site, Copper Center	L	350	14		●	●			●	Convenient rest area or overnight stop. Fishing for grayling.	86 B2
St. James Bay State Marine Park, Juneau	AW	10,220					●		●	Located off Lynn Canal. Undeveloped.	32 B2
Stariski State Recreation Site, Homer	L	30	13	●	●	●				Located on high bluff overlooking Cook Inlet with views of Aleutian Chain. Whale whatching.	62 A1
Sullivan Island State Marine Park, Juneau	AW	2,163							●	Located in Lynn Canal. Undeveloped.	32 A2
Summit Lake State Recreation Site, Palmer	L	360					●			Berry picking. Located in Hatcher Pass.	83 A4
Sunny Cove State Marine Park, Seward	AW	960							●	Vertical rock cliffs. Located on Fox Island in Resurrection Bay. Undeveloped.	64 A1
Surprise Cove State Marine Park, Whittier	AW	2,280	7				●		●	Popular anchorage. Short trail. Tide pools. Located in Cochrane Bay. Undeveloped.	72 A1
Taku Harbor State Marine Park, Juneau	AW	700							●	Located in Stephens Passage. Boat dock. Undeveloped.	33 D4
Tanana Valley State Forest, Fairbanks	L	1,786,330	1				●	●	●	Extensive, undeveloped area within Tanana River Basin. Hunting.	115 A4
Thom's Place State Marine Park, Wrangell	AW	1,198							●	Located on Wrangell Island. Undeveloped.	24 D2
Thumb Cove State Marine Park, Seward	AW	720							●	Views of Porcupine Glacier. Located in Resurrection Bay. Undeveloped.	71 D4
Tok River State Recreation Site, Tok	L	38	50	●	●	●	●			Very popular overnight rest area. Canoeing on Tok and Tanana Rivers.	108 C3
Tolsona Creek State Recreation Site, Glennallen	L	600	10		●		●		●	Rest area and overnight stop.	96 D3
Totem Bight State Historical Park, Ketchikan	W	11			●		●			Model coastal Indian village dedicated to southeastern Alaska Native cultures *(see Historic Sites/Museums)*.	20 C1
Upper Chatanika River State Recreation Site, Fairbanks	L	73	15		●	●			●	Access point for river trips *(see Float Trips)*.	125 D6
Willow Creek State Recreation Area, Willow	L	3,583	7	●	●	●			●	Fishing for grayling, rainbow trout; king, chum, silver and pink salmon.	82 A2
Wolf Lake State Recreation Site, Palmer	L	23	4	●	●		●		●	Swimming beach.	83 B4
Wood–Tikchik State Park, Dillingham	AW	1,555,200	3		●				●	Largest US state park. Remote, undeveloped wilderness. Rugged mountains to open tundra. Excellent fishing and boating.	56 B2
Worthington Glacier State Recreation Site, Valdez	L	113		●	●		●			High alpine tundra and many hanging glaciers. Trail leads to glacier *(see Unique Natural Features)*. Visitor center.	86 D1
Zeigler Cove State Marine Park, Whittier	AW	720	1						●	Protected anchorage. Located in Port Wells. Undeveloped.	72 A1

Historic Sites/Museums

For more information on historic sites and museums contact the Alaska Division of Tourism, Ninth Floor, State Office Building, Juneau, AK 99811, (907) 465-2010.

ALASKA HIGHWAY – Delta Junction – Page 116 D3 1,422-mile highway from Dawson Creek, British Columbia, to Delta Junction. Built 1942 in eight months by US Army Corps of Engineers for WWII military transport; originally called Alaska–Canada Military Highway (Alcan). Considered one of 20th century's great engineering achievements. Opened to public 1948.

ALASKA STATE MUSEUM – Juneau – Page 33 C4 Human and natural history. Native culture and art of Alaska. Over 150 wildlife and historical displays, including exhibits on Russian-American history, gold mining, Alaska purchase and Trans-Alaska Pipeline. Full-sized bald eagle nesting tree. Extensive archival photograph collection.

ALASKALAND – Fairbanks – Page 115 A5 44-acre pioneer theme park established 1967 by city to commemorate centennial of Alaska's purchase from Russia. Gold Rush Town features relocated historic buildings, including Wickersham House and Pioneer Museum; Mining Valley depicts Fairbanks gold mining; drydocked Yukon River sternwheeler S.S. *Nenana*, on National Register of Historic Places; Native Village.

ANCHORAGE MUSEUM OF HISTORY AND ART – Anchorage – Page 82 D3 Collections emphasize art, history and Native cultures of Alaska. Sculpture, paintings, works on paper, and traditional and contemporary crafts. Alaska Gallery includes exhibits on archaeology, exploration, Russian settlement, US purchase, gold rush era, WWII and statehood. Full-scale and miniature dioramas illustrate Native culture.

ATTU BATTLEFIELD – Attu Island – Page 140 A1 Site of only WWII battle on North American continent. Island captured by Japan in June 1942, then recaptured by US in three-week bloody and costly battle in May 1943. Loss caused Japan to secretly evacuate other occupied Aleutian island, Kiska, two months later. National Historic Landmark.

BARANOF MUSEUM–Kodiak–Page 45 A5 Collection of Russian, Aleut and Koniag objects from Kodiak and Aleutian Islands. Located in Erskine House, one of oldest Russian buildings in Alaska, built in 1790s as storehouse for sea otter pelts. National Historic Landmark.

BIG DELTA STATE HISTORICAL PARK – Delta Junction – Page 116 D3 Located along Tanana River and Valdez-to-Fairbanks Trail, important crossroad for travelers, traders, gold miners and military in early 1900s. Centerpiece, restored Rika's Roadhouse, functioned as gathering place, post office, fur exchange, restaurant and lodging house from 1909 to 1947. Museum in restored sod-roof log cabin, with displays of pioneer and Athabascan artifacts. *(See State Parklands.)*

CAPE KRUSENSTERN NATIONAL MONUMENT – Kotzebue – Page 132 A4 114 beach ridges record in time sequence estimated 6,000 years of prehistoric human use of coastline. Some archaeological findings older than well-known remains of ancient Greek civilizations on Mediterranean Sea. *(See National Parklands.)*

CARRIE McLAIN MEMORIAL MUSEUM – Nome – Page 132 D3 Displays and artifacts concentrating on Eskimo life and Nome gold rush *(see this section—Gold Rush Days)*. Other exhibits include Bering Land Bridge, Seward Peninsula minerals and history of dog mushing. Extensive photography collection.

CASTLE HILL STATE HISTORIC SITE – Sitka – Page 27 D3 Location of Tlingit Indian village until early 1800s, then site of various headquarters of Russian-American Company during Alaska's Russian occupation. Buildings included impressive Baranof's Castle (burned in 1894), named after first chief Russian manager Alexander Baranof. Site of official transfer of Alaska from Russia to America in 1867 and where first American flag flew. Also first place flag with 49 stars was raised when Alaska achieved statehood in 1959. Interpretive plaques. Panoramic views of Sitka Sound.

CLAUSEN MEMORIAL MUSEUM – Petersburg – Page 24 A1 Concentrates on area's ties to sea. Tlingit Indian and Norwegian pioneer artifacts. Displays of past and current fishing techniques. World record king salmon (126.5 pounds) and chum salmon (36 pounds). Re-created cannery owner's office.

CORDOVA MUSEUM AND HISTORICAL SOCIETY – Cordova – Page 74 B1 Exhibits of area Native and pioneer history. Displays on Copper River and Northwestern Railroad. Original Fresnel lens from Cape St. Elias Lighthouse. Eyak Indian and Chugach Eskimo artifacts.

CORRINGTON MUSEUM OF ALASKAN HISTORY – Skagway – Page 38 C2 History of Alaska from prehistoric times to present, using scrimshawed walrus tusks and original art.

DOG MUSHING MUSEUM – Fairbanks – Page 115 A5 Headquarters of Alaskan Dog Mushers' Association and North American championship race. Exhibit on dog mushing history. Live dog sled demonstrations; slides and videos of dog racing.

EAGLE HISTORIC DISTRICT – Eagle – Page 119 A6 Military, judicial, transportation and communications hub of turn-of-century interior Alaska. Closest American settlement to Klondike Gold Rush *(see this section)*. High point 1905 when polar explorer Roald Amundsen trekked from ice-locked ship in Arctic Ocean to telegraph discovery of Northwest Passage. More than 100 historic buildings remain, including federal courthouse, customs house and Ft. Egbert *(see this section)*. Walking tours conducted by Eagle Historical Society.

FOREST SERVICE INFORMATION CENTER – Juneau – Page 33 C4 Exhibits and films on southeast Alaska history and natural resources. Located in Centennial Hall.

FT. ABERCROMBIE STATE HISTORICAL PARK – Kodiak – Page 45 A5 Fort established in 1941 as part of North Pacific Coastal Defense to protect Kodiak Naval Air Station and Ft. Greely Garrison during WWII Aleutian Campaign. Closed 1945, abandoned 1947, state park established 1969. Remnants of guns and gun carriages, ammunition bunkers, observation platform and other structures. Self-guided walking tour. National Register of Historic Places.

FT. EGBERT – Eagle – Page 119 A6 Established 1899 to help prevent problems among miners during gold rush. High point 1903 under Lt. William "Billy" Mitchell as base for construction of 2,000-mile Washington–Alaska Military Cable and Telegraph System (WAMCATS), which provided first direct communication between Alaska and outside world. Restored and partially reconstructed buildings include water wagon shed, granary, quartermaster storehouse, NCO quarters and mule barn. Tours.

GOVERNOR'S MANSION – Juneau – Page 33 C4 Designed 1911 by James Knox Taylor, example of early 20th-century American architecture, with significant design features used to blend structure with site. First occupied 1913 by Territorial Governor Walter E. Clark.

IDITAROD NATIONAL HISTORIC TRAIL – Nome – Page 132 D3 Network of more than 2,300 miles of trails from Nome to Seward, first used by ancient hunters and then by early-20th-century gold seekers. Mail route, "Seward to Nome Mail Trail," until 1924. Named for Athabascan Indian village on Iditarod River near site of 1908 gold discovery. Most famous historic event 1925 when 20 dog mushers carried diptheria serum 674 miles over trail from Nenana to Nome in 127.5 hours. Annual 1,049-mile Iditarod Trail Sled Dog Race, "The Last Great Race," started 1967, commemorates 1925 event, runs from Anchorage to Nome every March. (Note: Length of historic trail and race checkpoints marked in Atlas; *see Legend*. For clarity, maps show trail parallel to railroad tracks, where they actually coincide.)

ISABEL MILLER MUSEUM – Sitka – Page 27 D3 Exhibits highlight local history and people. Eight-foot-square scale model of 1860s Sitka. Photographs, furniture, paintings and Russian tools. In Centennial Building.

JUNEAU–DOUGLAS CITY MUSEUM – Juneau – Page 33 C4 Exhibits and audio-visual presentations on area, featuring gold mining and cultural history. Tools and artifacts. Native art. Children's Discovery Room.

KENAI VISITOR AND CULTURAL CENTER – Kenai – Page 69 B5 Former Ft. Kenay Museum located in Bicentennial Building. Local and natural history of area. Native and Russian artifacts, including tools, photographs and church icons.

MUSEUM OF ALASKA TRANSPORTATION AND HISTORY – Palmer – Page 83 B4 Alaska history depicted through industrial and transportation development. Trains, planes, cars, trucks, farming equipment and watercraft. Several displays inside Alaska Railroad cars and diesel engine. Outdoor exhibits.

NANA MUSEUM OF THE ARCTIC – Kotzebue – Page 133 B4 "Living culture" museum. Demonstrations of Eskimo crafts including animal skin sewing and ivory carving. Traditional Native dancers. Diorama of arctic wildlife. Jade Mountain factory where jade products are made.

NATIONAL BANK OF ALASKA HERITAGE LIBRARY AND MUSEUM – Anchorage – Page 82 D3 Alaskan, Native and Russian art. Prehistoric artifacts and gold rush period displays. Book collection includes volumes on history, exploration and Native culture.

OLD SITKA STATE HISTORICAL PARK – Sitka – Page 27 D3 First settlement in southeast Alaska, established 1799 by Russian-American Company manager, Alexander Baranof. Burned by Tlingit Indians in 1802 and relocated to present-day location in 1804. Site marked by Russian Orthodox cross and interpretive plaque. Short trail and visitor center.

OSCAR ANDERSON HOUSE – Anchorage – Page 82 D3 Built 1915, believed to be first permanent residence built in newly established town. Constructed by civic and business leader Oscar Anderson. Occupied by Anderson family until 1974. Restored, with period furnishings. National Register of Historic Places.

POTTER SECTION HOUSE STATE HISTORIC SITE – Anchorage – Page 82 D3 Restored railroad service building along Alaska Railroad. Served as living quarters for track workers. Displays of Alaska railroad history. Outside exhibits feature railcar, personnel transport car and massive snowblower. Tours. Located at Mile 115 Seward Highway.

PRATT MUSEUM – Homer – Page 62 B1 Natural and cultural history of Kenai Peninsula and Kachemak Bay. Marine aquariums, botanical garden, Alaskan mammals, whale skeletons, Native tools and marine vessels.

SAMUEL K. FOX MUSEUM – Dillingham – Page 56 D3 Display of Yup'ik Eskimo arts and crafts. Traveling exhibits from other Alaska regions.

SHELDON JACKSON MUSEUM – Sitka – Page 27 D3 Excellent collection of artifacts, art and historical items representing Alaska's main ethnic groups, mostly obtained in late 1800s by missionary Sheldon Jackson. Native vehicles, hunting and fishing equipment, clothing, baskets and totem poles. Housed in first concrete building in territory, built 1895. Located on Sheldon Jackson College campus.

SHELDON MUSEUM & CULTURAL CENTER – Haines – Page 38 D1 Interpretation of Tlingit Indian culture and pioneer history of upper Lynn Canal. Gold rush memorabilia. Slide show and video. Guided tours.

SITKA NATIONAL HISTORICAL PARK – Sitka – Page 27 D3 Commemorates Battle of Sitka, last major conflict between Europeans and Alaskan Natives. Fought 1804 between Tlingits and Russian fur traders, battle signified end of Tlingit independence and establishment of Russian stronghold in North America. Two park units include site of Tlingit fort and battleground, Russian Bishop's House and collection of 28 totem poles exhibited along park's wooded pathways *(see Hiking)*. Visitor center. Access by boat and plane.

ST. MICHAEL'S CATHEDRAL – Sitka – Page 27 D3 Exact replica of 1840s structure destroyed by fire in 1966, rebuilt 1967–1976. Constructed with logs and handhewn planks in shape of cross. Original furnishings and icons, including Our Lady of Sitka, known as "Sitka Madonna."

STATE CAPITOL – Juneau – Page 33 C4 Six-story structure, built 1930 as Federal and Territorial Building, now houses governor's offices, state legislature and government agencies. Large pillars at front of building made of native marble from southeast Alaska quarry. Upper floors display photographs of early Juneau. Tours.

TANGLE LAKES ARCHEOLOGICAL DISTRICT – Paxon – Page 106 D2 With 400 recorded sites, 455,000-acre area contains one of highest concentrations of archaeological sites in Alaska. District may have supported human occupation 12,000–15,000 years ago. Evidence of Siberian cultures supports theory of migration across Bering Land Bridge. Located between Miles 15 and 45 Denali Highway. Popular recreation area. National Register of Historic Places.

TONGASS HISTORICAL MUSEUM – Ketchikan – Page 20 C1 More than 40 exhibits of area history and culture. Native culture and art, copper and gold mining, logging and fishing. Located in Centennial Building, commemorating 1867 purchase of Alaska from Russia.

TOTEM BIGHT STATE HISTORICAL PARK – Ketchikan – Page 20 C1 Replicas of 19th-century southeast Alaska Native community house and totem art providing 20th-century interpretation of Tlingit and Haida social customs, technology and art. Constructed 1938–1941 as joint US Forest Service–Civilian Conservation Corps project. Trail through rainforest to Clan House and 14 totem poles. National Register of Historic Places.

TOTEM HERITAGE CENTER – Ketchikan – Page 20 C1 Collection of 33 original, unrestored totem poles and fragments retrieved from original locations in Tlingit and Haida villages between Yakutat and British Columbia. Among last examples of art form flourishing between 18th and 20th centuries, now exhibited in specially constructed building. Guided tours and demonstrations. National Register of Historic Places.

TRANS-ALASKA PIPELINE – Fairbanks – Page 115 A5 800-mile-long, 48-inch-diameter oil pipeline from Prudhoe Bay oilfields to terminal in Valdez. Built 1974–1977 with participation by 70,000 people. Transports almost two million barrels of oil per day. Northern half of pipeline runs above ground to protect sensitive arctic permafrost and parallels Dalton Highway. Southern half parallels Richardson Highway. Elevated pipeline can be viewed from turnout north of Fairbanks at Mile 7 Steese Highway, or along Dalton Highway *(see Scenic Drives)*. Visitor information office at Alyeska Pipeline Terminal in Valdez offers interpretive displays and brochures. Tours of Valdez terminal and Prudhoe Bay pumping/production facilities available.

UNIVERSITY OF ALASKA MUSEUM – Fairbanks – Page 115 A5 Natural history of Alaska. Exhibits include wildlife, geology, and art, tools and clothing of Native and pioneer Alaskans. State's largest gold collection. Guided tours.

VALDEZ HERITAGE CENTER MUSEUM – Valdez – Page 85 D5 History of Valdez and surrounding area. Photographs of 1964 earthquake. Scale model of oil pipeline terminal in Valdez. Exhibit on 1989 Exxon *Valdez* oil spill. Replica of miner's cabin. Firefighting equipment.

WICKERSHAM STATE HISTORIC SITE – Juneau – Page 33 C4 Large Victorian house purchased in 1928 by James V. Wickersham, one of first judges and representatives to Congress for Territory of Alaska. Displays include Wickersham's Alaska collection of early histories, diaries and documents; historical photographs; period furnishings; and Native, Russian and pioneer artifacts. Located on Chicken Ridge, considered Juneau's "Nob Hill." National Register of Historic Places.

GOLD RUSH DAYS

When an 1897 issue of a Seattle newspaper reported a steamer from Alaska with prospectors and a "a ton of gold" on board from the Klondike River, it set off the last of the great gold rushes in America. Thousands of prospectors were attracted from all over, hoping to strike it rich. This section includes some of the state's many sites relating to gold, starting with that very intense period near the turn of the century.

CHILKOOT TRAIL – Dyea – Page 38 C2 Arduous 33-mile trail from Dyea over Chilkoot Pass to Bennett Lake in British Columbia. One of only three glacier-free corridors through Coast Range. Vital link first in Native trading during pre-gold rush period and then during Klondike Gold Rush of 1897–1898. Shortest and best-known route for thousands of gold-seeking "stampeders" on first leg of journey to goldfields. Prospectors finished rest of 600-mile trip to Klondike by boat on Yukon River. Trail abandoned 1899 with establishment of White Pass & Yukon Route Railroad *(see this section)*. Historic ruins, settlements and artifacts along way. National Register of Historic Places. *(See Hiking.)*

COLDFOOT GOLD CAMP – Coldfoot – Page 136 C3 Located in southern portion of Brooks Range, 58 miles north of Arctic Circle. One of northernmost gold mining camps, established about 1899 and deserted 1912 when miners rushed northward to new strike at nearby Wiseman. Standing and collapsed structures can be seen from dirt road off highway, as well as small cemetery for inhabitants of once-thriving camp. Interpretive center with photographs of Coldfoot and adjacent areas. Located at Mile 173.6 Dalton Highway.

CROW CREEK MINE – Girdwood – Page 71 A4 Example of turn-of-century gold mine. Eight original buildings include bunkhouse, mess hall and blacksmith's shop. Panning for gold. National Register of Historic Places.

DYEA – Dyea – Page 38 C2 Gateway to Chilkoot Pass, once rivaled Skagway as largest town in Alaska. Settlement rapidly declined after opening of White Pass & Yukon Route Railroad *(see this section)* in 1898, leaving hotels, banks and stores vacant. Remains include scattered foundation ruins, rotting stubs of once extensive wharfs and Slide Cemetery, where 60 victims of 1898 avalanche on Chilkoot Trail *(see this section)* lay buried. National Register of Historic Places.

GOLD DREDGE NO. 8 – Fairbanks – Page 115 A5 Five-deck 250-foot-long ship representative of large-scale gold mining in Fairbanks area. Built 1928, in use until 1959. Displaced 1,065 tons of rock and gravel as it plied rich goldfields of Pedro, Engineer and Goldstream Creeks. Located at Mile 9 Old Steese Highway. Tours.

GOLD RUSH CEMETERY – Skagway – Page 38 C2 Resting place for early Skagway residents including notorious con-man Jefferson Randolph "Soapy" Smith, killed 1898 in shootout with surveyor Frank Reid, also killed and buried here.

INDEPENDENCE MINE STATE HISTORICAL PARK – Palmer – Page 83 A4 Largest hard-rock or lode gold mine in southcentral Alaska. Produced over 150,000 ounces of gold by 1942, from claims covering almost 3,000 acres, employing over 300 people. Closed 1951, 801-acre park established 1970s. Walking tour includes bunkhouses, warehouses, commissary, manager's home, mess hall, assay office and tunnel entrance. Interpretive signs. Tours. Visitor center. Simulated mining tunnel with hard-rock display. National Register of Historic Places. *(See State Parklands.)*

KLONDIKE GOLD RUSH NATIONAL HISTORICAL PARK – Skagway – Page 38 C2 Preserved historic buildings and portions of Chilkoot and White Pass Trails *(see this section)* from period of Klondike Gold Rush. Skagway Historic District *(see this section). (See National Parklands.)*

NOME GOLD – Nome – Page 132 D3 Discovery of gold at Anvil and Snow Creeks in 1898 resulted in Alaska's greatest gold rush—in yield and number of people involved. Estimated 20,000 gold-seekers attracted to area previously inhabited by only handful of settlers, mined more than $60 million of gold by 1911 from area creeks and beaches. Miners still camp on beaches every summer and pan for gold. As many as 100 gold dredges, many currently in use, scattered throughout Seward Peninsula, with over 40 around Nome, some just north of airport.

SKAGWAY HISTORIC DISTRICT – Skagway – Page 38 C2 Heart of downtown Skagway designated part of Klondike Gold Rush National Historical Park *(see this section)*. Boardwalks, false-fronted buildings and horse-drawn wagons evoke gold-rush-era atmosphere. About 100 buildings remain including Pantheon Saloon, Lynch & Kennedy Dry Goods Store, Verbauwhede Confectionery, Captain William Moore Cabin and White Pass & Yukon Route Railroad Depot. Walking tours and interpretive programs. Visitor center. National Register of Historic Places.

TRAIL OF '98 MUSEUM – Skagway – Page 38 C2 Collection of Klondike Gold Rush and Native artifacts from period 1897–1899. Miners' tools, sleds, scrapbooks and photographs, clothing and gambling paraphernalia. Original Baldwin steam locomotive displayed outside. Located in Skagway City Hall, Alaska's oldest granite building.

WHITE PASS & YUKON ROUTE RAILROAD – Skagway – Page 38 C2 Narrow-gauge railway built 1898–1900 at peak of Klondike Gold Rush. First railroad in Alaska and northernmost in North America at time. Considered one of world's great engineering feats, climbs to 2,865 feet above sea level, with grades as steep as 3.9 percent. Served mining industry until 1980s, then switched to excursion service. 21-mile narrated trip to White Pass summit. Spectacular views include trestles, gorges and waterfalls.

WHITE PASS TRAIL – Skagway – Page 38 C2 Second most popular route during Klondike Gold Rush. 40-mile route from Skagway to Bennett Lake in British Columbia, less steep than Chilkoot Trail *(see this section)*, allowing use of pack horses to carry supplies. Also called Dead Horse Trail for more than 3,000 horses that died from starvation and overwork, many at Dead Horse Gulch along way. Wagon toll road to White Pass City improved travel, but White Pass & Yukon Route Railroad *(see this section)* replaced trail in 1898. Presently not accessible on foot, visible from turnouts along Klondike Highway and from WP&YR Railroad paralleling trail. National Register of Historic Places.

Hiking

This section includes a sampling of developed hiking trails in Alaska. These trails range from short, easy routes to long and extremely difficult climbs through remote mountain wilderness. Many trails are accessible only by boat or plane. Backcountry hiking (no marked trails) is also very popular and, in fact, the only way to access the majority of the state's parklands.

Be sure to make adequate preparations before any hike and always check trail conditions with the appropriate land managing agency. For more information, contact one of the Public Lands Information Centers as listed in Visitor Information Centers *on page 6.*

For additional trail listings, see National Parklands and State Parklands.

Note: *All distances are one-way unless they are otherwise indicated.*

CHILKOOT TRAIL – Klondike Gold Rush National Historical Park – 33-mile route – Page 38 B2 Trail extends from Dyea to Bennett, British Columbia. Long used by Chilkoot Indians as trading route, then by thousands during Klondike Gold Rush *(see Historic Sites/Museums—Gold Rush Days)*. Difficult but popular historic trail with extremely intimidating steep section at pass. Allow 3–5 days to complete. Many reminders of gold rush activity along route. Elevation Gain: 3,700 feet.

CIRCLE–FAIRBANKS HISTORIC TRAIL – Fairbanks – 58-mile route – Page 125 D6 Part of original transportation route used by Athabascan Indians, which ran between Circle City and Fairbanks. Traverses series of high ridgetops. Trailheads located at both ends: Fairbanks Creek Road four miles from Cleary Summit and Twelvemile Summit at Mile 86 Steese Highway. Not actively maintained. Elevation Gain: 1,700 feet.

COASTAL TRAIL – Caines Head State Recreation Area – 4.5-mile route – Page 71 D4 Leaves from parking area at Lowell Point. Important to time trip around tides: three-mile stretch between Tonsina Point and North Beach can only be hiked during low tide. Leave Seward at least two hours before low tide to avoid becoming stranded along route. Stay on designated trail. Camping shelter at end of trail in North Beach.

FULLER LAKES TRAIL – Kenai National Wildlife Refuge – 2.3-mile route – Page 70 C2 Begins 1.5 miles east of east end of Skilak Lake Road and 2.5 miles west of Russian River Ferry parking area. Trail provides access to Mystery Creek Unit of Kenai Wilderness. Fairly steep climb to Lower Fuller Lake with little elevation gain beyond. Several areas may be wet or muddy. Excellent views of Kenai Range along trail. Fishing. Elevation Gain: 1,400 feet.

GRANITE TORS TRAIL – Chena River Recreation Area – 15-mile loop – Page 116 A2 Trailhead at campground, Mile 39.5 Chena Hot Springs Road. Leads to Granite Tors *(see Unique Natural Features)*. Spectacular view from top. Part of trail rocky.

GREWINGK GLACIER – Kachemak Bay State Park – 3.2-mile route – Page 62 B2 Trailhead accessible from Kachemak Bay. Easy hike over flat terrain, through stands of spruce and cottonwood and across outwash of Grewingk Glacier. Superb views of glacier and surrounding area. Rock cairns mark trail across outwash. Caution: Access to glacial ice is difficult and hazardous.

HALIBUT POINT STATE RECREATION SITE – Halibut Point State Recreation Site – 0.5-mile loop – Page 27 D3 Begins at footbridge crossing Granite Creek. Two spur trails to beach and picnic shelter. Easy trail follows beach, then winds back into forest. Elevation Gain: 30 feet.

HARDING ICEFIELD TRAIL – Kenai Fjords National Park – 3.5-mile route – Page 71 D3 Trailhead at Ranger station. Hike provides spectacular views of Exit Glacier and Harding Icefield *(see Unique Natural Features)* as well as valley below. Steep and sometimes slippery terrain.

HISTORIC IDITAROD/CROW PASS TRAIL – Chugach State Park – 26-mile route – Page 83 D4 Leaves from Eagle River Visitor Center in Chugach State Park. Section of historic trail *(see Historic Sites/Museums)* formerly used as transportation and mail route between villages of Portage and Knik. Abandoned 1919 when railway was completed; reopened for hiking in 1971. Short day hikes available at both ends of trail. Trail ends at Crow Creek trailhead. Elevation Gain: 2,600 feet.

LAZY MOUNTAIN – Palmer – 4-mile route – Page 83 B4 Trail used in early 1940s as horsepacking trail for hunters. Entire Matanuska Valley from Sutton to Anchorage can be viewed from peak. Picnic area and rest rooms at trailhead. Elevation Gain: 3,520 feet.

LITTLE COAL CREEK TRAIL – Denali State Park – 4.5-mile route – Page 94 A1 Trailhead at parking lot, Mile 163.8 Parks Highway. Easy access to alpine country. Outstanding views from top of Indian Mountain. Option of continuing on trail along Kesugi Ridge route to Byers Lake Campground (27.4 miles, rated difficult). Elevation Gain: 3,300 feet.

MT. JUNEAU TRAIL – Juneau – 3-mile route – Page 33 C4 Begins one mile from beginning of Perseverance Trail *(see this section)*, at end of Basin Road. Danger of avalanche may persist until late spring. Extremely steep climb near end to summit; ice ax useful until early summer. Spectacular views of Juneau. Caution: Do not leave trail! Elevation Gain: 2,876 feet.

PERSEVERANCE TRAIL – Juneau – 3-mile route – Page 33 C4 Trailhead at end of Basin Road. Trail starts in cul-de-sac, follows gentle grade around horn of Mt. Juneau. Trail ends in clearing next to Gold Creek. Views of Ebner Falls *(see Unique Natural Features)*. Old mining ruins scattered throughout clearing. Use caution while exploring historic area. Great danger of avalanche in winter and early spring. Elevation Gain: 700 feet.

PINNELL MOUNTAIN – Steese National Conservation Area – 27.3-mile route – Page 126 C3 Clearly marked trail traverses series of alpine ridgetops entirely above timberline. Spectacular views. Steep and rugged in many areas. Allow at least three days. Accessible from two trailheads: Mile 85.6 or 107.3 Steese Highway. Small log emergency shelters located along trail. National Recreation Trail.

POINT BRIDGET TRAIL – Point Bridget State Park – 3.5-mile route – Page 32 B3 Trailhead at Mile 39 Glacier Highway, one mile north of North Bridget Cove sign. Trail passes through rainforest muskeg, meadows, old-growth rainforest and beach. Ends at Point Bridget. Panoramic view of Lynn Canal, Chilkat Range and mountains north and east of Berner's Bay.

SEDUCTION POINT – Chilkat State Park – 6.75-mile route – Page 38 D2 Scenic beach and forest walk. Outstanding views of Davidson Glacier with prolific bird and sea life along way. Allow 9–10 hours; plan to do last beach stretch at low or mid tide. Camping on cove east of Seduction Point.

SITKA NATIONAL HISTORICAL PARK TRAIL – Sitka National Historical Park – 1.5-mile route – Page 27 D3 Begins at visitor center. Two easy, maintained loops. Totem poles along loop to battleground and fort. Prime area to view fish spawning in Indian River during late summer and early fall. *(See Historic Sites/Museums.)*

SKI LOOP TRAIL – White Mountains National Recreation Area – 5-mile route – Page 125 D4 Trail begins at Mile 28 Elliott Highway. Follow Summit Trail for first two miles, then trail on right for 1.5 miles, then Wickersham Creek Trail for remaining 1.5 miles. Trail ascends for one mile, then descends for last four miles. Views of Alaska Range at overlook at mile 1. Year-round trail with some wet and muddy sections. Elevation Gain: 460 feet.

SKILAK LOOKOUT TRAIL – Kenai National Wildlife Refuge – 2.5-mile route – Page 70 C2 Begins three miles east of Upper Skilak Campground and two miles west of Hidden Lake Campground. Passes through spruce–cottonwood forest. Ends on knob overlooking Skilak Lake. Several steep sections. Spectacular views. No fishing. Elevation Gain: 750 feet.

SUMMIT TRAIL – White Mountains National Recreation Area – 20-mile route – Page 125 D4 Developed trail with boardwalk over wetter areas. Follows ridgeline northward and passes through treeless alpine tundra, then drops into spruce forests. Borealis–LeFevre Cabin located across Beaver Creek (reservations necessary). Use caution crossing creek. Elevation Gain: 900 feet.

TURNAGAIN ARM TRAIL – Chugach State Park – 9.4-mile route – Page 82 D3 Trailhead at Potter Section House State Historic Site *(see Historic Sites/Museums)* and park headquarters. Parallels coastline and Seward Highway, ends at Windy Corner. Scenic overlooks provide views of Chugach and Kenai Mountains. Favorite "first hike of the year" for many because snow clears in early spring. Well-developed and fairly easy to hike.

TWIN PEAKS TRAIL – Chugach State Park – 3.5-mile route – Page 83 C4 Trailhead at Eklutna Lake Campground. Popular well-maintained trail provides panoramic views of entire Eklutna Valley. Difficult hike with steep sections follows west side of Twin Peaks Mountain. Sheep often seen grazing in Goat Mountain bowl. Hikers can choose own route across tundra. Good berry picking.

CHUGACH NATIONAL FOREST TRAILS

BYRON GLACIER TRAIL – 0.8-mile route – Page 71 A5 Begins six miles down Portage Glacier Road (past Begich–Boggs Visitor Center). First half of trail flat, wide and well-maintained; second half rocky with small stream crossings. Close-up views of glacier with rugged mountains in all directions. Trail ends at snowfields below glacier. Good family outing. High avalanche hazard in winter. Elevation Gain: 100 feet.

LOST LAKE TRAIL – 7-mile route – Page 71 D4 Begins at gravel pits at Mile 5 Seward Highway. Good family trail with spectacular views. Provides access to alpine country where hike can be extended in almost any direction. Trail ends at Lost Lake, two miles above timberline. Elevation Gain: 1,820 feet.

McKINLEY LAKE TRAIL – 2.1-mile route – Page 74 C2 Begins at Mile 21 Copper River Highway. Easy and wide trail through lush, moss-covered mature spruce and hemlock forest. Tent camping near lake, and cabins at each end of trail (reservations required). Trail ends at McKinley Lake Recreation Cabin. Expect rain. Bear country. Good hunting and fishing. Elevation Gain: 25 feet.

PIPELINE LAKES TRAIL – 1.8-mile route – Page 74 C2 Trail begins at Mile 20.8 Copper River Highway. Short, easy hike through wet muskeg follows old water pipeline occasionally visible. Excellent trout and grayling fishing in numerous lakes along trail. Ends at junction with McKinley Lake Trail. Expect rain. Elevation Gain: 75 feet.

POWER CREEK TRAIL – 2.5-mile route – Page 74 B1 Trailhead located at end of Power Creek Road. Magnificent scenery. First 0.5 mile excellent for family outings—thereafter, hazards require caution. Potential side trips to view glaciers. Trail follows whitewater of Power Creek through narrow valley, ends at Power Creek Basin. Numerous side streams and waterfalls. Expect rain. Elevation Gain: 350 feet.

PTARMIGAN CREEK TRAIL – 3.5-mile route – Page 71 C4 Begins at Ptarmigan Creek Campground at Mile 23 Seward Highway. Fairly easy hike with good chance of seeing goats and sheep on mountain peaks and slopes. Ends at Ptarmigan Lake. Good fishing in lake and stream one mile below outlet. Avalanche hazard in winter. Elevation Gain: 255 feet.

RESURRECTION PASS TRAIL SYSTEM – 35.2-mile route – Page 71 A3 Begins five miles south of Hope. Popular trail offers beautiful scenery, good lake fishing and six public-use cabins (reservations required). Trail splits at mile 20.5: one direction leads to Schooner Bend ending at Mile 52.3 Sterling Highway; other leads across Devils Pass, ending at Mile 39 Seward Highway. Brown bear country. Elevation Gain: 2,400 feet.

RUSSIAN LAKES TRAIL – 21-mile route – Page 70 C3 Begins at Russian Lake Campground, Mile 52 Sterling Highway. First three miles to Lower Russian Lake good family trail. Trail continues to Upper Russian Lake and Cooper Lake. Public-use cabin on Upper Russian Lake (reservations required). Brown bear country. Good fishing in lakes. Elevation Gain: 768 feet.

TONGASS NATIONAL FOREST TRAILS

AMALGA (EAGLE GLACIER) TRAIL – 5.5-mile route – Page 32 B3 Trailhead at Mile 28.4 Glacier Highway, just past Eagle River. Begins at parking lot and passes under bridge leading toward Eagle Glacier. Several beaver ponds along way. Impressive views of glacier. Easy hike. Elevation Gain: 200 feet.

ANAN CREEK TRAIL (#448) – 1-mile route – Page 25 D3 Access by boat or floatplane. Begins in Anan Bay at recreation cabin. Easy trail parallels shore, offering good views of Anan Lagoon, ends at Anan Bear Observatory. (Note: Bears also use trail—make your presence known!) Elevation Gain: 100 feet.

CASCADE CREEK TRAIL – 4.5-mile route – Page 29 D4 Access by boat or plane. Trail begins at Cascade Creek Cabin, follows Cascade Creek and ends at Swan Lake. Difficult trail. Access to fishing and outstanding scenery. Elevation Gain: 1,514 feet.

DAN MOLLER TRAIL – 3-mile route – Page 33 C4 Small parking area with marked trailhead off Pioneer Avenue. Old road serves as first part of trail. Most of trail consists of elevated planks over muskegs, very slippery when wet or frosty. Popular for cross-country skiing. Avalanche-prone area. Trail ends at Dan Moller Cabin (reservations required). Elevation Gain: 1,600 feet.

DEER MOUNTAIN/JOHN MOUNTAIN TRAIL – 9.9-mile route – Page 20 C1 Trail begins at junction of Granite Basin and Ketchikan Dump Roads. Steep climb to summit with many switchbacks. Spectacular scenic overlooks to Ketchikan and Tongass Narrows. Trail continues past Deer Peak to John Mountain, ending at Lower Silvis Lake. Elevation Gain: 3,001 feet.

ELLA LAKE TRAIL – Misty Fiords National Monument – 2.5-mile route – Page 21 C3 Access by boat or floatplane. Begins in Ella Bay. Beach marker sign at trailhead visible from bay. Difficult trail runs through old second-growth forest, muskeg and marsh. Ends at Lower Ella Lake. Excellent trout and salmon fishing in Ella Creek. Elevation Gain: 254 feet.

HARVEY LAKE TRAIL – 0.5-mile route – Page 24 B1 Access by boat or plane. Begins at Duncan Canal and passes through old-growth Sitka spruce and western hemlock. Flat terrain. Remnants of mining activity near trailhead. Trail ends at Harvey Lake Cabin. Elevation Gain: 105 feet.

INDIAN RIVER TRAIL – 5.5-mile route – Page 27 D3 Begins at pumphouse/dam at end of Indian River Road and ends at base of Indian River Falls. Within walking distance of downtown Sitka. Trail follows Indian River, meandering through rainforest. Easy trail; elevation gain gradual. Elevation Gain: 700 feet.

PERSEVERANCE LAKE TRAIL – 2-mile route – Page 20 C1 Trail begins on Harriet Hunt Lake Road at parking lot. Easy trail crosses muskeg and old-growth forest. Good hiking surface on boardwalk tread. Swinging bridge crosses Ward Creek. Fishing in Perseverance Lake at trail's end. Elevation Gain: 450 feet.

PETERSBURG MOUNTAIN – 2.5-mile route – Page 24 A1 Access by boat to state dock. Trail begins across narrows from Petersburg. Difficult hike offers outstanding views of Petersburg and Coast Range Mountains, ending atop Narrows Peak. Elevation Gain: 2,750 feet.

PUNCHBOWL LAKE TRAIL – Misty Fiords National Monument – 0.75-mile route – Page 21 B3 Access by boat or floatplane. Trail begins at south end of Punchbowl Cove *(see Unique Natural Features)*. Steep trail with several switchbacks, very narrow with deep drops in places. Considered Misty Fiords' most scenic trail with views of cove and Punchbowl Creek waterfall. Trail ends at beginning of logjam on lake. Elevation Gain: 600 feet.

SALT CHUCK TRAIL – 1-mile route – Page 19 B4 Begins at south end of Lake No. 3 in old clearcut at edge of gravel. Historic sites of Salt Chuck and Rush and Brown Mines along trail. Trail follows banks of Ellen Creek for most of way, with spur trail crossing creek and looping around Ellen Lake. Ends at Salt Chuck ruins. Elevation Gain: 75 feet.

SHAKES HOT SPRINGS TRAIL (#625) – 0.3-mile route – Page 24 B2 Access by boat via Hot Springs Slough. Trail follows easy grade to Shakes Hot Springs Recreation Site containing two hot tub structures with changing rooms. Gravel surface part of way. Elevation Gain: 25 feet.

TWENTY-MILE SPUR TRAIL – 3-mile route – Page 19 C4 Begins off Craig–Klawock–Hollis Road, 0.25 miles east of Harris River bridge. Trail follows former logging road, in second-growth forest. Parallels Harris River to headwaters, ending at box canyon in Klawock Mountains. Also used by mountain-bikers and cross-country skiers. Elevation Gain: 100 feet.

WEST GLACIER TRAIL – 3.4-mile route – Page 33 C3 Begins on north side of parking lot. Most of trail below glacier trimline. Last section difficult to follow—look for cairns marking route. Ends at top of rock outcrop. Used for access to Mendenhall Glacier *(see Unique Natural Features)* by experienced ice climbers. Not recommended for inexperienced hikers. Elevation Gain: 1,300 feet.

Downhill Ski Areas

For more information on skiing contact the Alaska Division of Tourism, Ninth Floor, State Office Building, Juneau, AK 99811, (907) 465-2010.

NAME	LOCATION	PAGE & GRID	VERTICAL DROP	NUMBER OF RUNS	LIFTS	CROSS-COUNTRY TRAILS
Alpenglow	5 miles East of Anchorage	83 D3	1,500 feet	3	2 D-Chairs, 1 T-Bar	no
Alyeska Resort and Ski Area	35 miles South of Anchorage	71 A4	3,125 feet	60	4 D-Chairs, 1 Quad, 2 Rope Tows	yes
Cleary Summit	22 miles North of Fairbanks	125 D6	1,300 feet	21	2 T-Bars, 1 Platter	no
Eaglecrest Ski Area	Juneau	33 C3	1,400 feet	30	2 D-Chairs, 1 Platter	yes
Hilltop Ski Area	8 miles East of Anchorage	83 D3	294 feet	9	1 D-Chair, 1 Rope Tow	yes
Skiland	21 miles North of Fairbanks	125 D6	1,057 feet	26	1 D-Chair	no

Freshwater Fishing

To locate freshwater fishing spots in this Atlas, look on the appropriate page for the freshwater fishing symbol and corresponding four-digit number. This chart has been compiled with the assistance of the Alaska Department of Fish and Game. It is most important to be thoroughly familiar with all rules, regulations and restrictions before fishing in any area. For a copy of the current Alaska Sport Fishing Regulations Summary booklet or more information contact the department at Capital Office Park, 1255 West 8th Street, P.O. Box 3-2000, Juneau, AK 99802, (907) 465-4112.

Note: Symbols on the maps mark only the bodies of water; location does not necessarily indicate public access or the best fishing area.

ACCESS ABBREVIATIONS
B – boat   H – hike
F – fly   R – road

FISH SPECIES SYMBOLS
○ – wild   □ – hatchery   ☆ – wild/hatchery
● – most significant wild   ■ – most significant hatchery   ★ – most significant wild/hatchery

Column groups: SALMON (Chum, Coho, King, Pink, Sockeye) | TROUT (Brook, Cutthroat, Dolly Varden/Char, Lake, Rainbow, Steelhead) | OTHER (Burbot, Grayling, Northern Pike, Sheefish, Smelt, Whitefish, Razor Clams) | FACILITIES (Dock/Boat Ramp, Fuel/Water, Campground/Toilet, Public Cabin, Commercial Lodging)

Body of Water	Access	Page & Grid
4000 Aaron Creek	B/F	25 C3
4004 Admiralty Creek	B/F	33 D3
4008 Afognak Lake	F/B	53 D3
4012 Alagnak (Branch) R	R	58 D1
4016 Alexander Creek	F/B	82 B1
4020 Alexander, Lake	F/H	28 B1
4024 American River	R	45 B4
4028 Anan/Boulder Lakes	B/F	25 D3
4032 Anchor River	R	62 B1
4036 Anchorage Bowl Lks	R	82 D3
4040 Andreafsky River	B/F	130 B3
4044 Andrew Creek	B/F	24 B2
4048 Ankau Lagoon	R/B	34 B3
4052 Anvik River	R	131 A4
4056 Avoss Lake	BH/F	22 B2
4060 Ayakulik (Red) River	F	44 D1
4064 Baranof Lake	BH/F	27 D4
4066 Bear Creek	R	24 B1
4068 Berry Creek	R	107 B6
4076 Big Goat Creek	F	21 B3
4080 Big Lake	R	82 B3
4088 Birch Creek	R	127 A6
4092 Birch Lake	R	116 C1
4096 Bird Creek	R/H	83 D4
4100 Blossom/Wilson R	B/F	21 C3, 4
4104 Blue Lake	R/H	27 D3
4108 Bluff Cabin Lake	H	116 D3
4110 Bob Johnson Lake	R/H	136 C4
4112 Boulder Lake	H	106 D1
4116 Brooks River	F/B	50 B3
4120 Brushkana Creek	R	105 C4
4124 Buskin River	R	45 A4
4128 Butte Creek	H	105 D5
4132 Campbell Creek	R/H	82 D3
4136 Carroll Creek	B	20 B2
4140 Castle River	B/F	23 B4
4144 Caswell Creek	R	82 A3
4148 Chandler Lake	F	136 B2
4152 Chatanika River	R	125 D5
4156 Chatanika River	R	125 D6
4160 Chena Lake	R	115 A6
4164 Chena River	R	115 A6
4168 Chilkat Lake	B/F	38 C1
4172 Chilkat River System	R	38 C1
4176 Chilkoot Lake	R/B	38 C1
4180 Chilkoot River System	R	38 C1
4184 Chuitna River	F	81 D4
4188 Clarence Lake	F	95 B5
4192 Clark Area, Lake	F/B	67 D4
4196 Clear Creek	R	74 B3
4198 Clearwater Creek	R	116 D3
4200 Coal Mine Road Lakes	R/H	106 B3
4204 Coghill Lake	F	84 D2
4208 Connell/Talbot Lakes	R/H	20 C1
4212 Copper Lake	F	98 C1
4216 Cottonwood Creek	R/H	83 B3
4220 Cowee Creek	R	32 B3
4224 Craig Lake	H	107 B5
4228 Crescent Creek	R/H	71 C3
4232 Crooked Creek	R	69 D5
4236 Crooked Creek	R	106 D1
4240 Crosswind Lake	F	96 C2
4244 Dall River	F	136 D4
4248 Deep Creek	R	69 D4
4252 Deep Lake	F	96 C2
4260 Denali–Clearwater Cr	R	106 D1
4264 Deshka River	F/B/R	82 A2
4268 Dewey Lakes	H	38 C2
4272 Distin Lake	F/H	28 B1
4276 Donna Lake	H	107 A5
4280 Donna Lake, Little	H	107 A5
4284 Donnelly Lake	R	106 A3
4288 Duncan Saltchuck Cr	B/F	23 A4
4292 Dune Lake	F	114 C1
4296 Eagle River	R/H	83 D4
4300 Eagle River/Lake	B/F	25 D3, 4
4304 Eklutna Tail Race	R	83 C4
4308 Elusive Lake	R/H	136 B4
4312 Eshamy Lake/Creek	F/B	72 C1
4316 Essowah Lake	F	17 A3
4320 Eva, Lake	BH/F	27 C3
4324 Exchange Creek	F	24 D1
4328 Eyak River	R	74 C1
4332 Falls Creek	R	24 B1
4336 Fielding Lake	R	106 D3
4340 Filmore Lake System	F/B	17 C3
4344 Fish Creek	R	33 C3
4348 Fish Creek	R	82 C3
4352 Fish Creek (Hyder)	R	21 A4
4356 Fish Cr (Thorne Arm)	B	20 C2
4360 Florence Lake	F	27 A4
4364 Four Mile Lake	H	108 C3
4368 Frazer Lake/River	F	44 C1
4372 Galbraith Lake	R	136 B4
4376 George, Lake	B/F	107 A6
4380 Geskakmina Lake	F	113 B6
4384 Glacier Lake	H	106 D2
4388 Goodnews River	F	54 D2
4392 Goodpaster River	B	117 D4
4396 Goose Creek	R/H	93 D6
4400 Goulding Lakes	F	26 A1
4404 Gulkana River	B/R	96 B3
4408 Hamilton Creek	B/F	23 A4
4412 Harding Lake	R	116 C1
4416 Harding River	B/F	25 C3
4420 Harriet Hunt, Lake	R	20 C1
4424 Harris River	R	19 C4
4428 Hasselborg Lake	F/H	28 B1
4432 Herman Lake	H	37 C5

Body of Water	Access	Page & Grid
4436 Hess Creek	R	124 B1
4440 High Lake	F	85 A5
4444 Hoktaheen Lake	F	31 D4
4448 Holitna River	B/F	131 C6
4452 Hugh Smith Lake	B	21 D3
4456 Humpback Lake Syst	B/F	21 D3
4460 Iliamna Lk/Tributaries	F/B	59 B4
4464 Ingram Creek	R	71 A4
4468 Iniakuk Lake	F	136 C2
4472 Innoko River	B/F	131 B5
4476 Italio River	F	35 C4
4480 Itkillik Lake	R/H	136 B4
4484 Jan Lake	R	108 B1
4488 Jim Creek	R/H	83 B5
4492 Jim River	R	136 D3
4496 Jims Lake	F	28 B1
4500 Kadake Creek	B/F	23 A3
4504 Kah Sheets River Syst	B/F	24 B1
4508 Kanektok River	F	54 A1
4512 Kanuti River	R	136 D2
4516 Karluk River	R	44 B1
4520 Karta River System	B/F	19 B4
4524 Kasilof River	R/B	69 C5
4528 Katalla River	F	75 C4
4532 Kathleen, Lake	F	27 A4
4536 Kegan River System	F	20 D1
4540 Kenai Lake	F/R	71 C3
4544 Kenai River	B/F/R	70 C1
4548 Kepler–Bradley SRA	R/H	83 B4
4552 Ketchikan Creek	R	20 C1
4556 Klawock River System	R	19 B3
4560 Klutina Lake	R	86 B1
4564 Klutina River	R	86 A1
4568 Kobuk River	F	133 B6
4572 Kodiak I Roadside Lks	R/H	45 A4
4576 Kook Lake	F	27 B4
4580 Koole Lake	F/H	116 D1
4584 Koyukok R, Mid Fk	F	136 C4
4588 Koyukok River, S Fk	R	136 B1
4592 Kurupa Lake	F	136 B1
4596 Kustatan River	F	69 A4
4598 Kuzitrin River	R	132 C4
4600 Kvichak River	F/B	58 D2
4604 Lake Creek	F/B	82 A1
4608 Lake Louise Road Lks	R	96 D1
4612 Landmark Gap Lake	H	106 D2
4616 Lewis River	F	82 C1
4620 Lisa Lake	H	107 B5
4624 Little Harding Lake	R	116 C1
4628 Lost Lake	R	116 C1
4632 Lost River	R/H	35 C3
4636 Louise, Lake	R	96 C1
4640 Manzanita Lake Syst	B/F	21 B2
4644 Manzoni, Lake	F	21 B3
4648 Marten Lake System	B/F	25 C3
4652 Martin Lake	F	75 C3
4656 Martin River	F	75 C3
4660 McDonald Syst, Lake	B/F	20 A1
4664 McKinley Lake	R	74 C2
4668 Meadows Road Lakes	R/H	106 A3
4672 Mendeltna Creek	R	96 D1
4676 Minto Flats	R/B	124 D2
4680 Montana Creek	R	93 D6
4684 Montana Creek	R	33 C3
4688 Moose Creek	R	96 B3
4692 Moose River	B/F/R	70 B1
4696 Mulchatna River	F/B	58 A1
4700 Naha River System	B/F	20 B2
4704 Nakat Lake System	B/F	17 C3
4708 Naknek Lk/Bay of Is	F	51 B3
4712 Naknek River	B/R	50 B1
4716 Nakwasina River	F	27 C3
4720 Nancy Lake Rec Area	R/H	82 B2
4724 Newhalen River	F	59 A5
4728 Ninilchik River	R	69 D4
4732 Niukluk River	R	132 C3
4736 Noatak River	F	134 D4
4740 Nome River	R	132 D3
4744 Nowitna River	B/F	111 A4
4748 Nushagak River	F/B	57 D4
4752 Nuyakuk River	F	57 A4
4756 Ohmer Creek	R	24 B1
4760 Olds River	R/H	45 B4
4764 Orchard Lake	F/B	20 A2
4768 Pasagshak River	R	45 C5
4772 Pat's Lake System	R	24 C2
4776 Paxson Lake	R	96 A3
4780 Perseverance Lake	R/H	20 C1
4784 Peters Creek	R	93 D6
4788 Peters, Lake	F	137 A6
4792 Petersburg Creek/Lake	B/F	24 A1
4796 Peterson Creek	R	33 C3
4800 Piledriver Slough	R	115 B6
4804 Pilgrim River	R	132 C3
4808 Plotnikof Lake	F	22 B2
4812 Polly Creek	R	68 C2
4816 Poplar Grove Creek	R	97 C4
4820 Power Creek	R	74 B1
4824 Prudhoe Bay	R	135 D7
4828 Pullen Creek	R	38 C2
4832 Quartz Lake	R	116 D3
4836 Rainbow Lake	F/H	116 D2
4840 Rainbow Lake	F	20 B1
4844 Ravine/Bonnie Lakes	R	84 A1
4848 Ray River	R	124 A1
4852 Red Lake System	R	23 D4
4856 Reflection Lake	F/B	25 D3
4860 Rezanof Lake	F	22 B2
4864 Robertson #2 Lake	H	108 B1

FRESHWATER FISHING, continued

ACCESS ABBREVIATIONS
B – boat   H – hike
F – fly   R – road

FISH SPECIES SYMBOLS
○ – wild   □ – hatchery   ☆ – wild/hatchery
● – most significant wild   ■ – most significant hatchery   ★ – most significant wild/hatchery

Column headers: SALMON (Chum, Coho, King, Pink, Sockeye), TROUT (Brook, Cutthroat, Dolly Varden/Char, Lake, Rainbow, Steelhead), OTHER (Burbot, Grayling, Northern Pike, Sheefish, Smelt, Whitefish, Razor Clams), FACILITIES (Dock/Boat Ramp, Fuel/Water, Campground/Toilet, Public Cabin, Commercial Lodging), PAGE & GRID

No.	Body of Water	Access	Page & Grid
4868	Rock Creek	R	106 D2
4872	Roslyn Creek	R/H	45 B5
4876	Russian River	R/H	70 C3
4880	Sagavanirktok River	R	136 A4
4884	Salcha River	R	116 B2
4888	Salmon Bay System	F	24 C1
4892	Salmon Lake	R	132 D3
4896	Salonie Creek	R/H	45 B4
4900	Saltery Creek	F/H	45 B4
4904	Sarkar River System	R/F	19 A3
4908	Schrader, Lake	F	137 A6
4912	Scottie Creek	R	99 B6
4916	Sculpin Lake	R	87 B4
4920	Selawik River	F	133 B6
4924	Sevenmile Lake	R	106 D3
4928	Shaw Creek	R	116 C3
4932	Sheep Creek	R/B	93 D6
4936	Ship Creek	R	83 D3
4940	Silver Salmon Creek	F	68 D2
4944	Sinuk River	R	132 D3
4948	Sitkoh Creek/Lake	BH/F	27 B3
4952	Situk River	R	35 C3
4956	Skilak Lake	R/B/F	70 C2
4960	Sourdough Creek	R	97 B4
4964	Staney Creek	R	19 A3
4968	Summit Lake	R	106 D3
4972	Surge Lake	BH/F	31 D4
4976	Susitna Lake	B/F	96 C1
4980	Susitna River	F/B	82 B2
4984	Susitna River, Little	R/HB	83 B3
4988	Susitna River, Upper	F/B	93 C6
4992	Swan Lake	F/B	20 B2
4996	Swanson River	R/B	70 B1
5000	Swanson River Lakes	R/H	70 A2
5004	Swede Lake	H	96 A3
5008	Swede Lake, Little	H	106 D3
5012	Sweetwater System	R/F	19 A4
5016	Taiya/Dyea Rivers	R	38 B2
5020	Talachulitna River	F/B	81 A5
5024	Talarik Creek, Lower	F	59 B4
5028	Talkeetna River	B/F/R	94 C1

No.	Body of Water	Access	Page & Grid
5032	Tanada Lake	F	98 C2
5036	Tangle Lakes	R	96 A2
5040	Tebay River Drainage	F	87 C4
5044	Ten Mile Lake	R	106 D3
5048	Theodore River	F	82 C1
5052	Thoms Lake/Creek	B/F	24 D2
5056	Thorne River	R	19 A4
5060	Tikchik/Nuyakuk Lks	F	56 A2
5064	Togiak Lake	F/B	55 C4
5068	Tokun, Lake	F	75 C4
5072	Tolsona/Moose Lake	R	96 D2
5076	Triangle Lake	F	113 B6
5080	Tsiu River	F	76 D1
5084	Tulsona Creek	R	97 C4
5088	Turner Lake	F	33 C5
5092	Tustumena Lake	B/FH	69 D5
5096	Twentymile River	R/H	71 A5
5100	Twin Lake, East	F	113 C5
5104	Twin Lake, West	F	113 C5
5108	Twin Lakes	R/H	136 C4
5112	Tyee Lake	F	25 D4
5116	Tyone Lake	B/F	96 B1
5120	Uganik Lake System	F/B	44 B3
5124	Ugashik Lakes	F	42 B1
5128	Unalakleet River	F	131 A4
5132	Van Lake	R	87 C4
5136	Virginia Lake	B/F	24 C2
5140	Walker Lake	F	136 C1
5144	Walker Lake	F	37 C5
5148	Walker Lake System	B/F	21 A3
5152	Ward Lake System	F	20 C1
5156	Wasilla Cr/Rabbit Sl	R/H	83 B4
5160	Whipple Creek	R	20 C1
5164	Willow Creek	R/HB	82 A3
5168	Willow Creek, Little	R/B	82 A3
5172	Windfall Lake	F	33 B3
5176	Wood River Lakes	F/B	56 C2
5180	Wulik River	F	132 A4
5184	Yentna Drainage Lks	F/B	82 A1
5188	Yentna River	F/B	82 A1
5192	Young Lake	F	33 D4

Saltwater Fishing

To locate saltwater fishing spots in this Atlas, look on the appropriate page for the saltwater fishing symbol and corresponding four-digit number. This chart has been compiled with the assistance of the Alaska Department of Fish and Game. It is most important to be thoroughly familiar with all rules, regulations and restrictions before fishing in any area. For a copy of the current Alaska Sport Fishing Regulations Summary booklet or more information contact the department at Capital Office Park, 1255 West 8th Street, P.O. Box 3-2000, Juneau, AK 99802, (907) 465-4112.
Note: Symbols on the maps mark only the bodies of water; location does not necessarily indicate public access or the best fishing area.

ACCESS ABBREVIATIONS
B – boat   H – hike
F – fly   R – road

FISH SPECIES SYMBOLS
○ – wild   □ – hatchery   ☆ – wild/hatchery
● – most significant wild   ■ – most significant hatchery   ★ – most significant wild/hatchery

Column headers: BOAT (Chum Salmon, Coho Salmon, King Salmon, Pink Salmon, Sockeye Salmon, Halibut, Rockfish, Dolly Varden, Flounder/Sole/Other, Sheefish), SHORELINE (Chum Salmon, Coho Salmon, King Salmon, Pink Salmon, Sockeye Salmon, Halibut, Rockfish, Cutthroat Trout, Dolly Varden, Flounder/Sole/Other), FACILITIES (Dock/Boat Ramp, Fuel/Water, Campground/Toilet, Public Cabin, Commercial Lodging), PAGE & GRID

No.	Body of Water	Access	Page & Grid
6000	Auke Bay	R	33 C3
6004	Bell I/Yes Bay	F/B	20 A1, 2
6008	Billys Hole	B/F	72 A3
6012	Blind Slough	R/B	24 B1
6016	Caamano Point	B	20 C1
6020	Cape Strait	B	24 A1
6024	Carroll Inlet	B	20 C2
6028	Carroll Point	B	20 C2
6032	Chatham Strait	B/F	27 B4
6036	Chilkat Inlet	B/R	38 D2
6040	Chilkoot Inlet	B/R	38 D2
6044	Chiniak Bay	B/R	45 B5
6048	Clover Passage	B/R	20 C1
6052	Cochrane Bay	B/F	72 B1
6056	Coghill Lagoon	B/F	84 D2
6060	Cook Inlet	B/F/R	69 C4
6064	Cross Sound	B/F	31 D4
6068	Culross Passage	B/F	72 B1
6072	Eastern Passage	B	24 C2
6076	Elfin Cove	B/F	31 D5
6080	Eshamy Bay/Lagn	B/F	72 C2
6084	Esther Passage	B/F	72 A2
6088	Frederick Sound	B/F	28 D2
6092	Frederick Sound	B	24 A1
6096	Galena Bay	B/F	73 A4
6100	Gambier Bay	B/F	28 C2
6104	Gastineau Channel	B/R	33 D4
6108	Glacier Bay	B/F	31 A5
6112	Grindall Island	F/B	20 C1
6116	Hell's Hole	B/F	73 B5
6120	Herring Bay	B/F	20 C2
6124	Hinchinbrook I (N)	B/F	73 C4
6128	Hinchinbrook I (S)	B/F	73 C4
6132	Hoonah Sound	B/F	27 B3
6136	Icy Strait	B/F	32 C1
6140	Jackpot Bay	B/F	72 C1
6144	Kachemak Bay	S/F/R	62 B2
6148	Kalsin Bay	B/R	45 B5
6152	Kelp Bay	B/F	27 C4
6156	Khaz Bay	B/F	26 B1
6160	Knight Island	B/F	72 C2
6164	Long Bay	B/F	72 B1
6168	Lutak Inlet	B/R	38 C1

No.	Body of Water	Access	Page & Grid
6172	Lynn Canal	B	32 B2
6176	Main Bay	B/F	72 B1
6180	Middle Bay	B/R	45 B5
6184	Monashka Bay	B/R	45 A5
6192	Mountain Point	R/B	20 C1
6196	Neets Bay	B/F	20 A1
6200	Noyes Island	B	18 B2
6204	Passage Canal	B/F	71 A5
6206	Patton Bay	B/F	65 A5
6208	Peril Strait	B/F	27 C2
6212	Pigot Bay	B/F	72 A1
6216	Point Alava	B	20 D2
6220	Point Ellis	B	23 B3
6224	Port Banks	B/F	22 A1
6228	Port Chalmers	B/F	72 D3
6232	Port Frederick	B/F	32 D1
6236	Port Snettisham	B/F	28 A2
6240	Portage Cove	B/R	38 D2
6244	Pybus Bay	B/F	28 C1
6248	Redoubt Bay	B/F	22 A1
6252	Resurrection Bay	S/F/R	71 D4
6256	Salisbury Sound	B/F	27 D2
6260	San Alberto Bay	B	19 C3
6264	Shelter Island	B/F	32 C3
6268	Simpson Bay	B/F	74 B1
6272	Sitka Sound	B/R	27 D3
6276	Sitkoh Bay	B/F	27 B4
6280	Stephens Passage	B/F	28 B2
6284	Taiya Inlet	B/F	38 C2
6288	Taku Inlet	B/F	33 C4
6292	Tee Harbor	B/R	32 C3
6296	Thorne Bay	B	19 B4
6300	20 Fathom Bank	B	20 C1
6304	Unakwik Inlet	B/F	72 A2
6308	Ushk Bay	B/F	26 B2
6312	Valdez Arm	BF/R	85 D4
6316	Vallenar Point	B	20 C1
6320	Warm Springs Bay	B/F	27 D4
6324	Whale Bay	B/F	22 A1
6328	Women's Bay	B/R	45 B5
6332	Wrangell Narrows	R/B	24 B1
6336	Yakutat Bay	B/R	34 B3

11

Float Trips

The listings in this chart provide a sampling of the many float trips Alaska has to offer. Detailed descriptions, including all hazards, portages, current water conditions and land ownership must be obtained before starting out. For more information contact one of the Public Lands Information Centers listed in Visitor Information Centers on page 6.
Nine of Alaska's 25 National Wild and Scenic Rivers (NW&SR) *are included here. The remaining 16 are identified along the riverways in the Atlas. These rivers have been federally designated because of outstanding natural, cultural and/or recreational features.*

ABBREVIATIONS

Type of Craft	Access	Skill Level	
C–canoe	A–air	B–beginner	A–advanced
K–kayak	L–land	I–intermediate	E–expert
R–raft	W–water		

NAME, LOCATION	PAGE & GRID	LENGTH (miles)	TYPE OF CRAFT	ACCESS	SKILL LEVEL	WHITEWATER CLASS	PUT-IN	TAKE-OUT	COMMENTS
Aniakchak River	139 B4	32	R	A	B/A	I–IV	Surprise Lake	Aniakchak Bay	Spectacular trip from lake inside volcano, along boulder-lined river to saltwater bay. NW&SR.
Beaver Creek	126 C1	127	CKR	AL	B/I	I	Nome Cr, Mi 57 Steese Highway	via plane, Victoria Creek	Rolling hills, jagged White Mountains peaks, Yukon Flats marshes. NW&SR.
Birch Creek	126 C3	126	CKR	L	B/A	I–III	Mile 94.5 Steese Highway	Mile 147 Steese Highway	Upland plateaus, forested valleys and rolling hills. Class III rapids. NW&SR.
Chatanika River Trail	126 C1	60	CKR	L	B/I	I	Mile 66 Steese Highway	Mile 11 Elliot Highway	Clear-water stream paralleling highway. No major obstacles.
Chitina River	88 C2	62	KR	L	I	II–III	Kennicott River near McCarthy	O'Brien Creek near Chitina	Includes Kennicott and Nizina Rivers. Spectacular views of Wrangell Mountains.
Copper River	98 B1	244	CKR	ALW	I/A	II–IV	Slana River Bridge	Cordova Road at Flag Point	Wrangell Mountains, canyons, glaciers, Copper River Delta. Shorter trips possible.
Cross Admiralty Canoe Route	28 B1	32	CK	AW	B/A	—	Mole Harbor	Angoon	Scenic route across Admiralty Island linking eight lakes and Mitchell Bay. Several portages.
Delta River	106 D3	29	CKR	L	B/A	I–III	Tangle Lks, Mile 22 Denali Hwy	Mile 212.5 Richardson Hwy	Tundra-covered hills, steep slopes, rock cliffs. Alaska Range. NW&SR.
Eagle River, Upper	83 C4	13	CKR	L	I/A	I–III	Mile 7.5 or 9 Eagle River Road	Eagle River Campground	Glacial stream through Chugach Mountains. Easy access from Anchorage.
Fortymile River, Middle Fork	118 C2	90	CKR	AL	B/E	I–V	via plane, Joseph	O'Brien Creek Bridge	Deep, winding canyons. Forests. Mining ruins. Portage Class III–V rapids. Add 182 miles to Eagle. NW&SR.
Fortymile River, South Fork	109 A4	72	CKR	L	B/I	I–III	Mile 49 Taylor Highway	O'Brien Creek Bridge	Active gold mining area. Add 92 miles for trip to Eagle. NW&SR.
Gulkana River, Main Fork	96 A3	45	CKR	L	B/I	I–III	Paxson Lake Campground	Sourdough Campground	Wild but subdued scenery. Abundant wildlife. Highlight Canyon Rapids. Popular route. NW&SR.
Honker Divide Canoe Route	19 A4	30	CK	LW	A	—	Hatchery Creek Bridge	Public dock, Thorne Bay	Traverses series of lakes and Thorne River across Prince of Wales Island. Primitive. Very difficult.
Kobuk River	136 C1	125	CKR	A	I/A	II–IV	via plane, Walker Lake	via plane, Kobuk	Popular trip through wide valley and two scenic canyons. NW&SR.
Nancy Lake Canoe Trail System	82 B2	8	C	L	B/I	—	Mile 4.5 Nancy Lake Parkway	same as put-in	Chain of lakes in Link Lake Loop. Well-marked portages. Good weekend trip; longer trip possible.
Nenana River	105 C4	130	CKR	L	I/E	I–V	Mile 18 Denali Highway	Tenana River at Nenana	Scenic glacial river with sections of Class V whitewater. No canoes, upper and lower sections.
Noatak River	136 C1	396	CKR	A	B/I	I–II	via plane, headwaters Noatak River	via plane, Noatak	Wilderness trip through canyon, tundra and forest above Arctic Circle. NW&SR.
Nowitna River	100 A3	250	CKR	AW	B/I	I	via plane, Meadow Cr confluence	via plane, Yukon River	Trip through Nowitna NWR *(see Wildlife Refuges)*. Camping beaches. Rockhounding. NW&SR.
Squirrel River	133 A5	53	CKR	A	B/I	I	via plane, North Fork confluence	via plane, Kiana	Broad valley, tundra, 2,000-foot Kiana Hills. Good family trip. Above Arctic Circle.
Stikine River, North Arm Route	24 B1	18	CK	ALW	I/A	—	Mile 35.5 Mitkof Highway	Kakwan Point	Upriver paddling through spectacular steep-walled, glaciated valley. LeConte Glacier *(see Unique Natural Features)*.
Swan Lake Route	70 B1	60	CK	L	B/I	I	Swan Lake Road, E/W entrances	Moose River Bridge	30 lakes and forks of Moose River in Kenai NWR *(see Wildlife Refuges)*. Varied wildlife.
Swanson River Route	70 A2	80	CK	L	B/I	I–II	Paddle Lake	North Kenai Road Bridge	40 lakes and 46 miles of Swanson River in Kenai NWR *(see Wildlife Refuges)*. National Recreation Trail.
Tazlina River System	85 A4	74	KR	L	I/A	II–III	Mile 138 Glenn Highway	Mile 110 Richardson Hwy	Trip on Nelchina, Little Nelchina and Tazlina Rivers and Tazlina Lake. Wildlife.
Unalakleet River	133 D6	76	CKR	A	B	I	via plane, Tenmile Cr confluence	Unalakleet	Remote scenic area. Oxbows, marshes, gravel bars. Fishing for salmon, grayling and arctic char.
Upper Tangle Lake/Gulkana River, Mid Fk	106 D2	77	KR	L	B/I	I–III	Tangle River Campground	Sourdough Campground	Through tundra and forest of Alaska Range to Main Fork, Gulkana River. NW&SR.
Yukon River	119 A6	155	CKR	L	B/I	I	Taylor Highway, Eagle	Steese Highway, Circle	Scenic, traversable section of one of North America's longest rivers. Through Yukon–Charley Rivers Nat Preserve.

Boat Ramps

To locate boat ramps in this Atlas, look on the appropriate map for the boat ramp symbol and corresponding four-digit number.
This chart was compiled with the assistance of the Alaska Department of Fish and Game, Division of Sport Fish. For more information on boat ramps contact this agency at 1255 West 8th Street, P.O. Box 3-2000, Juneau, AK 99802, (907) 465-4180.

SURFACE ABBREVIATIONS

A–asphalt	G–gravel	S–sand
C–concrete	L–landing mat	W–wood planks

FACILITY	LOCATION	SURFACE	LANES	BOARDING DOCK	FEE	RESTROOMS	PICNIC AREA	CAMPGROUND	BOAT RENTAL	SMALL BOAT HARBOR	PARKING	PAGE & GRID
3000 Alaganik Slough	Mile 17 Copper River Highway	C	1			●		●				74 C2
3004 Aleknegik Boat Launch	Wood–Tikchik State Park	G	1			●					●	56 C2
3008 Amalga Harbor	Juneau	C	2	●	●	●					●	32 C3
3012 Anton Larsen Bay	Kodiak Island	C	1								●	45 A4
3016 Auke Bay	Juneau	C	2	●	●	●				●	●	33 C3
3020 Bar Harbor	Ketchikan	C	1	●		●				●		20 C1
3024 Beach Lake	Birchwood	G	1			●	●				●	83 C3
3028 Bernice Lake	Mile 10 North Kenai Road	G	1			●		●			●	69 B5
3032 Big Eddy Jetty	Kenai River, Mile 14	G	1			●		●				69 B5
3036 Big Lake East	Mile 52 Parks Highway	C	2			●	●	●				82 B3
3040 Big Lake Lodge	Big Lake	G	1			●						82 B3
3044 Bing Brown's Landing	Kenai River, Mile 39.5	G	1			●	●	●			●	70 B1
3048 Birch Lake	Mile 308 Richardson Highway	S	1			●						116 C1
3052 Bluffs on Susitna	Mile 86 Parks Highway	G	2		●	●					●	82 A2
3056 Boat Harbor	Dillingham	C	1		●					●	●	56 D3
3060 Bonnie Lake	Mile 83 Glenn Highway	G	1			●		●			●	84 A1
3064 Burkeshore Marina	Big Lake	C	2			●					●	82 B3
3068 Byers Lake Campground	Mile 147 Parks Highway	G	1			●	●	●			●	93 B6
3072 Centennial Park	Kenai River, Soldotna	C	1			●	●	●	●	●	●	69 C5
3076 Chatanika	Mile 39 Steese Highway	G	1			●						125 D6
3080 Chatanika River	Mile 11.4 Elliott Highway	G	1			●						125 D5
3084 Chena River State Recreation Site	University Avenue, Fairbanks	C	1			●	●	●			●	115 A5
3088 Chilkat State Park	Haines	C	1	●		●	●	●				38 D2
3092 Chitina River	Edgerton Highway	G	1									87 B4
3096 Christiansen Lake	Talkeetna	G	1	●		●	●				●	93 C6
3100 Clearwater Lake	Mile 269 Richardson Highway	C	1									116 D3
3104 Clearwater Creek	Mile 1415 Alaska Highway	C	1			●						117 D4
3108 Cordova Boat Harbor	Cordova	C	2	●		●				●	●	74 B1
3112 Crescent Harbor	Sitka	C	1			●				●	●	27 D3
3116 Cunningham Park	Lower Kenai River	L	1			●	●	●				69 B5
3120 Deep Creek	Ninilchik	C	2			●	●	●			●	69 D4
3124 Deshka Landing	Mile 67 Parks Highway	G	1		●						●	82 B2
3128 Dog Bay	Kodiak	C	1	●		●				●	●	45 A5
3132 Dot Brown's Fish Camp	Kenai River, Mile 43.3	G	1			●					●	70 C1
3136 Douglas Harbor	Douglas	C	1		●	●	●			●	●	33 C4
3140 Eagle Rock	Kenai River	G	1			●	●	●			●	69 B5
3144 Echo Cove	Juneau	C	1		●	●	●				●	32 B3
3148 Eyak River	Cordova	G	1			●						74 B1
3152 Fielding Lake State Recreation Site	Mile 200.5 Richardson Highway	C	1			●	●	●				106 D3
3156 Finger Lake	Wasilla	G	2	●		●	●	●			●	83 B4
3160 Fish Creek Marina	Big Lake	G	1				●	●	●		●	82 B3
3164 George Lake Lodge	Mile 1385 Alaska Highway	G	1									107 A5
3168 Goodpaster	Big Delta	C	1									116 D3
3172 Haines Harbor	Haines	C	1		●	●				●	●	38 D2
3176 Harding Lake	Mile 322 Richardson Highway	C	1			●	●	●			●	116 C1
3180 Harris Harbor	Juneau	C	1		●					●	●	33 C4
3184 Hidden Lake	Kenai Peninsula	G	1			●	●	●				70 C2
3188 Hollis	Prince of Wales Island	C	1									19 C4
3192 Homer Boat Harbor	Homer Spit	C	4	●		●		●		●	●	62 B2
3196 Hoonah Harbor	Hoonah	C	1	●						●		32 D2
3200 Hyder Harbor	Hyder	C	1	●						●		21 A4
3204 Iliamna Lake	Newhalen	G	1									59 B5
3208 Izaak Walton Campground	Moose/Kenai River	A	1			●	●	●	●			70 B1
3212 Jan Lake	Mile 1353.5 Alaska Highway	G	1			●						108 B1
3216 Jim's Landing	Kenai River, Mile 70	G	1			●	●	●			●	70 C2
3220 Johnson Lake	Mile 110 Sterling Highway	G	1			●	●	●			●	69 C5
3224 Kasilof Harbor	Lower Kasilof River	C	1	●		●					●	69 C5
3228 Kasilof River	Sterling Highway Bridge	C	1			●	●	●			●	69 C5
3232 Kasilof River, Upper	Tustumena Lake Outlet	G	1			●	●	●			●	69 D5
3236 Kenai Keys	Kenai River, Mile 43.5	G	1									70 C1
3240 Kenai Lake	Mile 41 Sterling Highway	G	1			●	●	●			●	71 C3
3244 Kenai Lake	Mile 104 Seward Highway	G	1			●					●	71 C4
3248 Kenai Lake Outlet	Cooper Landing	G	1									70 C3
3250 Kenai Riverbend Campground	Kenai River, Mile 13.8	G	1			●	●	●	●			69 B5
3252 Kenai, City Ramp	Lower Kenai River	C	2			●						69 B5
3256 Kepler Lake	Mile 37 Glenn Highway	G	1			●	●	●	●		●	83 B4
3260 King Run	Kenai River, Mile 15.3	G	1			●	●	●	●	●		69 B5
3264 Klawock River	Klawock	G	1							●		19 B3
3268 Klondike Inn	Big Lake	G	1			●	●		●		●	82 B3
3272 Knudson Cove	Ketchikan	C	2	●					●	●	●	20 C1
3276 Kodiak Boat Harbor	Kodiak	C	2	●						●	●	45 A5
3280 Lake Camp Access	Katmai National Park	G	1	●		●	●				●	50 B2
3284 Letnikof Cove	Haines	C	1							●		38 D2
3288 Little Susitna River	Wasilla	C	2	●	●	●	●	●			●	82 C2
3292 Long Lake	Mile 85 Glenn Highway	G	1			●		●			●	84 A1
3296 Longmare Lake	Kenai Peninsula	C	1								●	70 B1
3300 Lucile Lake	Mile 41 Parks Highway	G	1			●	●	●			●	83 B4
3304 Lutak Inlet	Haines	C	1		●						●	38 C2
3308 Manley Hot Springs	Manley Hot Springs	C	1			●	●				●	113 A5
3312 Matanuska Lake	Mile 35 Glenn Highway	G	1	●		●	●	●			●	83 B4
3316 Metlakatla	Metlakatla	C	1	●						●		20 D1
3320 Miller's Landing	Mile 57 Parks Highway	G	1			●	●	●			●	82 B3
3324 Mirror Lake	Mile 23 Glenn Highway	G	2			●	●				●	83 C4
3328 Mitkof Point	Petersburg	C	1								●	24 B1
3332 Mountain Point	Ketchikan	C	2									20 C1
3336 Naknek City Dock	Naknek	C	1									49 B5
3340 Naknek River	King Salmon	G	1						●		●	50 B1
3344 Nancy Lake	Mile 67 Parks Highway	C	1			●	●	●				82 B2
3348 Nenana	Nenana	C	1								●	114 B2
3352 Ninilchik Village	Lower Ninilchik River	C	1			●	●	●	●	●	●	69 D4
3356 Nordale	Chena River	G	1									115 A6
3360 North Cove	Craig	C	1							●	●	19 C3
3364 North Douglas	Juneau	C	1		●							33 C3
3368 Papkes Landing	Petersburg	C	1							●	●	24 B1
3372 Paxson Lake	Mile 173 Richardson Highway	C	1			●		●				96 A3
3376 Pelican Boat Launch	Pelican	G	1							●		26 A1
3380 Petersburg, North Harbor	Petersburg	W	1			●				●		24 A1
3384 Petersburg, South Harbor	Petersburg	C	1	●						●	●	24 A1
3388 Placer River	Portage	G	1								●	71 A5
3392 Poachers Cove	Kenai River, Mile 17.1	G	1			●	●	●	●	●		69 C5
3396 Port Valdez Harbor	Valdez	C	1			●				●		85 D5
3400 Portage Cove	Kake	C	1	●						●		23 A4
3404 Porters	Kenai River, Mile 15.2	G	1			●						69 B5
3408 Quartz Lake	Mile 277.8 Richardson Highway	C	1			●	●	●	●			116 D3
3416 Riverside Campground	Kenai River, Mile 17	G	1			●	●	●				69 B5
3420 Rocky Lake	Mile 52 Parks Highway	G	1			●	●	●			●	82 B3
3424 Salamatof, Lower	Kenai River, Mile 26.9	G	1								●	70 C1
3428 Salamatof, Upper	Kenai River, Mile 28.6	G	1									70 C1
3432 Salcha	Mile 325.3 Richardson Highway	C	1			●	●	●				116 C1
3436 Scout Lake Road	Kenai River, Mile 34.6	G	1								●	70 B1
3440 Sealing Cove	Sitka	C	1	●		●				●	●	27 D3
3444 Seventeenmile Lake	Jonesville	G	2				●				●	83 B5
3448 Seward Public Ramp	Seward	C	2	●		●	●	●		●	●	71 D4
3452 Shaw Creek	Mile 288.7 Richardson Highway	C	1		●							116 C2
3456 Ship Creek	Anchorage	G	1								●	82 D3
3460 Shoemaker Harbor	Wrangell	C	1	●			●	●		●	●	24 C2
3464 Situk River (Lower Landing)	Situk	G	1				●	●			●	35 C3
3468 Situk River/Nine Mile Bridge	Yakutat	G	1				●				●	35 B4
3472 Skagway Harbor	Skagway	C	2			●				●		38 C2
3476 Skilak Lake, Lower	Kenai Peninsula	L	1			●	●	●			●	70 C2
3480 Skilak Lake, Upper	Kenai Peninsula	L	1			●	●	●			●	70 C2
3484 Soldotna	Kenai River, Mile 16	G	1			●				●		69 B5
3488 Sourdough	Mile 148 Richardson Highway	G	2			●		●			●	96 B3
3492 South Rolly Lake	Mile 67 Parks Highway	G	1			●	●	●			●	82 B2
3496 Starrigavan	Old Sitka	C	1	●		●	●				●	27 D3
3500 Stormy Lake	North Kenai	C	1			●	●	●			●	69 A5
3504 Summit Lake	Mile 194 Richardson Highway	G	1			●					●	106 D3
3508 Susitna Landing	Mile 82 Parks Highway	G	5		●	●	●				●	82 A2
3512 Swiftwater Park and Ramp	Kenai River, Mile 23	C	1			●	●	●	●		●	69 C5
3516 Talkeetna	Mile 14 Talkeetna Spur	G	2			●					●	93 C6
3520 Tee Harbor	Juneau	G	1							●		32 C3
3524 Thorne Bay	Prince of Wales Island	C	1	●						●		19 B4
3528 Twentymile River	Portage	S	1								●	71 A5
3532 Upper Trail Lake	Mile 30 Seward Highway	G	1									71 B4
3536 Wasilla Lake	Mile 40 Parks Highway	G	1	●		●	●		●		●	83 B4
3540 Whittier Boat Harbor	Whittier	C	2	●		●				●	●	71 A5
3544 Willow Creek	Mile 72 Parks Highway	G	1			●	●	●			●	82 A2
3548 Wood River	Dillingham	C	1								●	56 D3
3552 Wrangell Harbor	Wrangell	A	1	●						●		24 C2
3556 Yakutat Harbor	Yakutat	C	1	●						●	●	35 B3
3560 Yukon River	Mile 56 Dalton Highway	C	1			●						124 A1

Unique Natural Features

Many of the features listed in this category are found within Alaska parks and forests. For more information on these areas see National Parklands and State Parklands.

ANIAKCHAK CALDERA – Aniakchak National Monument and Preserve – Page 139 B4 Six-mile-diameter, 2,000-foot-deep, explosive volcanic crater, one of world's largest. Resulted from collapse of huge volcano thousands of years ago, when 15.4 cubic miles of debris were hurled from its core and scattered for 20 miles on surrounding countryside. Caldera contains 2,200-foot cone, Vent Mountain, and Surprise Lake, headwaters of Aniakchak River *(see Float Trips)*. Caldera floor dotted with cinder cones, lava and ash flows and explosion pits. Last volcanic eruption in 1931. National Natural Landmark.

BAILEY BAY HOT SPRINGS – Tongass National Forest – Page 20 A1 Highest surface temperature of any known springs in southeast Alaska. Not altered significantly for recreation use; good opportunity for study of hot springs flora. Access on 2.2-mile trail. Shelter.

BLUE RIVER LAVA FLOW GEOLOGICAL AREA – Misty Fiords National Monument – Page 25 C4 9,500-acre area includes remains of lava flow which moved down Lava Fork and Blue River Valleys from Canada, creating Blue Lake and temporarily damming Unuk River which then carved channel through lava. Youngest-known lava flow in southeast Alaska.

CHITISTONE FALLS – Wrangell–St. Elias National Park and Preserve – Page 89 B3 Formed by Chitistone River dropping 300 feet over sheer wall. Located in Upper Chitistone Canyon.

COLUMBIA GLACIER – Chugach National Forest – Page 85 D4 One of largest tidewater glaciers in North America, 42 miles long and four miles wide at terminus. Actively retreating, last of 52 Alaskan tidewater glaciers to still fill length of its fiord. Cliffs of ice towering as high as 300 feet above water calve translucent, house-sized icebergs into Columbia Bay. Access by state ferry, charter boat or plane.

EBNER FALLS – Juneau – Page 33 C4 Scenic falls cascading down 3,576-foot Mt. Juneau to Gold Creek. Access on Perseverance Trail *(see Hiking)*.

EXIT GLACIER – Kenai Fjords National Park – Page 71 D3 Retreating remnant of larger glacier which once extended to Resurrection Bay. Descends 2,500 feet over three miles. From ranger station easy loop trails lead to base of glacier and rough-cut three-mile trail following glacier flank to Harding Icefield *(see this section and Hiking)*.

GLACIER BAY – Glacier Bay National Park and Preserve – Page 31 B5 16 tidewater glaciers, 12 actively calving icebergs into bay. Remnants of Little Ice Age which began 4,000 years ago. Mountains rise up to three vertical miles directly from bay. Access by boat or plane.

GRAND CANYON OF THE NOATAK – Noatak National Preserve – Page 133 A5 Strikingly scenic 65-mile-long canyon carved out by Noatak River *(see Float Trips)*. Migration route for plants and animals between subarctic and arctic environments.

GRANITE TORS – Chena River State Recreation Area – Page 116 A2 Grouping of tall granite spires rising from tundra. Some as high as 200 feet. Reached on Granite Tors Trail *(see Hiking)*.

GREAT KOBUK SAND DUNES – Kobuk Valley National Park – Page 133 A6 Sand created by grinding action of ancient glaciers, then carried to Kobuk Valley by wind and water, creating 25-square-mile dune area. Summer temperatures can exceed 90°Fahrenheit. Also Little Kobuk and Hunt River Dunes.

HARDING ICEFIELD – Kenai Fjords National Park – Page 70 D3 300-square-mile icefield most dominant park feature, one of four major icecaps in US. Discovered early 20th century when mapping team realized several coastal glaciers originated from same massive system. Snowclad surface interrupted only by isolated mountain peaks called nunataks, Eskimo word for "lonely peaks."

HUBBARD GLACIER – Wrangell–St. Elias National Park and Preserve – Page 37 B4 At 80 miles, one of North America's longest glaciers, beginning in Canada and terminating in Disenchantment Bay. Movement threatens to close off adjacent Russell Fiord, as temporarily happened in mid-1980s. Access by charter boat or plane.

ILIAMNA LAKE – Newhalen – Page 59 B5 Largest lake in state at 75 miles long, 20 miles across and 1,000 square miles. Freshwater harbor seals. Supports one of world's largest sockeye salmon runs. Located near Katmai National Park and Preserve.

ILIAMNA VOLCANO – Lake Clark National Park and Preserve – Page 68 D1 10,016-foot, active, cone-shaped stratovolcano, composed of layers of lava flows and pyroclastic rocks. Vented steam to more than 10,000 feet in 1978. Visible from eastern side of park. National Natural Landmark.

JUNEAU ICEFIELD – Juneau – Page 33 B4 1,500-square-mile icefield located in Coast Mountain Range. Supplies 39 glaciers, including Mendenhall *(see this section)*. Annual snowfall exceeds 100 feet.

LeCONTE GLACIER – Stikine–LeConte Wilderness – Page 24 A2 Originating from Stikine Icefield, southernmost tidewater glacier in North America. High volume of icebergs produced ice for refrigeration in 19th and early 20th centuries. Access by charter boat or plane.

MALASPINA GLACIER – Wrangell–St. Elias National Park and Preserve – Page 34 A2 North America's largest piedmont glacier, formed by other glaciers converging to form broad ice mass. Flows out of St. Elias Range between Icy and Yakutat Bays and covers 1,500-square-mile area, larger than state of Rhode Island. Carries so much glacial silt that plants and trees take hold on extremities, grow to maturity and topple over edge as glacier retreats. National Natural Landmark.

MATANUSKA GLACIER – Palmer – Page 84 B2 27 miles long, four miles wide at terminus and 1,000 feet thick. Stable enough to walk on. Access on private road. Good views from Matanuska Glacier State Recreation Site.

MENDENHALL GLACIER – Juneau – Page 33 C3 One of state's most accessible glaciers. 12 miles long, 1.5 miles wide, extending from Juneau Icefield *(see this section)* to Mendenhall Lake. Forward movement two feet per day, but retreating 25–30 feet annually due to melting. Six trails offer various viewpoints. Visitor center. Located in Mendenhall Glacier Recreation Area.

MT. EDGECUMBE – Kruzof Island – Page 26 D2 3,201-foot extinct volcano dominates island near Sitka. Activity since last ice age spanned several thousand years, leaving island with many unique volcanic formations. Inactive for last 200 years.

MT. McKINLEY – Denali National Park and Preserve – Page 103 D4 Highest point in North America. Mountain includes two separate peaks: South Peak, its true summit at 20,320 feet; North Peak, 19,470 feet. 18,000 feet above surrounding area, greater than Mt. Everest. Officially named for 25th US president, but called Denali, "High One" by Athabascan Native people. Part of Alaska Range. Permanent snowfields cover more than 50 percent of mountain. Often difficult to see; cloud-hidden as much as 75 percent of summer.

MT. ST. ELIAS – Wrangell–St. Elias National Park and Preserve – Page 36 A1 Second highest peak in US at 18,008 feet. Sited and recorded during 1741 Bering Expedition, first climbed in 1897. Part of St. Elias Range, one of world's highest coastal mountain ranges.

MT. WRANGELL – Wrangell–St. Elias National Park and Preserve – Page 97 D6 At 14,163 feet, highest active volcano in state and northernmost on Pacific Rim. Last erupted 1930. Viewed from nearby highways, plume of steam and ash-covered snow near summit visible on clear days.

MULDROW GLACIER – Denali National Park and Preserve – Page 103 C6 At 32 miles, longest glacier on north side of Alaska Range. Terminus covered with rock, soil and shrub growth. Experienced powerful surges in 1956, advancing more than four miles before slowing down by 1957. Descends from Mt. McKinley to within one mile from McKinley Park Road, between Eielson Visitor Center and Wonder Lake.

NEW EDDYSTONE ROCK – Misty Fiords National Monument – Page 21 B3 237-foot-high volcanic plug projecting from depths of Behm Canal. Made of basalt, part of volcanic vent where magma rose to surface repeatedly from bottom of canal.

NOGAHABARA DUNES – Koyukuk National Wildlife Refuge – Page 133 C7 10,000-acre active sand dune. Formed from wind-blown deposits about 10,000 years ago.

POLYCHROME PASS – Denali National Park and Preserve – Page 104 B1 Spectacular, multicolored landscape with shades of red, orange and purple. Created during the Ice Age by wind and water erosion. Located at Mile 45.9 McKinley Park Road.

PORTAGE GLACIER – Chugach National Forest – Page 71 B5 Six miles long, one mile wide at terminus, creating Portage Lake *(see this section)*. Spectacular views from Begich–Boggs Visitor Center, with picture windows, observation deck, simulated ice cave, interpretive displays and movie. Easy access from Seward Highway. One of state's most visited sites. Located in 8,600-acre Portage Glacier Recreation Area. Also Explorer, Middle and Byron Glaciers *(see Hiking)*.

PORTAGE LAKE – Chugach National Forest – Page 71 A5 Aquamarine, iceberg-filled lake, only decades old, formed by retreating Portage Glacier *(see this section)*. 1.7 miles long, approximately 600 feet deep. Dramatic views from Begich–Boggs Visitor Center. Warning: Climbing on unstable icebergs dangerous.

PUNCHBOWL COVE – Misty Fiords National Monument – Page 21 B3 Located in Rudyerd Bay. Spectacular cove and surrounding high cliffs formed by large glaciers. 3,150-foot vertical cliff on east side.

REDOUBT VOLCANO – Lake Clark National Park and Preserve – Page 68 C2 Active, cone-shaped stratovolcano. At 10,197 feet, second highest of 76 major volcanoes of Alaska Peninsula and Aleutian Islands. Numerous eruptions recorded from late 1700s to 1989, when steam and ash were blown to 35,000 feet. View from eastern side of park. Visible from Anchorage. National Natural Landmark.

TIDAL BORE – Anchorage – Page 71 A4 Steep-fronted tide crest, from one to six feet high, caused by tides flowing into constricted inlets at speeds up to 12 miles per hour; also called bore tide. 40-foot tide range of Cook Inlet increases effect as tides surge into both Turnagain and Knik Arms. Viewpoints in Turnagain Arm along Seward Highway about 30 miles south of Anchorage.

TOGIAK TUYA – Togiak National Wildlife Refuge – Page 55 D4 Two-mile-long, flat-topped volcano, formed when lava erupted under glacier and spread sideways. Rare geologic feature, located in Togiak Valley.

VALLEY OF 10,000 SMOKES – Katmai National Park and Preserve – Page 51 C4 Major eruption of Novarupta Volcano in 1912 left 40-square-mile area buried beneath volcanic ash deposits as deep as 700 feet. Deep, narrow gorges cut through ash by turbulent Ukak River. Valley named in 1916 by Robert Griggs of National Geographic Society upon seeing steam rising as high as 1,000 feet from thousands of fumaroles or small holes and cracks in ash. Only a few active vents remain today.

WHITE MOUNTAINS – White Mountains National Recreation Area – Page 125 B5 Unusual limestone peaks, pinnacles and cliffs, distinctly different from terrain of rest of state's interior.

WORTHINGTON GLACIER – Worthington Glacier State Recreation Site – Page 86 D1 3.8-mile-long, 1.5-mile-wide, three-fingered glacier originating from Girls Mountain. One-mile trail along edge of glacier. Access from Richardson Highway. One of state's most accessible glaciers. National Natural Landmark.

YUKON RIVER – Eagle – Page 119 B6 One of longest North American rivers, running 2,300 miles from Atlin Lake in British Columbia. Enters Alaska near Eagle, crosses state, empties into Bering Sea. 1,400 river miles in Alaska. Drainage basin 320,000 square miles, 193,000 in Alaska. *(See Float Trips.)*

ALSO IN ALASKA...

ARCTIC CIRCLE Line of latitude approximately 66°33' north of equator circumscribing northern frigid zone. Southernmost point at which sun does not set at summer solstice or rise at winter solstice. (Shown in Atlas from page 132 in western part of state to page 137 in the east. *See also Physical Relief map, pages 2–3 and Alaska Perspectives, page 4.*)

AURORA BOREALIS (NORTHERN LIGHTS) Charged particles produced by sunspot activity collide with gases in earth's upper atmosphere in northern latitudes, causing spectacular multicolored drapery- and arc-like patterns of light in night sky. Colors include red, yellow, violet and green and vary with intensity of interaction. Visible in varying degrees all around state; interior and far north considered best places for viewing, from August to May.

CONTINENTAL DIVIDE Imaginary dividing line from Seward Peninsula in west *(see page 132)*, through Brooks Range, to Canadian border in east *(see page 137)*, between watersheds of Arctic Ocean and Bering Sea. Separates Atlantic and Pacific Ocean drainage in lower 48 states. *(See also Physical Relief map, pages 2–3.)*

MIDNIGHT SUN Summer daylight hours increase with proximity to North Pole, because of earth's tilting on axis toward sun. Barrow most extreme location: no sunset for approximately 84 days (May–August) as sun circles just above horizon. However, no sunrise from mid-November to mid-January, as sun stays just below horizon, when earth is tilted in opposite direction.

MUSKEG Openings found between forest stands consisting of bog plant communities growing on deep peat and dominated by sphagnum mosses, sedges, rushes and shrubs. Sparse tree growth consists of hemlock and lodgepole pine in scrub form. Habitat for many plants; provides streamflow and home for wildlife. Found over much of state.

PERMAFROST Ground remaining frozen for two or more years. Continuous permafrost occurs primarily north of Arctic Circle *(see this section)* and in alpine regions, extending to depths of approximately 2,000 feet. Discontinuous permafrost in southern sections (including interior and southcentral regions) starts one to ten feet below surface, to depths of approximately 250 feet. Also extends many miles offshore beneath Beaufort Sea. *(See also Alaska Perspectives, page 4.)*

TAIGA Russian term meaning "land of little sticks," applied to areas of scant tree growth near Arctic Circle *(see this section)*. White and black spruce most common trees. Woods carpeted with mosses and lichens. Open areas filled with shrubs including dwarf birch, blueberry and willow. Found in southcentral and interior parts of state.

TUNDRA Treeless areas consisting of dwarfed shrubs and miniature wildflowers adapted to short growing season. Subsoils permanently frozen. Two types: moist and dry, with numerous gradations in between. Moist tundra may contain sedges, cottongrass and dwarfed shrubs. Dry tundra plants live scattered among barren rocks at higher elevations, growing close to ground in own microclimate. Wildflowers provide stunning summer displays; plants provide important food for wildlife. Found in arctic and subarctic regions.

Mountain Ranges

NAME	HIGHEST ELEVATION	PAGE & GRID
Ahklun Mountains	3,000 feet	55 C3
Alaska Range	20,320 feet	103 D4
Alatna Hills	3,020 feet	136 D2
Aleutian Range	7,585 feet	68 B2
Askinuk Mountains	2,342 feet	130 C2
Baird Mountains	4,300 feet	133 A5
Bendeleben Mountains	3,730 feet	132 C4
Brabazon Range	5,700 feet	35 C5
Brooks Range	8,025 feet	136 B2
Chigmit Mountains	5,000 feet	68 C1
Chugach Mountains	13,176 feet	84 C2
Coast Mountains	10,290 feet	33 B4
Darby Mountains	3,273 feet	133 D4
Davidson Mountains	6,210 feet	137 B5
De Long Mountains	4,915 feet	134 D3
Endicott Mountains	7,000 feet	136 C1
Fairweather Range	15,300 feet	30 B3
Igichuk Hills	2,010 feet	132 A4
Kaiyuh Mountains	2,844 feet	133 D7
Kenai Mountains	6,612 feet	62 C2
Kiglapak Mountains	1,070 feet	54 D1
Kigluaik Mountains	4,714 feet	132 D3
Kilbuck Mountains	3,600 feet	131 D4
Kokrines Hills	4,978 feet	121 D4
Kuskokwim Mountains	4,508 feet	101 C3
Lookout Ridge	2,344 feet	134 C4
Mentasta Mountains	8,235 feet	98 A1
Moore Mountains	3,000 feet	27 B2
Mulgrave Hills	2,285 feet	132 A4
Nulato Hills	3,411 feet	131 A4
Nutzotin Mountains	8,560 feet	99 C4
Philip Smith Mountains	8,048 feet	136 C3
Purcell Mountains	3,831 feet	133 B7
Ray Mountains	5,500 feet	122 A3
Robinson Mountains	9,603 feet	76 C2
Romanzof Mountains	9,060 feet	137 B4
Schwatka Mountains	6,500 feet	136 C1
Selawik Hills	3,307 feet	133 B5
Sheklukshuk Range	2,100 feet	133 B7
Shublik Mountains	5,685 feet	137 A4
Sischu Mountains	3,510 feet	111 D6
St. Elias Mountains	18,000 feet	36 C2
Talkeetna Mountains	8,800 feet	94 B2
Taylor Mountains	3,583 feet	131 D6
Waring Mountains	1,800 feet	133 B6
Waxell Ridge	10,000 feet	76 B1
White Mountains	5,000 feet	125 B5
Wrangell Mountains	16,390 feet	88 A1
York Mountains	2,349 feet	132 C2
Zane Hills	4,053 feet	133 B7

HIGHEST PEAKS

17 of the 20 highest peaks in the US are found in Alaska. These, plus two additional peaks over 14,000 feet, are listed here.

NAME	ELEVATION	PAGE & GRID
Mt. McKinley	20,320 feet	103 D4
Mt. St. Elias	18,008 feet	36 A1
Mt. Foraker	17,400 feet	93 A4
Mt. Bona	16,421 feet	89 C4
Mt. Blackburn	16,390 feet	88 B1
Mt. Sanford	16,237 feet	97 D6
South Buttress	15,885 feet	103 D4
Mt. Vancouver	15,700 feet	37 A4
Mt. Churchill	15,638 feet	89 C4
Mt. Fairweather	15,300 feet	30 A2
Mt. Hubbard	14,950 feet	37 A5
Mt. Bear	14,831 feet	89 C5
East Buttress	14,730 feet	103 D5
Mt. Hunter	14,573 feet	93 A4
Browne Tower	14,530 feet	103 D5
Mt. Alverstone	14,500 feet	37 A5
University Peak	14,470 feet	89 C4
Mt. Wrangell	14,163 feet	97 D6
Mt. Augusta	14,070 feet	36 A2

Wildlife Refuges

More than 80 million acres of Alaska public land have been set aside as wildlife refuges, under both federal and state management. These areas have been established for various purposes; among them, the protection of wildlife and habitats, the fulfillment of international migratory bird treaty obligations, the allowance of continued subsistence by local residents and to provide opportunities for interpretation, environmental education and recreation.

For more information on any of the areas listed in this section, contact one of the Public Lands Information Centers listed in Visitor Information Centers *on Page 6.*

NOTES ON WILDLIFE WATCHING

In General

Keep your distance: Observe animals from a safe distance. Use binoculars, spotting scope or telephoto lens for a closer look.

Don't hurry: Approach animals slowly and quietly. Avoid sudden movements.

Blend in: Wear muted colors. Avoid using scented soaps or perfumes.

Avoid disturbing animals: Especially females with their young.

Don't feed animals: Besides being dangerous, it's also against Alaska state law.

Never litter: Properly dispose of garbage. Wildlife can be endangered by discarded plastic and other refuse.

On Bear Watching

Avoid surprising bears: Look for signs of bears and make plenty of noise.

Avoid crowding bears: Respect their personal space.

Avoid attracting bears: This can inadvertently happen through improper handling of food or garbage.

Identify yourself: Talk to the bear in a normal voice. Wave your arms.

Don't run: You can't outrun a bear. Talk and raise your arms as mentioned above. Raise your voice and become more aggressive if the bear comes closer. Bang pots and pans.

Surrender: If a brown bear actually touches you, fall down and play dead. Lie flat on your stomach or curl up in a ball with your hands behind your neck. A brown bear will usually break off its attack when it feels the threat has been eliminated. If a black bear attacks you, fight back vigorously.

[Source: Alaska Department of Fish and Game pamphlets, "The Bears and You" and "Bear Facts." For copies or more information contact one of the Public Lands Information Centers on Page 6.]

ALASKA CHILKAT BALD EAGLE PRESERVE – Klukwan – 49,320 acres – Page 38 C1 Critical habitat for world's largest concentration of bald eagles. As many as 4,000 eagles attracted to area between late September and early December to feed on spawned-out salmon in ice-free waters of Chilkat River. Known as "Bald Eagle Council Grounds" due to eagles' habit of perching in trees in groups. Main viewing area between Miles 18 and 24 Haines Highway.

ALASKA PENINSULA NATIONAL WILDLIFE REFUGE – Chignik – 3,500,000 acres – Page 139 B4 Located on Pacific side of Alaska Peninsula. Varied landscape including active volcanoes, lakes, rivers, tundra and rugged coastline dominated by Aleutian Range. Showcase of animal and plant adaptation in arctic marine environment. Moose, caribou, wolves, brown bears and wolverines. Sea lions, seals, otters and whales. Ducks, geese and shorebirds. Renowned caribou and brown bear hunting. Outstanding fishing for king and silver salmon, arctic char, lake trout, northern pike and grayling. Hiking, boating and camping.

ANCHOR RIVER AND FRITZ CREEK STATE CRITICAL HABITAT AREA – Homer – 19,000 acres – Page 62 B1 Floodplains and lower hillside slopes of two river drainage systems. Habitats range from bog to spruce forest. One of only major moose overwintering areas on southern Kenai Peninsula, providing good willow browse for 20 percent of area population. Popular for year-round recreation including wildlife viewing, hunting, fishing, trapping and photography. Access from North Fork Road or trails from Ohlson Mountain Road.

ANCHORAGE COASTAL WILDLIFE REFUGE – Anchorage – 32,476 acres – Page 82 D3 16-mile area along coast encompassing tidal flats, marsh and alder–bog forest. Greatest number and diversity of birds in Anchorage area. Best viewing at Potter Marsh. Peak concentrations during spring migration. Nesting Canada geese during summer. Waterfowl hunting. Elevated boardwalk and interpretive signs. Access along Seward Highway.

ARCTIC NATIONAL WILDLIFE REFUGE – Oksrukuyik – 19,049,236 acres – Page 136 B4 Northern-most unit of National Wildlife Refuge System. Refuge encompasses spectacular assemblage of arctic plants, wildlife and landforms. Designed to cover range of 110,000-member Porcupine caribou herd. Musk-ox, Dall sheep, wolves, wolverines, polar and grizzly bears. Long severe winters; brief, intense summers. Snow-covered at least nine months of year. Annual plant and tree growth very slight. Rugged Brooks Range. Float trips, hiking, backpacking, hunting and fishing. Access by plane. Includes 8-million-acre Wilderness.

BECHAROF NATIONAL WILDLIFE REFUGE – King Salmon – 1,200,000 acres – Page 50 B2 Dominated by Becharof Lake, second largest lake in Alaska, surrounded by rolling hills, tundra wetlands and volcanic peaks. Lake produces one of world's largest salmon runs, attracting large brown bear population. Moose, caribou, wolves and wolverines. Sea lions, sea otters, seals and whales. Hunting for bear and caribou. Fishing for salmon, arctic char and grayling. Access by plane. Refuge includes 400,000-acre Wilderness.

CAPE NEWENHAM STATE GAME REFUGE – Platinum – 13,952 acres – Page 46 A1 Primary feature Chagvan Bay with vast eelgrass beds. Spring and fall stopovers by hundreds of thousands of ducks, geese and shorebirds. Area critical for black brant. No developed access.

CHILKAT RIVER STATE CRITICAL HABITAT AREA – Klukwan – 4,800 acres – Page 38 C1 Wide floodplain filled with braided stream channels, gravel bars and islands, located at confluence of Tsirku and Chilkat Rivers. Gathering spot for largest concentration of bald eagles in world *(see this section—Alaska Chilkat Bald Eagle Preserve)*. Also winter moose habitat. No visitor facilities. Access from Haines Highway.

CINDER RIVER STATE CRITICAL HABITAT AREA – Pilot Point – 25,856 acres – Page 41 C3 Large expanse of wetlands, tideflats and estuarine waters at mouth of Ugashik River on north shore of Alaska Peninsula. Large flocks of migrating waterbirds. Important area for cackling Canada geese. No public-use facilities. Access by small plane or boat.

CLAM GULCH STATE CRITICAL HABITAT AREA – Kasilof – 2,560 acres – Page 69 C5 Intertidal area consisting of long, narrow, sandy belt extending over 30 miles along lower Cook Inlet. Popular razor clamming area. Salmon fishing in Deep Creek from May to July. Access from numerous points along Sterling Highway. Public campground nearby.

COPPER RIVER DELTA STATE CRITICAL HABITAT AREA – Cordova – 597,120 acres – Page 74 B1 Vast 35-mile-wide complex of wetlands and tidelands bisected by Copper River. Largest contiguous Pacific coast wetlands. Resting and feeding area for over 20 million migrating shorebirds, including the entire Pacific coast population of dunlins and western sandpipers. Also entire population of dusky Canada geese and large number of trumpeter swans. Greatest species diversity found in May. Waterfowl, moose and bear hunting; trapping, salmon fishing and clamming. Access by plane, boat or from Copper River Highway.

CREAMER'S FIELD MIGRATORY WATERFOWL REFUGE – Fairbanks – 1,664 acres – Page 115 A5 Variety of habitats including fields, bog, lake, forest and former dairy farm. Best known for spring and fall concentrations of migrating ducks, geese and cranes. Two-mile, self-guided nature path with moose-viewing tower. Access from College and Farmer's Loop Roads in Fairbanks.

DELTA JUNCTION BISON RANGE – Delta Junction – Page 106 B3 72,000-acre tract established to protect American bison brought to area from Montana in 1920s. Herd currently numbers about 350. Bison can be seen with binoculars from viewpoint at Mile 241.3 Richardson Highway. Interpretive display.

DUDE CREEK STATE CRITICAL HABITAT AREA – Gustavus – 4,083 acres – Page 32 C1 Open, wet meadow habitat, bisected by forest-fringed Dude Creek. Key resting area for migrating lesser sandhill cranes, especially during September. Popular year-round recreation area. No public-use facilities. Access from Good River Road.

EGEGIK STATE CRITICAL HABITAT AREA – Egegik – 8,064 acres – Page 49 D4 Extensive tideflats and wetlands at mouth of Egegik River in Egegik Bay. Large flocks of migrating waterbirds, including sea and dabbling ducks and geese, and shorebirds in spring and fall. No public-use facilites. Access by small plane or boat.

FOX RIVER FLATS STATE CRITICAL HABITAT AREA – Homer – 7,104 acres – Page 62 A3 Low-lying marshlands and tidal flats extending from head of Kachemak Bay. Primary value as staging area for thousands of migrating waterfowl and shorebirds in spring and fall. Popular for waterfowl hunting. No public-use facilities. Access on steep switchback trail from Homer East End Road out of Homer.

GOOSE BAY STATE GAME REFUGE – Anchorage – 10,880 acres – Page 82 C3 Wetlands drained by Goose Creek. Important spring and fall stopover for migrating waterfowl. Good area for fall hunting. Inland access points along Knik–Goose Bay Road.

INNOKO NATIONAL WILDLIFE REFUGE – McGrath – 3,850,000 acres – Page 131 A6 Two separate sections encompassing most of Innoko River basin. Extensive wetlands provide nesting habitat for more than 250,000 waterfowl. Wolves, black and grizzly bears, caribou and furbearers, including large beaver population. Hunting for moose and black bear. Fishing for northern pike. Float trips. Access by plane or boat. Includes 1.2-million-acre Wilderness.

IZEMBEK NATIONAL WILDLIFE REFUGE – Cold Bay – 320,893 acres – Page 138 C2 Located on tip of Alaska Peninsula facing Bering Sea. Landscape of glacier-capped volcanoes, valleys and tundra uplands. Large eelgrass bed in Izembek Lagoon haven for migratory birds, including emperor geese and world population of black brant. Wintering Steller's eider and sea ducks. Brown bear, caribou, ptarmigan and furbearers. Hunting for waterfowl, ptarmigan and caribou. Access by boat or on foot, with very limited access by road from Cold Bay. Includes 300,000-acre Wilderness.

IZEMBEK STATE GAME REFUGE – Cold Bay – 181,440 acres – Page 138 C2 Izembek Lagoon, with one of world's largest eelgrass beds, provides important feeding and staging habitat for millions of migrating waterfowl and other birds from North America, Asia and Pacific. Primary species: black brant, emperor geese and Steller's eiders. Road access from Cold Bay.

KACHEMAK BAY STATE CRITICAL HABITAT AREA - Homer - 222,080 acres - Page 62 B2 Includes all of Kachemak Bay, a large, highly productive, ice-free estuarine environment with diverse and abundant marine life. Tens of thousands of feeding waterfowl, shorebirds and seabirds in spring, summer and fall. Marine mammals year-round. Popular location for halibut and salmon fishing. Easy access along Homer Spit.

KALGIN ISLAND STATE CRITICAL HABITAT AREA – Kalgin Island – 3,520 acres – Page 69 C4 Remote area located on Kalgin Island in Cook Inlet. Spring and fall resting and feeding habitat for waterfowl and shorebirds. No public-use facilities. Access by boat or chartered plane.

KANUTI NATIONAL WILDLIFE REFUGE – Allakaket – 1,430,000 acres – Page 136 D2 Vast, remote wetland basin straddling Arctic Circle, composed of Kanuti Flats and rolling plains of Kanuti and Koyukuk Rivers. Nesting habitat for waterfowl, primarily Canada and white-fronted geese and ducks. Critical refuge during times of drought in traditional breeding areas. Moose, black and grizzly bears, wolves and wolverines. Fishing for northern pike and grayling. Access by plane from Fairbanks.

KENAI NATIONAL WILDLIFE REFUGE – Soldotna – 1,970,000 acres – Page 69 C5 Western slopes of Kenai Mountains and forested lowlands bordering Cook Inlet. Includes all Alaska habitat types—tundra, mountains, wetlands and forests. Originally established to preserve large moose population. Also Dall sheep, mountain goat, caribou, coyotes, wolves, grizzly and black bears, lynx and wolverines. Excellent fishing for numerous species. Over 200 miles of trails and routes including Swanson River Route *(see Float Trips)*. Access from Sterling Highway. Includes 1.4-million acre Wilderness.

KODIAK NATIONAL WILDLIFE REFUGE – Kodiak – 1,865,000 acres – Page 45 A3 Area covers two-thirds of Kodiak Island and portion of Afognak Island, including mountains, bays, inlets and wetlands. Originally established to protect brown bear habitat. Two million seabirds. Large numbers of bald eagles year-round. Rafting and camping. Cabins. Fishing for all five Pacific salmon species. Renowned for brown bear hunting. Access by boat or plane.

KOYUKUK NATIONAL WILDLIFE REFUGE – Galena – 3,550,000 acres – Page 133 D7 Extensive floodplain including 14 rivers, hundreds of creeks and 15,000 lakes. Refuge provides habitat for salmon, beaver and waterfowl. 400,000 migrating ducks and geese in fall. Black and grizzly bears, moose, wolves, caribou and furbearers. Nogahabara Dunes *(see Unique Natural Features)*. Hunting for moose. Fishing for northern pike and grayling. Access by plane. Includes 400,000-acre Wilderness.

McNEIL RIVER STATE GAME SANCTUARY – 80 mi. W of Homer – 83,840 acres – Page 60 D1 Rolling shrub and grasslands extending from coast upstream to above McNeil River Falls. Renowned for unique concentration of brown bears. Each summer, as many as 100 bears come from as far as 30 miles to feed on migrating salmon attempting to navigate falls. Access by small plane or boat. Permit required. National Natural Landmark.

MENDENHALL WETLANDS STATE GAME REFUGE – Juneau – 3,789 acres – Page 33 C4 Wetlands, tidelands and submerged lands along Gastineau Channel. Best known for Canada geese, ducks and bald eagles seen feeding along shoreline year-round. Popular for wildlife viewing, boating, fishing, hunting and horseback riding. Scenic turnout, viewing platform and interpretive signs. Access from several points along Egan Drive.

MINTO FLATS STATE GAME REFUGE – Nenana – 500,000 acres – Page 114 B2 Large expanse of low-lying wetlands dotted with numerous lakes, oxbows and potholes. Spring and fall migratory bird stop. High density duck and swan nesting. Also fish, furbearer and big game populations. Popular for fishing, hunting and trapping. Access from Murphy Dome Road and Parks Highway or by boat on Tanana River.

NOWITNA NATIONAL WILDLIFE REFUGE – Ruby – 1,560,000 acres – Page 110 B2 Forested lowlands, hills, lakes, marshes, ponds and streams in central Yukon River Valley. Dominant feature Nowitna River, designated National Wild and Scenic River *(see Float Trips)*. Waterfowl protection primary purpose. Black bears, moose and furbearers. Popular for moose and bear hunting. Fishing for northern pike and sheefish. Access by plane.

PALMER HAY FLATS STATE GAME REFUGE – Matanuska – 26,048 acres – Page 83 B4 45-square-mile complex of forest, wetlands, tidal sloughs, lakes and tideflats. Hay flats major stopover for migrating waterfowl. Popular waterfowl hunting and fishing area. Access by boat from Glenn Highway at Knik River Bridge.

PILOT POINT STATE CRITICAL HABITAT AREA – Pilot Point – 46,016 acres – Page 41 B4 Estuarine wetlands environment at mouth of several rivers in Ugashik Bay. Stopover for large flocks of migrating waterbirds, including ducks, geese and shorebirds. Important fall feeding and staging habitat for cackling Canada geese. No public-use facilities. Access by small boat or plane.

PORT HEIDEN STATE CRITICAL HABITAT AREA – Port Heiden – 72,128 acres – Page 139 B4 Extensive estuarine environment of tideflats and wetlands along shores of large bay, Port Heiden. Large flocks of migrating waterbirds, including ducks, geese and shorebirds in spring and fall. No developed access.

PORT MOLLER STATE CRITICAL HABITAT AREA – Port Moller – 127,296 acres – Page 138 C3 Located along shores of Port Moller, large bay on north shore of Alaska Peninsula. Stopover for hundreds of thousands of migrating ducks (eiders and other seaducks), geese (emperors) and shorebirds in spring and fall. Access by plane or boat.

REDOUBT BAY STATE CRITICAL HABITAT AREA – 40 mi. SW of Anchorage – 183,640 acres – Page 69 A4 268-square-mile, low-lying expanse of wetlands on west side of Cook Inlet. Resting and feeding area for hundreds of thousands of migrating waterfowl and summer nesting area for ducks, geese and swans. Best known as nesting ground for Tule white-fronted geese. Brown bears during salmon spawning season. Winter moose habitat. Very popular waterfowl hunting area. Access by plane or boat.

SELAWIK NATIONAL WILDLIFE REFUGE – Kotzebue – 2,150,000 acres – Page 133 B6 Estuaries, lakes, river deltas and tundra slopes straddling Arctic Circle. Prominent feature tundra wetlands between Waring Mountains and Selawik Hills, supporting abundance of waterbirds, waterfowl and mammals. Hundreds of thousands of nesting ducks. Moose, grizzly bear, furbearers and wintering caribou. Sheefish, whitefish, grayling and northern pike. Portions of Selawik River designated Wild and Scenic River. River rafting. Evidence of human, animal and plant migration still exists where Bering Land Bridge once crossed from Asia. Access by boat or plane. Includes 240,000-acre Wilderness.

STAN PRICE STATE WILDLIFE SANCTUARY – Admiralty Island – 613 acres – Page 28 A1 Tidelands and submerged lands along Pack Creek. Well-known location for watching brown bears. As many as 30 bears gather during July and August to feed on spawning salmon. Permit required. Access by floatplane or boat.

SUSITNA FLATS STATE GAME REFUGE – Anchorage – 300,800 acres – Page 82 C2 Expansive coastal lowlands bisected by Susitna River. Primary attraction spring and fall concentrations of migrating waterfowl and shorebirds. Popular for waterfowl hunting. Access by floatplane or boat.

TETLIN NATIONAL WILDLIFE REFUGE – Tok – 700,000 acres – Page 99 B6 Located in Upper Tanana River Valley encompassing thousands of lakes and ponds interspersed with rolling hills, forests and snowcapped mountains. One of highest densities of nesting waterfowl in Alaska. 143 nesting and 47 migrating bird species. Spectacular views of migrating sandhill cranes in spring and fall. Arctic and common loon, osprey, bald eagle and trumpeter swan. Hunting for moose and waterfowl. Fishing for northern pike, burbot and grayling. Two campgrounds and two cabins. Visitor center. Access along 70 miles of Alaska Highway.

TOGIAK NATIONAL WILDLIFE REFUGE – Dillingham – 4,105,000 acres – Page 56 D2 Mountain crags, fast-flowing rivers, deep lakes, estuaries, coastal lagoons, sea cliffs and sandy beaches. Resting and breeding area for migrating waterfowl and shorebirds. Spotted seals, walrus and seven whale species. 1,500 miles of streams and rivers for spawning salmon. River rafting. Excellent fishing for salmon and trout. Hunting for brown bear. Access by plane. Includes 2.3-million-acre Wilderness. *(See Unique Natural Features.)*

ALASKA MARITIME NATIONAL WILDLIFE REFUGE

With the most diverse wildlife species of all Alaska refuges, this 4.5-million-acre area encompasses more than 2,500 islands, islets, rocks and headlands. Divided into five units (listed below), the refuge extends from the Arctic Ocean to southeastern Alaska, including most lands in the Aleutian Islands and the Gulf of Alaska. 2.6 million acres are designated Wilderness.

In addition to thousands of sea mammals, including sea lions, seals, walruses and sea otters, 80 percent of the 50 million seabirds nesting in Alaska inhabit this area. Birds congregate in "bird cities" or colonies, each species having a specialized nesting site—rock ledge, crevice, boulder rubble, pinnacle or burrow—allowing them to use small areas of land. The 38 bird species using the refuge include puffins, murres, auklets, kittiwakes and storm-petrels.

For more information contact the refuge headquarters at 202 Pioneer Avenue, Homer, AK 99603, (907) 235-6546.

ALASKA PENINSULA UNIT – Sand Point – 139 B5 More than 700 islands, islets and rocks on south side of Alaska Peninsula. Many very small islands, including Semidi and Shumagin Islands and Sandman Reefs, support spectacular bird colonies.

ALEUTIAN ISLANDS UNIT–Amchitka Island – 140 D3 Volcanic, treeless island chain. Nesting area for tufted puffins, rare whiskered auklet and endangered Aleutian Canada goose. Asiatic species on central and western islands. WWII and Aleut historic sites.

BERING SEA UNIT – St. Matthew Island – 139 A4 Several islands and headlands on Norton Sound and extensive wilderness on St. Matthew Island. Well-known seabird cliffs and fur seal rookeries on Pribilof Islands and Hagemeister Island.

CHUKCHI SEA UNIT – Point Hope–134 D1 Many barrier islands along Chukchi Sea, Capes Lisburne and Thompson and Chamisso Island in Kotzebue Sound. High escarpments on Lisburne Peninsula host largest seabird colonies along Alaska's northern coast.

GULF OF ALASKA UNIT – Port William – 53 A4 Includes islands surrounding Kodiak and Afognak Islands; Duck and Chisik Islands in Cook Inlet; Barren, Pye and Chiswell Islands off Kenai Peninsula; and Forrester, Hazy and St. Lazaria Islands of southeastern Alaska. Most accessible sea lion rookeries and seabird colonies in refuge. Charter boats, lodging and campgrounds available in Sitka, Seward and Homer.

TRADING BAY STATE GAME REFUGE – Shirleyville – 160,960 acres – Page 81 D4   Large, tidally influenced coastal marsh fed by six rivers. Used by thousands of waterfowl during spring and fall migration and for nesting during summer months. Fishing and waterfowl, moose and bear hunting. Access by small plane, boat or road from Tyonek.

TUGIDAK ISLAND STATE CRITICAL HABITAT AREA – Tugidak Island – 50,240 acres – Page 64 D1   Remote, uninhabited, treeless island with shallow lagoon and barrier spit at northern end. Renowned for one of largest harbor seal pupping and haulout areas in world. Also large concentrations of migrating and ground nesting birds. No public-use facilities. Access by floatplane from Kodiak Island.

WALRUS ISLANDS STATE GAME SANCTUARY – Walrus Islands – 9,728 acres – Page 47 B4   Group of seven craggy islands fronted by rocky beaches and steep sea cliffs. Best known, Round Island, only regularly used land-based walrus haulout on southern Bering Sea, where 8,000–12,000 male walruses return each spring. Also nesting ground for nearly 450,000 seabirds. Access by charter boat or floatplane, May–September. Permit required.

WILLOW MOUNTAIN STATE CRITICAL HABITAT AREA – Willow – 22,270 acres – Page 82 A3   In Talkeetna Mountains, established to protect high-quality moose habitat. As many as 1,000 moose seen along mid-level mountain slopes in summer, fall and early winter. Access on Peters–Purches Trail off Fishhook–Willow Road or Willow Mountain Trail off Willer–Kash Road.

YAKATAGA STATE GAME REFUGE – Cape Yakataga – 82,000 acres – Page 76 D2   Isolated, coastal lowlands surrounded by Chugach Mountains to north and glaciers, east and west. Critical mountain goat and moose winter habitat. Hundreds of wintering bald eagles. Rich salmon spawning and rearing habitat. Hunting for moose, black and brown bear, mountain goat and waterfowl. Fishing for coho salmon. Access by plane or boat.

YUKON DELTA NATIONAL WILDLIFE REFUGE – Bethel – 19,624,458 acres – Page 131 D4   Treeless, wetland plain dominated by Yukon and Kuskokwim Rivers. Noted for wildlife variety and abundance. Nesting and feeding habitat for more than 750,000 swans and geese, two million ducks and 100 million shorebirds and waterfowl.

Moose, caribou, black and grizzly bears and wolves. Herds of musk-ox and reindeer on 1.1-million-acre Nunivak Island. 42 Eskimo villages. Hunting, fishing, hiking and boating. Access by boat or plane. Includes 1.9-million-acre Wilderness.

YUKON FLATS NATIONAL WILDLIFE REFUGE – Fort Yukon – 8,630,000 acres – Page 137 D6   Most northerly point reached by Yukon River, where waters spread unconfined through vast floodplain. 40,000 lakes and ponds. One of highest waterfowl nesting densities in North America. Two million migrating ducks and geese. Longest salmon spawning run in US. Moose, caribou, wolves, black and grizzly bears. Canoe, kayak and rafting trips. Fishing for northern pike. Access by plane.

Alaska Marine Highway System

The Alaska Marine Highway System is a fleet of eight ferries, owned and operated by the state of Alaska. This fleet provides year-round service to southeast and southwest parts of the state, covering 3,500 miles, including 32 ports. Most of the ferries carry vehicles as well as passengers, and offer food, observation lounges and staterooms. The vessels range in length from the 148-foot flagship M/V *Columbia* to the 193-foot M/V *Bartlett*. USDA Forest Service naturalists ride the larger ferries in summer, offering interpretive programs.

The ferries cover two separate routes which have been plotted in detail in this Atlas. The Southeast System offers trips from Bellingham, Washington, and Prince Rupert, British Columbia, up the Inside Passage to the northern tip of the Inside Passage. Stops at communities along the way include Ketchikan, Wrangell, Petersburg, Sitka and Juneau.

The Southwest System serves Prince William Sound, the Kenai Peninsula and Kodiak Island, including stops at Cordova, Valdez, Whittier, Seward, Seldovia, Homer, Kodiak and Port Lions. Service to remote ports of the Aleutian Chain is available May–September, including stops at Chignik, Sand Point, King Cove, Cold Bay and Dutch Harbor.

There are no connecting routes between the Southeast and Southwest Systems. Travelers can get from one system to the other overland via the road system; for example: Haines to Valdez, Haines to Fairbanks or Haines to Anchorage (see Mileage Chart, page 5, for distances).

Routes, schedules and tariffs vary according to time of year. Reservations are required on all ferries for both passengers and vehicles. For more information contact the Alaska Marine Highway System at P.O. Box 25535, Juneau, AK 99802-5535, 1-800-642-0066; in Canada, (907) 465-3941.

A sampling of routes with approximate running times and traveling distances (measured in nautical miles) follows.

Route	Time/Distance
Bellingham, WA–Ketchikan	36 hours/619 miles
Prince Rupert, BC–Ketchikan	6 hours/92 miles
Ketchikan–Wrangell	5.7 hours/88 miles
Wrangell–Petersburg	3 hours/40 miles
Petersburg–Juneau/Auke Bay	7.75 hours/120 miles
Juneau/Auke Bay–Haines	4.5 hours/68 miles
Haines–Skagway	1 hour/14 miles
Juneau/Auke Bay–Sitka	8.7 hours/131 miles
Petersburg–Sitka	10 hours/156 miles
Homer–Kodiak	12 hours/155 miles
Homer–Dutch Harbor	72 hours/875 miles
Whittier–Valdez	7 hours/90 miles
Seward–Kodiak	12 hours/200 miles
Seward–Valdez	12 hours/200 miles

Scenic Drives

Alaska's highways provide access to adventure and endless scenic wonder—mountains, rivers, glaciers, parks, forests and wildlife. Many of the state's major roads have been included here. While most roads are well-maintained, road surfaces and conditions may vary, and some may require high-clearance vehicles. Be sure to check ahead for road and weather conditions before starting out. For more information contact one of the Public Lands Information Centers listed in Visitor Information Centers on page 6.

NAME	LENGTH	TRIP START	TRIP END	PAGE & GRID	COMMENTS
Alaska Highway	1422 miles	Delta Junction	Dawson Creek, BC	116 D3	Historic highway (see Historic Sites/Museums). Open and maintained year-round. Only 302 miles actually within Alaska.
Denali Highway	133 miles	Paxson	Cantwell	106 D3	Original travel route to Denali National Park. Outstanding scenery. Gravel road most of length.
Elliott Highway	156 miles	Fox	Manley Hot Springs	115 A5	Well-maintained gravel road with steep hills and sharp turns. Parallels Trans-Alaska Pipeline for short distance.
George Parks Highway	324 miles	Matanuska	Fairbanks	83 B4	Heavily traveled, paved highway. Access to Denali National Park.
Glacier Highway	40 miles	Juneau	Echo Cove	33 C4	Follows Favorite Channel northward. Views of Chilkat Range. Gravel road last eight miles to Echo Cove.
Glenn Highway	124 miles	Anchorage	Tok	82 D3	Paved, heavily traveled road. Views of Talkeetna and Wrangell Ranges. Last 125 miles known as Tok Cut-off.
James Dalton Highway	416 miles	Livengood	Arctic Ocean	124 C3	Rough gravel road parallels Trans-Alaska Pipeline. Drive with headlights on at all times. Restricted use past Mile 211.
McCarthy Road	61 miles	Chitina Ranger Station	McCarthy	87 B4	Gravel road follows abandoned railroad bed. First 22 miles within Wrangell–St. Elias National Park.
Nabesna Road	46 miles	Slana Ranger Station	Nabesna	98 B1	Gravel road. Most of drive in Wrangell–St. Elias National Park. Last four miles to Nabesna not maintained (may be impassible).
Richardson Highway	368 miles	Valdez	Fairbanks	85 D5	Paved road leading through Alaska Range and Chugach Mountains. Passes spectacular glaciers.
Seward Highway	127 miles	Anchorage	Seward	82 D3	Passes through Kenai Mountains. Views of Chugach Mountains and Cook Inlet.
Steese Highway	162 miles	Fairbanks	Circle	115 A5	Used by gold rush prospectors to freight supplies by dog sled and wagon. Interior Alaska's oldest travel route.
Sterling Highway	137 miles	Junction with Seward Hwy	Homer	71 B3	Winds through Kenai Mountains in Kenai Peninsula. Excellent fishing opportunities along route.
Taylor Highway	160 miles	Tetlin Junction	Eagle	108 C3	Gravel road with steep hills and hairpin curves. Climbs three times to over 3,500 feet.

Hunting

Alaska is divided into 26 State Game Management Units within which various species can be hunted. For information on a specific unit call the closest regional office of the Alaska Department of Fish and Game, Division of Wildlife Conservation, as indicated below. Refer to the locater map below for approximate unit locations. Information provided here is subject to change. It is most important to be thoroughly familiar with all rules, regulations and restrictions before hunting in any area. For a copy of the current Alaska State Hunting Regulations booklet or more information contact any of the offices listed here.

UNIT	BIG GAME											FUR ANIMALS					SMALL GAME/MIGRATORY BIRDS			GEESE									
	BLACK BEAR	BROWN BEAR	BISON	CARIBOU	DEER	ELK	GOAT	MOOSE	MUSK-OX	SHEEP	WOLF	WOLVERINE	COYOTE	ARCTIC FOX	RED FOX	LYNX	SQUIRREL	BRANT	CRANES	DUCKS	CANADA	SNOW	WHITE-FRONTED	GROUSE	HARE	PTARMIGAN	SEA DUCKS	SNIPE	TUNDRA SWANS

GAME MANAGEMENT UNIT LOCATER MAP

OUTER ALEUTIANS

ALASKA DEPARTMENT OF FISH AND GAME OFFICES

Headquarters
Capital Office Park, 1255 West 8th Street, P.O. Box 25526, Juneau, AK 99802-5526, (907) 465-4190 .... Page 33 C4

Regional Offices
Douglas Island Center Building, 802 3rd Street, P.O. Box 240020, Douglas, AK 99824, (907) 465-4265 ...... Page 33 C4
333 Raspberry Road, Anchorage, AK 99518, (907) 267-2180 .... Page 82 D3
1300 College Road, Fairbanks, AK 99701, (907) 456-5156 .... Page 115 A5

INSET 1

134°00'
55°00'

A

North Rks

Lowrie Island

Cape Horn Rks
North
Sea Lion Rk

**ALASKA MARITIME NWR
(FORRESTER ISLAND WILDERNESS)**

Butler Rk

Eagle Hbr

Ruins

Wood Cove

Forrester Island

Petrel Island

South Rk

Camp Cove
Little Deer Lake
Welcome Pt
Lake Welcome

Welcome Cove
Waterfall Lake

White Pt
Augustine Bay
Waterfall Bay

Cape Augustine
Gourd I
Rockwell Pt

Gold Hbr

Beak Pt

Gooseneck Hbr

Gooseneck Pt

Ritter Pt

Cape Magdalena

NAT FOR BDY

INDEFINITE BDY

B

UNITED STATES
CANADA

P A C I F I C

54°30'53"
134°00'

Continue on Page 20

INSET 2

132°00'
55°00'

Continue on Page 17, Inset 1

Ingraham Pt

Ingraham Bay
Scott Pt

C

Hidden Bay

TONGASS NATIONAL FOREST

Kendrick Islands

Drick

Kendrick Bay

Gardner Bay

Orca Island Pt

McLean Arm
Lt McLean Pt

PRINCE OF WALES ISLAND

C L A R E N C E   S T R A I T

Stone Rock

Huaji Cliff

ANNETTE ISLAND IND RES

Pt Davison

Hotspur I
Spur

Pelice Strait
Tamgas Reef

Cow I

Vegas Is
Werlick I

Niquette Hbr

Pt Percy

Percy Is

Seal I

Point Pt White

Sealing Reef

Sealed Passage

Bee Rocks

Hassler Reef

Dog Bay
Dog I
Duck Islands

Bona Bay
Pond Bay

Reef Hbr

Flag Pt

DUKE   ISLAND

TONGASS

Morse Cove
Duke Hill
Duke Pt

Ray Anchorage

Hall Cove

Mt Lazaro

Judd Harbor

Foul

Kelp I

Son
East Island

Cape Northumberland

Vancouver I

Sister Islands

White Rock

West Rock

Club Rocks

Yellow Rocks

Barren I Lt

REVILLAGIGEDO   CHANNEL

ALASKA MARINE HWY

Kirk I

De Long Islands

D

UNITED STATES
CANADA

INDEFINITE BDY

NAT FOR BDY

East Devil Rock

West Devil Rock

P A C I F I C

EXCLUSIVE ECONOMIC ZONE LIMIT

O C E A N

Zayas Island
157

Jacinto Pt

CAAMANO

Celestial Reef

© DeLorme

54°30'
132°00'

KILOMETERS 5   0   5   10   15   20

MILES 1 0 1 2 3 4 5 6 7 8 9 10 11 12

Continue on Page 16, Inset 2

OCEAN

Continue on Page 21

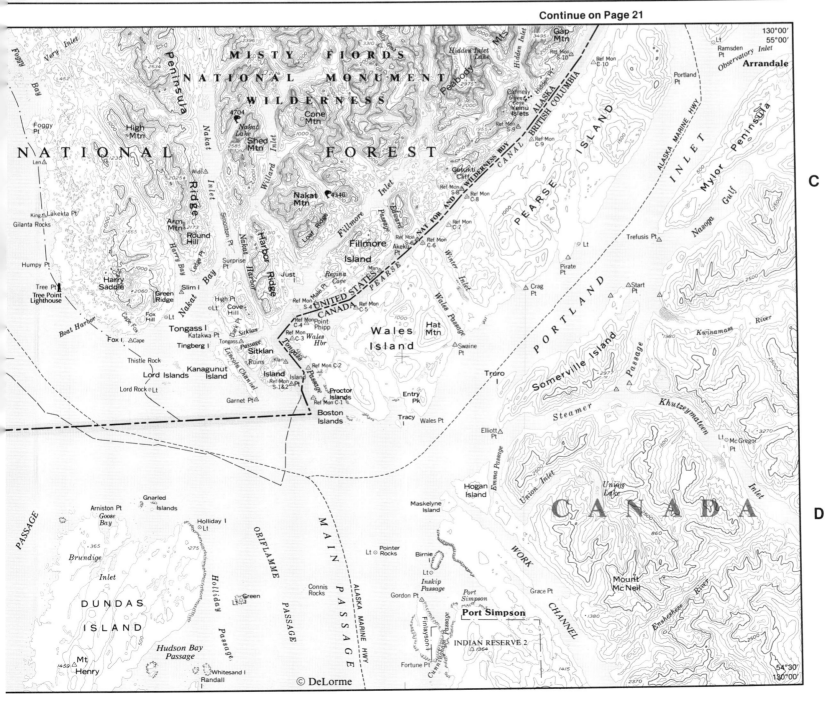

© DeLorme

Scale 1:300,000
1 inch represents 4.8 miles

Contour interval
200 feet (61 meters)

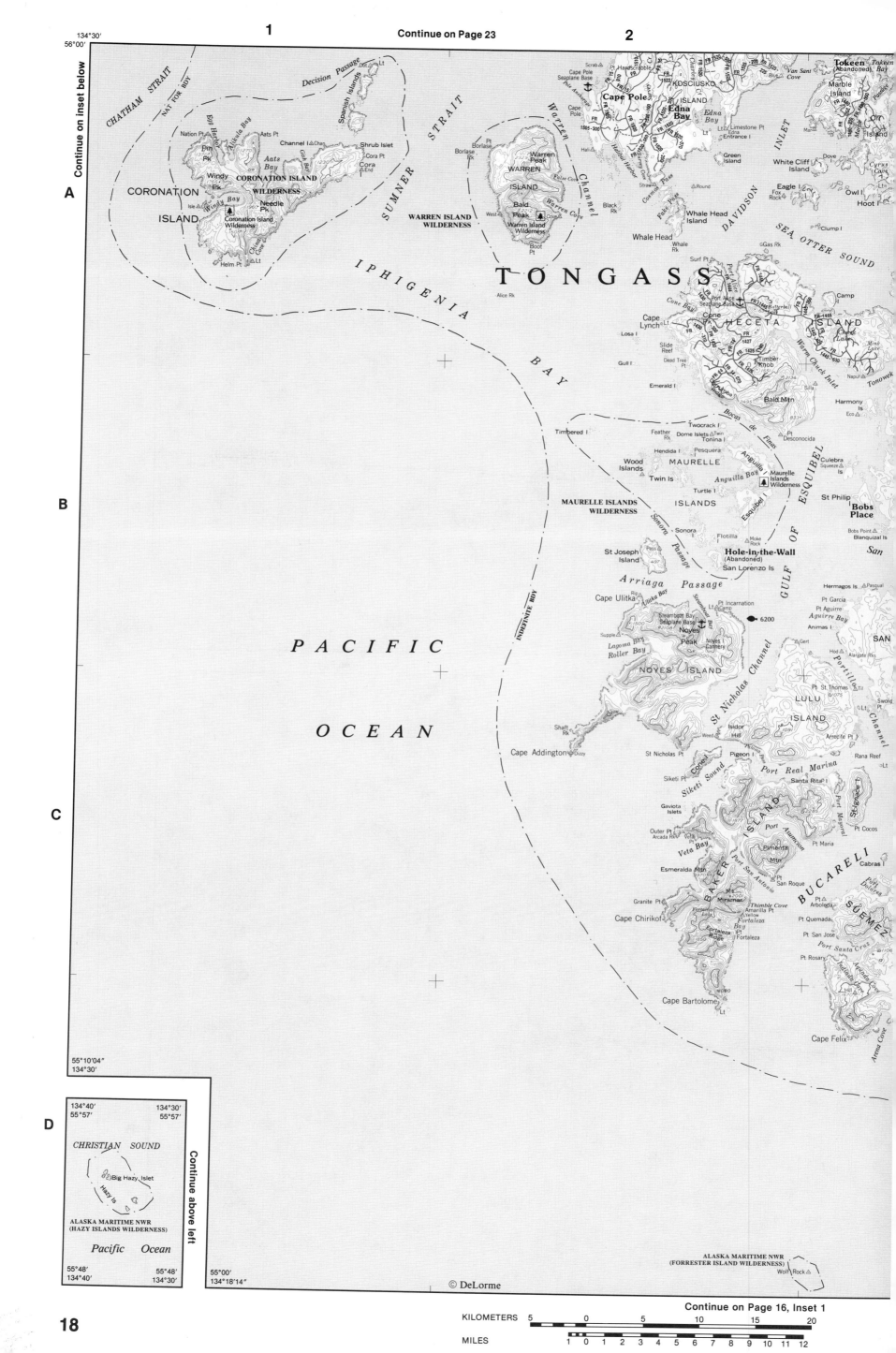

134°30'
56°00'

Continue on inset below

1   **2**

CHATHAM STRAIT

Decision Passage

Spanish Islands

Lt

Nation Pt

Aats Pt

Channel I   Chan

Shrub Islet

Pin Pk

Aats Bay

Cora Pt
Cora △End

Windy
Pk

CORONATION ISLAND
WILDERNESS

A

CORONATION

Isle △

Needle Pk

Windy Bay

ISLAND

Coronation Island
Wilderness

Helm Pt   △Lt

SUMNER STRAIT

WARREN CHANNEL

Cape Pole
Seaplane Base

Cape Pole

KOSCIUSKO
ISLAND

Edna
Bay

Edna Bay

Cape Pole

Limestone Pt
Edna
Entrance I

Lt

Green Island

Tokeen
(Abandoned)

Marble Island

Orn
Island

Van Sant
Cove

Marble

Pt
Borlase

Borlase
Rk

WARREN
PEAK

WARREN

False Cove

Warren Cove

ISLAND

West

Bald
Peak

Cove

Warren Island
Wilderness

WARREN ISLAND
WILDERNESS

Boot
Pt

Black Rk

Whale Head
Island

Whale Head

Whale
Rk

White Cliff
Island

Green Island

Dove

Eagle I
Fox
Rock

Owl I

Hoot

Halibut Harbour

DAVIDSON

INLET

SEA OTTER SOUND

△Round

Clump I

Gas Rk

T O N G A S S

IPHIGENIA

Alice Rk

BAY

Surf Pt

Port Alice
Seaplane Base

Cape
Lynch Lt

Cone Bluff

Cone

HECETA

Camp

ISLAND

Warm Chuck Inlet

Losa I

Slide
Reef

Dead Tree I

Timber
Knob

Mink
Creek
Lake

Napul

Gull I

Emerald I

Bald Mtn

Harmony
Is
Eco

Tonowek

Bocas de Finas

Timbered I

Twocrack I

Feather
Rk

Dome Islets △Twin
Tonina I

Pt
Desconocida

MAURELLE

Hendida I

Pesquera

Anguilla

Culebra
Is

Wood
Islands

B

Twin Is

Anguilla Bay

Maurelle
Islands
Wilderness

Turtle I

Esquibel

ISLANDS

St Philip

GULF OF ESQUIBEL

Bobs
Place

MAURELLE ISLANDS
WILDERNESS

Sonora
Passage

Sonora

Flotilla

Moke
Rock

Bobs Point △
Blanquizal Is

San

St Joseph
Island

Pass △
497

Hole-in-the-Wall
(Abandoned)
San Lorenzo Is

Hermagos Is
△Pasqual

Arriaga Passage

Cape Ulitka

Aliuka Bay

Pt Incarnation
Camp

Pt Garcia

Pt Aguirre
Aguirre Bay

Animas I

Supple △

Steamboat Bay
Seaplane Base
92106

Lagoma Bay
Roller Bay

Noyes
Peak

Noyes
Cannery

⚓ 6200

Gert

Hod △
Alargate Rks

SAN

P A C I F I C

NOYES **ISLAND**

St Nicholas Channel

Isidor
Hill

Weed Rk

Portilla Channel

LULU

ISLAND

Arrecife Pt

Rana Reef

O C E A N

Shaft
Rk

Cape Addington   Dizzy

St Nicholas Pt

Pigeon I

Coronados

Siketi Pt

Siketi Sound

Port Real Marina

Santa Rita

Pt Cocos

Cabras I

Gaviota
Islets

Outer Pt
Arcada Rk

Veta Bay

BAKER **ISLAND**

Port
Asuncion

Pimenta
Mtn

Pt Maria

Esmeralda Pt

Pt San Antonio

Pt San Roque

BUCARELI

Pt
Arboleda

Granite Pt

Pt
Miramar

Thimble Cove
Amarilla
Yellow
Pt

Pt Quemada

SUEMEZ

Cape Chirikof

Fortaleza
Bay
Fortaleza
Ridge
Fortaleza

Pt San Jose

Port Santa Cruz

Pt Rosary

C

55°10'04"
134°30'

Cape Bartolome

Lt

Cape Felix

Arena Cove

Continue above left

134°40'
55°57'

134°30'
55°57'

D

CHRISTIAN SOUND

Big Hazy Islet

Hazy Is

ALASKA MARITIME NWR
(HAZY ISLANDS WILDERNESS)

Pacific Ocean

55°48'
134°40'

55°00'
134°18'14"

55°48'
134°30'

ALASKA MARITIME NWR
(FORRESTER ISLAND WILDERNESS)

Wolf Rock △

© DeLorme

18

KILOMETERS   5   0   5   10   15   20

MILES   1 0 1 2 3 4 5 6 7 8 9 10 11 12

Continue on Page 16, Inset 1

A

B

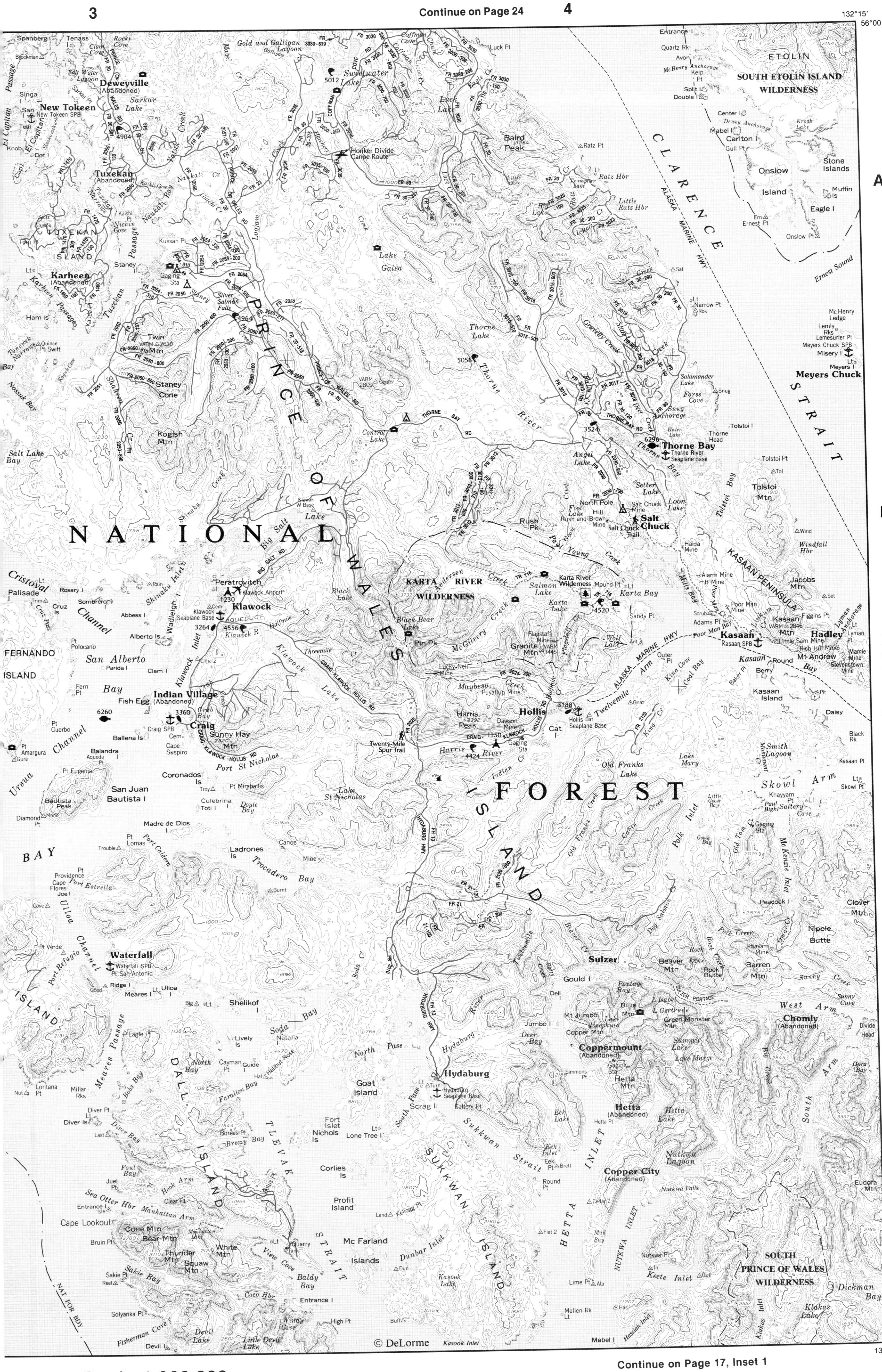

Continue on Page 20

C

D

PRINCE OF WALES

NATIONAL

FOREST ISLAND

KARTA RIVER WILDERNESS

SOUTH ETOLIN ISLAND WILDERNESS

CLARENCE STRAIT

KASAAN PENINSULA

TUXEKAN ISLAND

FERNANDO ISLAND

DALL ISLAND

BAY

SOUTH PRINCE OF WALES WILDERNESS

Deweyville (Abandoned)
New Tokeen
Tuxekan (Abandoned)
Karheen (Abandoned)
Klawock
Craig
Indian Village (Abandoned)
Thorne Bay
Salt Chuck
Meyers Chuck
Kasaan
Hadley
Hollis
Sulzer
Waterfall
Hydaburg
Coppermount (Abandoned)
Chomly (Abandoned)
Hetta (Abandoned)
Copper City (Abandoned)
Peratrovitch

Scale 1:300,000
1 inch represents 4.8 miles

Contour interval
200 feet (61 meters)

© DeLorme

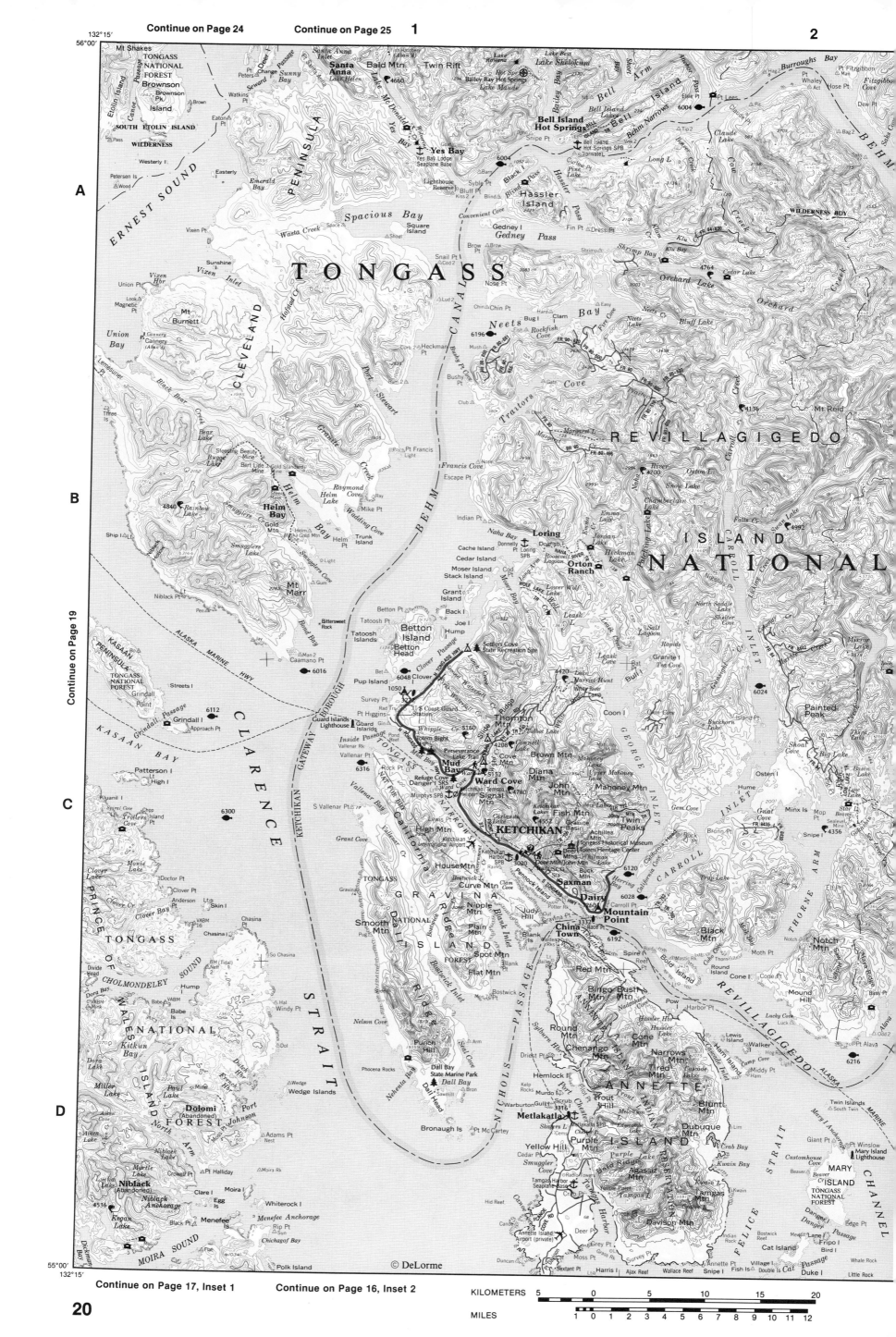

Continue on Page 19

© DeLorme

KILOMETERS 5 0 5 10 15 20

MILES 1 0 1 2 3 4 5 6 7 8 9 10 11 12

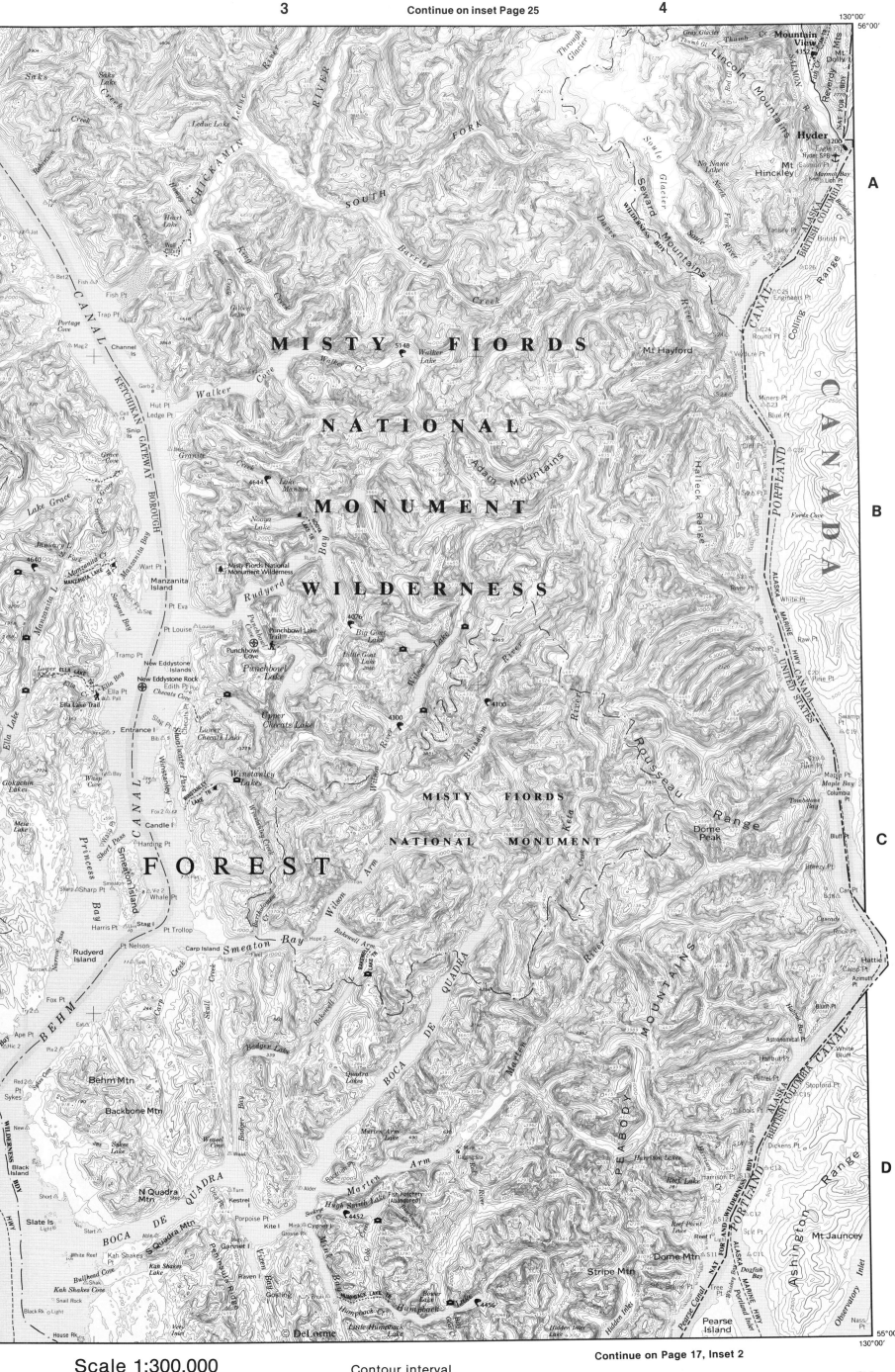

Scale 1:300,000
1 inch represents 4.8 miles

Contour interval
200 feet (61 meters)

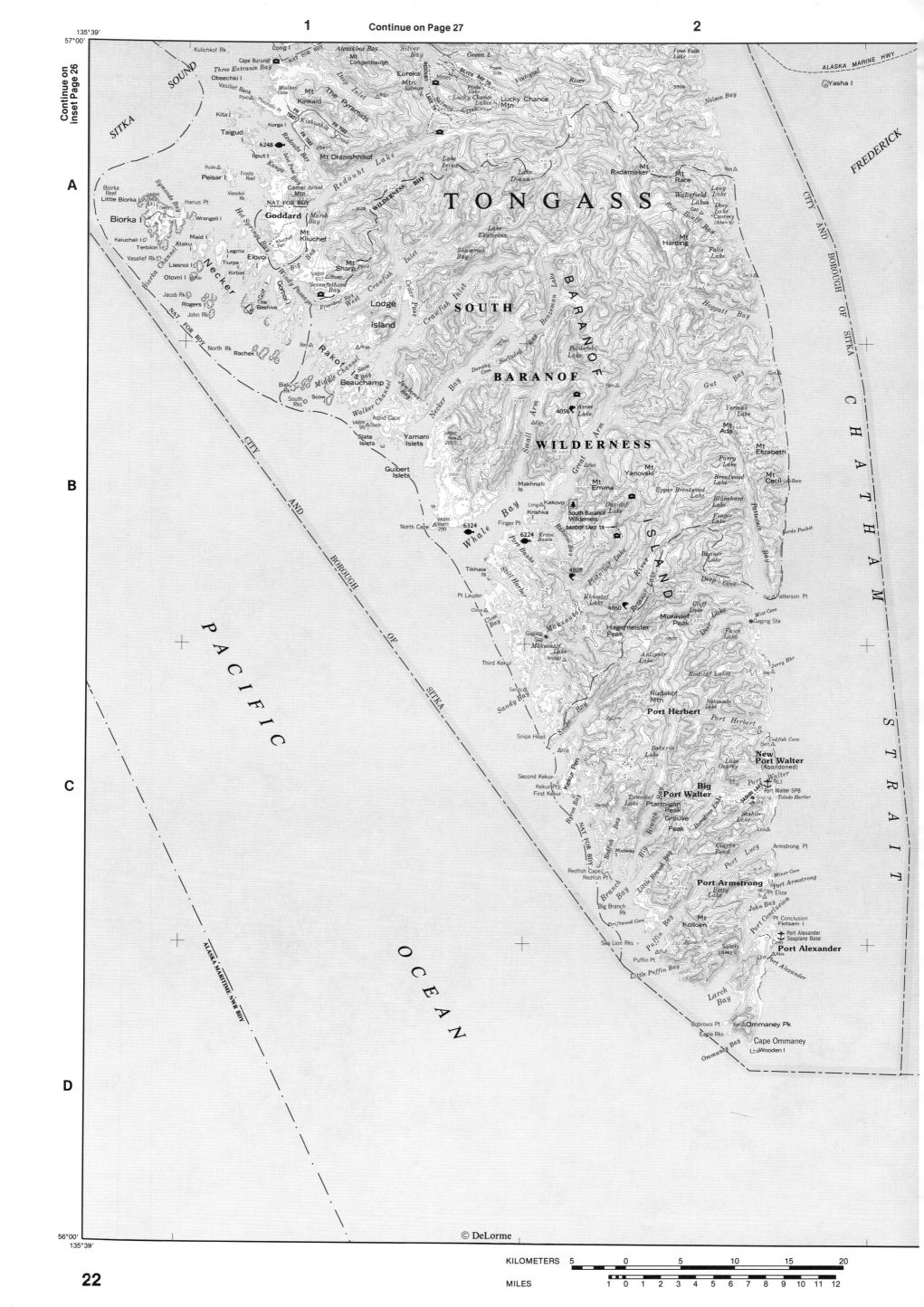

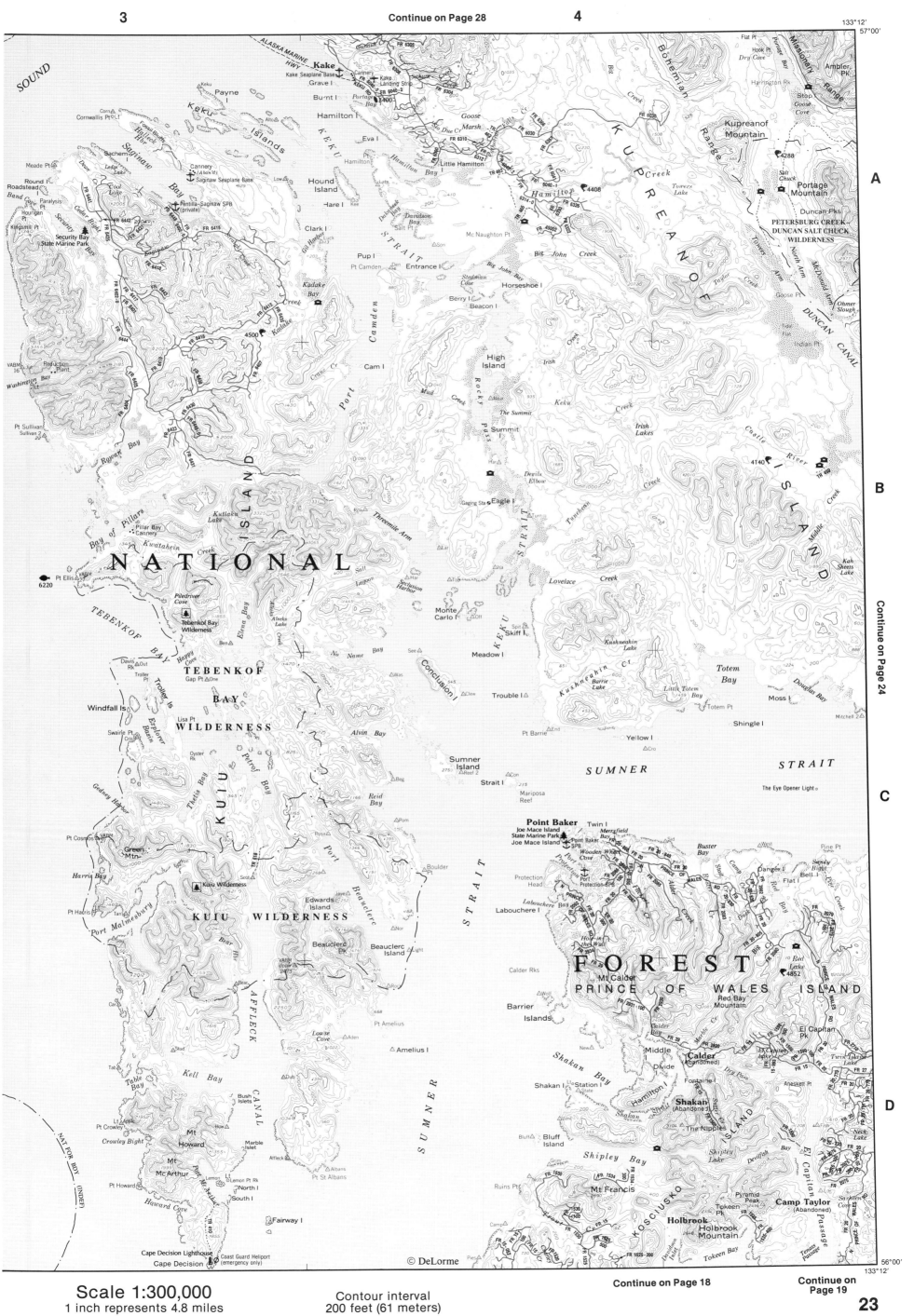

Continue on Page 24

Continue on Page 18

Continue on Page 19

© DeLorme

Scale 1:300,000
1 inch represents 4.8 miles

Contour interval
200 feet (61 meters)

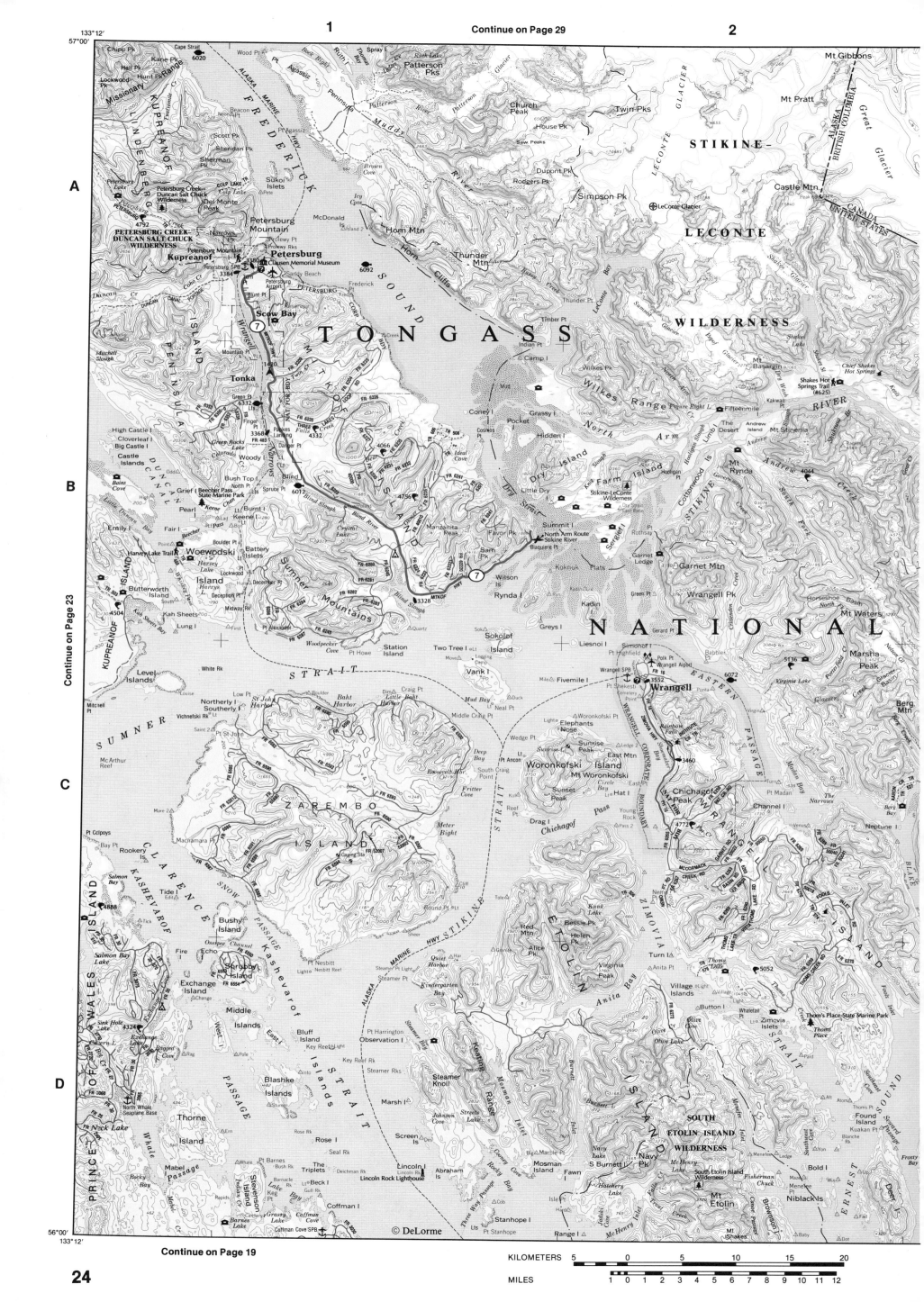

Continue on Page 23

© DeLorme

KILOMETERS 5   0   5   10   15   20

MILES 1 0 1 2 3 4 5 6 7 8 9 10 11 12

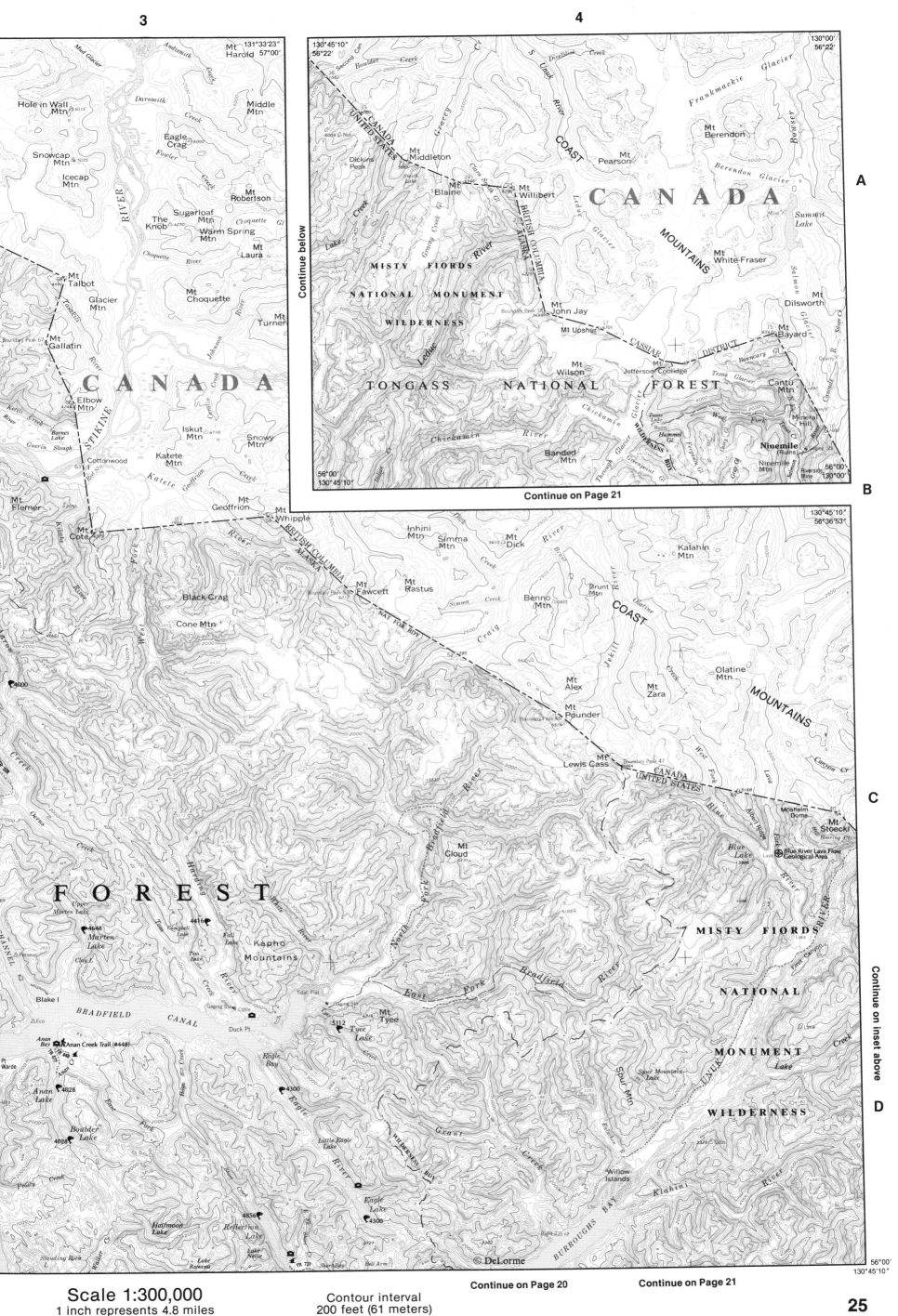

Scale 1:300,000
1 inch represents 4.8 miles

Contour interval
200 feet (61 meters)

Continue on Page 21

Continue on Page 20

Continue on Page 21

© DeLorme

136°40'
58°00'

A

B

C

D

57°06'06"
136°40'

YAKOBI ISLAND

Surge Bay
Takanis Bay
Takanis Peak
Takanis Pen
Cape Cross
Cross
Pt Satchrun
Squid Bay
Mindalina I
Greentop
Pt Theodore
Pinnacle Pk
Pinnacle Mtn
Star Rk
Urey Pks
Porcupine Is
Berthe Bay
Post
Middle I
Little Bay
Dry Pass
Cape Dearborn
Hill
Hogan
Pt Hogan
Cape Edward
Edward Is
Kukkan Bay
Kukkan Passage
White Sisters
Myriad Is
Black I
Brown Rk
Granite Is
Outer Rks
6156

El Nido Peak
Apex Mtn
Mt Raatikainen
Yakobi
Mt Hill
Cub Mtn
Lost Cove
Lt
North Mtn
Lake Morris
White Sulphur Sprs
Mt Barnesis
Mt Douglas
Mt Pinta
Pinta Bay
Goon Dip Mtn
Lock
Lydonia
Surveyor Pass
Williams Hill
Pole Pt
Open Passage
Tonalite Pass
Smooth Channel
Rough Channel
Khaz Bay
Deuce I
Ramp I
Baird I
Khaz Pass
Khaz Head
Khaz Breakers
Khaz Pt
Pt Slocum

Sunnyside
Wedge Mtn
Pelican
Pelican Seaplane Base
Pegmatite Mtn
Pass Mtn
Mineral Mtn
Apex Mine
Goose Lake
Logging Camp
Mine Mtn
Big Chief Mtn
Mt Crowther
Goulding Lakes
4400
Goulding Harbor
Whitestripe Mtn
Hirst Mtn
Black Mtn
Kimshan Cove
Doolth Mtn
Freeburn Mtn
Rust Mtn
Chichagof
Klag Bay
Klag
Twin
Sister Lake
Flat Top Mtn
Takeena Pen
Fort Arm
Falcon Arm
Slocum Arm
Waterfall Lake
Cobol
Island Cove
Flat Cove
Hidden Cove
Fortuna Strait
Fortuna Reefs
Klokachef I
Klokachef Pt
Pt Leo

CHICHAGOF

TONGASS

WILDERNESS

West Chichagof-Yakobi Wilderness
Lake Suloia
Suloia Bay
Suloia Pt
Schulze Head

Portage
Bell
Port Frederick
The Narrows
Salt Lake Bay
Salt Chuck
Hub I
Long I

Moser Island
South Arm
North Arm
Reynard Pt
Patterson Bay
Rust Lake
Pinnacle Pk
White Cliff Pt
Kook Cove

Ushk Bay
6308

Salisbury Sound
6256
Sinitsin
Morskoi Rk
Sea Rk
Pt Kruzof
Cape Georgiana
Mt Georgiana
Kalinin Pt
Eagle Rk
Sealion Cove
SEALION COVE TR
Sealion Is
Twin Pt
Pt Amelia
Pt Mary
Slaughter I
Storm
SHELIKOF BAY
Shell Mtn
Beaver Pt
Crater Ridge
Mount Edgecumbe
Mt Edgecumbe
EDGECUMBE TR
Neva Bay
Engano Pt
Shoals
Lava
Tower

KRUZOF ISLAND

Scraggy Is
Kane Is
Haywood
Partofshikof Island
Kresto
Gilmer Bay
Mud Bay
Port Krestof

PACIFIC OCEAN

ALASKA MARITIME NWR BDY

CITY AND BOROUGH OF SITKA

ALASKA MARINE HWY

Lisianski Inlet
Lisianski Strait
Lisianski River
West
North Arm

© DeLorme

Continue below right

136°00'
57°00'
Kruzof I
Sitka Pt
St Lazaria Is
135°39'
57°00'
Cape Edgecumbe
TONGASS NAT FOR
ALASKA MARITIME NWR
CITY AND BOROUGH OF SITKA
SITKA SOUND
PACIFIC OCEAN
56°55'
136°00'
56°55'
135°39'

57°00'
136°16'46"

Continue on inset left

26

KILOMETERS 5 0 5 10 15 20
MILES 1 0 1 2 3 4 5 6 7 8 9 10 11 12

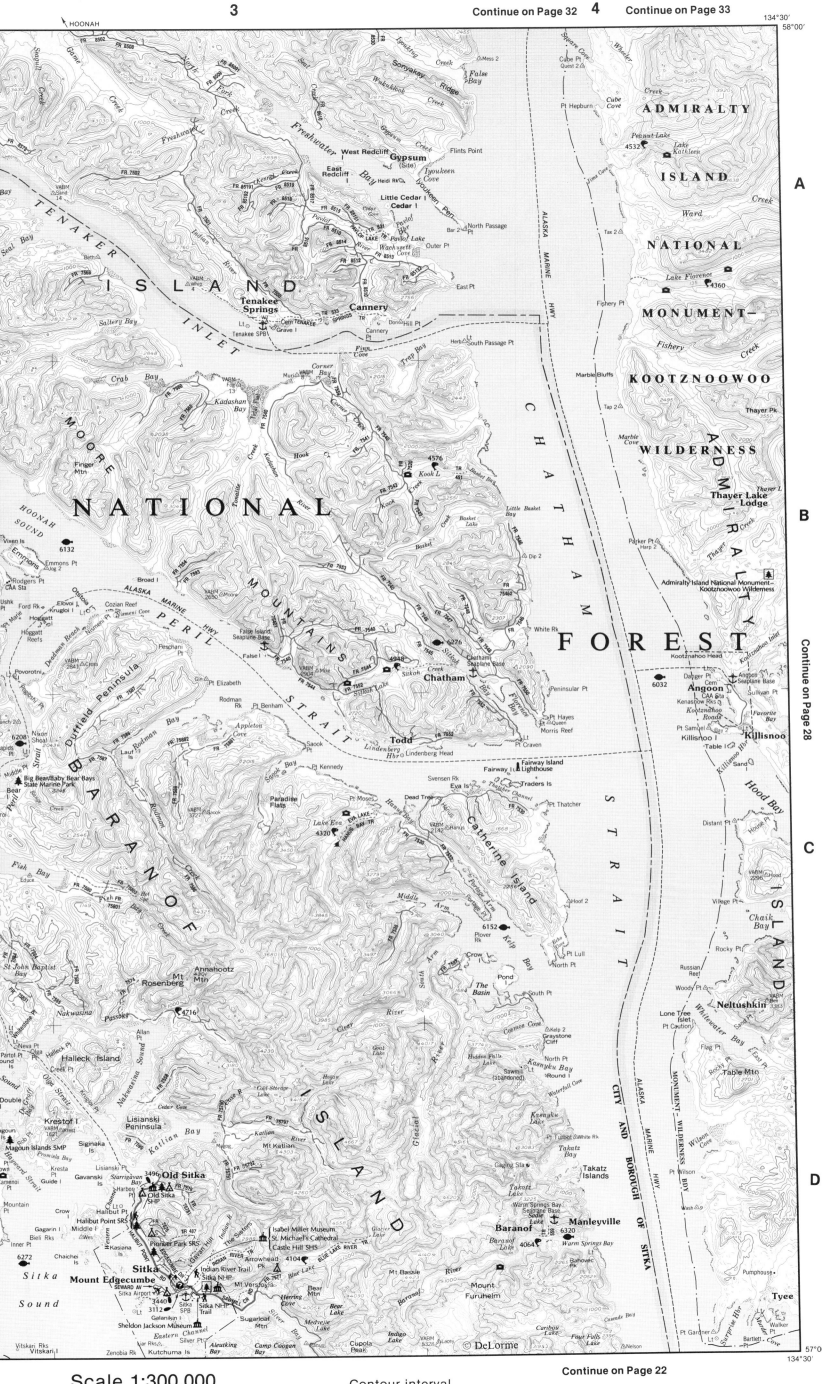

3   Continue on Page 32   4   Continue on Page 33

Continue on Page 28

Scale 1:300,000
1 inch represents 4.8 miles

Contour interval
200 feet (61 meters)

© DeLorme

Continue on Page 22

134°30'
58°00'

A

B

Continue on Page 27

C

D

57°00'
134°30'

TONGASS

ADMIRALTY ISLAND

KOOTZNOOWOO WILDERNESS

NATIONAL MONUMENT WILDERNESS

NATIONAL MONUMENT

STEPHENS PASSAGE

SEYMOUR CANAL

GLASS PENINSULA

SNETTISHAM PENINSULA

TRACY ARM

ENDICOTT

CHUCK RIVER WILDERNESS

Snettisham

Sumdum

Windham

PORT HOUGHTON

FREDERICK SOUND

KUPREANOF ISLAND

Swan Cove
Swan I
Stan Price State Wildlife Sanctuary
Bear Observatories
Windfall
Camp Shaheen
Hasselborg Homestead
Yellow Bear Mtn
Hood Bay
Soapberry Mtn
Bear Pass Mtn
Kanaiku Mtn
Middle Mtn
Pybus Lake
Favorite Bay
Kootznahoo Inlet
Mitchell Bay
Thayer Lake
Thayer Mtn
Mt Distin
Yeek-Sha Mtn
Pleasant Bay
Mole Harbor
Lake Alexander
Cross Admiralty Canoe Route
Gambier Bay
Gambier Island
West Brother Island
East Brother Island
The Brothers
San Juan Islands
Pybus Bay
Point Pybus
Deer Pt
Eliza Harbor
Bliss Lake
Mt Saffran
Herring Bay
Pt Brightman
Cape Bendel
Turn Mtn
Turnabout Island
Pt Macartney
Kekw Strait
Pt White
Carroll I

Port Snettisham
Pt Styleman
Pt Anmer
Meigs Peak
Gilbert Bay
Sweetheart Cr
Upper Sweetheart L
Lower Sweetheart L
Icefall Lake
Mt Sumdum
Sumdum Gl
Holkham Bay
Harbor I
Round Islet
Sand Spit
Tracy Arm–Fords Terror Wilderness
Sumdum I
Bushy Is
Thistle Ledge
Dry Bay
Pt Lookout
Pt League
Lighthouse Reserve
Taylor L
The Narrows
Windham Bay
Pt Windham
Pt Hobart
Hobart Bay
Sunset Island
Sunset Cove
Rocky Pt
The Twins
Entrance Island SPB
Entrance I
Alice Lake
The Salt Chuck
McDonald Rk
Sail Island
Akusha I
Pt Walpole
Crow I
Robert Is
Walter I
Rabbit I
The Five Fingers
Five Finger Lighthouse
Coast Guard Heliport (emergency only)
Fort Pt
Foot I
McNairy Pt
Bill Pt
Bartlett Pt
Whitney Island
Storm Is
Duck Pt
Cape Fanshaw
Mt Fanshaw
Fanshaw Bay
Canoe Pt
Fanshaw Range
Dahlgren Peak
Jamestown Peak
Saranac Peak
Alaska Pk
Tangent Pk
Bay Pt Knoll

Washburn Peak
Wheeler Peak
Randolph Peak
Morse Pk
Faust
Dorn
Flaw Pt
Midway Pt
Midway Islands
Station Pt
Fool Inlet
Mist I
River Pt
Sentinel I
Whiting R

ALASKA MARINE HWY

KILOMETERS   5   0   5   10   15   20
MILES   1 0 1 2 3 4 5 6 7 8 9 10 11 12

© DeLorme

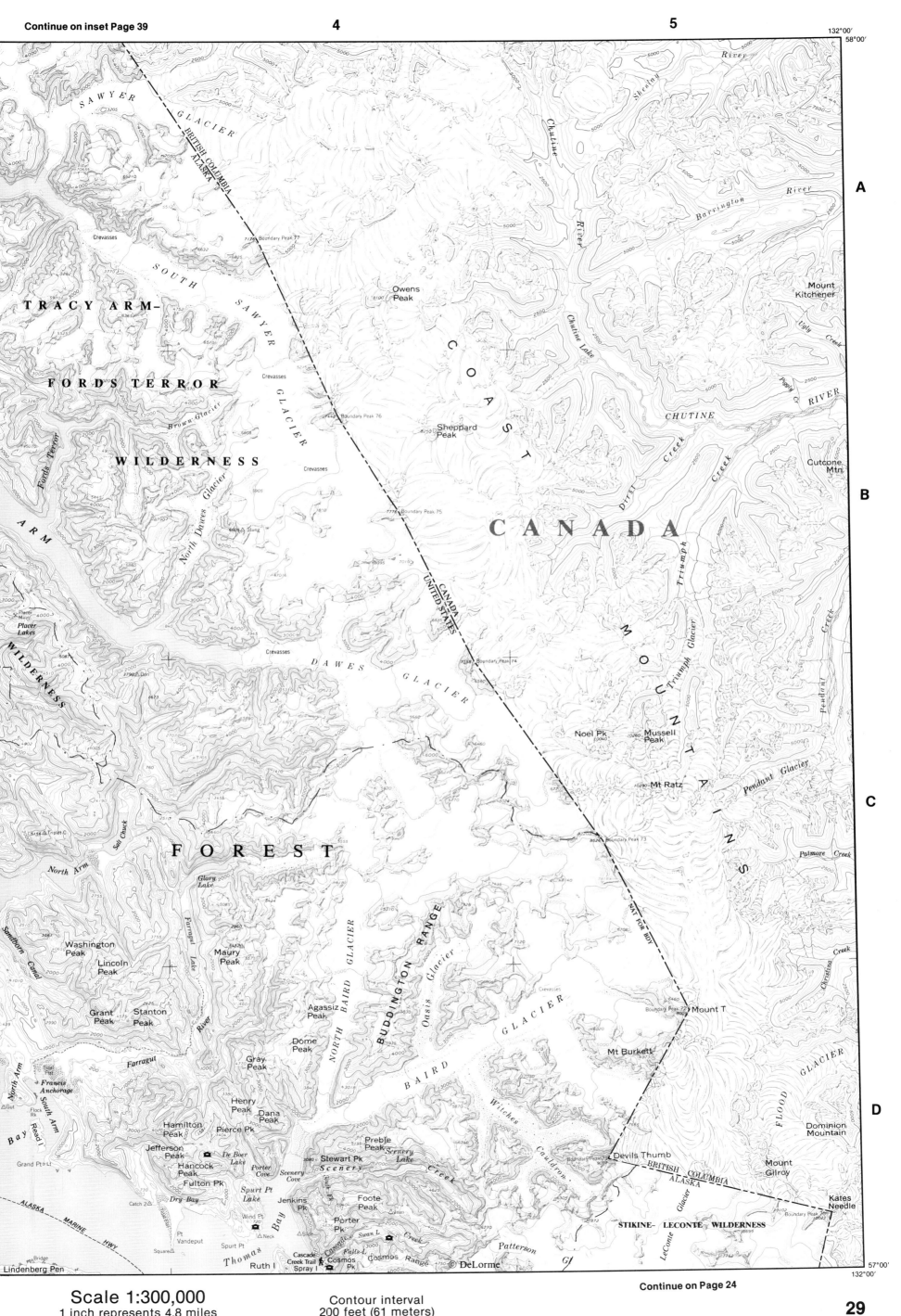

132°00'
58°00'

A

B

C

D

57°00'
132°00'

Scale 1:300,000
1 inch represents 4.8 miles

Contour interval
200 feet (61 meters)

Continue on Page 24

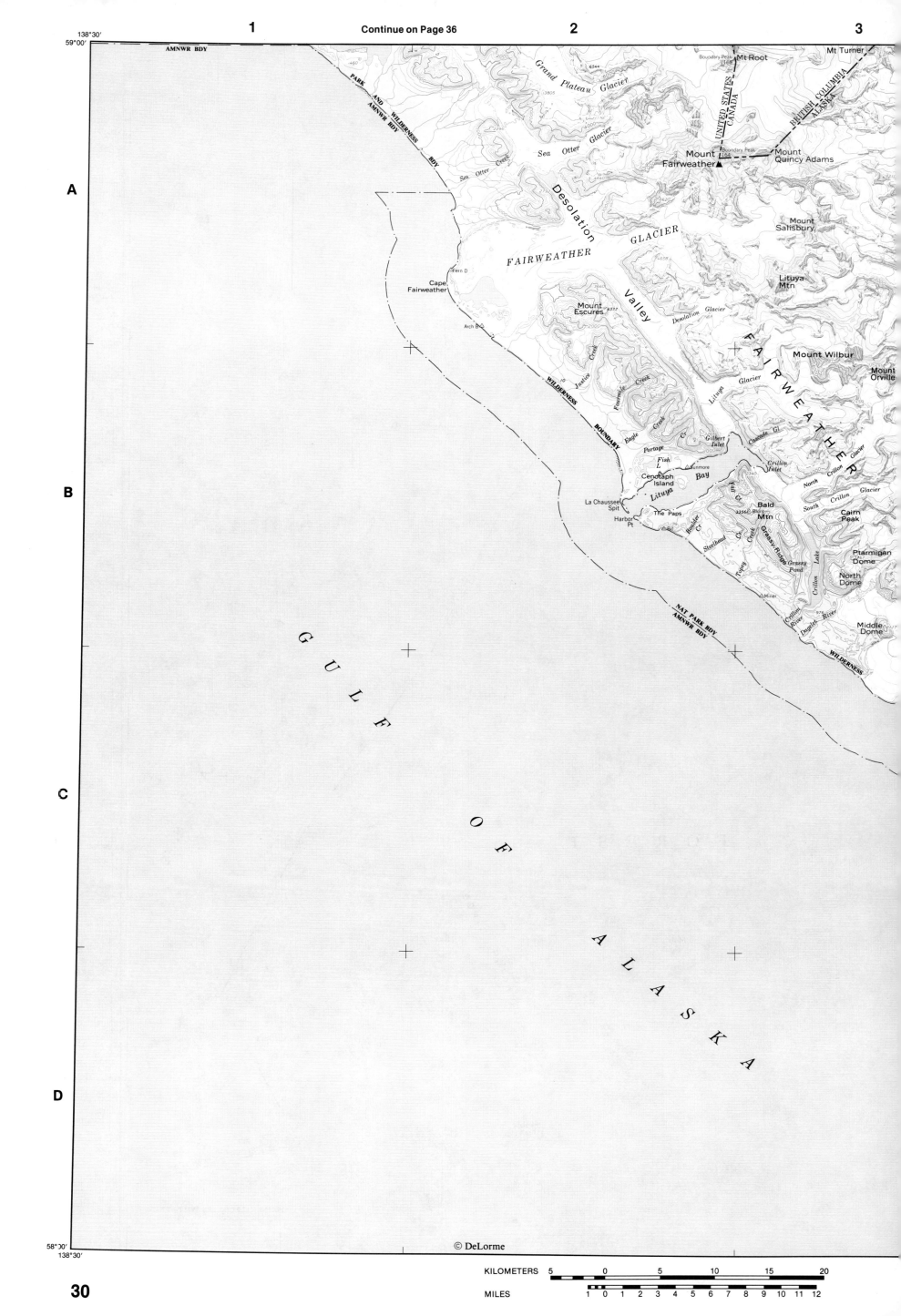

138°30'
59°00'

AMNWR BDY

PARK AND WILDERNESS AMNWR BDY

BDY

A

UNITED STATES
CANADA

BRITISH COLUMBIA
ALASKA

Grand Plateau Glacier

6544

Boundary Peak
4662 Mt Root

Mt Turner

Sea Otter Glacier

Sea Otter Creek

Mount
Fairweather ▲

Boundary Peak
4664

Mount
Quincy Adams

Mount
Salisbury

Desolation

GLACIER

FAIRWEATHER

Valley

Lituya
Mtn

Cape
Fairweather

Fern D

Mount
Escures

Desolation Glacier

Arch B D

FAIRWEATHER

Mount Wilbur

WILDERNESS

Justice Creek

Fourmile Creek

Eagle Creek

Lituya Glacier

Mount
Orville

Portage

Fish
L

Gilbert
Inlet

Chocate Gl

BOUNDARY

Cenotaph
Island

Gunmore

Crillon
Inlet

North Crillon Glacier

B

Bay

Lituya

South Crillon Glacier

La Chaussee
Spit

The Paps

Bald
Mtn

Cairn
Peak

Harbor
Pt

Bd

Boulder Cr

Grassy Ridge Creek

Grassy
Pond

Ptarmigan
Dome

Steelhead

Crillon Creek

Topsy

Grassy Lake

North
Dome

Miner

NAT PARK BDY
AMNWR BDY

Crillon River

Doplet River

Middle
Dome

WILDERNESS

G U L F

O F

A L A S K A

C

D

58°30'
138°30'

© DeLorme

KILOMETERS 5   0   5   10   15   20

MILES   1 0 1 2 3 4 5 6 7 8 9 10 11 12

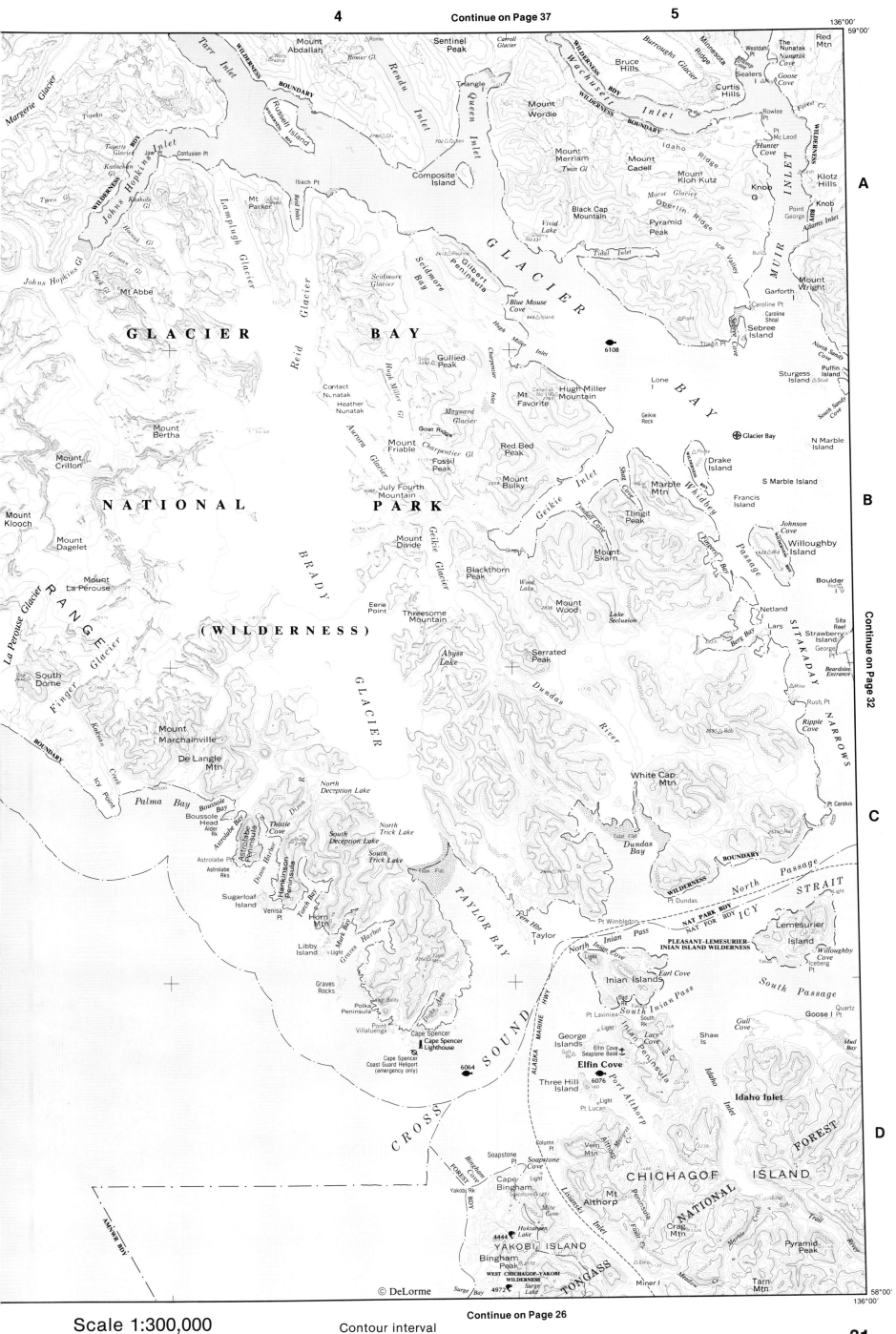

Continue on Page 32

Continue on Page 26

Scale 1:300,000
1 inch represents 4.8 miles

Contour interval
200 feet (61 meters)

© DeLorme

136°00'
59°00'

1   **2**   **3**

A

B

C

D

Continue on Page 31

HAINES BOROUGH
CITY AND BOROUGH OF JUNEAU

Snow Dome
Mt Elder
Canyon
Casement Glacier
Berg Mtn
Girdled Gl
NAT PARK AND FOR BDY WILDERNESS BDY

GLACIER BAY
ADAMS INLET
Tree Mtn
Mt Young
Granite Creek
Berg Creek
Main Valley

Mt Case
Endicott Gap
Endicott Lake
Endicott River
HAINES BOROUGH
CHILKAT

Eldred Rock Coast Guard
Heliport (emergency only)
Eldred Rock
Eldred Rock Lighthouse
Island

Rescue Harbor
Sullivan Island
State Marine Park
SULLIVAN ISLAND
STATE MARINE PARK
Sullivan Rock

Kakuhan Range
Lions Head Mountain

Berners Bay
Antler River
Gilkey River
Evelyn Lake
Antler Lake

Comet
Pt Sherman
Point Sherman Lighthouse
Sherman Rk

ENDICOTT RIVER
WILDERNESS
Endicott River Wilderness
Endicott River

Puffin Island
Miller Peak
Sandy Cove
Sandy Cove Wolf
Spokane Cove
Leland Islands

Beartrack Cove
Flapjack Island
GLACIER BAY
Beartrack River
Link Island
Kidney Island
Strawberry
Spider Island
Beardslee Islands
Beardslee Entrance
Young Island
Secret Bay
Lester Island
Bartlett Cove
Bartlett River
Bartlett Lake
Salmon River

MT PARK AND FOR WILDERNESS BDY

TONGASS
NATIONAL

Lance Pt
William Henry Bay

Yang Webster Peak

6172

Danger Pt

POINT BRIDGET
STATE PARK
Point Bridget
Point Bridget State Park
Point Bridget Trail
3144
Tongass National Forest

Mab Island
Bridget Cove
4220
Yankee Basin

7

St James Bay
State Marine Park
St Brothers
ST JAMES BAY
STATE MARINE PARK
Whidbey Pt
St James Point
Volcanic Peak

CITY AND HAINES BOROUGH

Vanderbilt Reef
North I
Benjamin Island
Sentinel Island
Sentinel Island Lighthouse
Little Island
Ralston Island
Punk I
Poundstone Rock

Lynn Sisters

Nun Mtn

CITY AND BOROUGH OF JUNEAU

LYNN CANAL

Mount Golub

MARINE HWY

Lincoln Island

Amalga
(Eagle Glacier)
Dotsons Landing
Gull
Bird 3008
Gruening SHP
St Terese
Hump Island
6264
Shelter Island State Marine Park
Aaron Island
Coghlan Island
6292
3520
Lena Cove
Lincoln Anchorage

SAGINAW CHANNEL

Pt Retreat
Point Retreat Lighthouse
Barlow Islands
False Pt Retreat

Shelter Island
Barlow Cove
Mansfield
Piling
Symonds
Strauss Rk

GLACIER BAY
NATIONAL PARK

Glacier Bay
National Park and Preserve
Radio Towers
Lagoon
Bartlett Cove SPB
DUDE CREEK
STATE CRITICAL
HABITAT AREA
Dude Creek
State Critical
Habitat Area
Gustavus Airport
GUSTAVUS AIRPORT
GUSTAVUS RIVER
Salmon River

Gustavus
Pt Gustavus
E Base
Lights
Berry

Icy Passage
Pt Gustavus
Ancon Rk

Excursion Inlet
Seaplane Base
Excursion Inlet
Neva Lake

Camp 26

Teardrop Lake

Stephens Passage
Lone Mtn
Green Mtn

NAT PARK BDY
NAT FOR BDY
NAT PARK BDY

ALASKA MARINE HWY

PLEASANT-LEMESURIER-
INIAN ISLAND WILDERNESS
Pleasant Island
Pleasant-Lemesurier-
Inian Islands Wilderness
The Knob
Boss 2
Pleasant Island Reef

Noon Pt
Porpoise Is
Light Por

FR 8580
FR 8581
FR 8553
FR 8551

Funter
Funter Bay State Marine Park
Funter Bay SPB
Funter Station
Robert Barron Peak

ICY
STRAIT
Adolphus 2
Lt Pt Adolphus
Pinta Cove
6136
Damp

Eagle Pt
Harry I
Burger Pt
Flynn Cove

TONGASS
Chicken Creek

NATIONAL
Godkin Channel
Hoonah I
Scraggy I
Pinta Rock
Crist Pt

FOREST
Day
Crm
Mud

Naked I
The Kittens
Clear Pt
Funter Bay
Rat
Doc
Couverden Rock
No Use Ledge
Ansley
Entrance
Pt Couverden
Rocky I
The Sisters
Sisters Reef

Snowy Mountain

PENINSULA

ALASKA
MARINE
HWY

Mud Bay
Gallagher
Creek
Creek
Halibut
Port Frederick
Pt Sophia
6232
Halibut Rk
Cannery Point
Light Spasski I
Spasski I
Neck Pt
Spasski Bay
Pulizzi I

Hawk Inlet
SPB (private)

TONGASS

CHICHAGOF
Neka River
Humpback Creek
FR 8540
FR 8401
Hoonah
3196
Hoonah SPB
Pitt I
Hoonah Landing Strip
Long I
Game
FR 8502
Neck

Piledriver Cove
Game Cove
Pt Marsden
Calm Pt
Lighths

CHATHAM STRAIT

Neka Mtn
PORT FREDERICK
FR 8530
FR 8503
Elephant Mtn
Whitestone Hbr
Pt Augusta
Lines Is

ISLAND
Neka Bay
Neka I
N Bight
Chimney Rock
S Bight
Burnt Pt
Fred I
FR 8502
FR 8503
FR 8513
FR 8513
FR 8504
FR 8530

Tenakee Inlet
Eight Fathom Bight
Midway Rocks

© DeLorme

58°00'
136°00'

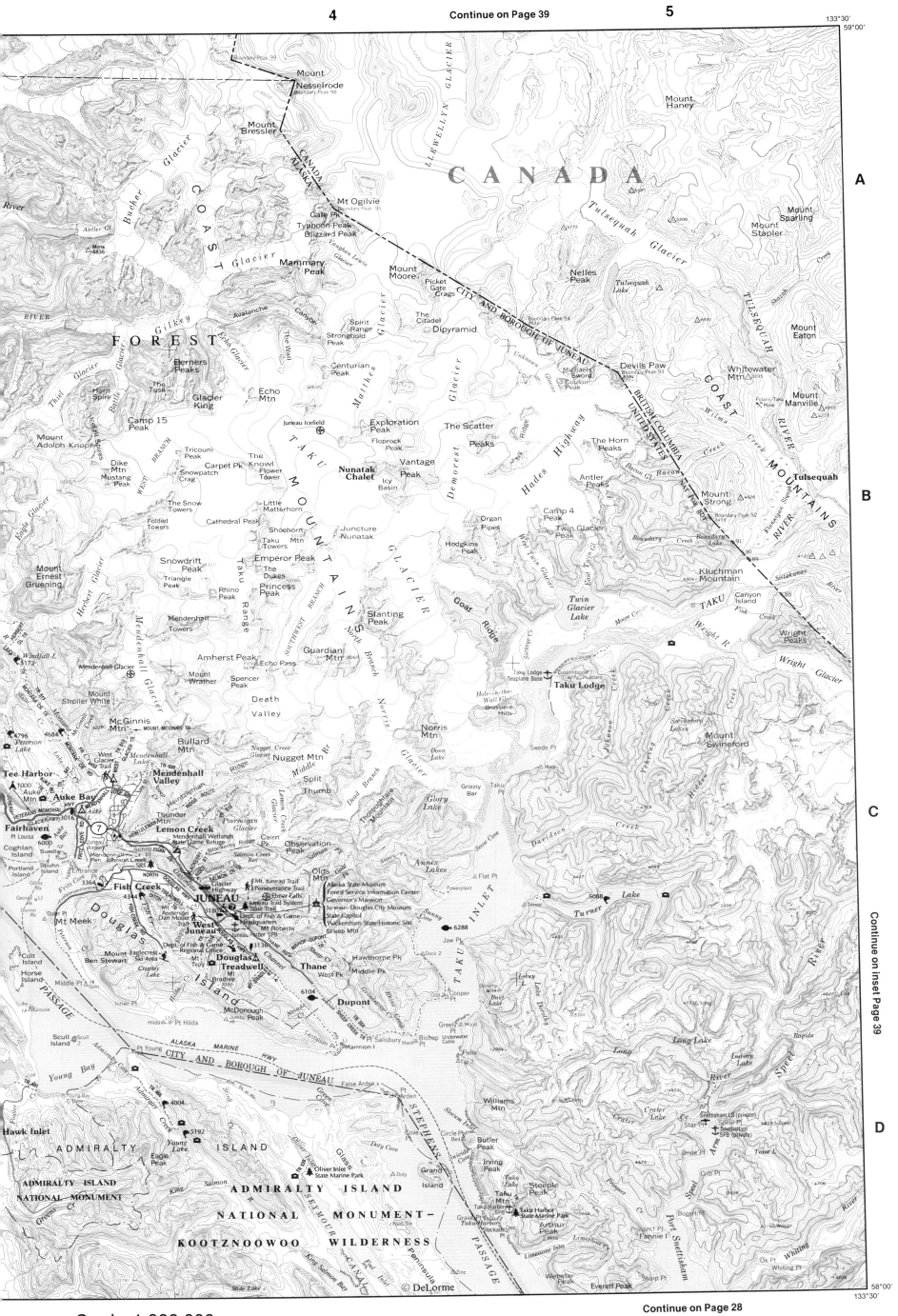

Continue on inset Page 39

Continue on Page 28

Scale 1:300,000
1 inch represents 4.8 miles

Contour interval
200 feet (61 meters)

141°00'
60°00'

W R A N G E L L - S A I N T   E L I A S

N A T I O N A L   P A R K

(W I L D E R N E S S)

M A L A S P I N A   G L A C I E R

A

⊕ Malaspina Glacier

Hayden Glacier
Floral Pass
Floral Hills
Lucia Nunatak
Lucia Glacier
Terrace Pt
Amphitheater Knob
Blizhr

WRANGELL–

NATIONAL PARK BDY
NATIONAL PRESERVE BDY
Kwik Stream
Samis
Lund

GRAND

SAINT ELIAS

WASH

NATIONAL

Malaspina Lake

Esker Stream
Strawberry Island

PRESERVE

RIVER

R. Kame Str
Sudden
Schooner Beach
350 Malaspina SW Base

Continue on inset below

Beach No 6
Cape Sitkagi
Fountain Str
Sitkagi   Bluffs NAT PARK AND WILDERNESS BDY
AMNWR BDY
WILDERNESS BDY
Mushy Stream
Alder Stream
Manby Stream
Pt Manby

Y A K U T A T

B

6336

Pt Munoz
Khantaak
Seal
Rurik Harbor
Pt Carrew
661
Monti Bay
Ocean Cape
Phipps Peninsula
Ocean Cape Lt
Kardy L Summit
FR 9965
4048

C

G   U   L   F

O   F

59°16'01"
141°00'

Continue on Page 77

142°00'
60°00'

141°00'
60°00'

Big River
Priest River
Watson Cr
Drill Hole
Big 18
Icy Bay LS
Icy Cape
Guyot Bay
Claybluff Pt
I C Y   B A Y
Gull Island
Caetani R
M A L A S P I N A

I C Y
Tsimpshian Point
Moraine I
Moraine Reef
Point Riou Spit
Riou Bay
Ridge 106
Drill Hole
Pt Riou
Sacred Lake
YAHTSE RIVER
YANA STREAM
G L A C I E R

D

G U L F   O F   A L A S K A

WRANGELL-SAINT ELIAS NATIONAL PARK
WRANGELL-SAINT ELIAS NATIONAL PARK

Continue above left

© DeLorme

59°45'
142°00'

59°45'
141°00'

59°00'
139°59'

KILOMETERS 5   0   5   10   15   20

MILES   1 0 1 2 3 4 5 6 7 8 9 10 11 12

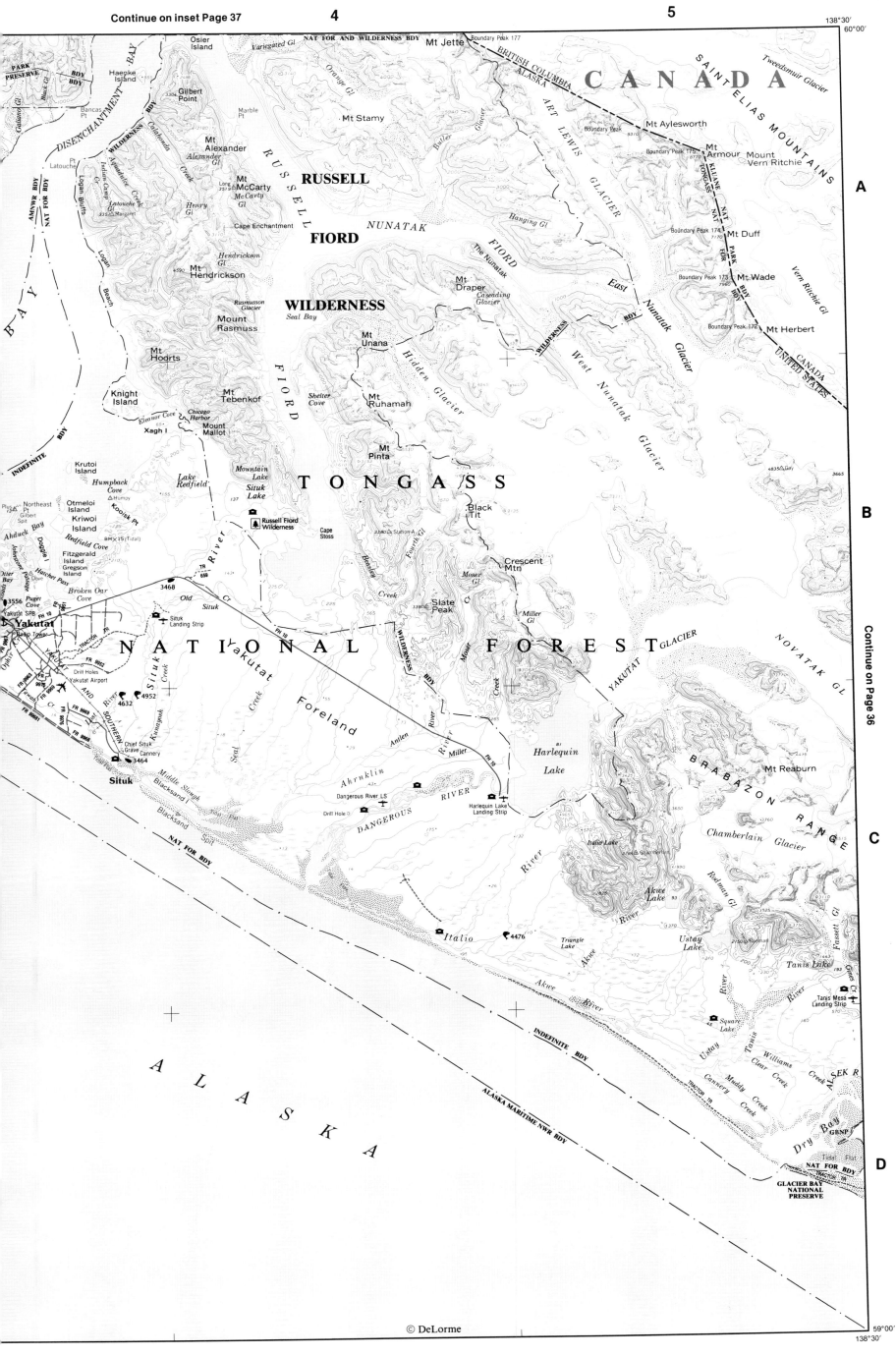

Continue on Page 36

Scale 1:300,000
1 inch represents 4.8 miles

Contour interval
200 feet (61 meters)

© DeLorme

138°30'
60°00'
138°19'16"
60°00'

141°00'
60°22'

KLUANE   **NATIONAL**

Mt Jeannette
Mt Bering
Mt Baird
Mt Malaspina

SEWARD
Mt Irving

Mt Newton
Russell Col
CAN
US

Boundary Peak 183
Mt Augusta

Mt St Elias
Mt. St. Elias 18008

PARK

Mt Eaton
Corwin Cliffs

C A N A D A

Newton Glacier

Haydon Peak
Boundary Peak 185

Augusta Gl

GLACIER

Mt Owen

YUKON TERRITORY
ALASKA

Cascade Gl
Dome Pass

Boundary Peak 184

Tweedsmuir Glacier

Boundary Peak 18
Mt Cook

Continue on Page 77

LIBBEY GLACIER
Agassiz Lakes

Agassiz GLACIER

Samovar Hills

Oily Lake

SEWARD

Pt Glorious
Pinnacle Pass Hills

Pinnacle Gl
Pinnacle Pass

WRANGELL-   **SAINT**   **ELIAS**

Chaix Hills
Moore Nunatak

WRANGELL SAINT ELIAS

Hitchcock Gl
Hitchcock Hills

Marvine Glacier

Hayden Gl

Vern Ritchie Gl

M A L A S P I N A

G L A C I E R

Blossom Gl

Flora Hills

60°00'
141°00'

Blossom Island

Continue on Page 34

CANADA
UNITED STATES

A
B
C
D

Bar Lake

Noisy

ALSEK

RIVER

TONGASS

Range

Tomahnous Creek

Continue on Page 35

NATIONAL

Reynolds Gl

TATSHENSHINI

Boundary
Bdy Pk
Bdy Pk 171
Bdy Pk 170

FOREST

NOVATAK GLACIER

ALSEK

RIVER

Melt Cr

Ninetyeighter Creek

Twaggh Cr

Basement Creek

Flower
Quib

Cub

Nolund Glacier

SAINT

Towagh

Creek

BRABAZON

RANGE

Alser
Creek

Melbern Gl

BRITISH COLUMBIA
ALASKA

Pentice
Pentice Ridge

Ice Cabs

Creek

Basement

Good

ELIAS

Kanamoxt

MELBERN

Martin Gl

NAT PARK AND WILDERNESS BDY

GLACIER   **BAY**

Konamoxt

GLACIER

Tikke

Canyon Glacier
Creek

Gl

Sittrosue Gl

Bay Gl

Jarl Gl

Melbern Lake

Emile Creek
Split
Gl

Cabin
Slough

NATIONAL

WILDERNESS BDY

Boundary Peak 167

Spur
Blonds Bench

ALSEK

RIVER

East Gateway Knob

Alsek Glacier

Mt Hay

Mount Jarl

MOUNTAINS

Alsek River Landing Strip
First Rapids

Bear Island

GLACIER   **BAY**

PARK

TONGASS NATIONAL FOREST

East Alsek River Landing Strip

NATIONAL

River

Lower Doame Lake

Mount Lodge

Mount Eliza

Deception Hills

PRESERVE BDY

PRESERVE

Upper Doame Lake

Boundary Peak 166

(WILDERNESS)

NAT PARK AND WILDERNESS BDY

Deception
South Fork
Clear Creek

GRAND PLATEAU GLACIER

CANADA
UNITED STATES

GULF OF ALASKA

Mount Watson

Boundary Peak 162
Mt Turner

Ferris

GRAND

Eliz

© DeLorme

59°00'
138°30'

Continue on Page 30

KILOMETERS   5   0   5   10   15   20

MILES   1 0 1 2 3 4 5 6 7 8 9 10 11 12

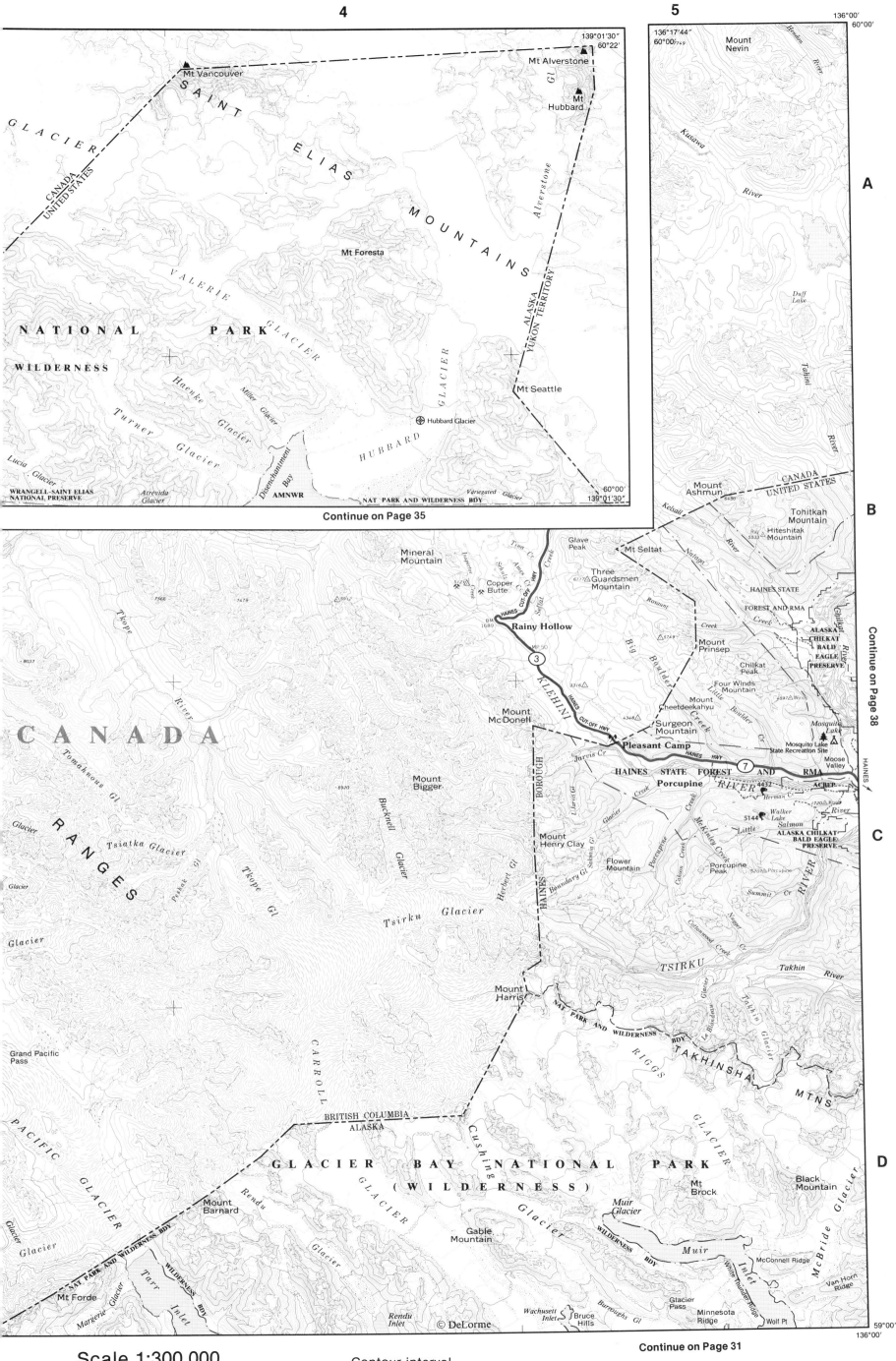

136°17'44"
60°00'
749

Mount
Nevin

Kusawa

River

A

Duff
Lake

Tahini

River

139°01'30"
60°22'
▲ Mt Alverstone

▲ Mt Vancouver

S A I N T   E L I A S   M O U N T A I N S

G L A C I E R

CANADA
UNITED STATES

Mt Foresta

V A L E R I E   G L A C I E R

N A T I O N A L   P A R K

W I L D E R N E S S

Haenke   Glacier

Miller Glacier

Turner   Glacier

Lucia   Glacier

WRANGELL-SAINT ELIAS
NATIONAL PRESERVE

Atrevida
Glacier

Disenchantment
Bay

AMNWR

HUBBARD

Hubbard Glacier ⊕

Mt Seattle

Variegated   Glacier

NAT PARK AND WILDERNESS BDY

G L A C I E R

ALASKA
YUKON TERRITORY

Alverstone

▲ Mt
Hubbard

60°00'
139°01'30"

Continue on Page 35

Mount
Ashmun

CANADA
UNITED STATES

Tohitkah
Mountain

6450

Hiteshitak
Mountain

5523

B

HAINES STATE

FOREST AND RMA

Creek

ALASKA
CHILKAT
BALD
EAGLE
PRESERVE

Continue on Page 38

HAINES

Glave
Peak

Mineral
Mountain

Copper
Butte

5273

599

Inspector

Creek

Schuls

Ames   Cr

Tinn   Cr.

Mt Seltat

Three
Guardsmen
Mountain

4777

Nataga

River

Kelsall

River

Mount
Prinsep

Chilkat
Peak

5749

Four Winds
Mountain

Mount
Cheetdeekahyu

4348

Surgeon
Mountain

4827   Winds

Mosquito
Lake

Mosquito Lake
State Recreation Site

Moose
Valley

Creek

Little

Boulder

Big

Boulder

Rosunt

Creek

BM
1689

Rainy Hollow

③

MP 50

HAINES CUT-OFF HWY

Seltat

K L E H I N I

HAINES   CUT-OFF   HWY

2316

Mount
McDonell

Pleasant Camp

⑦

HAINES   HWY

HAINES

HAINES STATE FOREST AND RMA

Porcupine

RIVER

4432

ACRF

Herman   Cr

Walker
Lake

1720   Kub

ALASKA CHILKAT
BALD EAGLE
PRESERVE

5144

Little

Salmon

C

T h o p e

River

7566

7479

8037

C A N A D A

R A N G E S

Tomahnous Gl.

Tsiatka Glacier

Psbuk Gl.

Glacier

Glacier

Thope Gl.

Bucknell

Glacier

Mount
Bigger

8920

Mount
Harris

Herbert Gl.

Tsirku   Glacier

BOROUGH

HAINES

Jarvis Cr

Llarvis Gl.

Boundary Gl.

Saltatus Gl

Mount
Henry Clay

Flower
Mountain

Creek

McKinley   Creek

Little

Porcupine

Cikon

Cottonwood   Cr.

Porcupine
Peak

5207   Porcupine

Summit   Cr

Nugget   Cr.

Takhin   River

Le Blondeau

Takhin   Gl.

Takhin   Glacier

T S I R K U

R I G G S

T A K H I N S H A

M T N S

G L A C I E R

Mt
Brock

Black
Mountain

Glacier

D

Grand Pacific
Pass

P A C I F I C

Glacier

CARROLL

BRITISH COLUMBIA
ALASKA

Mount
Barnard

Rendu

Glacier

Mt Forde

Margerie   Glacier

Tarr

NAT PARK AND WILDERNESS BDY

WILDERNESS   BDY

Tarr

Glacier

Inlet

Cushing

Glacier

G L A C I E R   B A Y   N A T I O N A L   P A R K

(W I L D E R N E S S)

Gable
Mountain

Glacier

Rendu
Inlet

© DeLorme

Wachusett
Inlet

Bruce
Hills

Burroughs Gl.

NAT PARK AND WILDERNESS BDY

WILDERNESS   BDY

Muir
Glacier

Muir

Glacier Pass

Minnesota
Ridge

McConnell Ridge

Inlet

White Thunder Ridge

Van Horn
Ridge

Wolf Pt

McBride Glacier

Continue on Page 31

136°00'
59°00'

Scale 1:300,000
1 inch represents 4.8 miles

Contour interval
200 feet (61 meters)

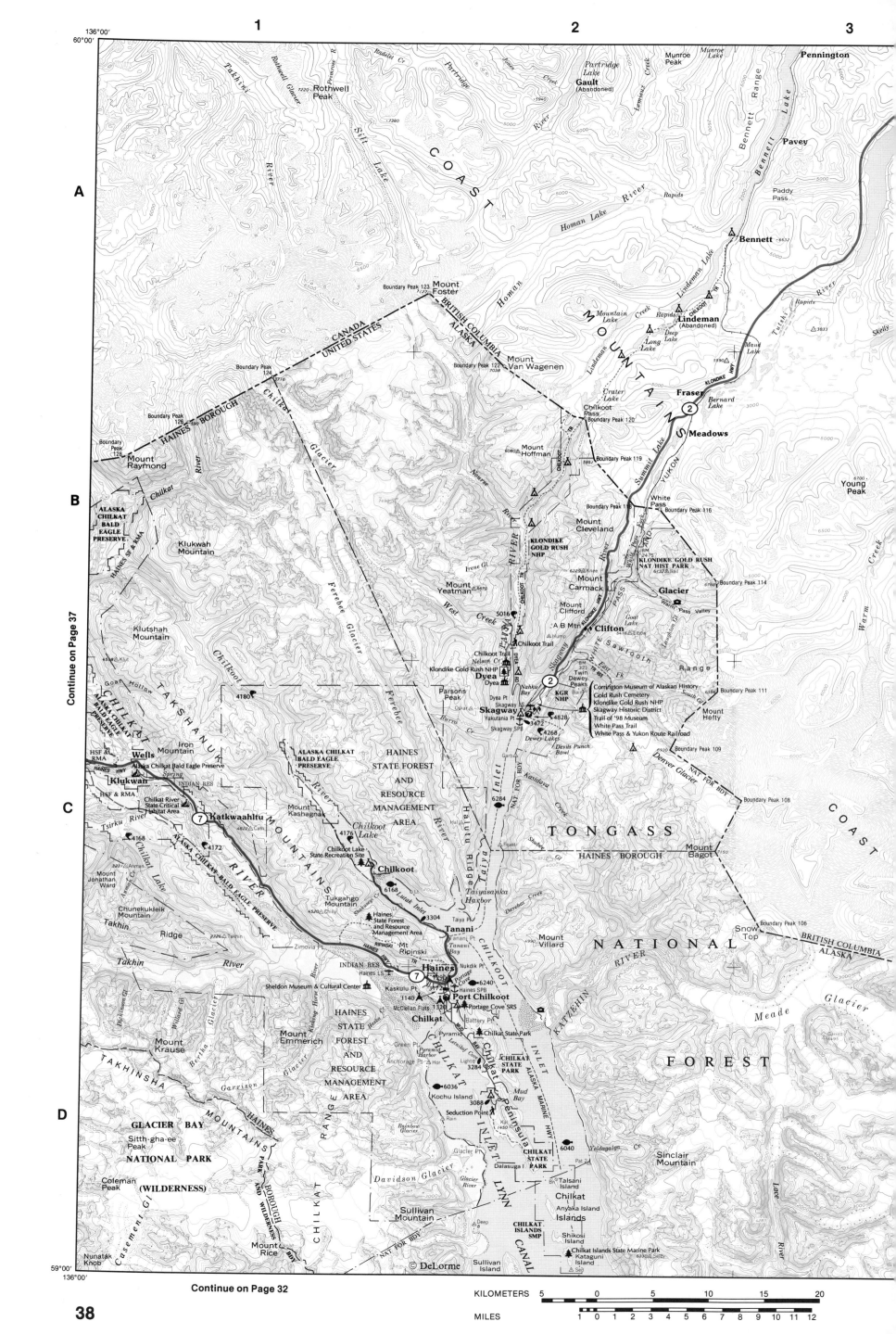

Continue on Page 37

Continue on Page 32

© DeLorme

KILOMETERS 5 0 5 10 15 20

MILES 1 0 1 2 3 4 5 6 7 8 9 10 11 12

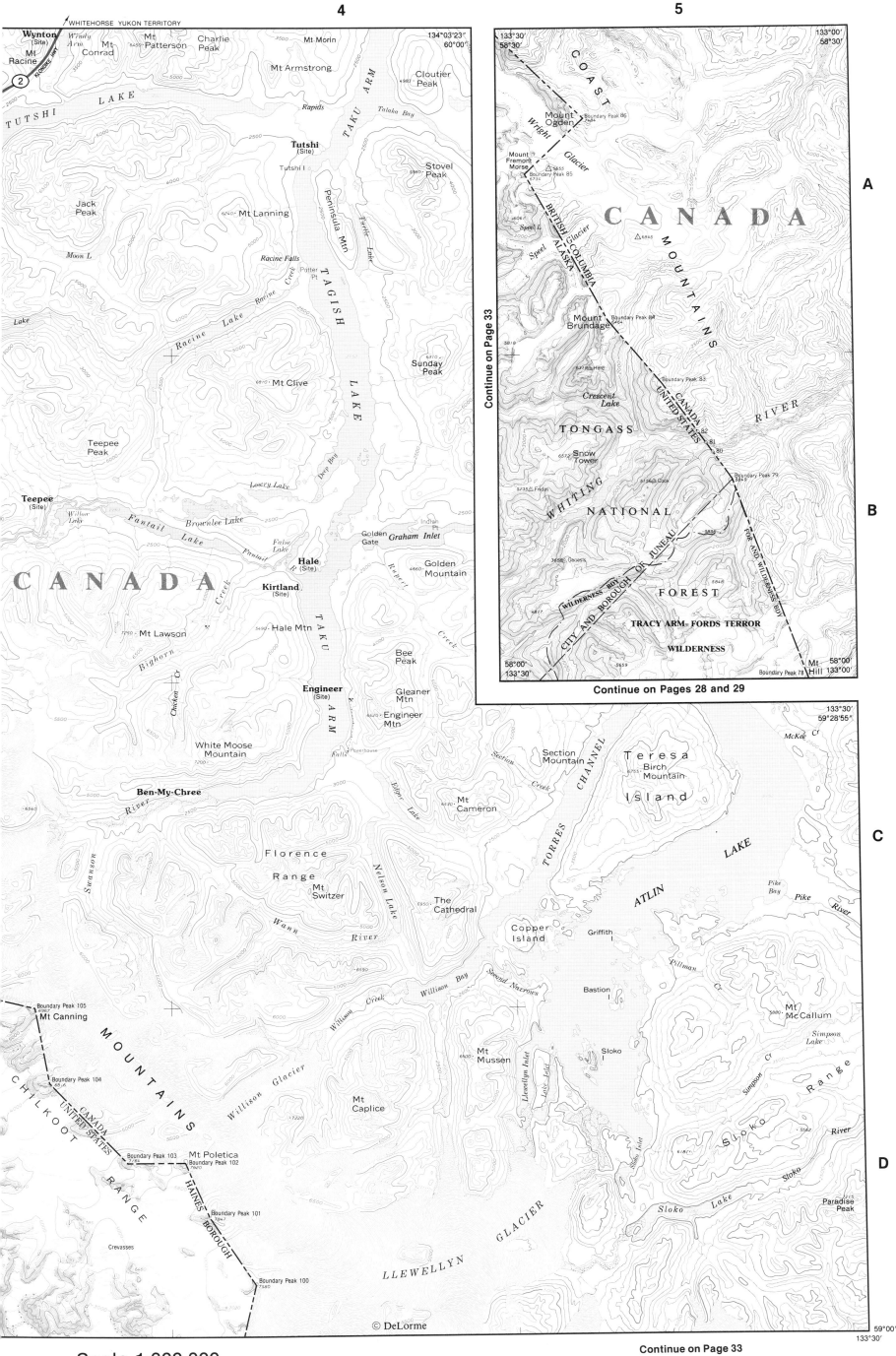

Continue on Page 33

Continue on Pages 28 and 29

Continue on Page 33

© DeLorme

Scale 1:300,000
1 inch represents 4.8 miles

Contour interval
200 feet (61 meters)

155°30'
58°00'

A

B

B R I S T O L

B   A   Y

C

LAKE AND PENINSULA BOROUGH

Sherry
75

Hook Lagoon

29

24 Quirt

D

59 Teck   93

Mud

© DeLorme

57°00'
159°30'

Continue on Page 139

40

| KILOMETERS | 5 | 0 | 5 | 10 | 15 | 20 |

| MILES | 1 0 1 | 2 | 3 | 4 | 5 | 6 | 7 | 8 | 9 | 10 | 11 | 12 |

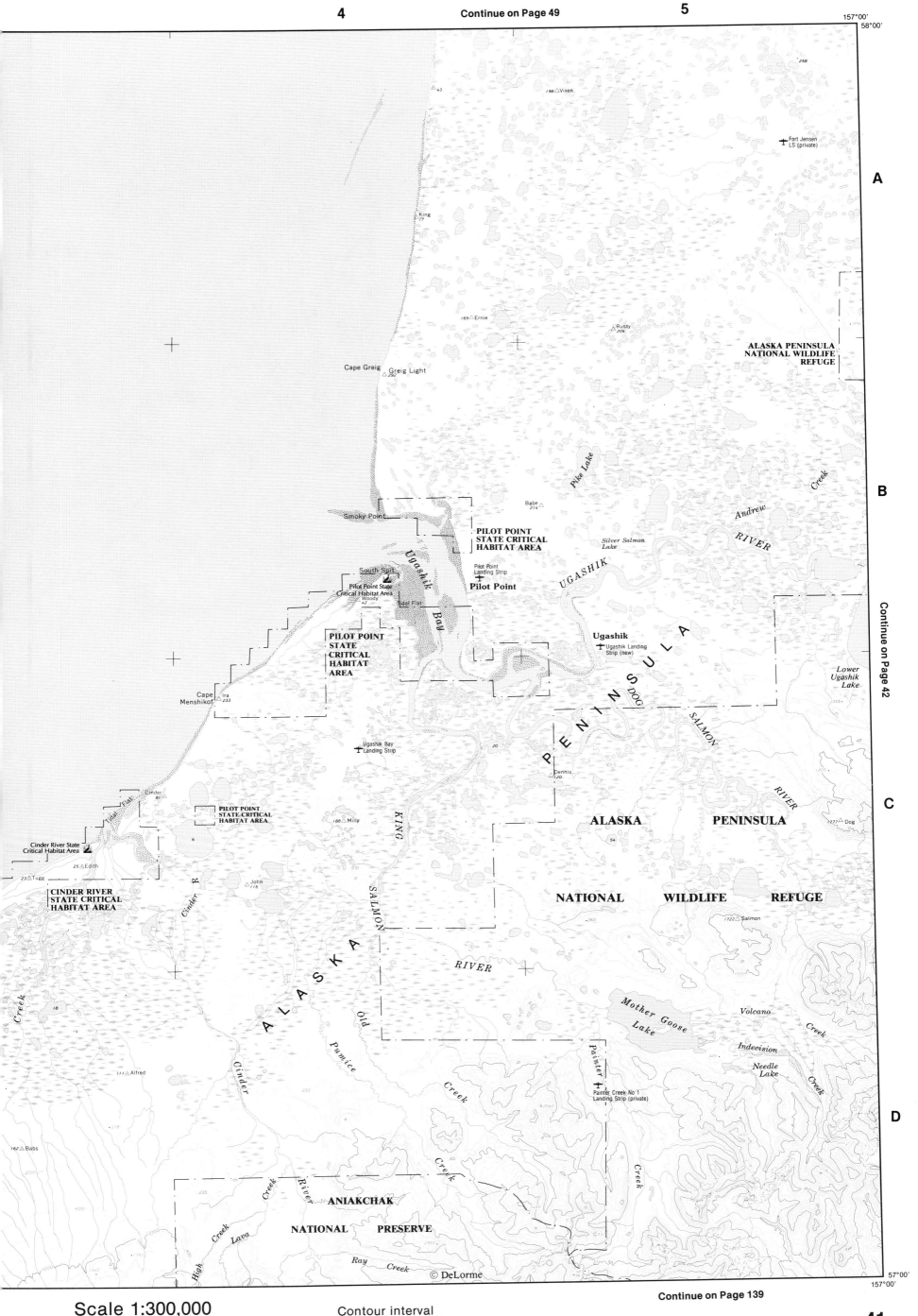

157°00'
58°00'

A

**ALASKA PENINSULA
NATIONAL WILDLIFE
REFUGE**

B

Continue on Page 42

**PILOT POINT
STATE CRITICAL
HABITAT AREA**

Pilot Point

Ugashik

**PILOT POINT
STATE
CRITICAL
HABITAT
AREA**

ALASKA   PENINSULA

C

**PILOT POINT
STATE CRITICAL
HABITAT AREA**

**Cinder River State
Critical Habitat Area**

**CINDER RIVER
STATE CRITICAL
HABITAT AREA**

NATIONAL   WILDLIFE   REFUGE

ALASKA

Mother Goose
Lake

D

ANIAKCHAK

NATIONAL   PRESERVE

© DeLorme

57°00'
157°00'

Continue on Page 139

Scale 1:300,000
1 inch represents 4.8 miles

Contour interval
200 feet (61 meters)

41

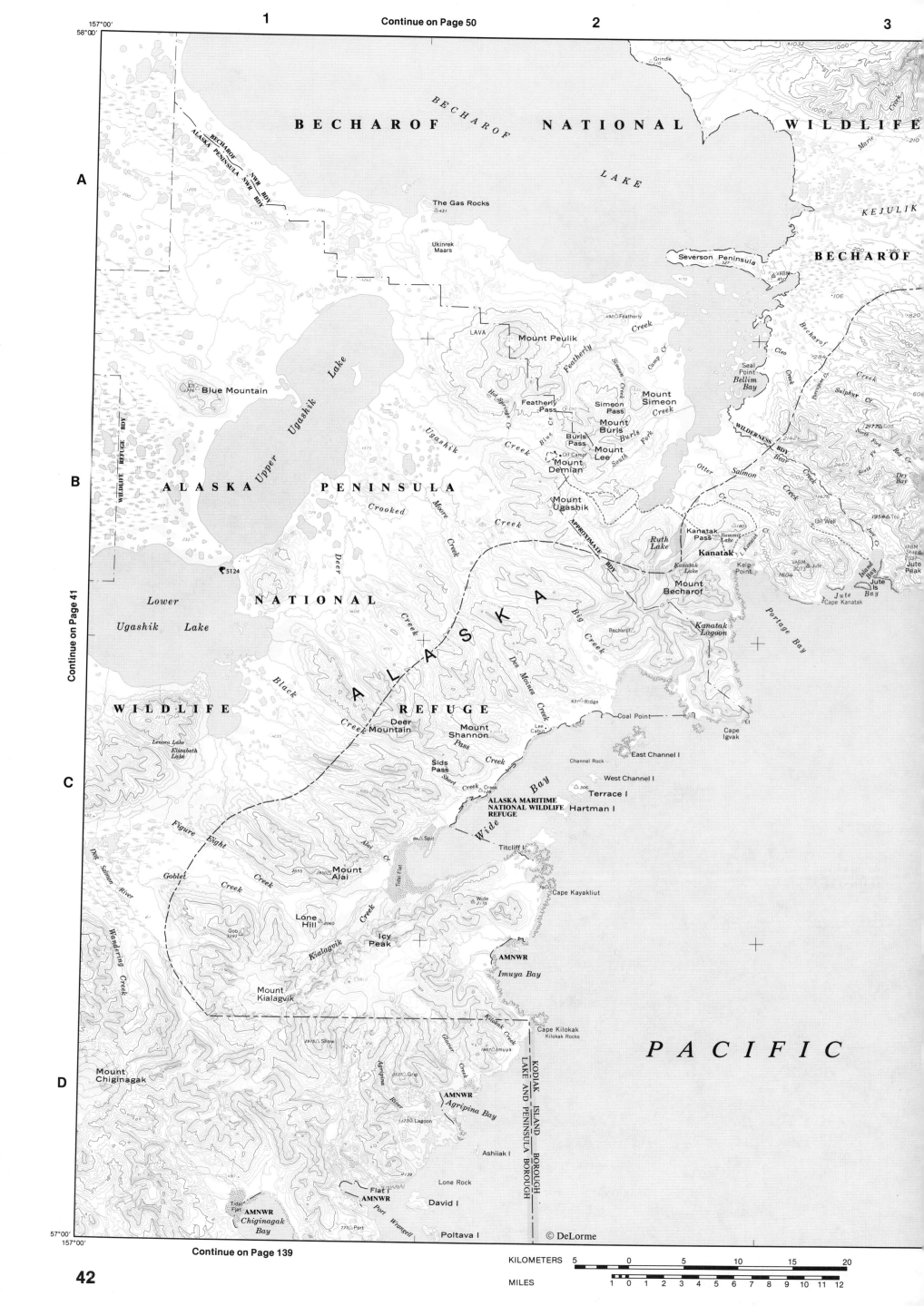

BECHAROF   NATIONAL   WILDLIFE

A

BECHAROF   NATIONAL   LAKE

KEJULIK

BECHAROF

The Gas Rocks
△431

Severson Peninsula
327

Ukinrek
Maars

△492 Featherly   Creek

LAVA   Mount Peulik

Seal
Point
Bellim
Bay

Cleo

Featherly   Creek

Camp Cr

Mount
Simeon

Blue Mountain   EHO
△376

Simeon
Pass

Mount
Burls   Simeon
Creek

Featherly
Pass

B

ALASKA   Upper   Ugashik   Lake

PENINSULA

Burls
Pass   Mount
Lee

Mount
Demian

WILDERNESS   BDY

Crooked

Moore   Creek

Mount
Ugashik

APPROXIMATE   BDY

Kanatak
Pass

Ruth
Lake

Kanatak
Lake   **Kanatak**

Deer   Creek

△5124

Kelp
Point

NATIONAL

Mount
Becharof

Jute

C

Lower
Ugashik   Lake

Black   Creek

ALASKA   REFUGE

Big   Creek

Becharof   Kanatak
Lagoon

Portage Bay

WILDLIFE

Lenora Lake
Elizabeth
Lake

Deer
Mountain

Mount
Shannon
Pass

Des Moines Creek

637△Ridge

Coal Point

Cape
Igvak

Sids Pass

Lee
Cabin

East Channel I

Short   Creek   Creek

Channel Rock

West Channel I

Figure   Eight

Alai Cr

Wide   Bay

△306   Terrace I

ALASKA MARITIME
NATIONAL WILDLIFE
REFUGE   Hartman I

Goblet

Creek   Creek

Tidal Flat

Spit

Titcliff I

Mount
Alai

D

Dog Salmon River

Gob
△3293

Lone
Hill

Kialagvik   Creek

Icy
Peak

Wide
△2175   Cape Kayakliut

AMNWR

Imuya Bay

Wandering   Creek

Mount
Kialagvik

Kilokak Creek

Cape Kilokak
Kilokak Rocks

PACIFIC

Mount
Chiginagak

△Snow

Agripina   River   Grip

△Imuya

KODIAK   ISLAND   AND   PENINSULA   BOROUGH

AMNWR
Agripina Bay

Lagoon

Ashiiak I

Flat I
AMNWR

Lone Rock

David I

AMNWR
Chiginagak
Bay   Tidal Flat

Port Wrangell

△Port

Poltava I

© DeLorme

Continue on Page 41

Continue on Page 139

KILOMETERS   5   0   5   10   15   20

MILES   1 0 1 2 3 4 5 6 7 8 9 10 11 12

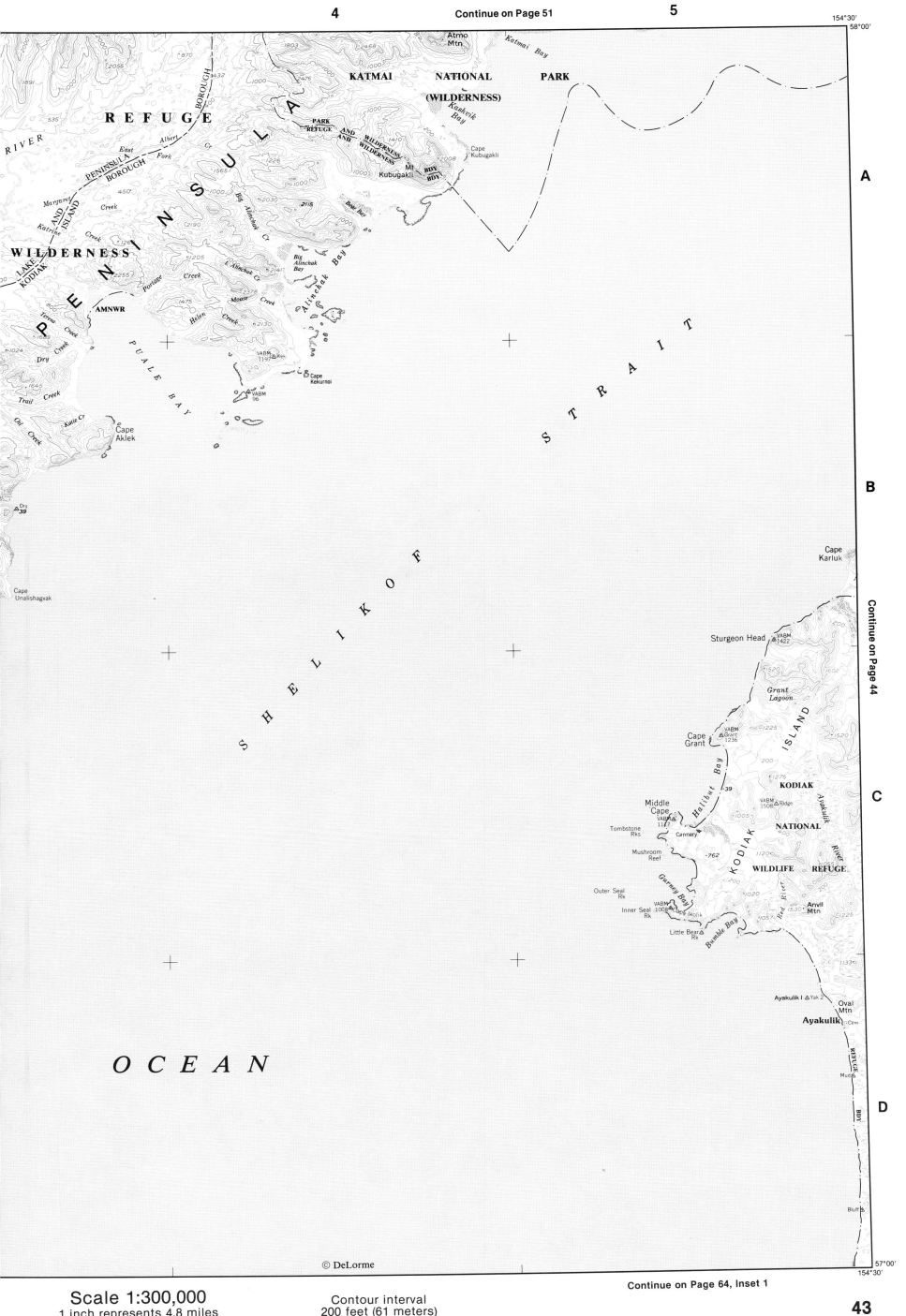

Continue on Page 44

Continue on Page 64, Inset 1

Scale 1:300,000
1 inch represents 4.8 miles

Contour interval
200 feet (61 meters)

154°30'
58°00'

KATMAI NATIONAL PARK

Outlet Cape

Cape Uganik

KODIAK NATIONAL

Noisy Islands

VIEKODA

Seiba Pt

Uganik Island

UGANIK PASSAGE

Miners Pt

California Creek

Campbell Lagoon

Broken Pt

WILDLIFE REFUGE

Mesa Rks East Pt

A

S T R A I T

Twocone Pt

Cape Ugat

West Pt

S H E L I K O F

Cape Kuliuk

Little River

Saddle Mtn

Little River Lake

Cannery

Village

West Point Village Seaplane Base Cannery

Green I

Rock Pt

Northeast Arm

Dog Ear Mtn Helmet Mtn

Port O'Brien

Cannery

San Jaun (Uganik) SPB

Sally I

Packers Spit

Bluff

East Arm

Mink Pt

Sheep I

Chief Pt

Chief Cove

Bird Rk

Pile

Hook Pt

Saltery

South Arm

Gaging Sta

Uganik

Mush Lake

SPIRIDON BAY

Spiridon Lake

Gaging Sta

Wolcott Reef

Rocky Pt

Bear

Harvester I

Clover Rks Last

Thistle Rk

Ditto Is

Telrod Cove

5120

Uganik Lake

Light Cape Uyak Northeast Harbor

Sevenmile Beach

Uyak

Cormorant Rk

YABM 844

Anguk I

Carlsen Reef

B

Tanglefoot Bay

Karluk Anchorage

Karluk Lagoon

K A R L U K

Stan

UYAK BAY

Carlsen

Zachar Bay

Browns Lagoon

Cannery

WILDLIFE

Karluk

4516

Karluk Landing Strip

BOUNDARY

Larsen Bay

RIVER

Larsen Bay

Larsen Bay Landing Strip

Cem

Face

Amook Island

Amook Bay

Amook Bay Seaplane Base (private)

REFUGE BOUNDARY

Sturgeon River

Moraine Cr

Cottonwood Creek

Tent Pt

Bear

Aleutian Rk

Twins

Alf I

Stream 2

N A T I O N A L

K O D I A K

Koning Glacier

C

Ayakulik

Grassy Pt

Alder Creek

Karluk Lake Seaplane Base

Camp I Island Pt

Thumb L

Gaging Sta

North Fk

K O D I A K

Koniag Peak

Karluk Lake

Halfway Cr

Tree Pt

Salmon Cr

E Fk

Thumb River

Trap 2

Eagle Cr

Bluff Pt

Mount Shuman

Long Cr

Barbara Pt

Canyon Creek

Meadow Cr

Stony Pt

Falls

Falls Creek

Creek

Mt Myrtle

4060

River

Red Lake

4368

Fraser Lake

Oseade Cr

O'Malley Lake

CORPORATE BOUNDARY

Sitkalidak Passage

Old Harbor LS

Old Harbor

Falls

Dog Salmon

Akalura L

Akalura Creek

2064

Dog Salmon Creek

Cannery

Olga Bay Seaplane Base

Stockholm Pt

Cannery Anchor Cove

Spit

Grayback Mtn

Horse Marine Lagoon

Horse Marine Lake

Alpine Cove

Barling Bay

D

VABM 171

Stormy Pt

OLGA BAY

Stintz Bluffs

Bank

Bear Rk Bruin Reef

Ivor Pt Ivor Cove

REFUGE BDY

Nunamiut

John I

Cape Liakik

Avalik Creek

Sitkalidak

Natalia Peninsula

Fish and Wildlife Service Upper Station

Olga Cr

South Olga Lakes

Olga Narrows

Moser Peninsula

Swan

Splitrock Pt

Paul's Reef

DEADMAN BAY

Kaiugnak Bay

Cape Kasiak

Natalia Pt

Natalia Bay

Sitkalidak Lagoon

KODIAK NATIONAL WILDLIFE REFUGE

Moser Bay

Shag Rock

SPB Rock

Chirp Cove

Cannery

Luchek Mtn

Happys Mtn

Trap Pt

Hepburn Peninsula

Sulua Bay

Bald

Shelf

VABM 463

Kiavak Bay

Tallapoosa Shoal

Rolling Bay

Puffin I

57°00'
154°30'

© DeLorme

KODIAK NWR

Continue on Page 43

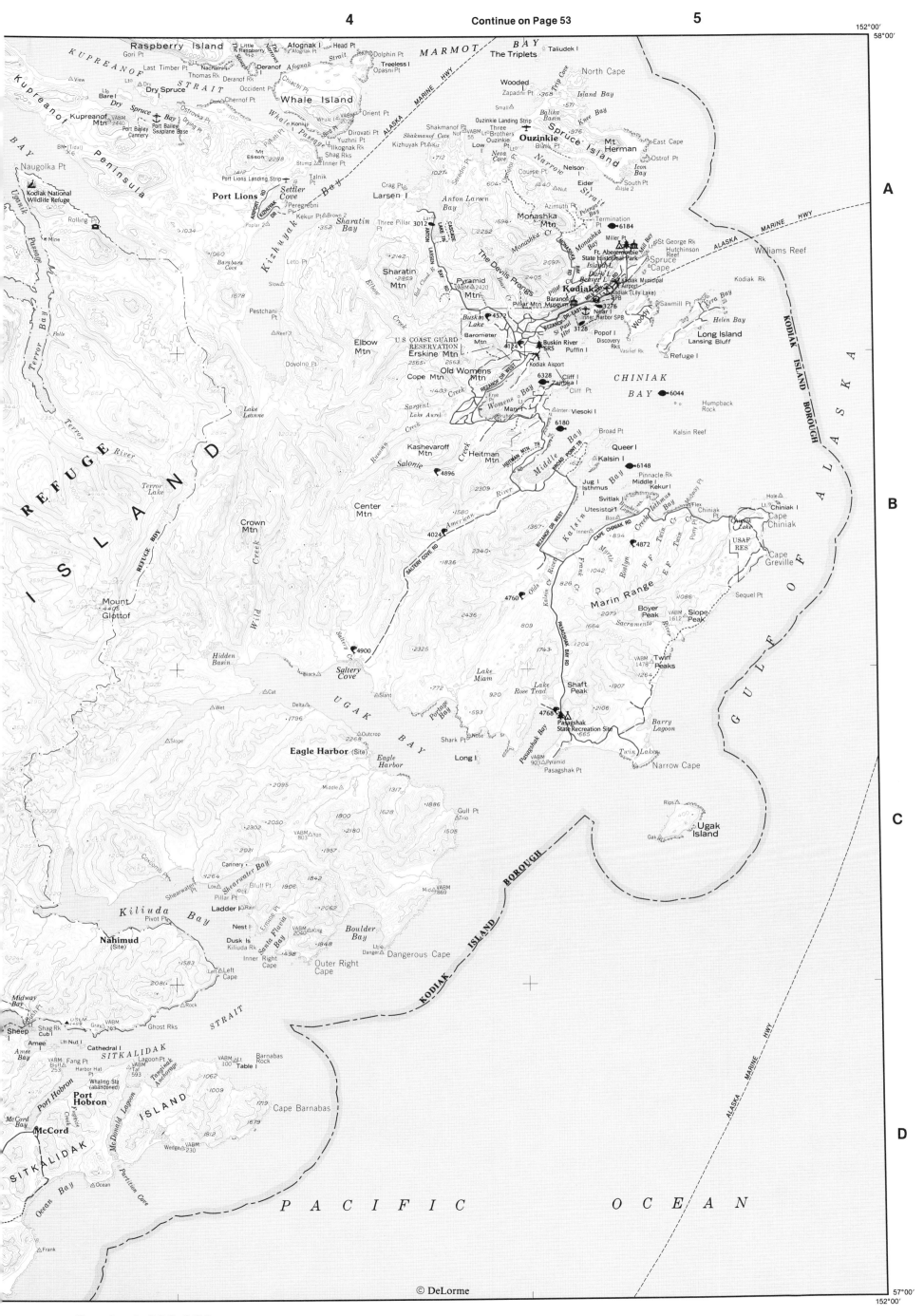

Scale 1:300,000
1 inch represents 4.8 miles

Contour interval
200 feet (61 meters)

© DeLorme

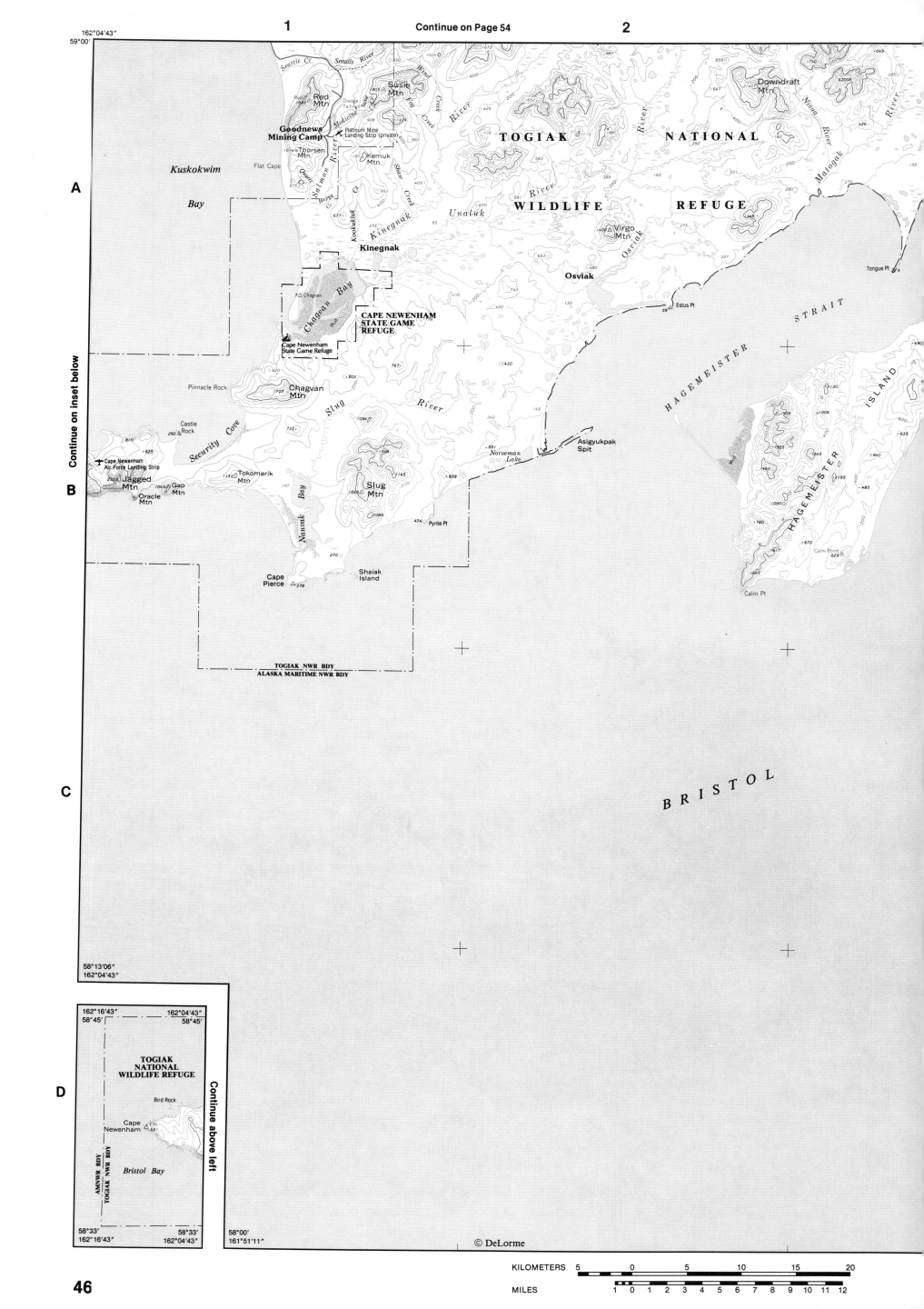

162°04'43"
59°00'

Seattle Cr. Smalls River

A

Kuskokwim

Bay

Red
Mtn

Susie
Mtn

**Goodnews
Mining Camp**

Platinum Mine
Landing Strip (private)

Thorsen
Mtn

Kemuk
Mtn

Flat Cape

TOGIAK   **NATIONAL**

WILDLIFE   **REFUGE**

Unaluk

Virgo
Mtn

Downdraft
Mtn

Tongue Pt

Kinegnak

Chagvan

Continue on inset below

Chagvan Bay

**CAPE NEWENHAM
STATE GAME
REFUGE**

Osviak

Cape Newenham
State Game Refuge

Estus Pt

HAGEMEISTER *STRAIT*

Pinnacle Rock

Chagvan
Mtn

Castle
Rock

Security Cove

Slug *River*

Norseman
Lake

Asigyukpak
Spit

HAGEMEISTER *ISLAND*

B

Cape Newenham
Air Force Landing Strip

Jagged
Mtn

Oracle
Mtn

Gap
Mtn

Tokomarik
Mtn

*Nanvak
Bay*

Slug
Mtn

Pyrite Pt

Calm Point

Cape
Pierce

Shaiak
Island

Calm Pt

C

B R I S T O L

58°13'06"
162°04'43"

162°16'43"
58°45'

162°04'43"
58°45'

D

**TOGIAK
NATIONAL
WILDLIFE REFUGE**

Bird Rock

Cape
Newenham

Continue above left

AMNWR BDY
TOGIAK NWR BDY

Bristol Bay

58°33'
162°16'43"

58°33'
162°04'43"

TOGIAK NWR BDY
ALASKA MARITIME NWR BDY

58°00'
161°51'11"

© DeLorme

KILOMETERS 5   0   5   10   15   20

MILES 1 0 1 2 3 4 5 6 7 8 9 10 11 12

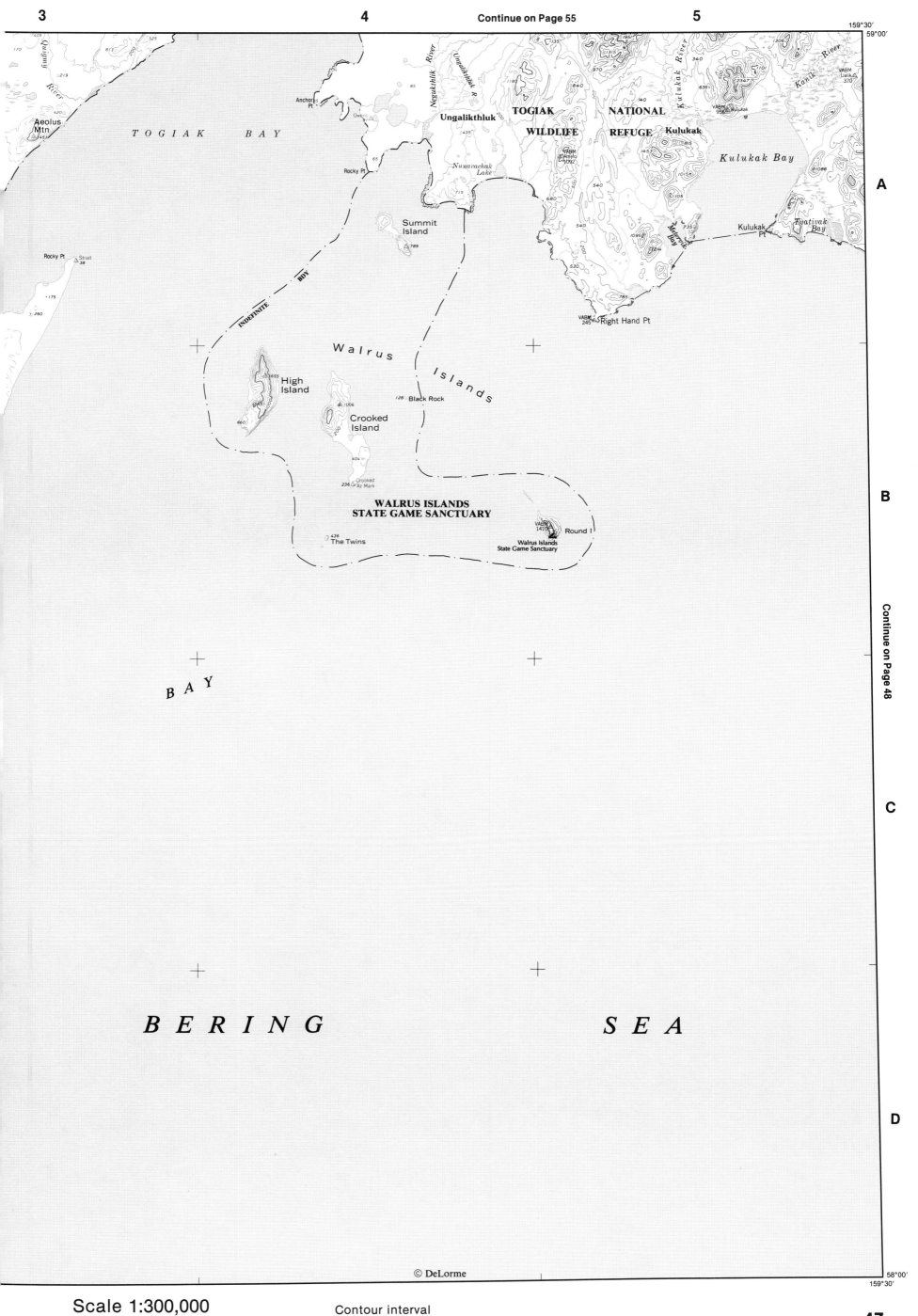

159°30'
59°00'

T O G I A K   B A Y

Aeolus
Mtn
·445

Anchorer
Pt

Owen

Rocky Pt

Ungalikthluk
TOGIAK
WILDLIFE

NATIONAL

REFUGE

Kulukak

Kulukak Bay

VABM
Ualik 370

A

Rocky Pt
·38
Strait

·175

·260

*Nunavachak
Lake*

Summit
Island
▲789

Right Hand Pt
VABM
245

Kulukak
Pt

*Avativak
Bay*

W a l r u s

I s l a n d s

High
Island

Crooked
Island

Black Rock

WALRUS ISLANDS
STATE GAME SANCTUARY

The Twins

Round I
VABM
1410

Walrus Islands
State Game Sanctuary

B

Continue on Page 48

C

B A Y

D

B E R I N G   *S E A*

© DeLorme

58°00'
159°30'

Scale 1:300,000
1 inch represents 4.8 miles

Contour interval
200 feet (61 meters)

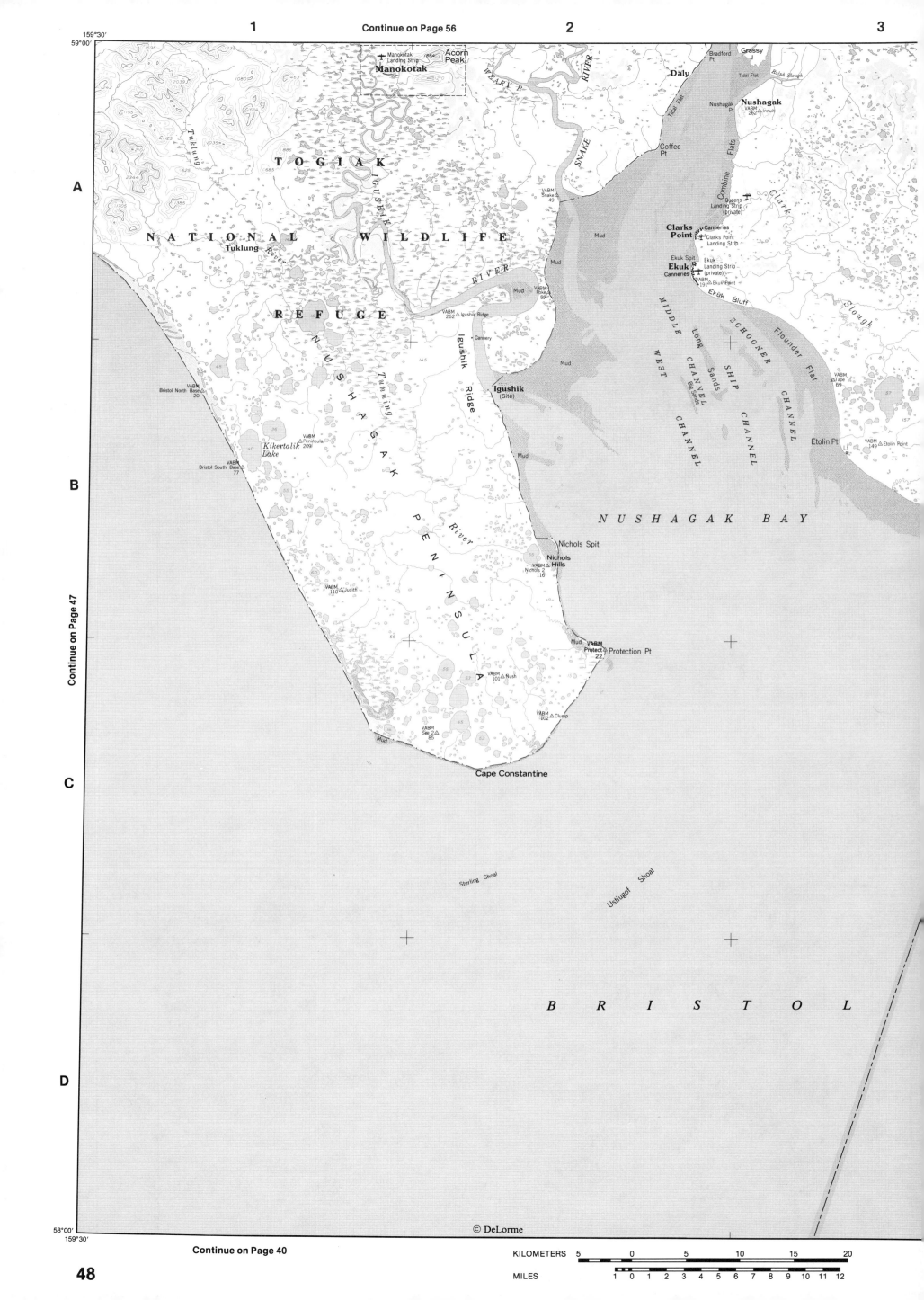

Continue on Page 47

Continue on Page 40

© DeLorme

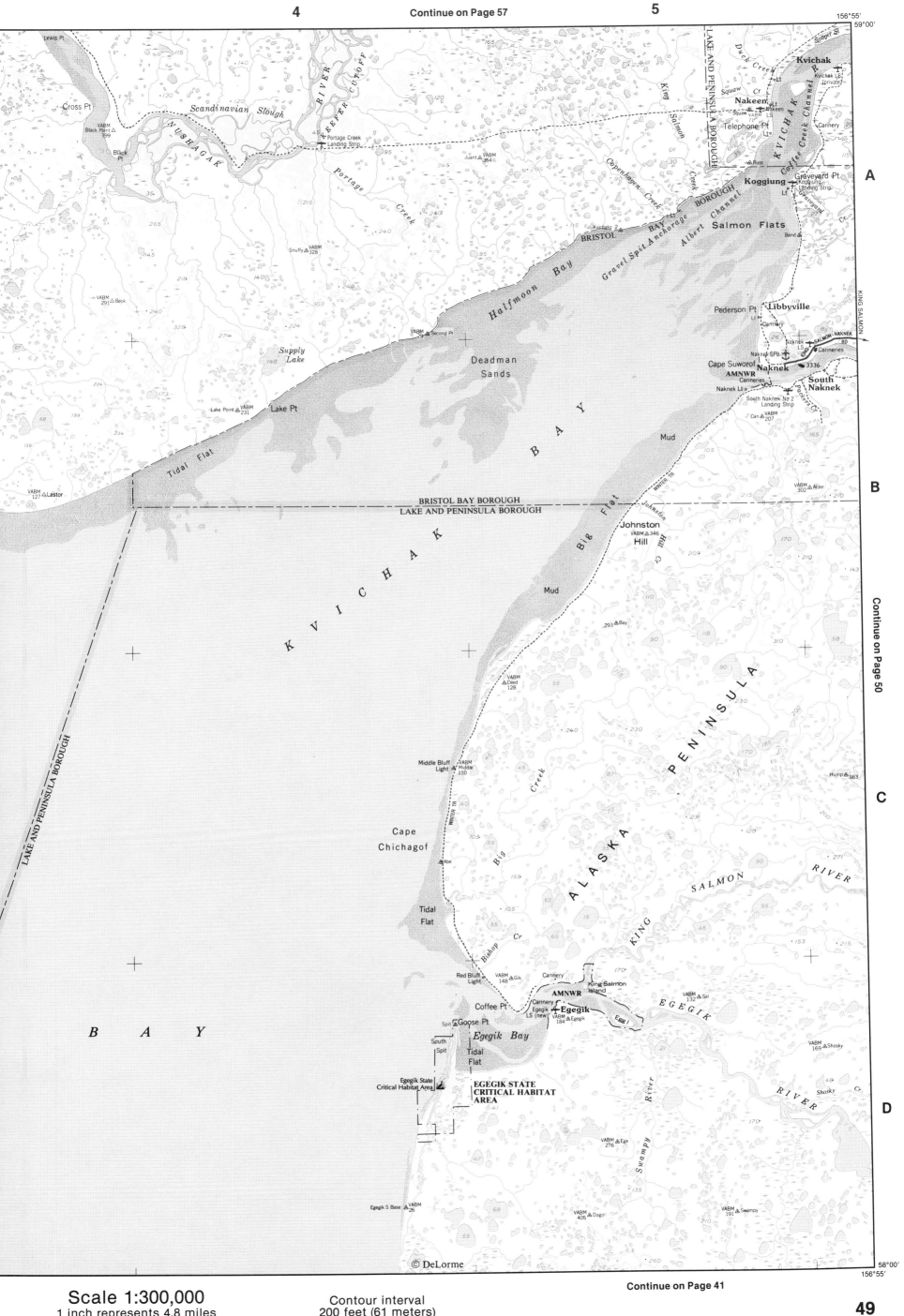

Continue on Page 50

Continue on Page 41

Scale 1:300,000
1 inch represents 4.8 miles

Contour interval
200 feet (61 meters)

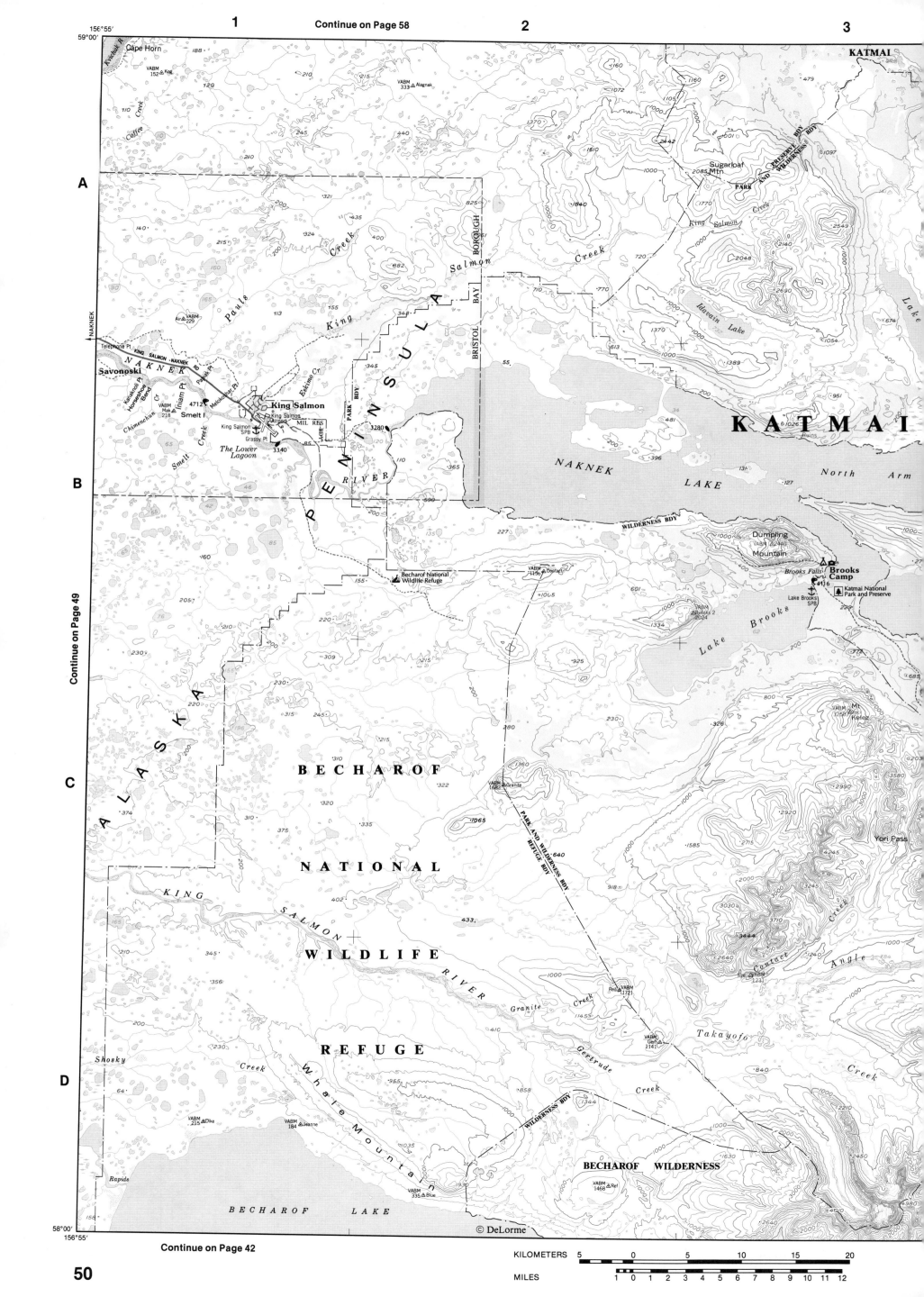

156°55'
59°00'

KATMAI

Kvichak R.

Cape Horn

·188

·152 △Yok

·120

·110

Coffee

Creek

VABM
333 △Alagnak

·215

·210

·1160

1160

·479

·1072

·1105

·1000

·1370

·600

·8097

A

·245

·31

·435

·324

·400

·215

·200

·150

·165

·180

·113

·140

Pauls

Creek

King

825

·682

·155

·Air △VABM
229

·348

Salmon

348·

Creek

·1610

·2442

·1770

Sugarloaf
Mtn
·2085

King Salmon

·1000

·840

Creek

·2549

·720

·1000

·2140

NAKNEK

·115

Eskimo Cr.

·345

·710

·770

·613

·2690

·2048

·400

·1370

·1000

·1054

·1389

NAKNEK

Telephone Pt.

KING SALMON-NAKNEK
RD

Savonoski

Kenaknoll Pt.
Horseshoe
Bend

VABM
Mak △
218

4712

King Salmon

Tiniam Pt.

Smelt

Chimenchan

·55

Melokhar Pt.

Grassy Pt.

King Salmon
SPB

King Salmon
Airport

MIL RES

3280

·55

·481

·396

·200

·1026

K A T M A I

PENINSULA

PARK BDY

BRISTOL BAY

BOROUGH

Salmon

B

The Lower
Lagoon

3340

·85

·46

·42

·200

·365

·110

·120

590·

NAKNEK

LAKE

·127

·13k

North Arm

·1000

·1000

Smelt
Creek

RIVER

·85

·160

·85

·227

WILDERNESS BDY

Dumpling
Mountain
VABM 440

·1000

Brooks Falls

Brooks
Camp
416

Katmai National
Park and Preserve

Continue on Page 49

·76

·205

·230

·196

·315

·220

·210

·309

·215

·155

Becharof National
Wildlife Refuge

·105.5

VABM
115 △Costor

·601·

VABM
Brooks 2
2024

Lake Brooks
SPB

Lake

·1334

·800

·685

·774

·2990

·3580

VABM Mt.
△3752 Kelez

C

ALASKA

·374

·230

·220

·245

·310

·375

·320

·322

·310

·335

·1065

·245

B E C H A R O F

N A T I O N A L

·925

·230

380·

PARK AND WILDERNESS BDY

REFUGE BDY

918·

VABM
△1082 △Granite

·326

·1585

·2715

·2920

·3245

·3030

·3710

·3444

·2640

Yori Pass

·2203

·4245

·2640

·1240

Contact

King

SALMON

402·

433·

·356

W I L D L I F E

R I V E R

Granite

·1455

Creek

·410

·1000

Red △VABM
1721

VABM
Geri △141

Takayofo

·840

·2210

·1000

·1000

Creek

·840

Angle

·2450

·165

·345

·356

·374

R E F U G E

Shosky

·64

VABM
215 △Dike

·200

Creek

·230

VABM
184 △Jeanne

·955·

Gertrude

Creek

·858

·1344

WILDERNESS BDY

·1000

·1000

·1630

BECHAROF WILDERNESS

VABM
1468 △Ref

D

·1035

Whale Mountain

·210

Rapids

·158

BECHAROF   LAKE

VABM
335 △Blue

·1930

·2640

© DeLorme

58°00'
156°55'

Continue on Page 42

KILOMETERS 5 0 5 10 15 20

MILES 1 0 1 2 3 4 5 6 7 8 9 10 11 12

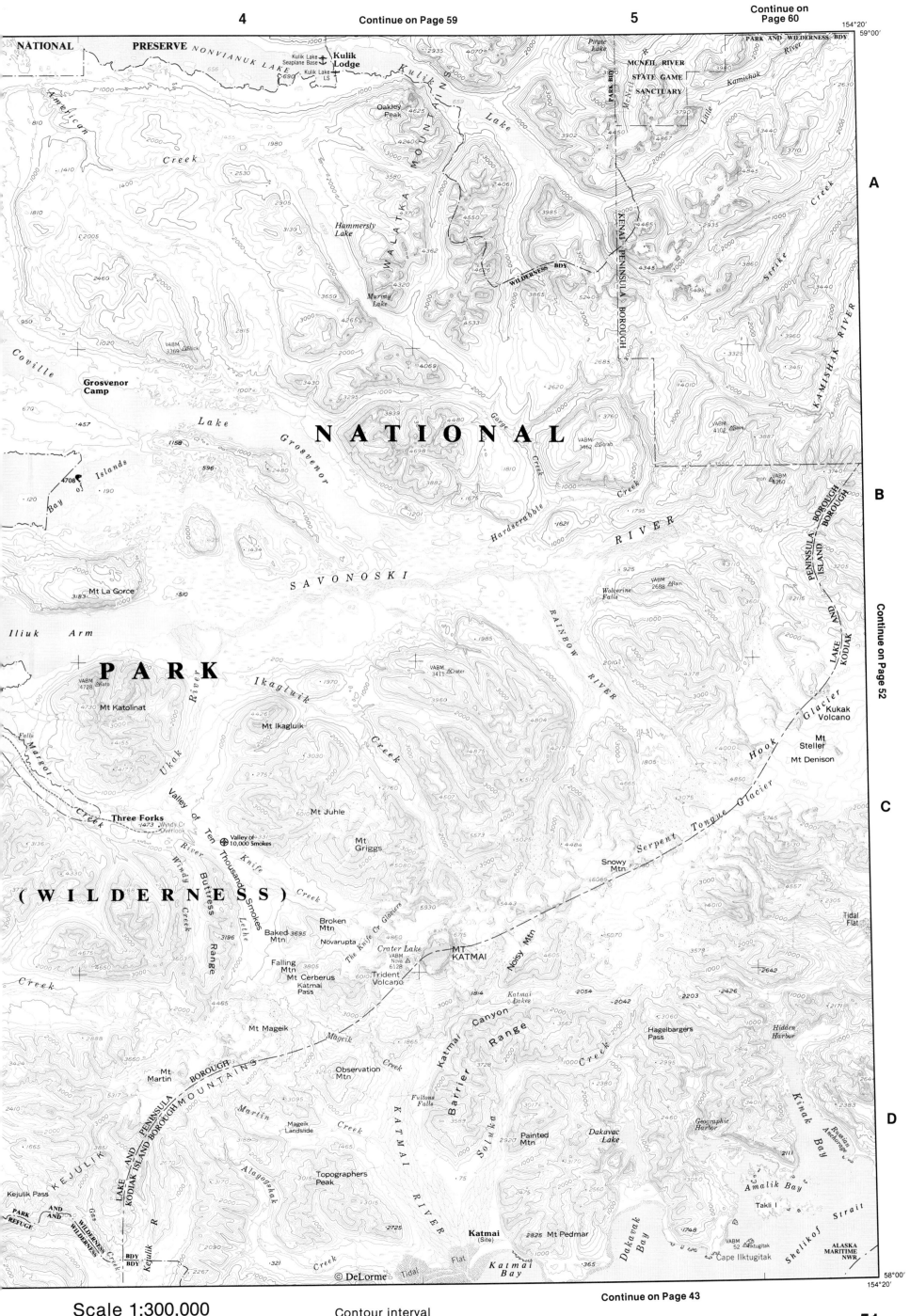

Continue on Page 52

Scale 1:300,000
1 inch represents 4.8 miles

Contour interval
200 feet (61 meters)

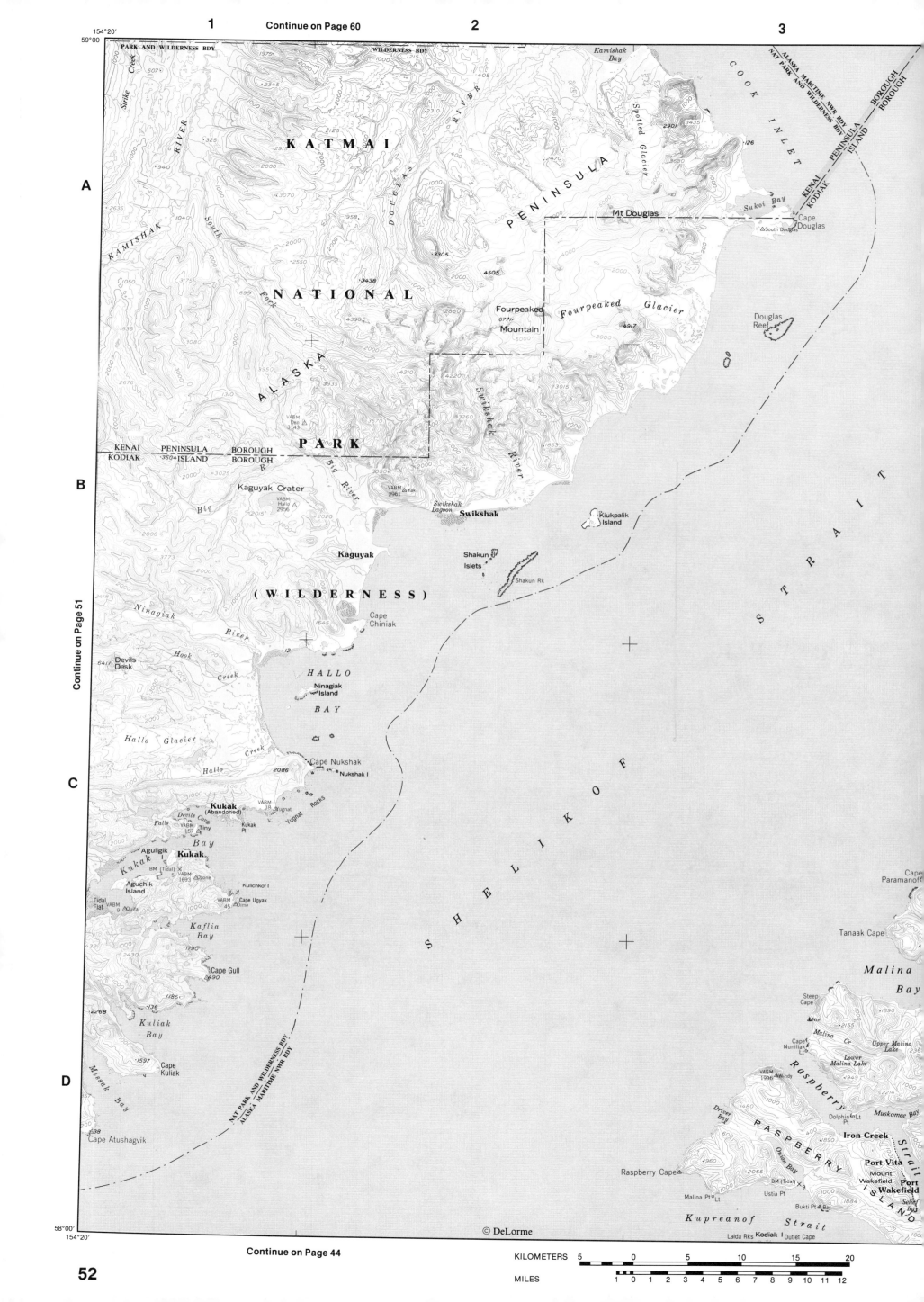

Continue on Page 60

Continue on Page 51

Continue on Page 44

© DeLorme

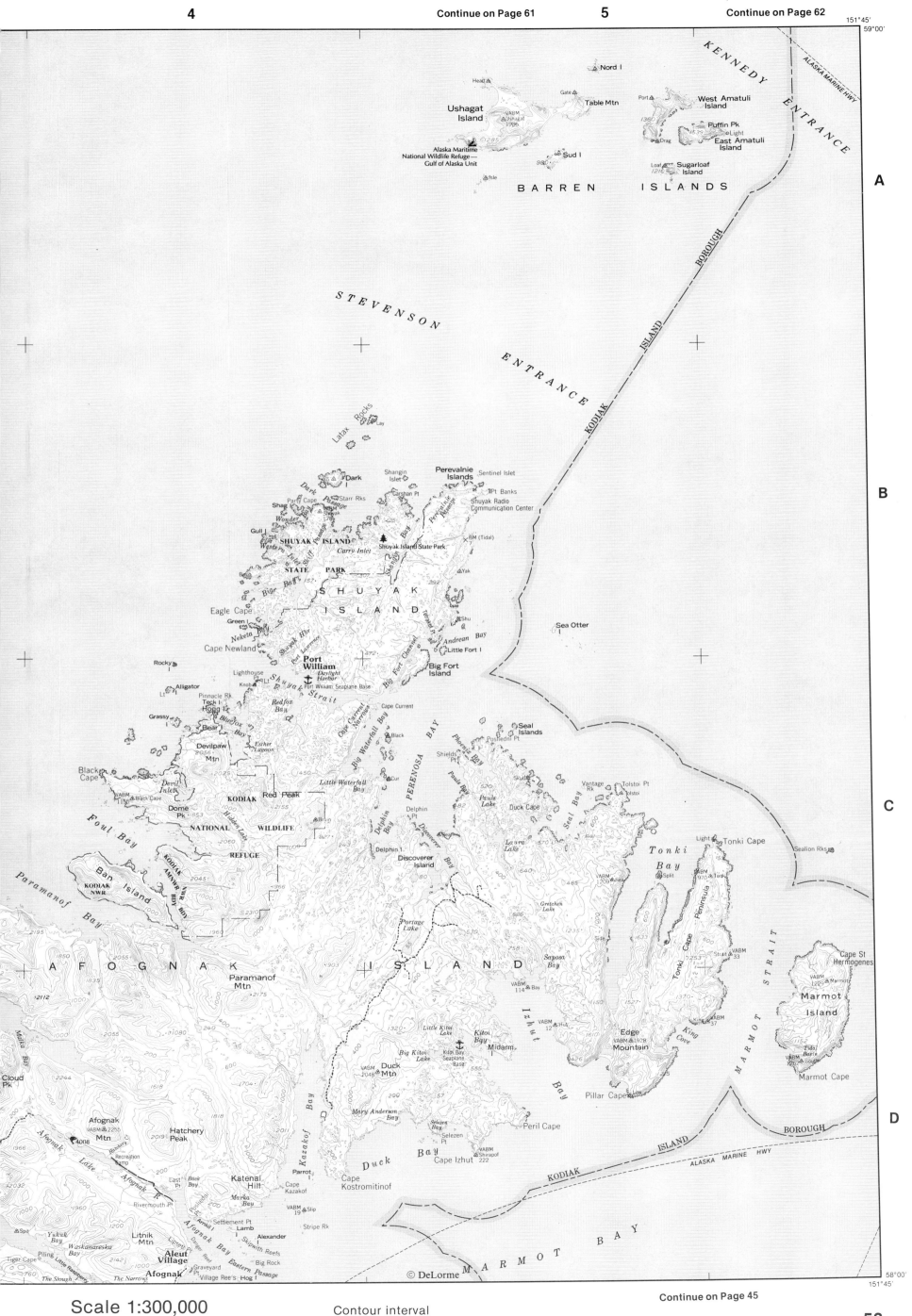

Scale 1:300,000
1 inch represents 4.8 miles

Contour interval
200 feet (61 meters)

162°11'14"
60°00'

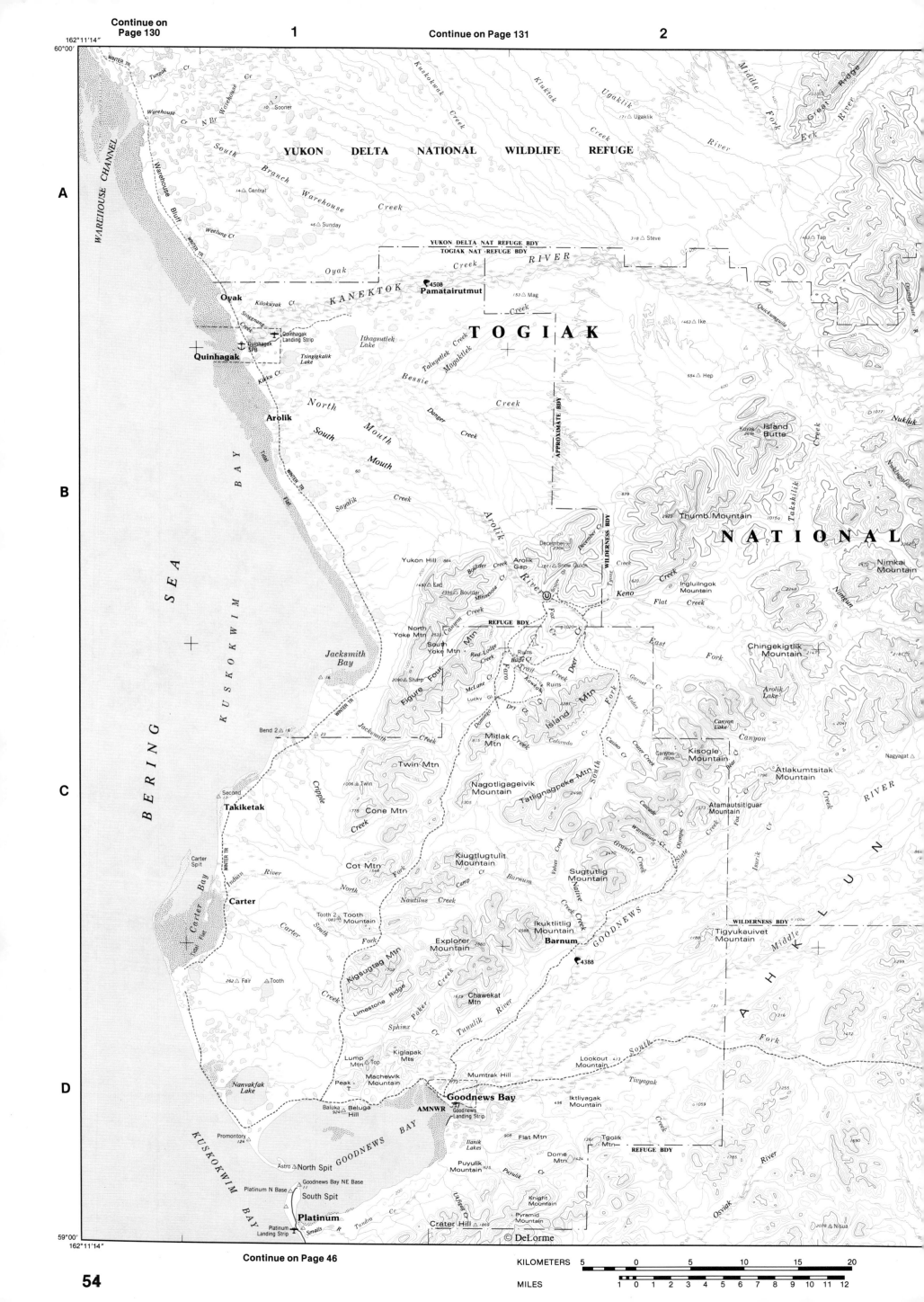

A

B

C

D

59°00'
162°11'14"

YUKON   DELTA   NATIONAL   WILDLIFE   REFUGE

WAREHOUSE CHANNEL

Tungok   Cr

Warehouse

Warehouse
Cr

N Br Warehouse   Cr

Sooner

South

Branch   Warehouse   Creek

Central

Weelung Cr

Sunday

Oyak

Oyak

Quinhagak

Arolik

YUKON DELTA NAT REFUGE BDY
TOGIAK NAT REFUGE BDY

KANEKTOK

Kilokuyak Ct

Stoxynung
Creek

Kiku Cr

Quinhagak
Landing Strip

Quinhagak
SPB

Tsingigkalik
Lake

Ithagsutlek
Lake

Pamatairutmut
4508

RIVER

Creek

Mag

Steve

Tap

Kuskokwak

Creek

Kliuktak

Creek

Ugaklik

Creek

Ugaklik

Quickumguila

Ike

Middle

Fork

Eek

River

Great

Ridge

River

Olungokhale

T O G I A K

Bessie

Danger

Talwetlek Creek

Magaklek

Creek

Creek

Hep

Island
Butte

Kayak

Nukluk

Takshilik

Creek

BERING

SEA

KUSKOKWIM

BAY

North

South

Mouth

Mouth

Creek

Sayalik   Creek

Arolik

River

Jacksmith
Bay

Yukon Hill

End

Boulder
Minnewa

Boulder Creek

Creek

Arolik
Gap

Snow Gulch

APPROXIMATE BDY

WILDERNESS BDY

December

December

Snow   Fox

Keno

Tunu

Flat

Creek

Creek

Thumb Mountain

NATIONAL

Nimkai
Mountain

Ningun

Creek

Ingluilngok
Mountain

Chingekigtlik
Mountain

Arolik
Lake

North
Yoke Mtn

South
Yoke Mtn

Red Lodge
Creek

Canyon
Mtn

Bidie Cr

Ruins

Trail

McLane

Lucky Gl

Faro

REFUGE BDY

East

Fork

Garnet

Cr

Canyon
Lake

Nagyagat

Atlakumtsitak
Mountain

RIVER

Figure Four

Sharp

Domingo

Dry Ct

Kowish

Deer

Ruins

Island

Mtn

Colorado

Miles Cr

South   Fork

Crater Creek

Casino Cr

Canyon

Canyon

Kisogle
Mountain

Atamautsitiguar
Mountain

Second

Bend 2

Jacksmith
Creek

Twin Mtn

Twin

Mitlak
Mtn

Nagotligageivik
Mountain

Tatlignagpeke Mtn

Cascade Cr

Watermute Cr

Slate Cr

Olympic

Fox Cr

Isurik Cr

Atamautsitliguar
Mountain

Takiketak

Cripple

Creek

Cone Mtn

Cot Mtn

Kiugtlugtulit
Mountain

Sugtutlig
Mountain

Granite Creek

Native Creek

WILDERNESS BDY

K

L

U

N

A   H   K

Carter
Spit

Carter
Bay

Carter

Indian   River

North   Fork

Nautilus   Creek

Camp

Barnum

Creek

Velvet Cr

Tigyukauivet
Mountain

Middle

Fork

Takiketak

Tooth 2

Tooth
Mountain

Carter   South   Fork

Tooth Mountain

Explorer
Mountain

Ikuktlitlig
Mountain

Barnum

4388

GOODNEWS

Tidal Flat

Fair

Tooth

Kigsugtag Mtn

Creek

Poker   Cr

Limestone Ridge

Chawekat
Mtn

River

Tiviyagak

Creek

Tunulik

Sphinx Cr

Kiglapak
Mts

Lump Mtn Top

Peak T

Machewik
Mountain

Mumtrak Hill

Lookout
Mountain

South   Fork

Nanvakfak
Lake

Promontory

Baluka

Beluga
Hill

AMNWR

Goodnews Bay

Goodnews
Landing Strip

Iktliyagak
Mountain

Flat Mtn

Tgolik Mtn

REFUGE BDY

KUSKOKWIM   BAY

Astro

North Spit

Platinum N Base

Goodnews Bay NE Base

South Spit

Platinum

Platinum
Landing Strip

Smalls

Tunulik Cr

Puyulik
Mountain

Puyulik

Ilanik
Lakes

Ukfigat Cr

Dome
Mtn

Knight
Mountain

Pyramid
Mountain

Crater Hill

Osviuk

Nisua

© DeLorme

KILOMETERS 5   0   5   10   15   20

MILES   1 0 1 2 3 4 5 6 7 8 9 10 11 12

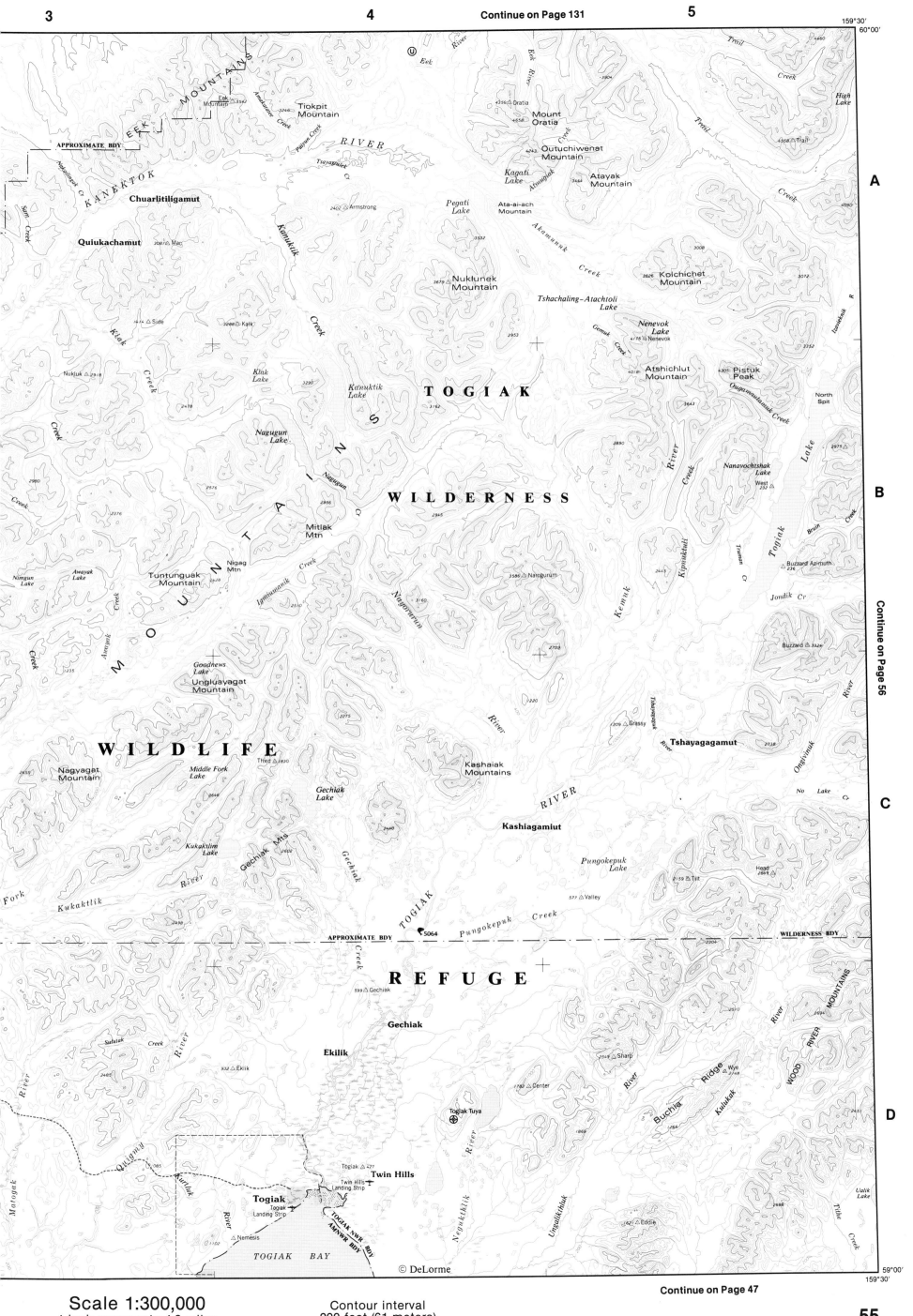

159°30'
60°00'

A

Chuarlitiligamut

Quiukachamut

KANEKTOK

MOUNTAINS

EEK

Eek Mountain

Tiokpit Mountain

RIVER

Tsayaguliet Cr

Armstrong

Pegati Lake

Ata-ai-ach Mountain

Mount Oratia

Outuchiwenat Mountain

Atayak Mountain

Kagati Lake

Akamunuk Creek

Nuklunek Mountain

Tshachaling-Atachtoli Lake

Kolchichet Mountain

Nenevok Lake

Atshichlut Mountain

Pistuk Peak

North Spit

B

Kanuktik Lake

Klak Lake

Nagugun Lake

Kanuktik Creek

WILDERNESS

TOGIAK

Nanavochtshak Lake

West

Togiak Lake

Bruin

Klak Creek

Nukluk

Side

Kalk

Nimgun Lake

Awayak Lake

Mitlak Mtn

Nigag Mtn

Tuntunguak Mountain

MOUNTAINS

Igmiunanik Creek

Narogurum

Kemuk

Kipmikluli

Truman Cr

Buzzard Azimuth

C

Goodnews Lake

Ungluayagat Mountain

Nagomanun

River

Grassy

Buzzard

Jondik Cr

Tshayagagamut

Ongivinuk River

Nagyagat Mountain

WILDLIFE

Middle Fork Lake

Third

Gechiak Lake

Kashaiak Mountains

Kashiagamiut

RIVER

Pungokepuk Lake

No Lake

Cr

Head

Tilt

Kukaktlim Lake

Gechiak Mts

Gechiak

Valley

Kukaktlik River

TOGIAK

APPROXIMATE BDY

5064

Pungokepuk Creek

WILDERNESS BDY

Fork

Gechiak Creek

REFUGE

Gechiak

WOOD RIVER MOUNTAINS

Sharp

River

Buchia Ridge

Wye

Kulukak

D

Suluiak Creek River

Eklik

Ekilik

Center

Togiak Tuya

Quigmiut

Kanluk River

Togiak

Togiak Landing Strip

Twin Hills Landing Strip

Twin Hills

Togiak NWR BDY

Togiak River

Neguklmlik River

Ungalikthluk River

Eddie

Ualik Lake

Matogak River

Nemesis

TOGIAK BAY

AMNWR BDY

© DeLorme

Ugashik Creek

159°00'
59°00'
159°30'

Continue on Page 56

Continue on Page 47

Scale 1:300,000
1 inch represents 4.8 miles

Contour interval
200 feet (61 meters)

55

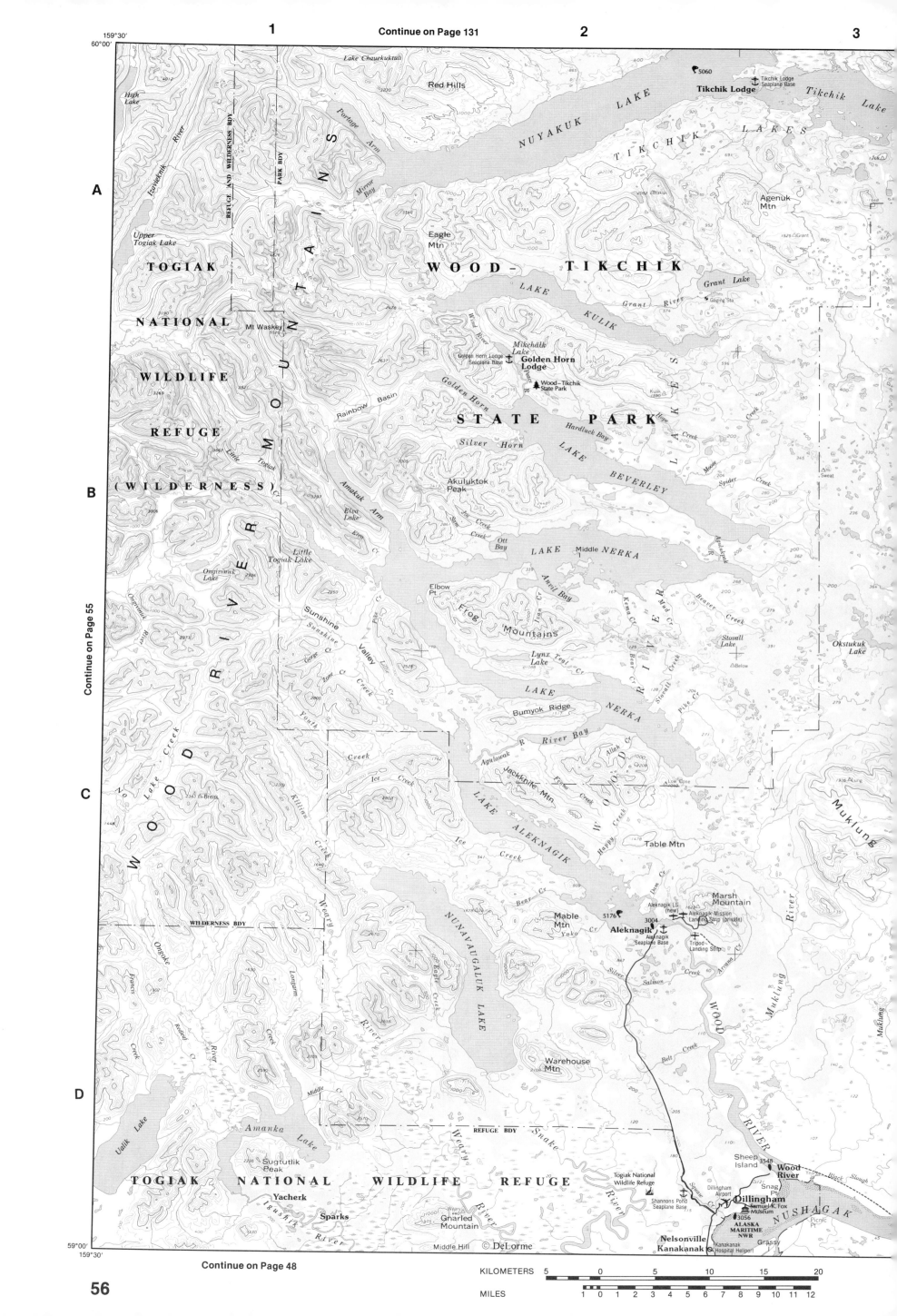

159°30'
60°00'

A

TOGIAK

Lake Chauekuktuli

Red Hills

High
Lake

Portage
Arm

Igushik

River

Mirror
Bay

Park Bdy

REFUGE AND WILDERNESS BDY

Upper
Togiak Lake

Eagle
Mtn

WOOD — **TIKCHIK**

NUYAKUK LAKE

5060
Tikchik Lodge Tikchik Lodge
Seaplane Base

TIKCHIK

LAKES

Tikchik
Lake

Agenuk
Mtn

Grant Lake

LAKE   KULIK

Grant   River

Gaging Sta

NATIONAL

Mt Waskey

Mikchalk
Lake

Golden Horn Lodge
Seaplane Base

**Golden Horn
Lodge**

Wood–Tikchik
State Park

LAKES

Kulik
Creek

WILDLIFE

Rainbow   Basin

Golden Horn

STATE   PARK

Hardluck Bay

Hope

Creek

Moose

Spider   Creek

Sweat

REFUGE

Little Togiak

Silver Horn

LAKE BEVERLEY

B

(WILDERNESS)

Amakuk Arm

Akuluktok
Peak

Joe Creek

Strm

Ott
Bay

Agulakpak   R.

Elva
Lake

Elva

Creek

LAKE Middle NERKA

Ongivinuk
Lake

Little
Togiak Lake

Elbow
Pt

Frog
'Mountains

Anvil Bay

Kema Cr

Mud Cr

Beaver   Creek

Stovall
Lake

Okstukuk
Lake

Ongivinuk   River

Sunshine

Sunshine

Gorge Cr

Zone Cr

Valley

Little

Creek

Pike Cr

Youth

Creek

Lynx Tent
Lake

LAKE

NERKA

Stovall Creek

Bar Cr

Pike Cr

Below

Ice Cone

MOUNTAINS

C

No Lake Creek

Break

Ice   Creek

Bumyok Ridge

Agulowak   R.

River Bay

Allah Cr

Happy   Creek

Jackknife
Mtn

Fisher   Creek

Table Mtn

Muklung

Kilbuck

Creek

Ice   Creek

LAKE ALEKNAGIK

WOOD

RIVER

Weary

WILDERNESS BDY

Bear Cr

Marsh
Mountain

5176   Aleknagik LS
(new)

Aleknagik Mission
Landing Strip (private)

Mable
Mtn

3004

Aleknagik

Aleknagik
Seaplane Base

Tripod
Landing Strip

Omoke

Francis

Redfield Cr

Longarm

Creek

Eagle Creek

River

NUNAVAUGALUK LAKE

Yako Cr

Silver

Salmon

Creek

Aroona Cr

WOOD

Muklung

River

Muklung

Belt Creek

D

Ualik Lake

Amanka Lake

Iguigig River

Middle

Weary

River

Warehouse
Mtn

REFUGE BDY

Snake

TOGIAK   NATIONAL   WILDLIFE   REFUGE

Sugtutlik
Peak

Yacherk

Sparks

Gharled
Mountain

Middle Hill

© DeLorme

Weary

River

Snake

River

Togiak National
Wildlife Refuge

Shannons Pond
Seaplane Base

Dillingham
Airport

Dillingham

Samuel K. Fox
Museum

3056

**ALASKA
MARITIME
NWR**

Nelsonville
Kanakanak

Kanakanak
Hospital Heliport

Sheep
Island

3548

**Wood
River**

Snag
Pt

Black

Slough

NUSHAGAK

Grassy

Picnic
Pt

RIVER

59°00'
159°30'

Continue on Page 55

KILOMETERS 5   0   5   10   15   20

MILES   1 0 1 2 3 4 5 6 7 8 9 10 11 12

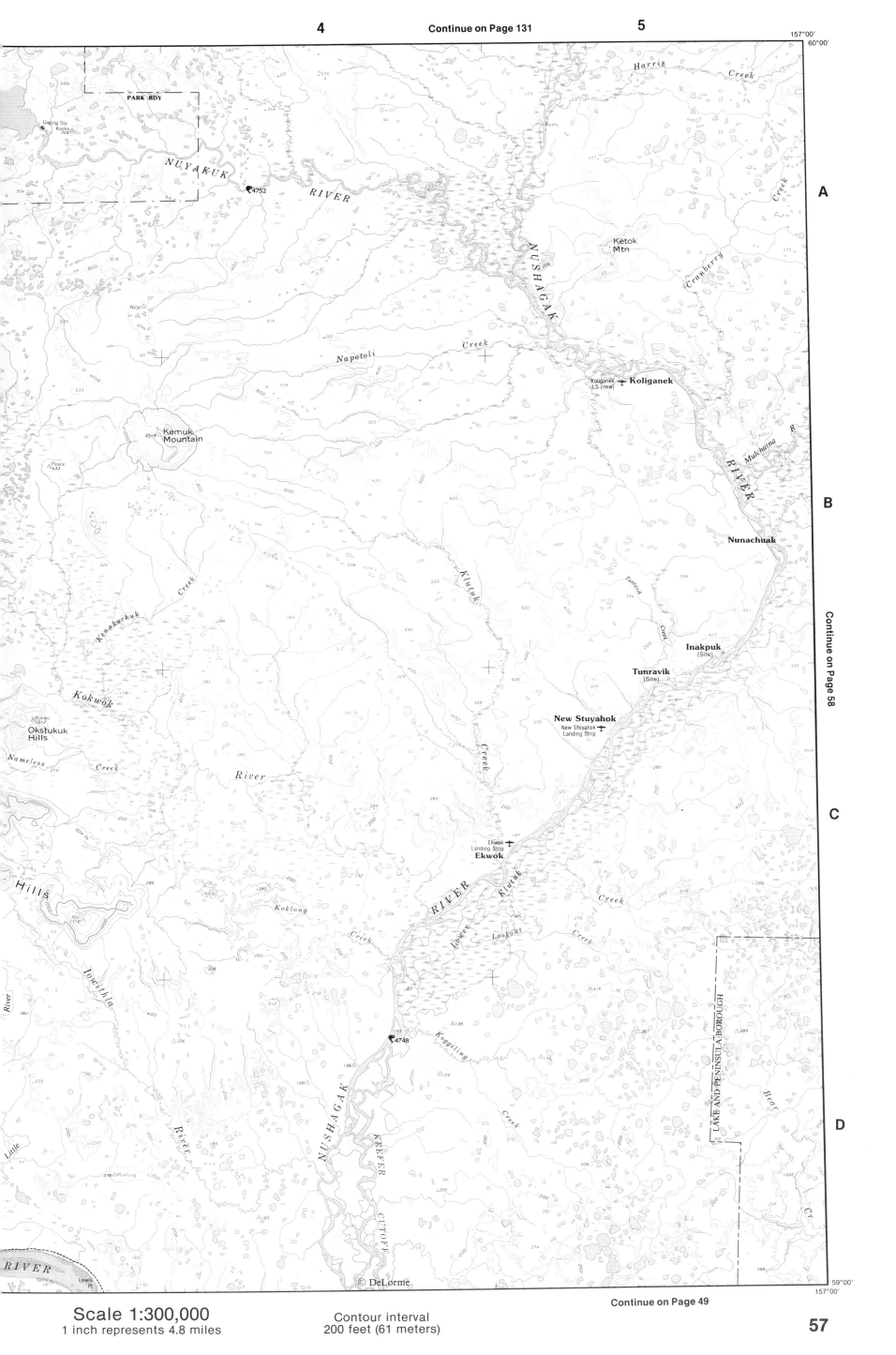

Continue on Page 58

Scale 1:300,000
1 inch represents 4.8 miles

Contour interval
200 feet (61 meters)

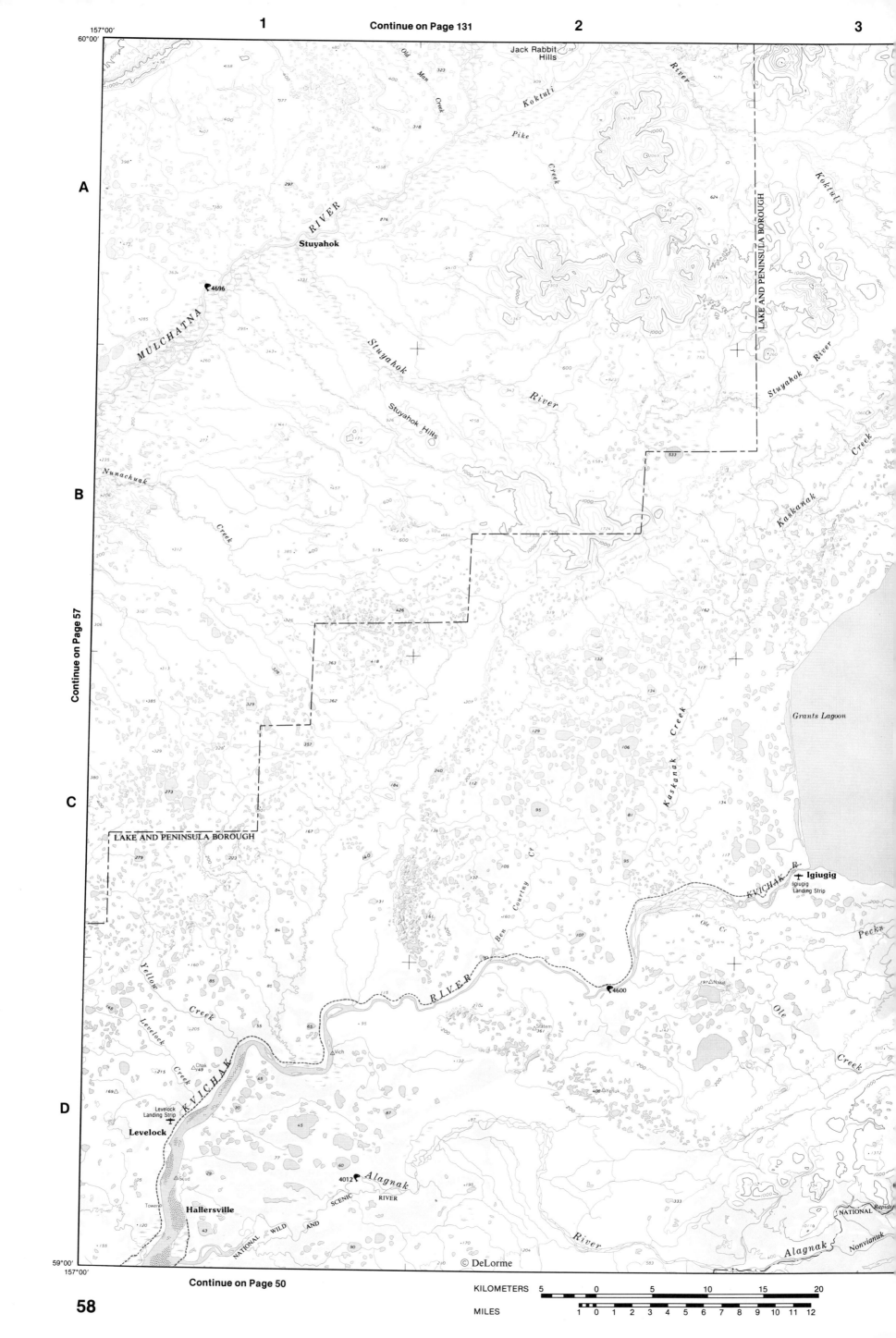

157°00'
60°00'

A

B

Continue on Page 57

C

D

59°00'
157°00'

Jack Rabbit
Hills

Koktuli

River

Koktuli

Pike

Creek

LAKE AND PENINSULA BOROUGH

Stuyahok River

RIVER

Stuyahok

4696

MULCHATNA

Stuyahok

River

Stuyahok Hills

Kaskanak Creek

Nunachuak

Creek

Kaskanak Creek

Grants Lagoon

LAKE AND PENINSULA BOROUGH

Ben

Courtny

Cr

Ole Cr

KVICHAK R. **Igiugig**
Igiugig
Landing Strip

Pecks

Yellow

Creek

RIVER

4600

Nskd

Statem

Ole

Creek

Levelock

Creek

Chak

KVICHAK

Yelluk

Scud

Levelock
Landing Strip

Levelock

4012 **Alagnak**

RIVER

Hallersville

Towers

SCENIC

NATIONAL WILD AND

River

NATIONAL

Rapids

Alagnak

Nonvianuk

© DeLorme

KILOMETERS   5   0   5   10   15   20

MILES   1 0 1 2 3 4 5 6 7 8 9 10 11 12

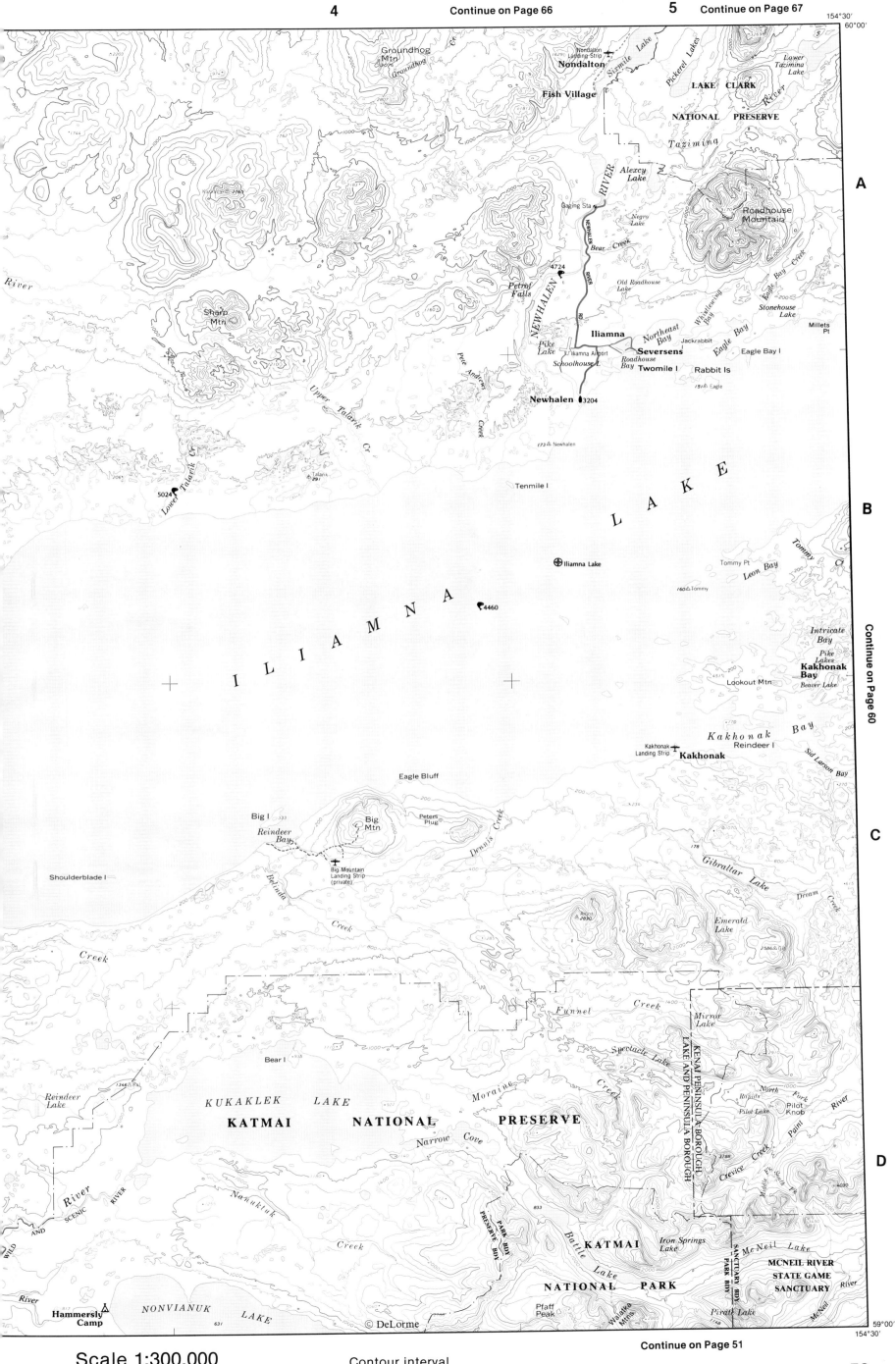

154°30'
60°00'

A

B

Continue on Page 60

C

D

59°00'
154°30'

Scale 1:300,000
1 inch represents 4.8 miles

Contour interval
200 feet (61 meters)

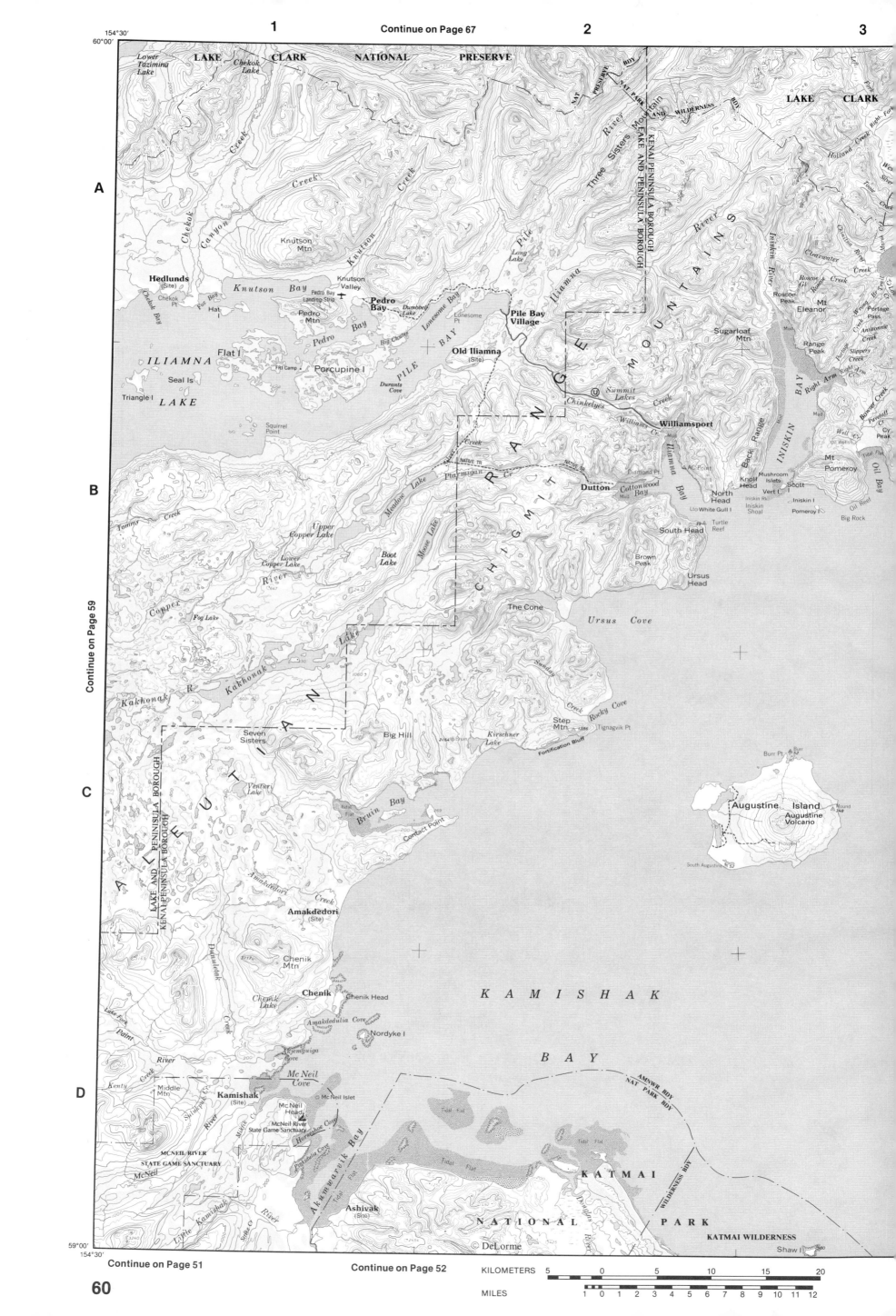

154°30'
60°00'

LAKE CLARK NATIONAL PRESERVE

LAKE CLARK

Lower Tazimina Lake

Chekok Lake

A

Chekok Creek

Creek

Knutson Creek

Canyon

Chekok Canyon

Three Sisters Mountain

NAT PARK

PRESERVE BDY

NAT PARK AND WILDERNESS BDY

KENAI PENINSULA BOROUGH

LAKE AND PENINSULA BOROUGH

Iliamna River

Mountains

Holland

Clearwater Creek

Knutson Mtn

Knutson Valley

Long Lake

Pile Creek

Roscoe's Gl

Roscoe Peak

Mt Eleanor

Hedlunds (Site)

Chekok Pt

Fox Bay

Knutson Bay

Hat

Pedro Bay Landing Strip

Pedro Bay

Dumbbell Lake

Pile Bay Village

Sugarloaf Mtn

Range Peak

Antntonnie Creek

Portage Pass

Slippers Creek

Pedro Mtn

Pedro Bay

Lonesome Pt

Lonesome Bay

Old Iliamna (Site)

Chinkelyes Creek

Summit Lakes

Williams Cr

Williamsport

Bower Creek

Paveloff

Cy Peak

Well I

ILIAMNA

Flat I

Chekok Bay

Seal Is

Triangle I

LAKE

Porcupine I

FRI Camp

Duranta Cove

Big Chats

PILE BAY

RANGE

CHIGMIT

Diamond Pt

Dutton

Cottonwood Bay

North Head

Knoll Head

Scott

Mushroom Islets

Vert I

Iniskin Rk

Iniskin I

Pomeroy I

Mt Pomeroy

Oil Bay

Oil Reef

Big Rock

Squirrel Point

Creek

Ptarmigan Creek

NATIVE TR

NATIVE TR

Mendone Lake

INISKIN BAY

Back Range

Iliamna Bay

Llo White Gull I

South Head

Turtle Reef

B

Tommy Creek

Upper Copper Lake

Moose Lake

Boot Lake

Brown Peak

Ursus Head

Continue on Page 59

Lower Copper Lake

Copper River

Fog Lake

Copper

Kakhonak

R

Kakhonak

The Cone

Ursus Cove

1060

Seven Sisters

Big Hill

Kirschner Lake

Step Mtn

Creek

Rocky Cove

Tignagvik Pt

Fortification Bluff

Burr Pt

Burr

52

C

AKUTLIAN

LAKE AND PENINSULA BOROUGH

KENAI PENINSULA BOROUGH

Venturi Lake

Bruin Bay

Tidal Flat

Contact Point

Augustine Island

Augustine Volcano

Mound 368

Amakdedori Creek

South Augustine 52

Amakdedori (Site)

Paauleak Creek

Chenik Mtn

K A M I S H A K

Chenik

Chenik Lake

Chenik Head

Amakdedulia Cove

Nordyke I

B A Y

Lake Fork Point

Aljemguiga Cove

River

D

Kenty Creek

Middle Mtn

Sldvsak River

Kamishak (Site)

Mc Neil Cove

McNeil Head

Mc Neil Islet

McNeil River State Game Sanctuary

Horseshoe Cove

AMNWR BDY

NAT PARK BDY

Tidal Flat

WILDERNESS BDY

Tidal Flat

KATMAI

MCNEIL RIVER STATE GAME SANCTUARY

McNeil

Little Kamishak River

Spike Cr

Akumwarvik Bay

Paralulia Cove

Tidal Flat

Ashivak (Site)

Tidal Flat

NATIONAL

Douglas River

PARK

KATMAI WILDERNESS

© DeLorme

Shaw I

59°00'
154°30'

Continue on Page 51

Continue on Page 52

KILOMETERS 5   0   5   10   15   20

MILES   1 0 1 2 3 4 5 6 7 8 9 10 11 12

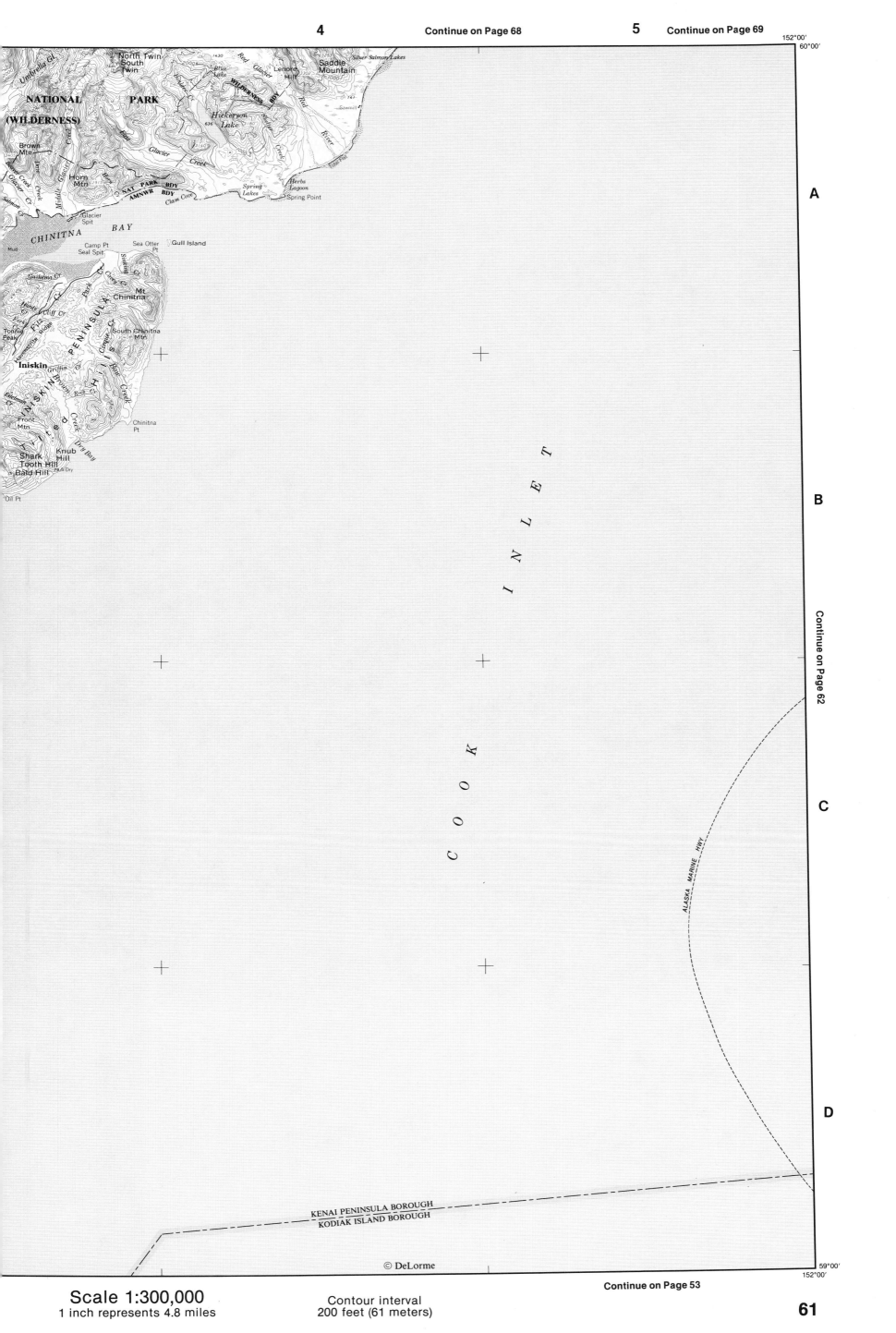

152°00'
60°00'

A

B

Continue on Page 62

C

D

NATIONAL PARK
(WILDERNESS)

Brown Mtn

Horn Mtn

NAT PARK BDY
AMNWR BDY

Glacier Spit
Clam Cove

CHINITNA BAY

Mud

Camp Pt
Seal Spit
Sea Otter Pt
Gull Island

North Twin
South Twin

Red Glacier
Blue Lake

Hickerson Lake

Lenore Hill
Saddle Mountain

Silver Salmon Lakes

Spring Lakes
Herbs Lagoon
Spring Point

Sawmill

Iniskin

Mt Chinitna

South Chinitna Mtn

Tonnie Peak

Front Mtn

Shark Tooth Hill
Knub Hill
Bald Hill

Oil Pt

Chinitna Pt

Dry Bay

C O O K   I N L E T

ALASKA MARINE HWY

KENAI PENINSULA BOROUGH
KODIAK ISLAND BOROUGH

© DeLorme

59°00'
152°00'

Continue on Page 53

Scale 1:300,000
1 inch represents 4.8 miles

Contour interval
200 feet (61 meters)

NINILCHIK

152°00'
60°00'

CLAM GULCH STATE CRITICAL HABITAT AREA

A

Happy Valley

Cape Starichkof

Wells

Stariski State Recreation Site

Anchor Point

Anchor Point

Anchor River SRA

North Fork

Anchor River State Recreation Site

Anchor River and Fritz Creek State Critical Habitat Area

Epperson Knob

S Beaver

Ohlson Mtn

Twitter Creek

Lookout Mountain

Crossman Ridge

Lilly L

C O O K   I N L E T

Ninilchik Dome

North Fork

K E N A I

ANCHOR RIVER AND FRITZ CREEK STATE CRITICAL HABITAT AREA

Bald Mountain

Fritz Creek

GREER RD

HOMER EAST END RD

EAST END RD

Ptarmigan Head

Caribou Hills

Boxcar Hills

Caribou Lake

Clearwater

Eagle Lake

Cavanaugh Fox River Landing Strip (private)

Kachemak Silo

FOX RIVER FLATS STATE CRITICAL HABITAT AREA

Fox River Flats State Critical Habitat Area

Chugachik Island

Bear Island

Bear Cove Farm (private)

Bradley Lake

Sheep

K E N A I

B

Diamond Ridge

Kachemak City

Millers Landing

Kachemak Bay State Critical Habitat Area

Bluff Point

Pratt Museum

Homer

Homer Airport

Homer SPB

PIONEER RD

OCEAN DR

Coal Bay

6144

KACHEMAK   BAY   STATE   CRITICAL   HABITAT   AREA

3192 Coal Point

Archimandritof Shoals

Gull Island

Sixty foot Rock

Cohen Island

Peterson Bay

Aurora Lagoon

Grewingk Glacier

Mallard Bay

Neptune Bay

McKeon Flats

Anisom Point

Peterson Pt

Ismailof Island

China Poot Lake

Kachemak Bay State Park and Wilderness Park

PARK BDY   HABITAT AREA

Portlock Glacier

Dixon Glacier

K E N A I

Iceworm Peak

K A C H E M A K

Yukon Island

Hesketh Island

Grass Island Herring Is

Eldred Passage

Little Tutka Bay

Sadie Cove

Tutka Bay

KACHEMAK SCHA

K A C H E M A K B A Y S T A T E P A R K

Wosnesenski Glacier

Doroshin Gl

Glacier

Petrof Glacier

C

Barabara Point

Nubble Point

MacDonald Spit

Seldovia Point

Kasitsna Bay

Kasitsna

Jakolof Bay Landing Strip

Jakolof Bay

Point Naskowhak

Seldovia Lagoon

Seldovia Landing Strip

Seldovia

Seldovia Seaplane Base

Point Pogibshi

Powder Island

Dangerous

Dangerous Cape Reef

Dangerous Cape

Bird Reef

English Bay Reef

English Bay

Port Graham

Passage I

Russian Pt

Johnson Slough

Port Graham

English Bay LS

Port Graham Landing Strip

Flat Islands

Point Bede

Magnet Rock

Mount Bede

Indian Village

Red Mountain

Seldovia Lake

Rocky River

Windy River

Wind River

Jakolof Creek

KACHEMAK SCHA

Brown Mountain

Westdahl Cove

Long Island

K A C H E M A K B A Y S T A T E W I L D E R N E S S P A R K

West Arm

Port Dick Cr

Tonsina Bay

Taylor Bay

Takoma Cove

Sunday Harbor

Front Point

Koyuktolik Bay

Mount Mills

Rocky Lake

Picnic Harbor

Port Dick

Okentula Bay

Gore Peak

BM Tidal 16

Rocky Bay

Arch Rock

Gore Point

Chrome

Portlock

Cone Mountain

Rock Mountain

Windy Bay

Badger Hill

Chugach Bay

Gore Rock

KENAI PENINSULA BOROUGH

D

Cape Elizabeth

Elizabeth Island

Nagahut Rocks

Perl Island

Perl Rock

East Chugach Island

Chugach Island

C H U G A C H   I S L A N D S

Chugach Passage

Dora Reef

KODIAK ISLAND
BOROUGH

ALASKA MARINE HWY

K E N N E D Y   E N T R A N C E

ALASKA MARINE HWY

© DeLorme

59°00'
152°00'

Continue on Page 69
Continue on Page 61
Continue on Page 53

KILOMETERS   5   0   5   10   15   20

MILES   1 0 1 2 3 4 5 6 7 8 9 10 11 12

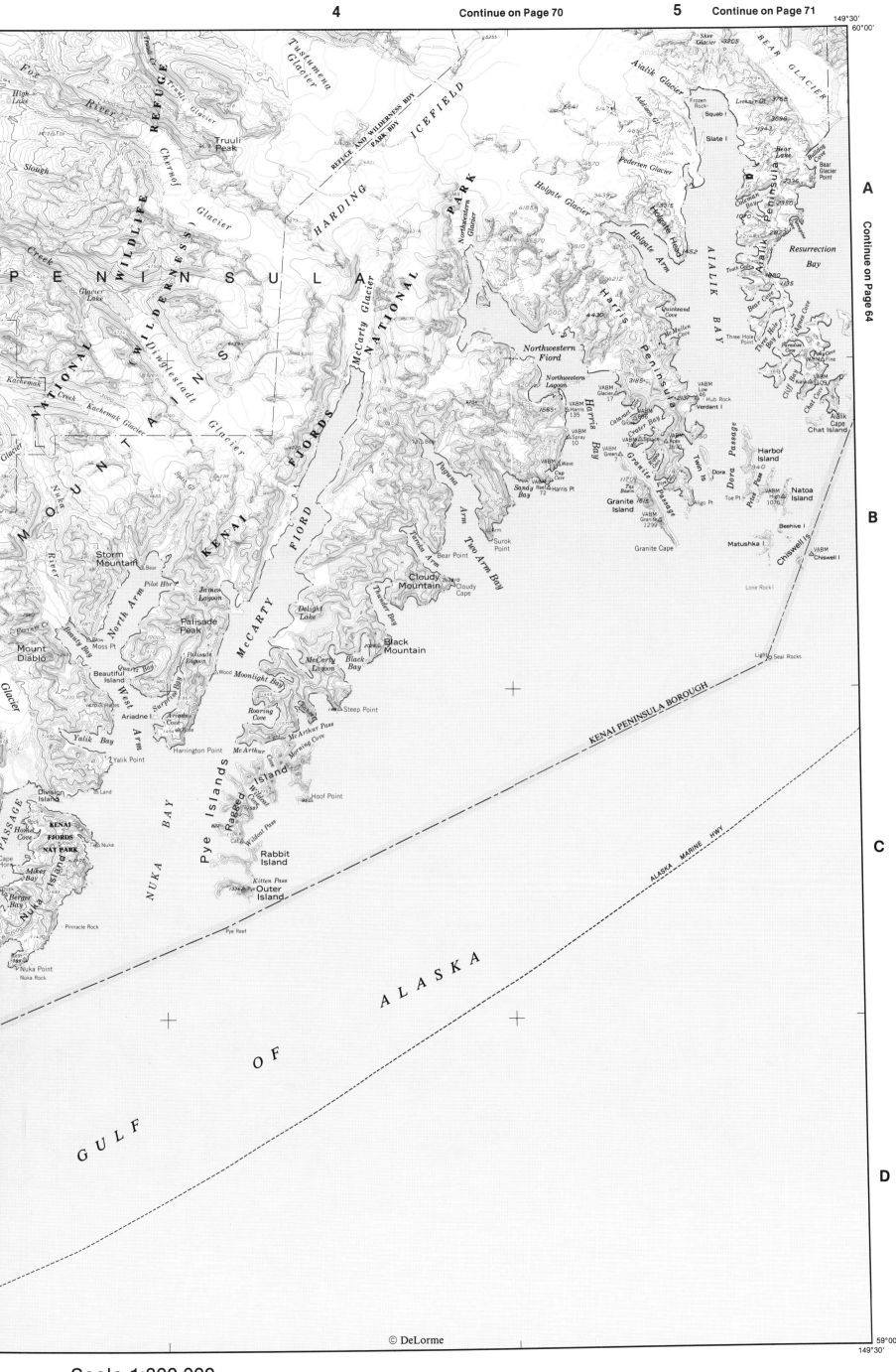

149°30'
60°00'

A

Continue on Page 64

B

C

D

59°00'
149°30'

© DeLorme

Scale 1:300,000
1 inch represents 4.8 miles

Contour interval
200 feet (61 meters)

149°30'
60°00'

Callisto Pk
3223
Caines Head
CAINES HEAD
STATE REC AREA
Lighthouse
Porcupine
Glacier
Talus Bay
Anchor
Cove
Safety Cove
Excelsior
Glacier
325
Goat
Harbor
CHUGACH
NAT FOR
VABM
Pug 23
PORT
BAINBRIDGE

Humpy
Cove
Hat I
Safety Cove
State Marine Park
Fault
Point
Whidbey
Bay
Mt Fairfield
Puget
Bay
Cape
Puget
Pt Elrington

VABM
15
VABM
476
VABM
118
Dry Harbor
Day Harbor
Johnstone Bay
Cape Junken

Sunny
Cove
Sunny Cove
State Marine Park
Hive I
Driftwood Bay
State Marine Park
Cape
Mansfield
Cape
Fairfield
Pinnacle
Rock

CHUGACH   NATIONAL   FOREST

KENAI   PENINSULA   BOROUGH

Rugged
Island
Cape
Resurrection
Light
Barwell I

RESURRECTION   BAY

BLYING   SOUND

GULF   OF

Light Pilot Rock

ALASKA   MARINE   HWY

ALASKA MARINE HWY

Continue on Page 63

59°38'06"
149°30'

Continue on Page 44

155°02'32"
57°00'

INSET 1

Low Cape
KODIAK   NATIONAL   WILDLIFE
REFUGE
KODIAK
Tungulara
Mountain
Moser
Peninsula
KNWR
Fox I
Hepburn
Peninsula
KODIAK
NWR

Kelp
Sukhoi
Lagoon
KODIAK   ISLAND
Akhiok
Akhiok
Landing Strip
Miller I
Camp Cove
Nelson
Reef
Cape
Hepburn
Shag Bluff

Sukhoi Bay
Round Hill
Akhiok I
Akhiok Reef
Portage

Rodman
30
Alitak
SPB
Twin Pks
White Rk
Cannery Drake Head
Egg I
Alitak   Bay
Sedanka Bay

Alitak
Lagoon
Tanner Head
Cape Alitak
Alitak Shoal
KODIAK
NATIONAL

GULF
Hawk
Bluff
KODIAK
690

Cape Trinity
Russian   Harbor
GEESE

Aiaktalik
Aiaktalik
Island
Cove
Gosling I
Geese

Sundstrom I
Aiak I

OF

Sitkinak   Strait

Dolina
Valley Point 2
Flat Point 2
Whirlpool Pt

Red Bluff 2
Tidal Flat
Tugidak Island
E Base
Exposed
Wreck
Sitkinak
Dome

TUGIDAK ISLAND
STATE CRITICAL HABITAT AREA
Bag Point 2
Radio
Tower
Landing Strip
(abandoned)
Mark
Lake
Island

Sitkinak
Lagoon

Tugidak   Island
BM (Tidal)
Pyramid 2

TRINITY   ISLANDS

Tugidak Island State
Critical Habitat Area
Dry Rock
Ocean View

56°23'
155°02'32"

© DeLorme

KILOMETERS   5   0   5   10   15   20
MILES   1 0 1 2 3 4 5 6 7 8 9 10 11 12

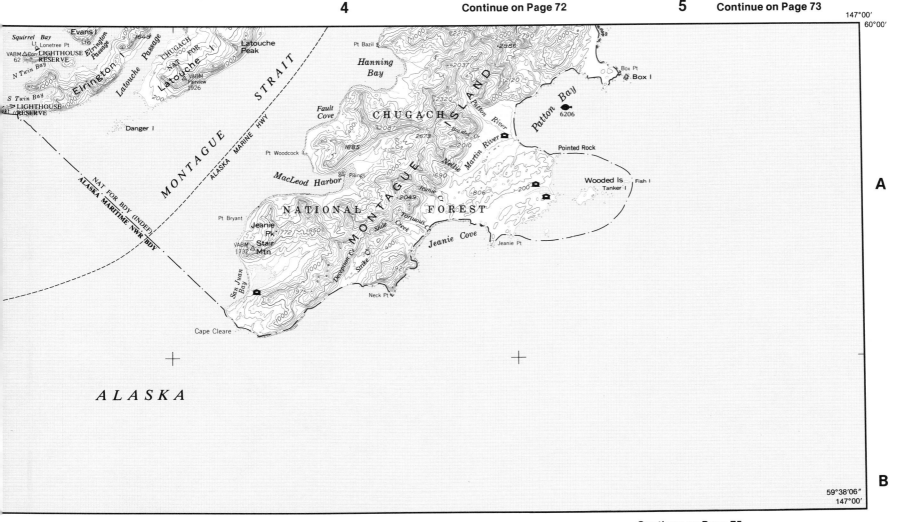

Continue on Page 44

Continue on Page 75

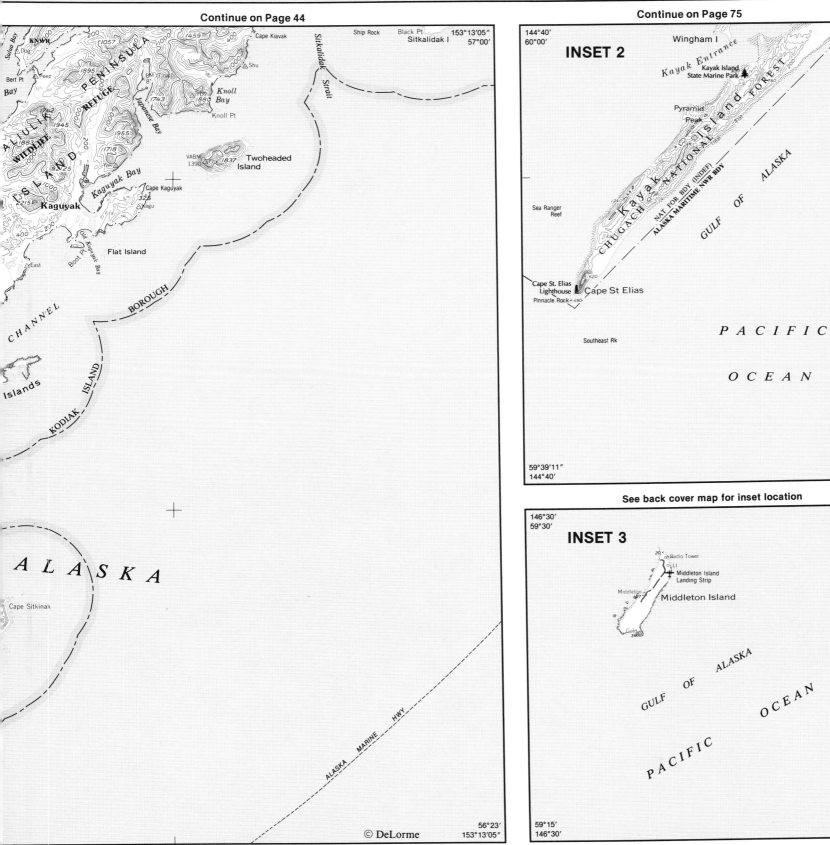

See back cover map for inset location

Scale 1:300,000
1 inch represents 4.8 miles

Contour interval
200 feet (61 meters)

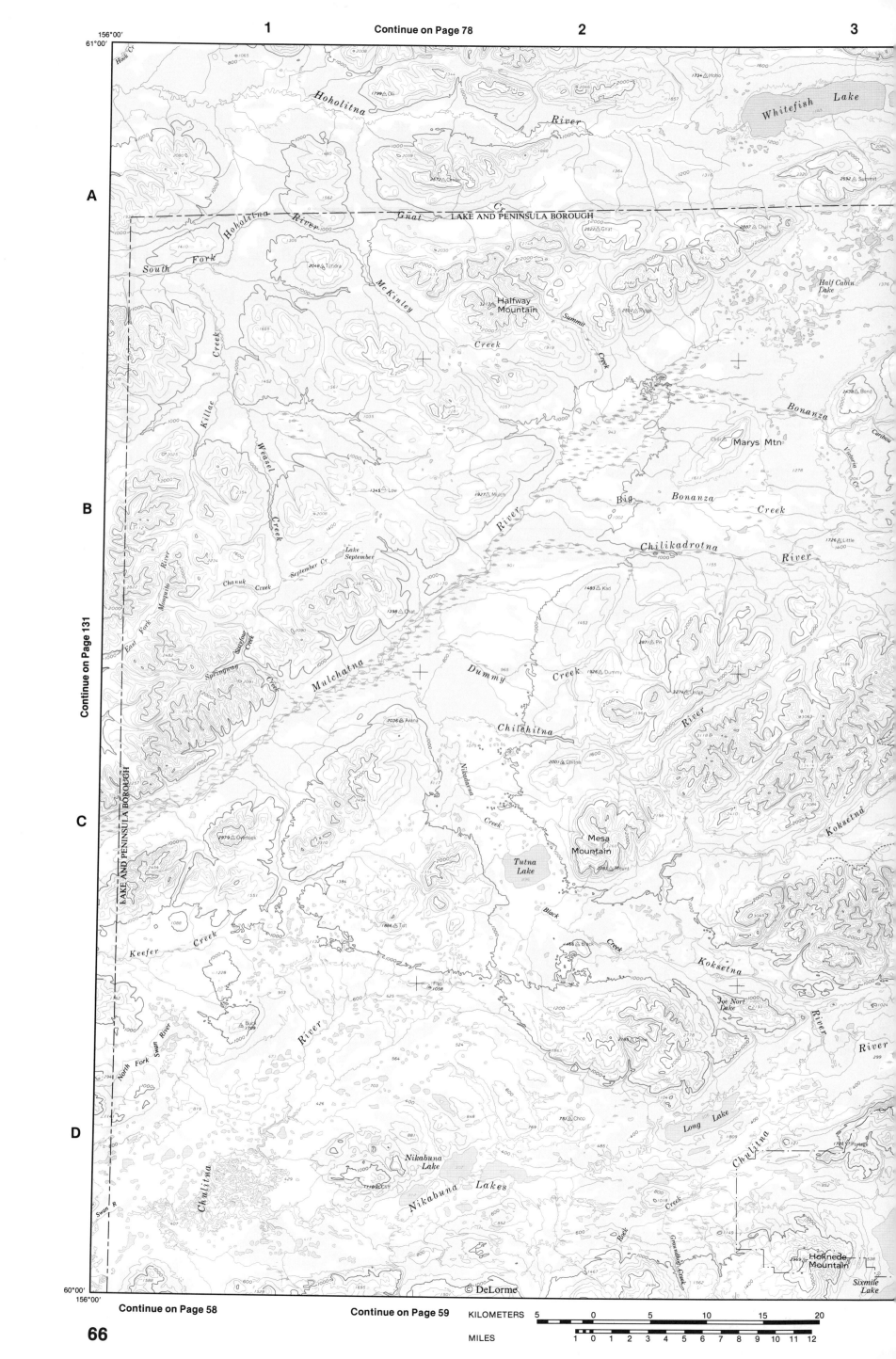

Continue on Page 131

KILOMETERS   5   0   5   10   15   20

MILES   1 0 1 2 3 4 5 6 7 8 9 10 11 12

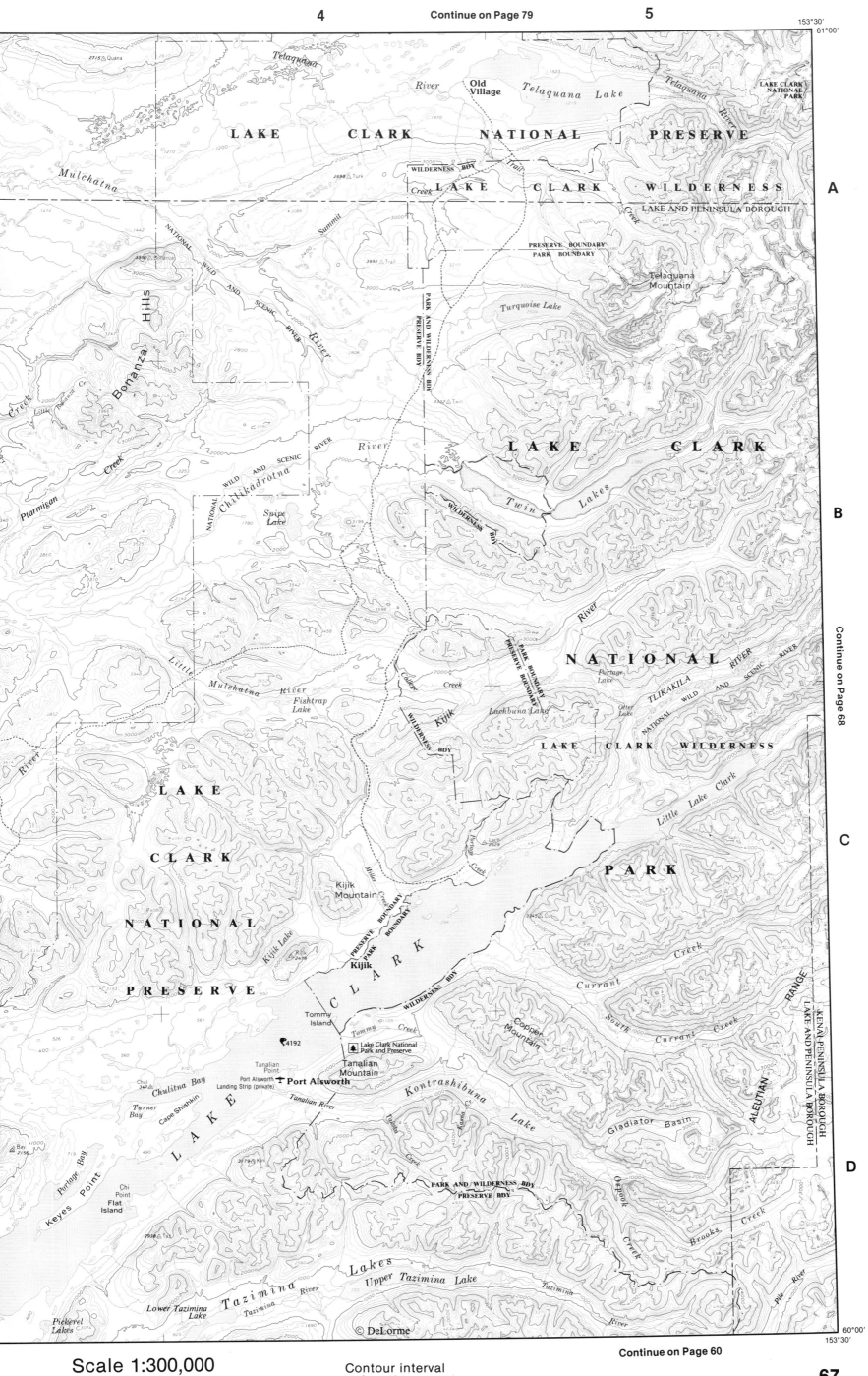

153°30'
61°00'

A

LAKE CLARK NATIONAL PARK

LAKE CLARK NATIONAL PRESERVE

LAKE CLARK WILDERNESS

LAKE AND PENINSULA BOROUGH

PRESERVE BOUNDARY
PARK BOUNDARY

Telaquana Lake

Telaquana River

Old Village

River

Turk

Creek

Quana

Telaquana
Mountain

Turquoise Lake

Twin

Bonanza Hills

Bonanza

NATIONAL WILD AND SCENIC RIVER

River

Mulchatna

Little Bonanza Cr

Creek

Ptarmigan

Chilikadrotna River

Snipe Lake

River

Trail

Summit

Twin

LAKE CLARK

Lakes

NATIONAL

Continue on Page 68

B

PARK AND WILDERNESS BDY

PARK BOUNDARY
PRESERVE BOUNDARY

WILDERNESS BDY

River

Portage
Lake

Otter
Lake

Lachbuna Lake

TLIKAKILA NATIONAL WILD AND SCENIC RIVER

LAKE CLARK WILDERNESS

Little

Mulchatna

River

Fishtrap
Lake

College

Creek

Kijik

WILDERNESS BDY

Little

Lake Clark

LAKE

CLARK

NATIONAL

PRESERVE

River

Kijik Lake

Kijik Mountain

Kijik

Miller

Creek

Portage

Creek

Currant

Creek

PARK

South Currant Creek

Currant

Creek

Copper Mountain

Cur

C

WILDERNESS BDY

PRESERVE BOUNDARY
PARK BOUNDARY

KENAI PENINSULA BOROUGH
LAKE AND PENINSULA BOROUGH

ALEUTIAN RANGE

Kijik

Tommy Island

4192

Lake Clark National
Park and Preserve

Tommy

Creek

Kontrashibuna Lake

Gladiator Basin

Tanalian
Point

Tanalian
Mountain

Port Alsworth
Landing Strip (private)

Port Alsworth

Tanalian River

Chulitna Bay

Chul

Turner
Bay

Cape Shishkin

LAKE

CLARK

Tokitha Creek

Kijik Creek

Brooks Creek

Osprook Creek

D

Bay

Portage Bay

Keyes Point

Chi
Point

Flat
Island

Pickerel
Lakes

Taz

Lakes

Tazimina River

Lower Tazimina
Lake

Tazimina

Upper Tazimina Lake

Tazimina

PARK AND WILDERNESS BDY
PRESERVE BDY

River

Pile Creek

© DeLorme

60°00'
153°30'

Continue on Page 60

Scale 1:300,000
1 inch represents 4.8 miles

Contour interval
200 feet (61 meters)

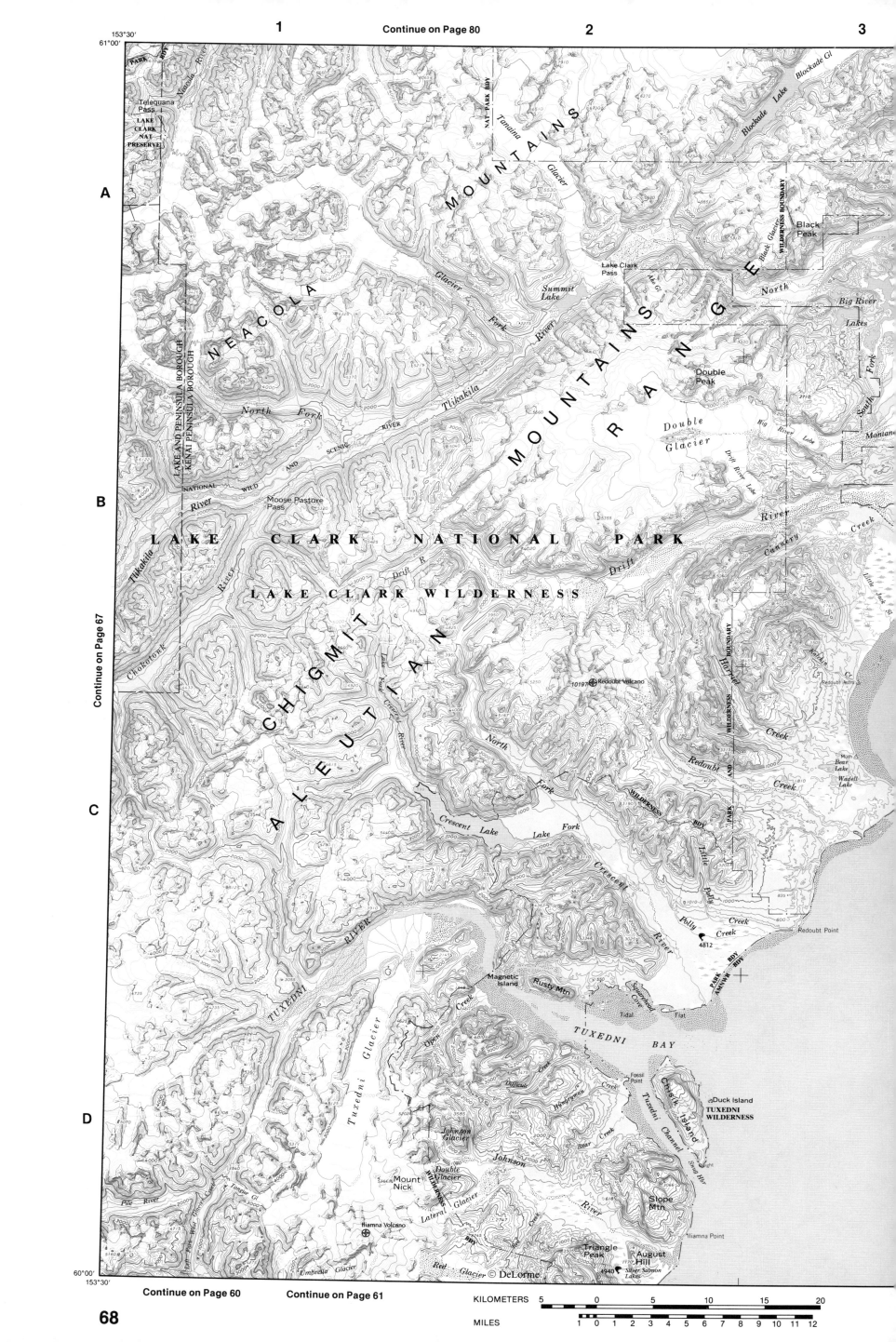

153°30'
61°00'

Tanaina Glacier

NAT PARK BDY

Blockade Gl

Blockade Lake

Telequana Pass

LAKE CLARK NAT PRESERVE

PARK BDY

Naqula River

A

MOUNTAINS

Black Glaciers Boundary

WILDERNESS BOUNDARY

Black Peak

Lake Clark Pass

Aku Gl

North

Big River

Summit Lake

Glacier Fork

River

Lakes

Double Peak

NEACOLA

M O U N T A I N S

South Fork

North Fork

Tlikakila

LAKE AND PENINSULA BOROUGH

KENAI PENINSULA BOROUGH

RIVER

R A N G E

Double Glacier

Big River Lobe

Drift River Lobe

Montana

SCENIC

B

River

Moose Pasture Pass

WILD

Drift R

Drift

Cannery

Creek

L A K E   C L A R K   N A T I O N A L   P A R K

Tlikakila

NATIONAL

River

L A K E   C L A R K   W I L D E R N E S S

Little Jack Sl

Chokotonk

River

WILDERNESS BOUNDARY

C H I G M I T

Redoubt Volcano

10197

Redoubt Astro

Redoubt

A L E U T I A N

Lake Fork

North

Fork

Crescent

River

WILDERNESS

Moth Bear Lake

Creek

Wadell Lake

C

Crescent Lake

Lake Fork

BDY

PARK AND

Little

Polly

Creek

Crescent

River

Polly

Creek

Redoubt Point

4812

RIVER

Magnetic Island

Rusty Mtn

Squarehead Cove

Tidal

Flat

T U X E D N I

B A Y

Creek

Open

Creek

Tuxedni Glacier

Fossil Point

Cisik Island

Duck Island

TUXEDNI WILDERNESS

D

Difficult

Creek

Tuxedni Channel

Creek

Johnson Glacier

Bear

River

Johnson

Slope Mtn

Double Glacier

Mount Nick

WILDERNESS

Lateral Glacier

Creek

Iliamna Volcano

BDY

Tongue Gl

Pile River

Red

Glacier

© DeLorme

Triangle Peak

August Hill

4940

Iliamna Point

Silver Salmon Lakes

Umbrella Glacier

60°00'
153°30'

Continue on Page 67

KILOMETERS 5   0   5   10   15   20

MILES   1 0 1 2 3 4 5 6 7 8 9 10 11 12

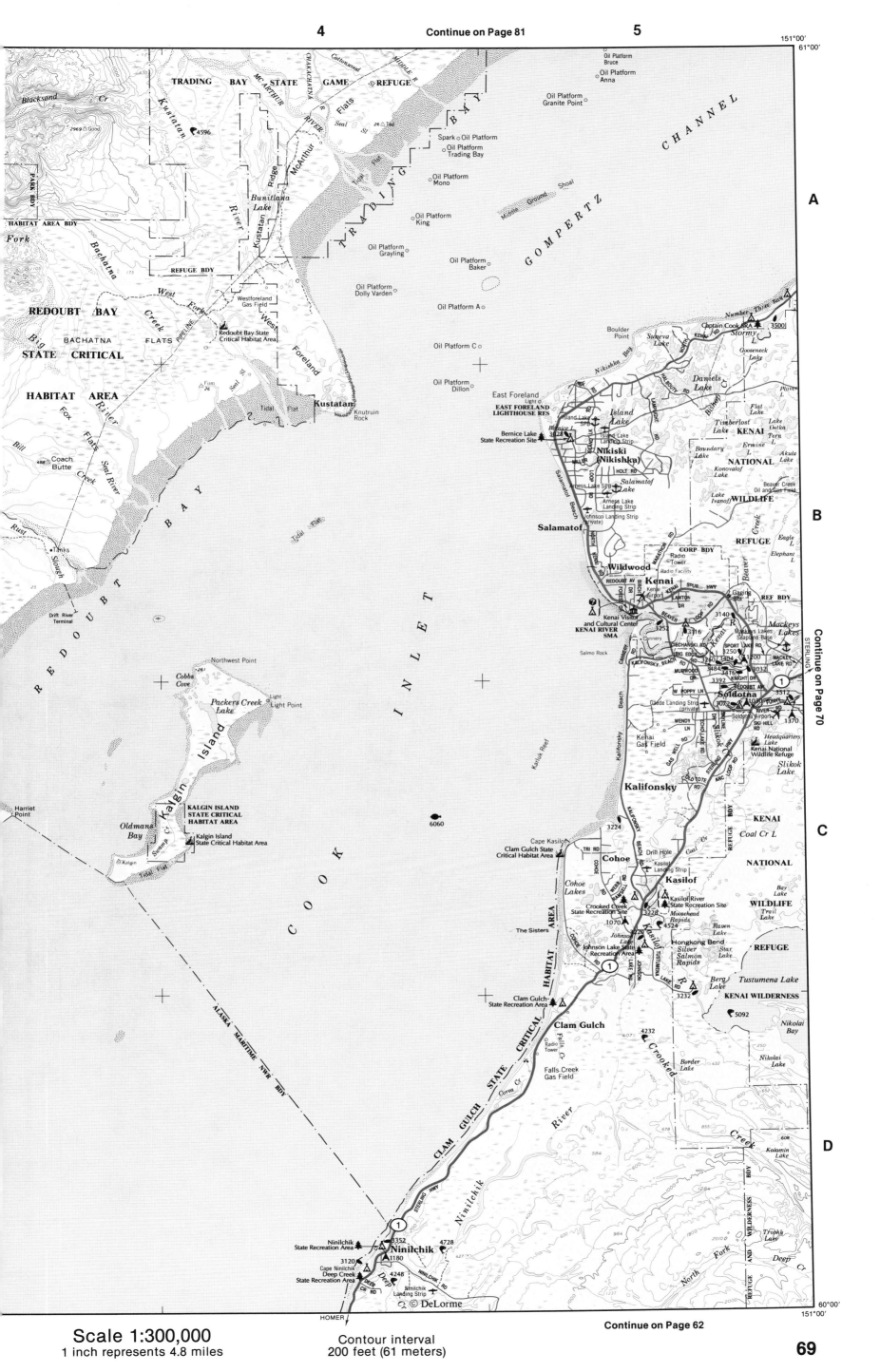

Continue on Page 70

Scale 1:300,000
1 inch represents 4.8 miles

Contour interval
200 feet (61 meters)

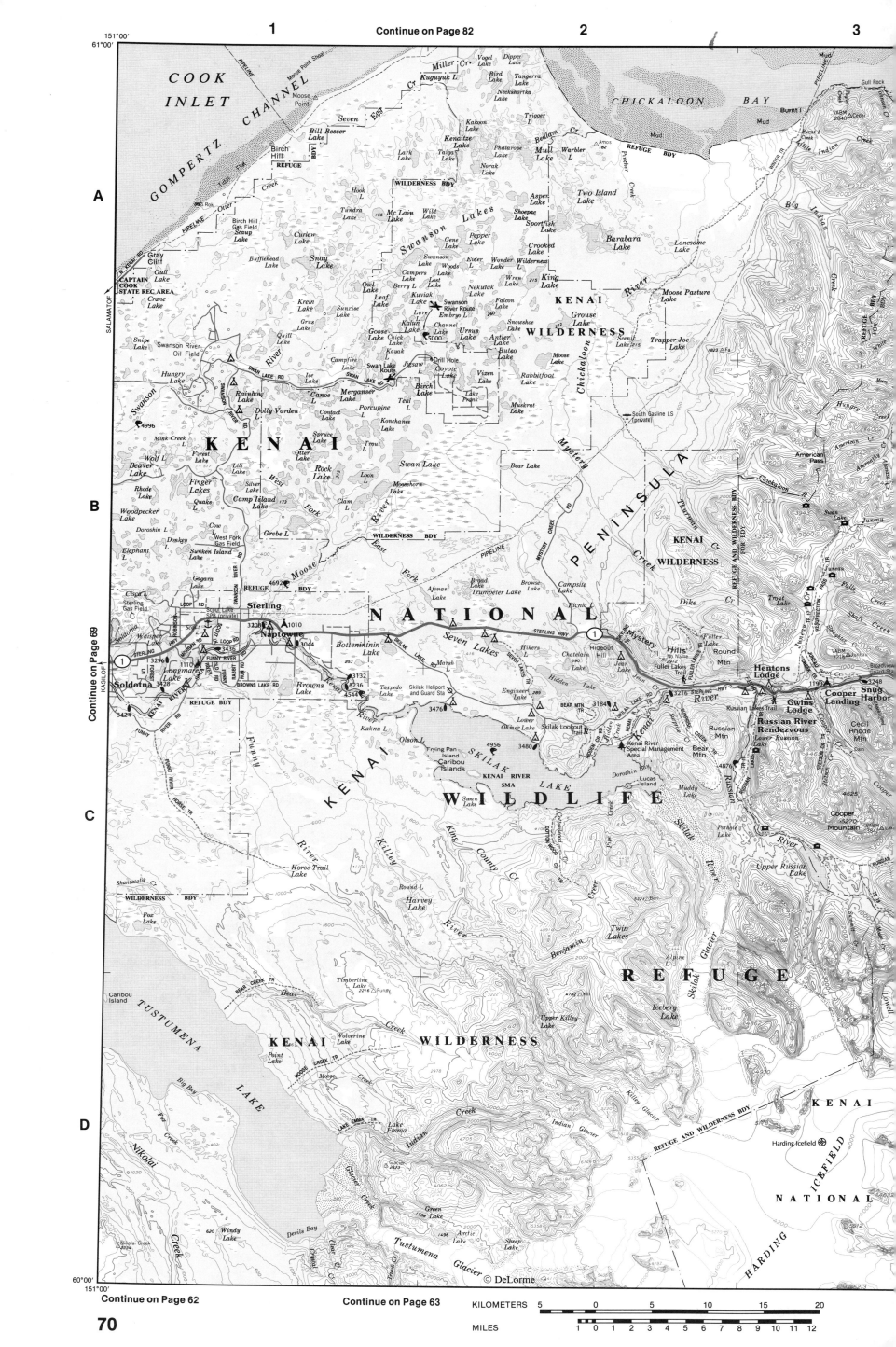

151°00'
61°00'

COOK

INLET

CHICKALOON   BAY

GOMPERTZ   CHANNEL

Swanson   Lakes

KENAI

WILDERNESS

KENAI

KENAI

PENINSULA

KENAI
WILDERNESS

NATIONAL

Soldotna

Sterling

Naptowne

Cooper
Landing

Snug
Harbor

Hentons
Lodge

Gwins
Lodge

Russian River
Rendezvous

KENAI

WILDLIFE

KENAI
RIVER
SMA

WILDERNESS

KENAI

REFUGE

NATIONAL

TUSTUMENA

LAKE

HARDING

ICEFIELD

Harding Icefield

REFUGE AND WILDERNESS BDY

60°00'
151°00'

Continue on Page 69
Continue on Page 62   Continue on Page 63

70

KILOMETERS   5   0   5   10   15   20

MILES   1 0 1 2 3 4 5 6 7 8 9 10 11 12

© DeLorme

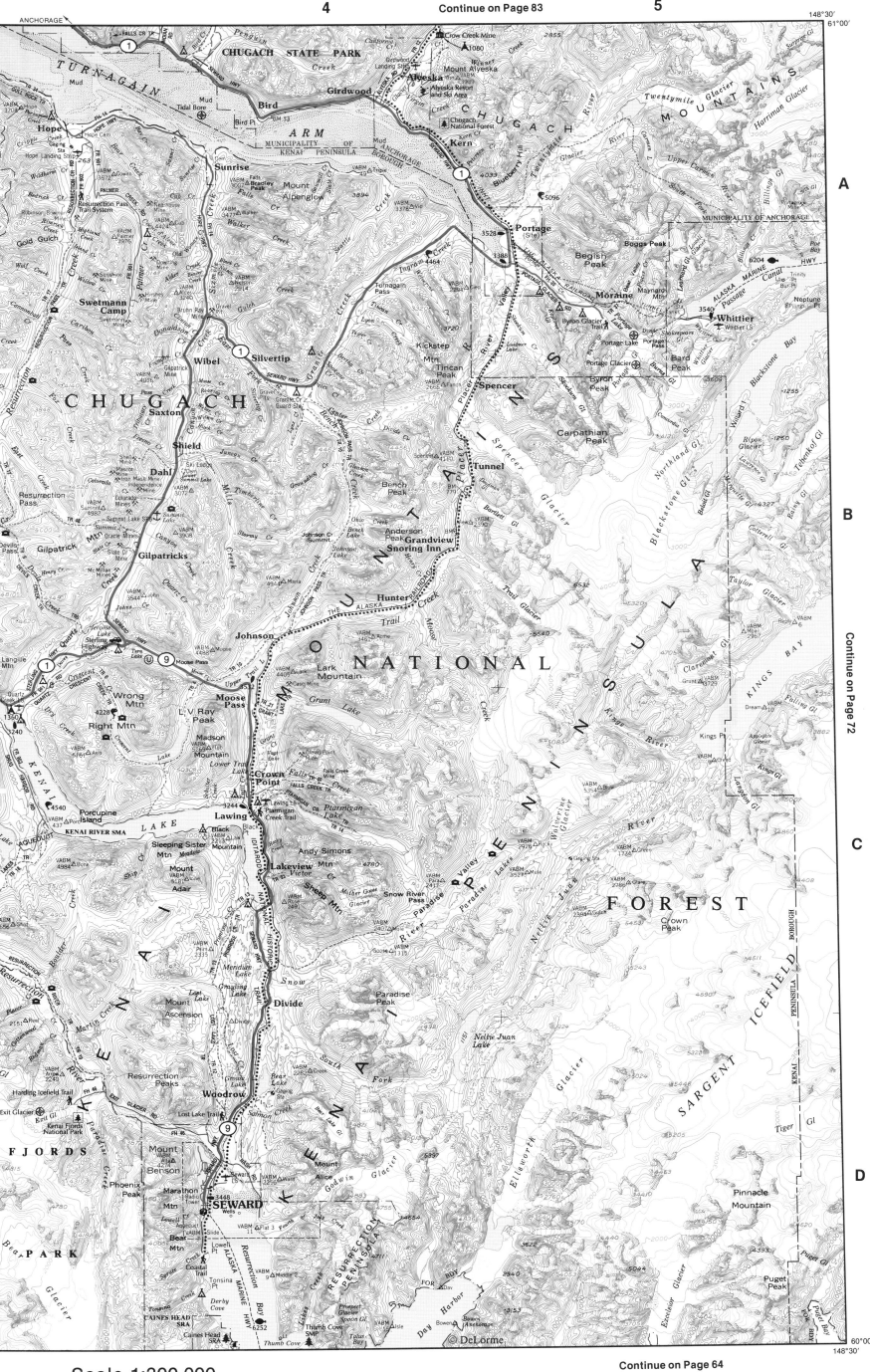

Continue on Page 72

Continue on Page 64

Scale 1:300,000
1 inch represents 4.8 miles

Contour interval
200 feet (61 meters)

148°30'
61°00'

A

Harriman Fiord
Roaring Gl
Bettles Bay State Marine Park
Harrison Lagoon
Golden
Golden Lake
Davis Lake
Jonah Bay
Birch
Block Island
Billys Hole
Schrader I
6008

MUNICIPALITY OF ANCHORAGE

Hobo 22
Hummer
Chest 17
-1759
2057
Granite B
Granite Bay SMP
GRANITE BAY STATE MARINE PARK

PORT WELLS

Esther Island

UNAKWIK INLET

Wells Bay

Siwash Bay
Siwash Island
Inlet
Eaglek Glacier
Waterfall
Cascade Bay
Cascade Island
Nurse
Derickson Bay

6304
4085
2484
-1752
-978
Fairmount Island
Mueller Cove
1119
Olsen Cove
Olsen Island
Little Fairmount Island
Outpost Island

Pigot Gl
3652
-2274
4543
6212
Zeigler Cove State Marine Park
2569
Logging Camp
Entry Cove State Marine Park
Squirrel I
Decision Slope
Pt Pigot
Pt Pigot Light
Decision Point State Marine Park
Strong Pt
Blackstone Pt

SOUTH ESTHER ISLAND STATE MARINE PARK
Esther Rock
Pt Esther
Esther Island Light
Hodgkins Pt

Quillian Bay
South Esther Island State Marine Park
6084
Squid
E Flank Island
W Flank Island
Bald Head
Chris I

Kiniklik
Eaglek
Ketch
Kiniklik I
Eaglek Island
Little Axel Lind Island
Axel Lind Island
Jenny Is Mack
John

ALASKA MARINE HWY
Wells Passage
Egg Rocks
Fool I
CAA Radio Range Sta
Dutch Group
Oil Tank

Storey Island
Tall

B

Uncle
Surprise Cove State Marine Park
Surprise Cove
Prize
SURPRISE COVE STATE MARINE PARK

Tebenkof Gl
Cochrane Bay
Split
Amber
28
Pt Culross
Bob
Culross Bay
Hidden Bay

Culross Island

Perry Passage
Tipping Pt
West Twin Bay
East Twin Bay
Bald 2
Pt Perry
Perry
Perry Island
Billings
Bush Pt
Rest
South Bay
Meares Pt
Duck
Perry Island Seaplane Base
Lone Passage
Lone Island
Lone Pt
Lone
Waver

Liljegren Passage
Elk Head Pt
Peak Island
Jason
Flow
Cadet
McPherson Passage
Cabin Bay
McPherson Bay
East Pt

Naked Island
Outside Bay
Bass Harbor
Naked 2
Tuft
Agnes
Naked I

Horse
6052
6164
Lake Shrode
Kraut
Match
6068
Lake Jack
There
2016
Long
Rebel
Goose Bay
2196
624
Said
Applegate I
Wire
13

CHUGACH

PRINCE

WILLIAM

C

W Esther Inlet
Unite
Mink I
Nell
Coxcomb Pt
Quart
Greystone Bay
Deep Bay
Mace
Derickson Bay
Money
Neck
Orgah
E Esther Inlet
Shady Cove
Division Pt

PORT

NELLIE JUAN

Port Nellie Juan
Aqueduct
McClure Bay
First
Foul Bay
6176
LIGHTHOUSE RESERVE

Blue Fiord
Falls Lake
Falls Bay
Crafton Island
Eshamy Peak
Gunboat Lagoon
Eshamy Bay
6080
Eshamy Lake
Eshamy Lagoon
4312
Rubber Boot Lake
Pt Nowell

Storm
Pt Eleanor
Northwest Bay
Upper Passage
Eleanor
Flower
Clove
Ingot Island
Block I
Entrance I
Sphinx Island
Lower Passage
Fish Bay
Louis Bay
Little Smith Island
Smith I
LIGHTHOUSE RESERVE

6160

NATIONAL

Saddle Pk
Enan Lake
Contact Gl
Nellie Juan Glacier
Zone
Ultramarine Gl
Jackpot Ladder
Jackpot Bay

Island Passage
Herring Pt
Herring Bay
Shoulder Pt
Surf Cove
Surf Lake
Otter Lake
Slip
Pennsylvania Rock
Seal Island
Seal
Manning Rocks

Sargent Icefield
Princeton Glacier
6140
Toga
Delenia Island
Jackpot
Jackpot Center
Icy
Chenega Island

Junction I
Daagerous Passage
Marked Bay
Evan Bay
Granite Bay
Channel Rock
Lower Herring Bay
Aguliak Is
Johnson Bay
Squirrel Bay
Cannery
Mountain
Port Audrey
West Arm
South Arm
Bay of Isles
Short Arm
Knight
Iron Mtn
Rua Cove
Yellow Cliffs

Applegate Rock

STRAIT

D

Chenega Glacier
Nassau Fiord
Nassau
Berg
Cliff
1732
Sober
-1306
Verdant Island
Chenega (Site)
Chenega Cem
Chenega Pt
New Year Islands
Clam Is
Rocky Pt
Rocky Range
Cat Head
Drier Pass
Mummy I
Barnes Cove
Chase I
Northeast Cove
Cannery
Mary Bay

Copper Bay
Fishery
Deer Cove
Squire
Long Channel
Lucky Bay
Snug Harbor
Discovery Pt

KNIGHT

FOREST

Putnam Pt
Bump
Green
Green Island
Channel I
6228
Little Green Island
Trey

Tiger Gl
Icy Bay
Claw Peak
2650
Dual Head
Whale Bay
-1357
Pt Countess
Sage
Baird
Bainbridge
Pleiades Islands
Point of Rocks
Squire
Squire Bay
Mummy Bay
Thumb Bay
Horn Mtn
Oceanic
Little Bay
Hogan Bay

MONTAGUE

The Needle

2920
2461
Kit
Alex
Tower
Flemming Island
Gage I
Ship I
Bear
Outer
Paohat

Knight Island Passage

Shelter Bay
Evans Pt
Iktua Rks
Bishop Rk
Evans Pt

Bainbridge Passage

2008

60°00'
148°30'

Bainbridge Gl
Bainbridge
4395
1749
Pt Waters
Thrush
Hogg Pt
Hogg Bay
Bainbridge Island
Helo
Swanson Bay
Auk Bay
Goat Harbor
Port Pyke
Swanson

Prince of Wales

Evans Island
Crab Bay
Crab Bay
Port Ashton
San Juan Cannery
Bettles
Latouche (Site)
Radio
Chicken
Horseshoe Bay
State Marine Park
Horseshoe Bay
Latouche Island
Gibbon Peak
Mt Beatson
Port Crawford
Pt Grace
Procession Rocks
Squirrel Bay
Elrington Passage
Elrington I
Lake Hayden
Broom Buttes
Reynolds Peak
Purple Bluff
ALASKA MARINE HWY

MONTAGUE

AMNWR BDY

© DeLorme

KILOMETERS   5   0   5   10   15   20
MILES   1 0 1 2 3 4 5 6 7 8 9 10 11 12

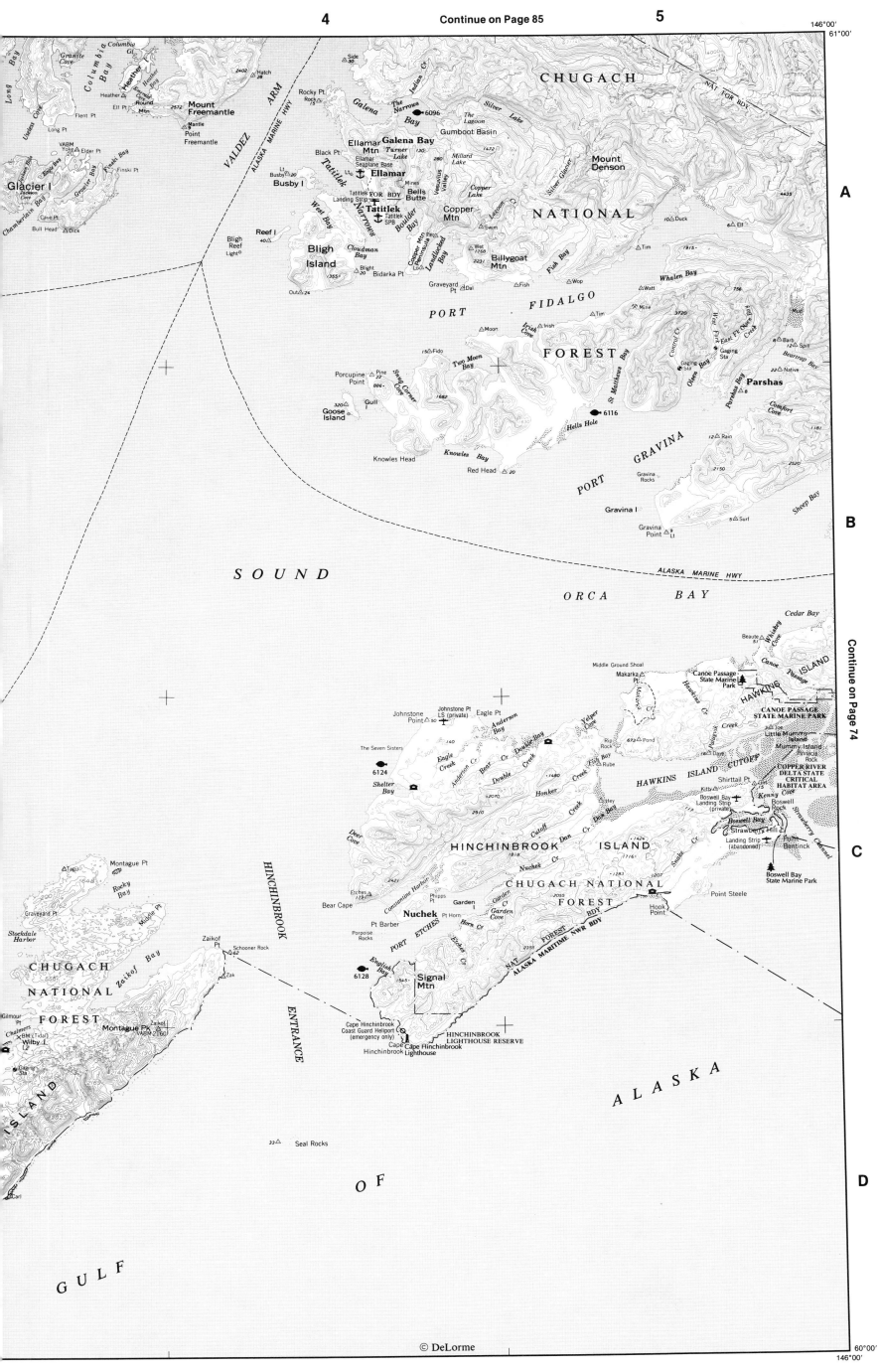

Continue on Page 74

© DeLorme

Meteorite
Mtn

Brown
Basin

Browns Glacier

Wortmans Glacier

Deserted Glacier

Tasnuna Glacier

Woodworth Glacier

Schwan Glacier

Whiting Falls

Schwan

Bremner

Dead Creek

A

Gravina River

NAT FOR BDY

CHUGACH

Cordova Glacier

Cordova Peak

Rude Lake

RUDE RIVER

CHUGACH

Heney Glacier

Mc Cune Cr

Shiels Cr

Gl

Sheep Bay

Sahlin Lagoon
Sahlin Lake

Sheep Creek

Koppen Cr

Simpson Creek

Raging Creek

Rogue Creek

Robinson Falls Cr

Nelson Bay

W Base
Sacre
E Base

Mount Kelly

Snyder Mtn

Shephard Glacier

SCOTT GLACIER

NATIONAL

Mount Williams

Mount O'Neel

CHILDS GLACIER

Grinnell Glacier

B

Simpson Bay

Bomb Pt
Simpson 2

Hanks
Gatherer Rock

Fox Pt

Milton Lake

Channel Is

The Narrows

ALASKA MARINE HWY

Narrows

Shepard Pt

North

Humpback

Bluff

Observation

Power Creek Trail

Gaging Sta

Ohman Falls

Ibeck Creek

4820

GLACIER

Mount Murchison

Goodwin Glacier

SHERIDAN GLACIER

Sherman Glacier

Fickett Glacier

4196

10

Windy Bay

Shipyard Bay

Cordova Museum and Historical Society

Spike
Stump

Mud Bay

Deep Cr
Deep Bay

Greatest Channel

Knot Pt

Aux

Orca

Grass I

Mt Eyak

Crater Lake

Eyak Lake

Ibex

Siamese Lakes

Scott Lake

Star

Shattered Peak

Saddlebag Glacier

Pyramid Peak

Sharp

Hawkins Island

Cordova
Municipal Airport

Tripod Hill

Mavis I

Saddle

Eyak
CB

Boy Scout

Eyak

Boy Scout

Lake Elsner

Skp

C

Hidden Cove

Big Pt

Hartney Bay

ORCA INLET

Bluff Pt

Treat

Cordova

Mount Eccles

Heney Cr

Heney Range

Heney Pk

2876

Cordova

Crystal Falls

4328

Eyak River

Government Sl

Eyak

Copper River Delta State Critical Habitat Area

Merle K Smith Airport

COPPER RIVER HWY

GLACIER

McKinley Peak

Pipeline Lakes Trail

Pipeline

McKinley Lake Trail

McKinley Lake

4664

Alaganik

Borrow Pit

Flag Point

Long Island

Heart Island

Round Island

Hooke Channel

SHEEP

Gravel Pt

Radio Towers

Twin Rocks

1400 Falls

Pt Whitshed

Government Rock

Mud

Mud

Sand

COPPER

RIVER

DELTA

STATE

COPPER RIVER DELTA STATE CRITICAL HABITAT

Alaganik Slough

Pete

PETE DAHL SLOUGH

Queen

Walhalla

Gut Steven Slough

CASTLE ISLAND SLOUGH

Castle Island

STOREY SLOUGH

Storey

KOKINHENIK SLOUGH

Kokinhenik BRANCH

Kokinhenik I

COPPER

RIVER

DELTA

Cottonwood Pt

Mud

Sand

Egg Islands

Egg Island Channel

Sand

Copper Sands

CRITICAL HABITAT AREA

Grass

Grass Island Bar

Kolinhenik Bar

HABITAT BDY

Strawberry Reef

D

NAT FOR BDY
AMNWR BDY

GULF   OF   ALASKA

© DeLorme

KILOMETERS   5   0   5   10   15   20

MILES   1 0 1 2 3 4 5 6 7 8 9 10 11 12

Continue on Page 73

143°30'
61°00'

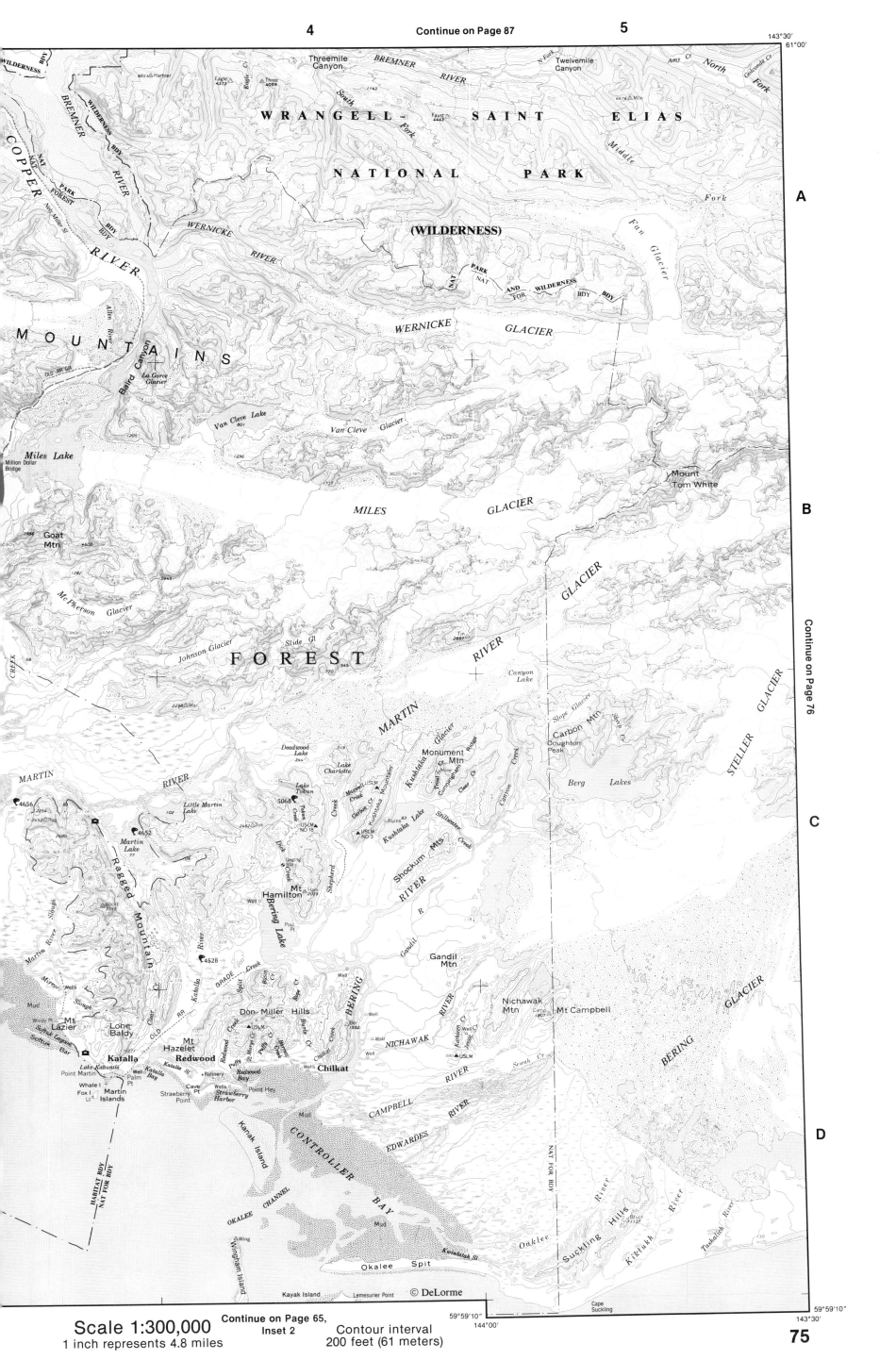

WRANGELL - SAINT ELIAS

NATIONAL PARK

(WILDERNESS)

A

B

Continue on Page 76

C

D

WERNICKE GLACIER

MILES GLACIER

GLACIER

MARTIN RIVER

STELLER GLACIER

FOREST

COPPER RIVER

MOUNTAINS

BREMNER RIVER

Miles Lake
Million Dollar
Bridge

Goat Mtn

Mt Pherson Glacier

Johnson Glacier

Slide Gl

Van Cleve Lake

Van Cleve Glacier

Mount
Tom White

Carbon Mtn
Doughton
Peak

Berg Lakes

Slope Glacier

Canyon Lake

MARTIN RIVER

Deadwood
Lake

Lake
Charlotte

Lake
Tokun

Monument
Mtn

Kushtaka Mountain

Shokum Mts

BERING GLACIER

Little Martin
Lake

Martin
Lake

Ragged Mountain

Mt
Hamilton

Bering Lake

Kushtaka Lake

Gandil
Mtn

Nichawak
Mtn   Mt Campbell

Don Miller Hills

Mt
Lazier

Lone Baldy

Mt
Hazelet
Redwood

Katalla

Chilkat

NICHAWAK RIVER

CAMPBELL RIVER

EDWARDES

Martin
Islands

Kanak Island

CONTROLLER BAY

Suckling Hills

OKALEE CHANNEL

Okalee Spit

Wingham Island

Kayak Island   Lemesurier Point

© DeLorme

Cape
Suckling

59°59'10"
143°30'

59°59'10"
144°00'

Continue on Page 65,
Inset 2

Scale 1:300,000
1 inch represents 4.8 miles

Contour interval
200 feet (61 meters)

143°30'
61°00'

A

WRANGELL – SAINT ELIAS

Ptarmigan Creek
N Fork
North Fork Lobe
Middle Fork Lobe
Tana Lobe
WEST FORK
TANA RIVER
GRANITE

CHUGACH MOUNTAINS

Bremner Glacier

Barkley Lake
Ross Green Lake
THOMPSON RIDGE
Needle Mountain

Mount Hawkins

B

PARK AND WILDERNESS BDY

STELLER GLACIER

WAXELL

Mt Steller

RIDGE

WRANGELL – SAINT ELIAS

BAGLEY
ICE

Juniper Island

Khitrov Hills

Natural Arch

BARKLEY
Mount Miller

C

BERING GLACIER

GLACIER

McIntosh Peak

Grindle Hills

Hanna Lake

ROBINSON

River

River

Leeper

NAT PARK

KALIAKH

Kulthieth

DUKTOTH RIVER

Dahlgren

Duktoth Mtn

D

YAKATAGA STATE GAME REFUGE

East Fork
West Fork

Tsiu River
Tsivat River

Oil Well

Sunshine Point
Odor Creek
Hope Creek

Kulthieth Mountain

Chiuki River
Yakataga State Game Refuge
RIVER

Cotton Creek
Boulder Creek
North Channel
Yakataga River

Midtimber Lake
Don

Beacon
Yakataga Landing Strip
Cape Yakataga
Radio Facility
Watson Peak
Cape Yakataga
South Channel
Mink Cr
Brower
Hamilton

GULF OF ALASKA

60°00'
143°30'

© DeLorme

Continue on Page 75

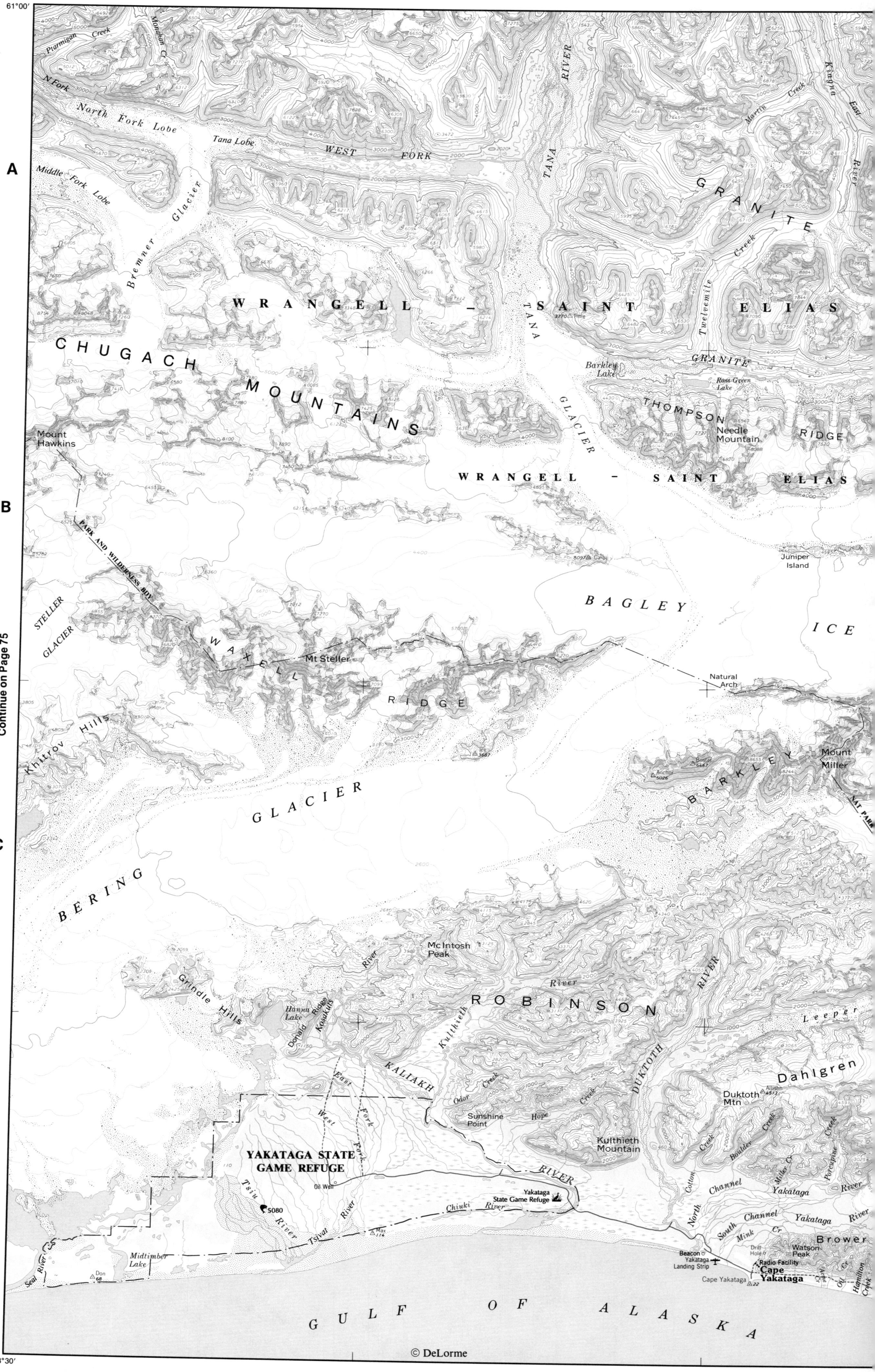

KILOMETERS 5 0 5 10 15 20
MILES 1 0 1 2 3 4 5 6 7 8 9 10 11 12

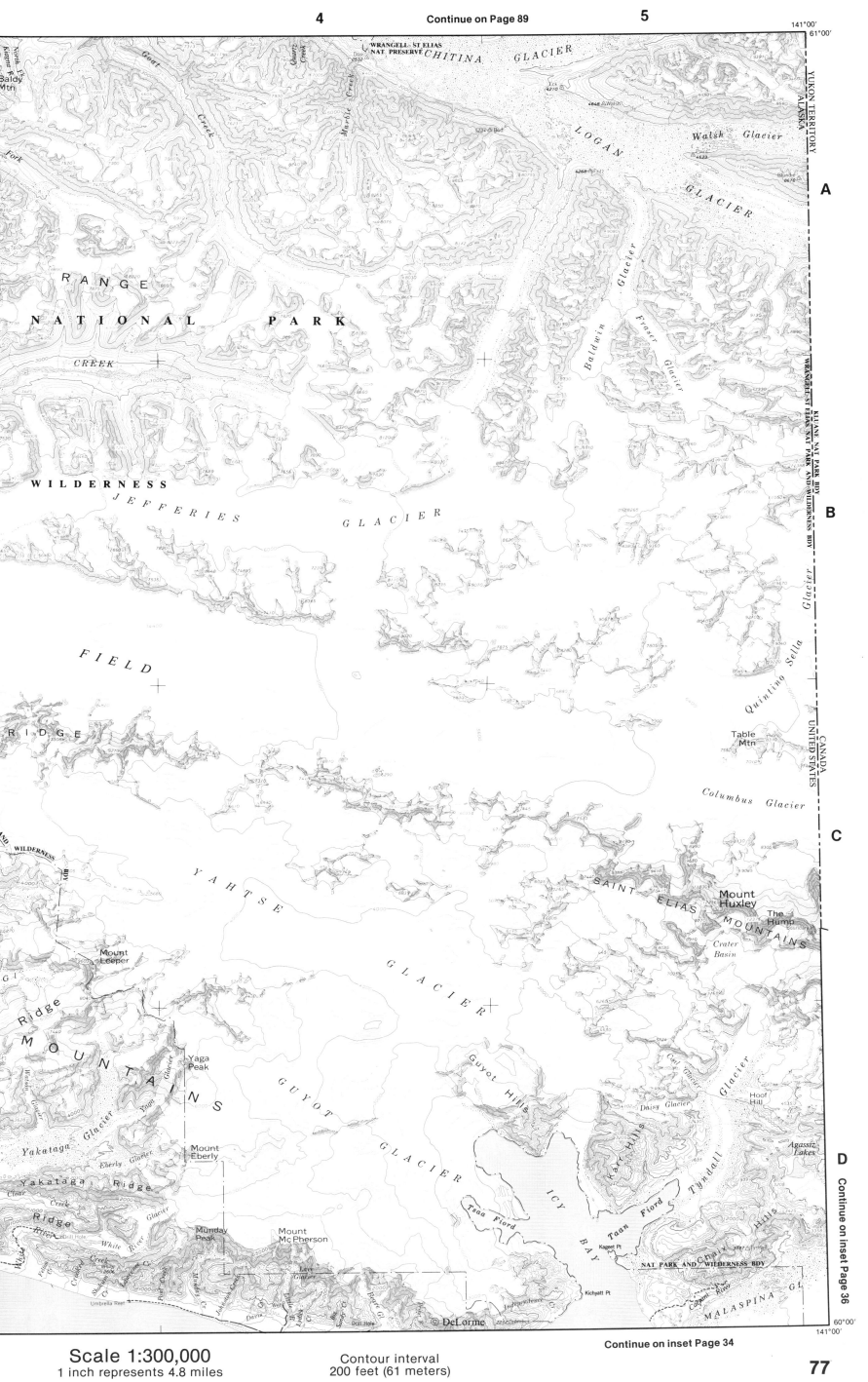

141°00'
61°00'

YUKON TERRITORY
ALASKA

A

WRANGELL-ST ELIAS NAT PARK AND WILDERNESS BDY

KLUANE NAT PARK BDY

B

CANADA
UNITED STATES

C

D

Continue on inset Page 36

60°00'
141°00'

Continue on inset Page 34

Scale 1:300,000
1 inch represents 4.8 miles

Contour interval
200 feet (61 meters)

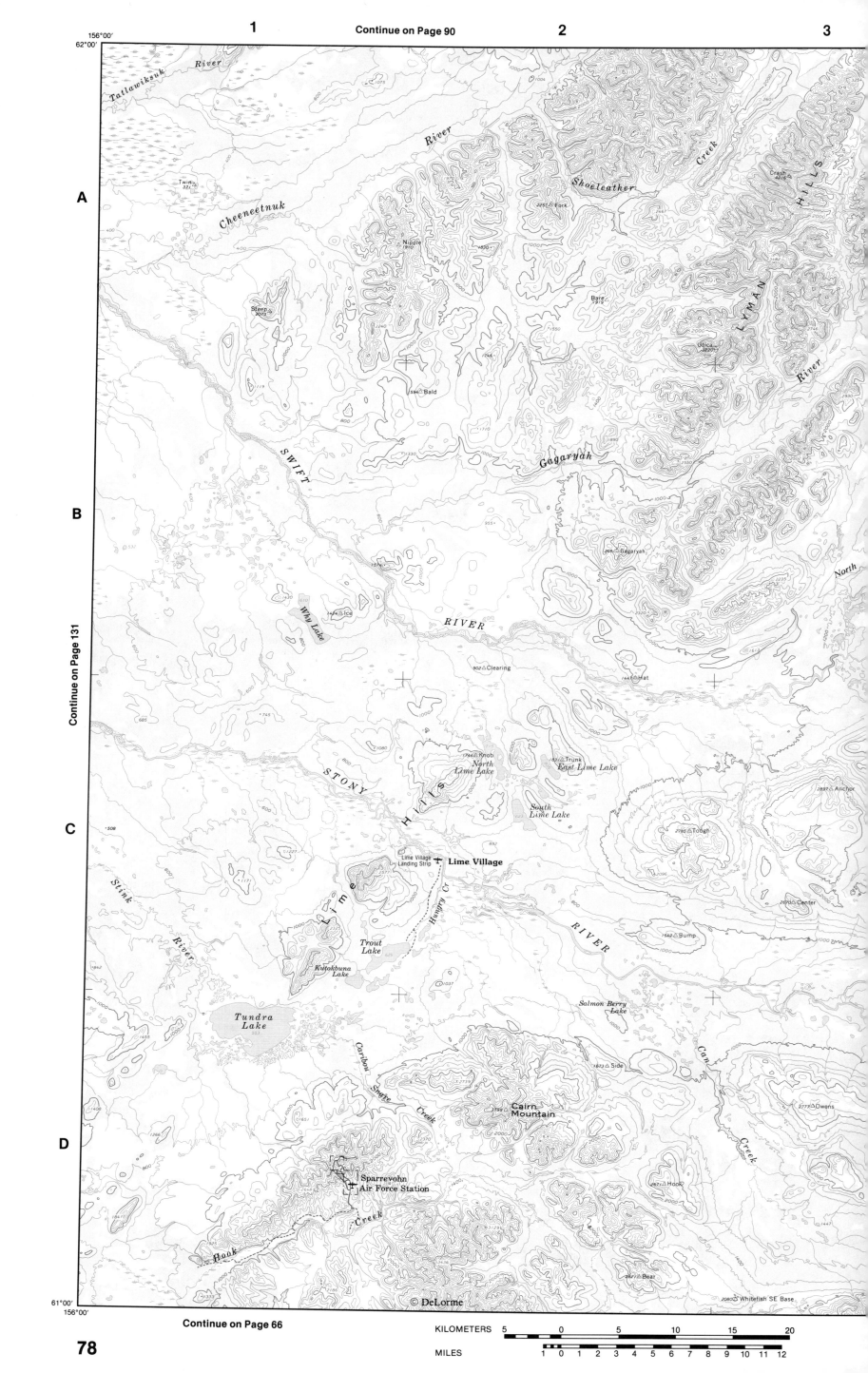

Continue on Page 131

© DeLorme

KILOMETERS   5   0   5   10   15   20

MILES   1 0 1 2 3 4 5 6 7 8 9 10 11 12

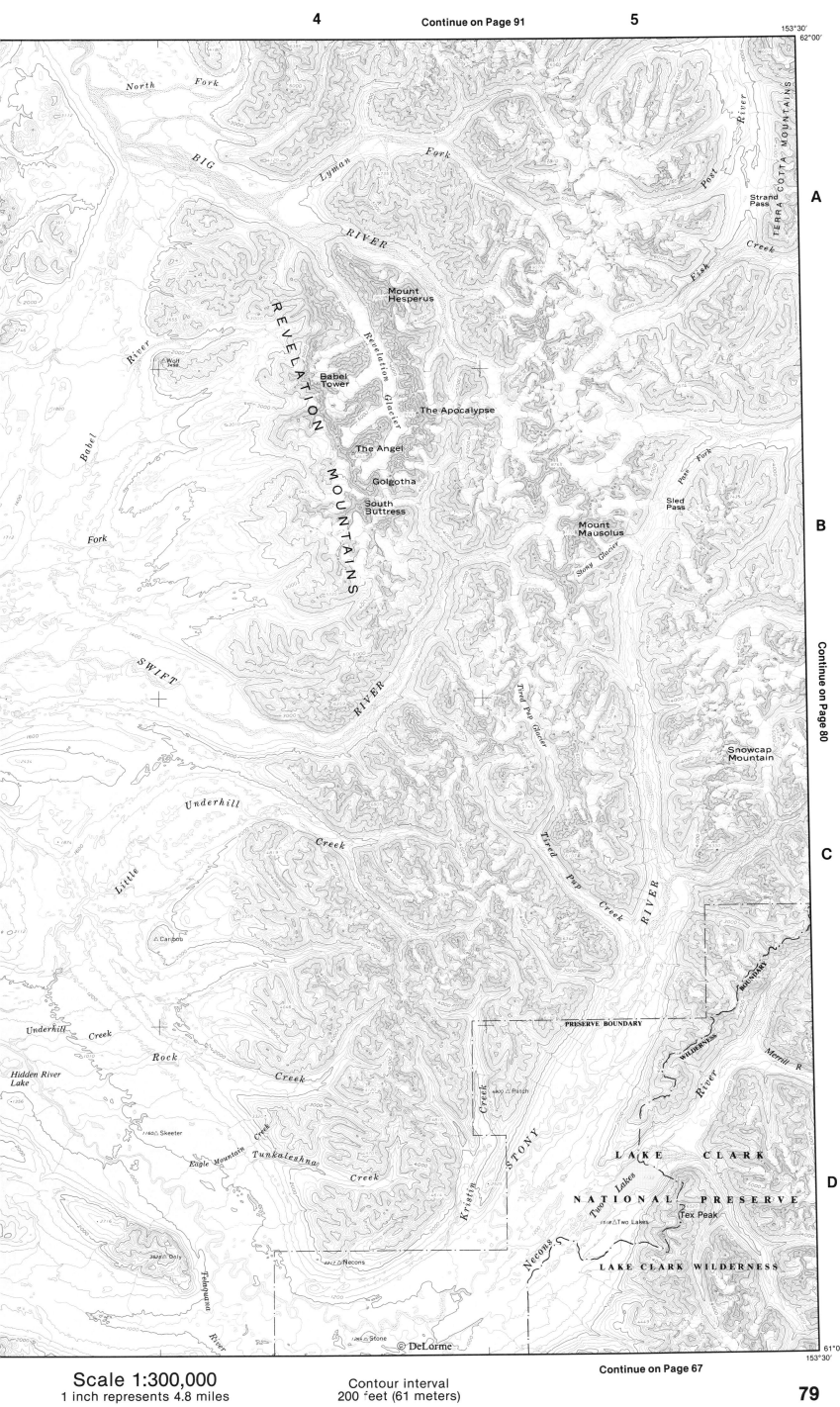

153°30'
62°00'

A

B

Continue on Page 80

C

D

61°00'
153°30'

Scale 1:300,000
1 inch represents 4.8 miles

Contour interval
200 feet (61 meters)

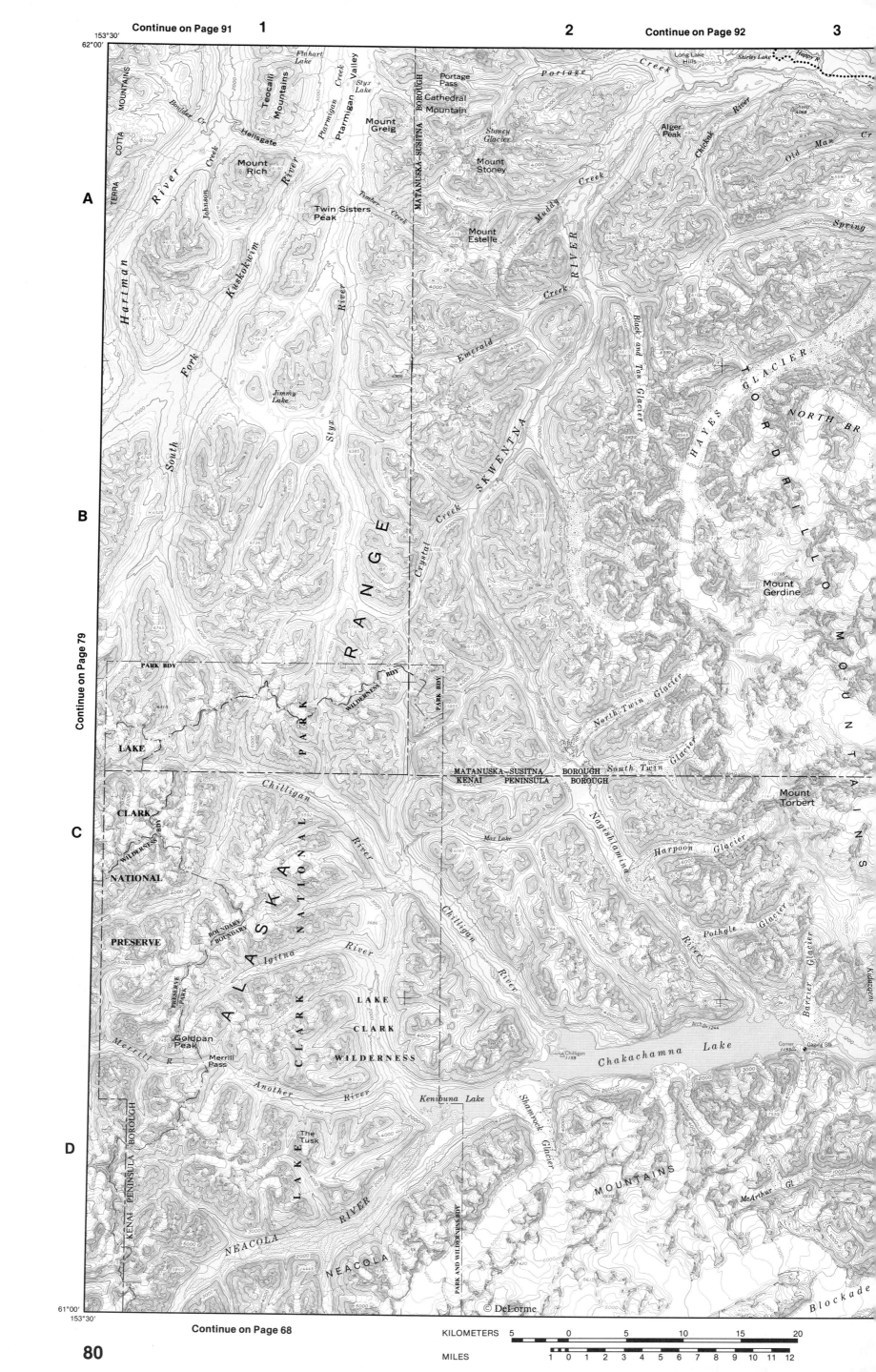

153°30'
62°00'

A

B

Continue on Page 79

C

D

61°00'
153°30'

TERRA COTTA MOUNTAINS

Hartman River

Bonilieu Cr.

Johnson Creek

Kuskokwim River

South Fork

Styx River

Jimmy Lake

Teocalli Mountains

Flinhart Lake

Ptarmigan Creek Valley

Styx Lake

Ptarmigan Creek

Mount Greig

Hellsgate

Mount Rich

Twin Sisters Peak

Timber Creek

MATANUSKA–SUSITNA BOROUGH

Portage Pass

Cathedral Mountain

Mount Stoney

Stoney Glacier

Mount Estelle

Emerald Creek

Crystal Creek

SKWENTNA RIVER

Maddy Creek

Portage Creek

Long Lake Hills

Shirley Lake

Happy R.

Alger Peak

Chichak River

Old Man Cr.

Spring

HAYES GLACIER

TORDRILLO MOUNTAINS

NORTH BR

Black and Tan Glacier

Mount Gerdine

North Twin Glacier

South Twin Glacier

Mount Torbert

PARK BDY

WILDERNESS BDY

PARK BDY

LAKE

PARK RANGE

MATANUSKA–SUSITNA BOROUGH
KENAI PENINSULA BOROUGH

CLARK

NATIONAL

PRESERVE

WILDERNESS BDY

BOUNDARY

PRESERVE PARK

Merrill R.

Goldpan Peak

Merrill Pass

Chilligan River

Igitna River

Another River

ALASKA

CLARK NATIONAL

LAKE CLARK WILDERNESS

The Tusk

NEACOLA RIVER

NEACOLA

Chilligan River

Max Lake

Nagishlamina

Harpoon Glacier

Pothole Glacier

River

Chakachamna Lake

Kenibuna Lake

Shamrock Glacier

MOUNTAINS

Barrier Glacier

Kidazqeni

McArthur Gl.

Blockade

© DeLorme

Continue on Page 68

KILOMETERS   5   0   5   10   15   20

MILES   1   0   1   2   3   4   5   6   7   8   9   10   11   12

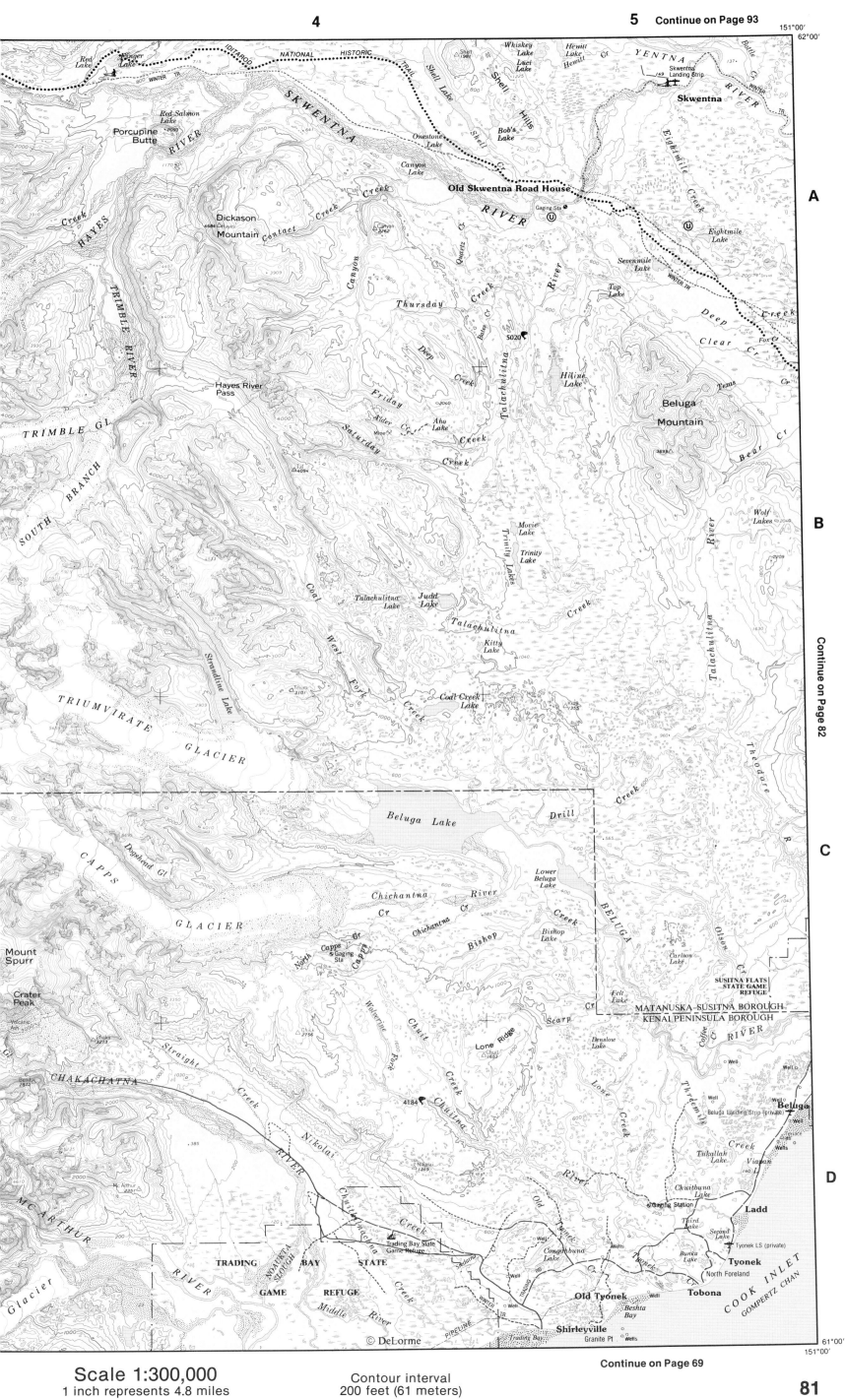

151°00'
62°00'

A

B

Continue on Page 82

C

D

61°00'
151°00'

Continue on Page 69

Scale 1:300,000
1 inch represents 4.8 miles

Contour interval
200 feet (61 meters)

© DeLorme

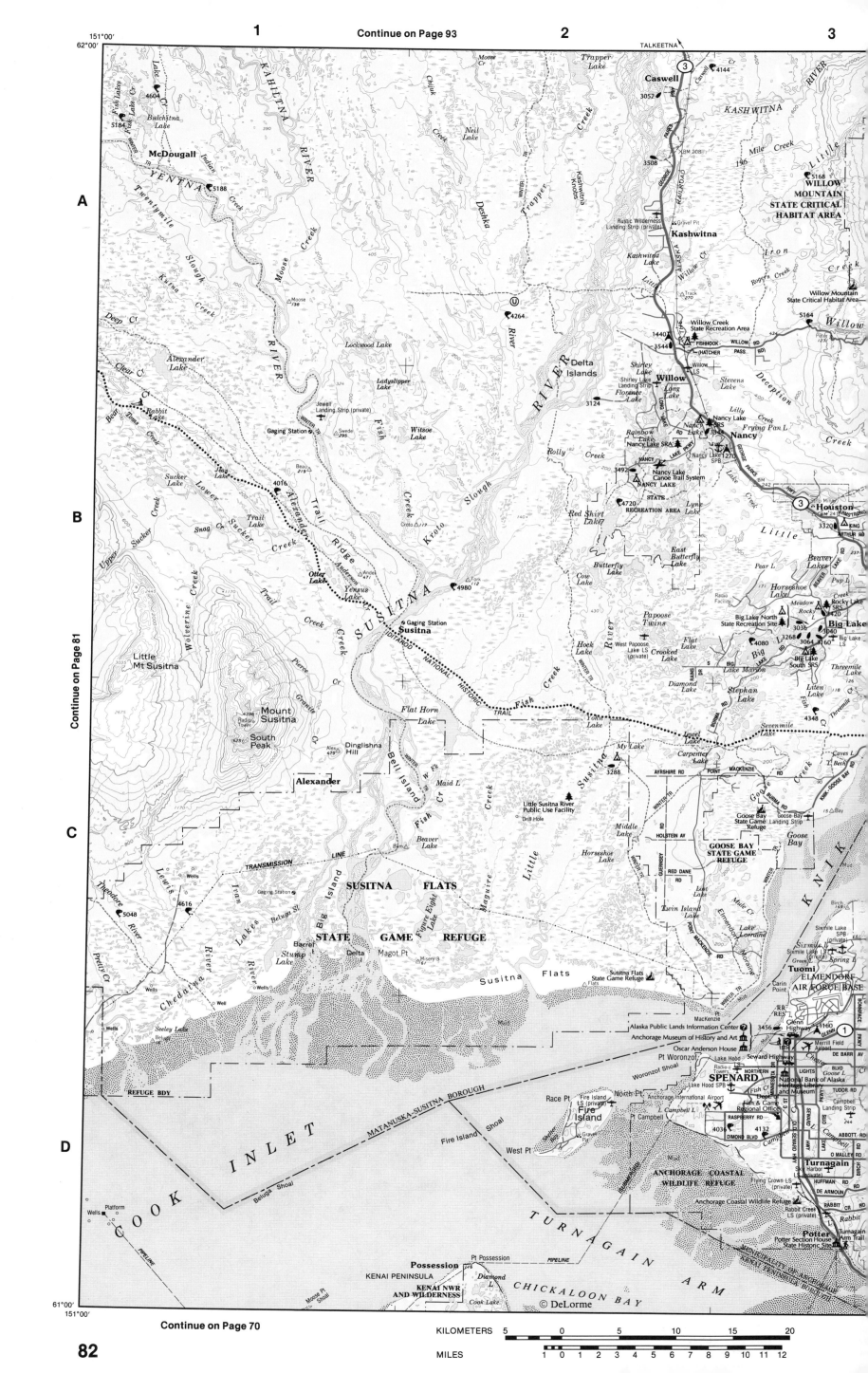

Continue on Page 93

Continue on Page 81

151°00'
62°00'

A

B

C

D

61°00'
151°00'

KILOMETERS   5   0   5   10   15   20

MILES   1 0 1 2 3 4 5 6 7 8 9 10 11 12

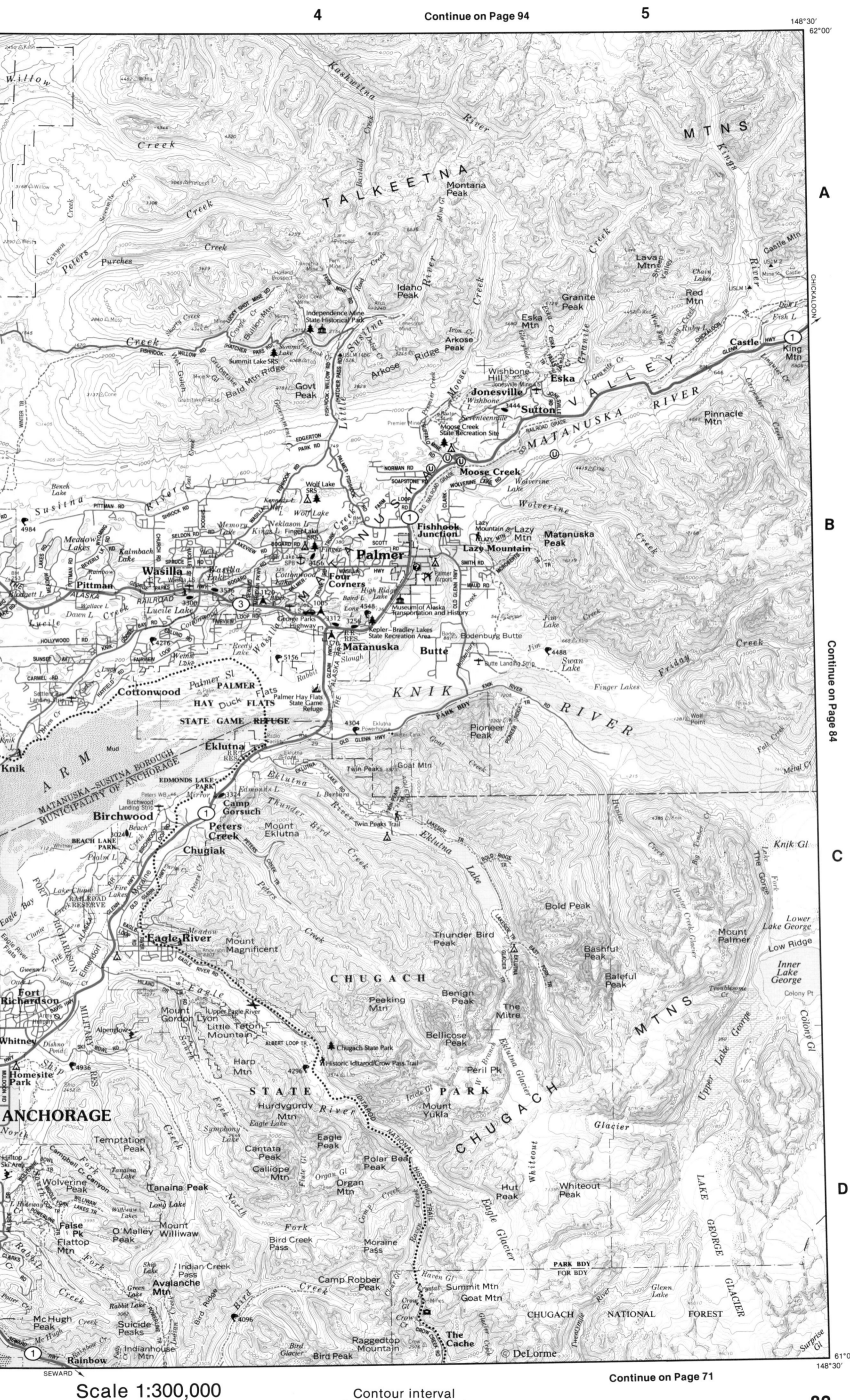

Continue on Page 94

Continue on Page 84

Continue on Page 71

Scale 1:300,000
1 inch represents 4.8 miles

Contour interval
200 feet (61 meters)

© DeLorme

83

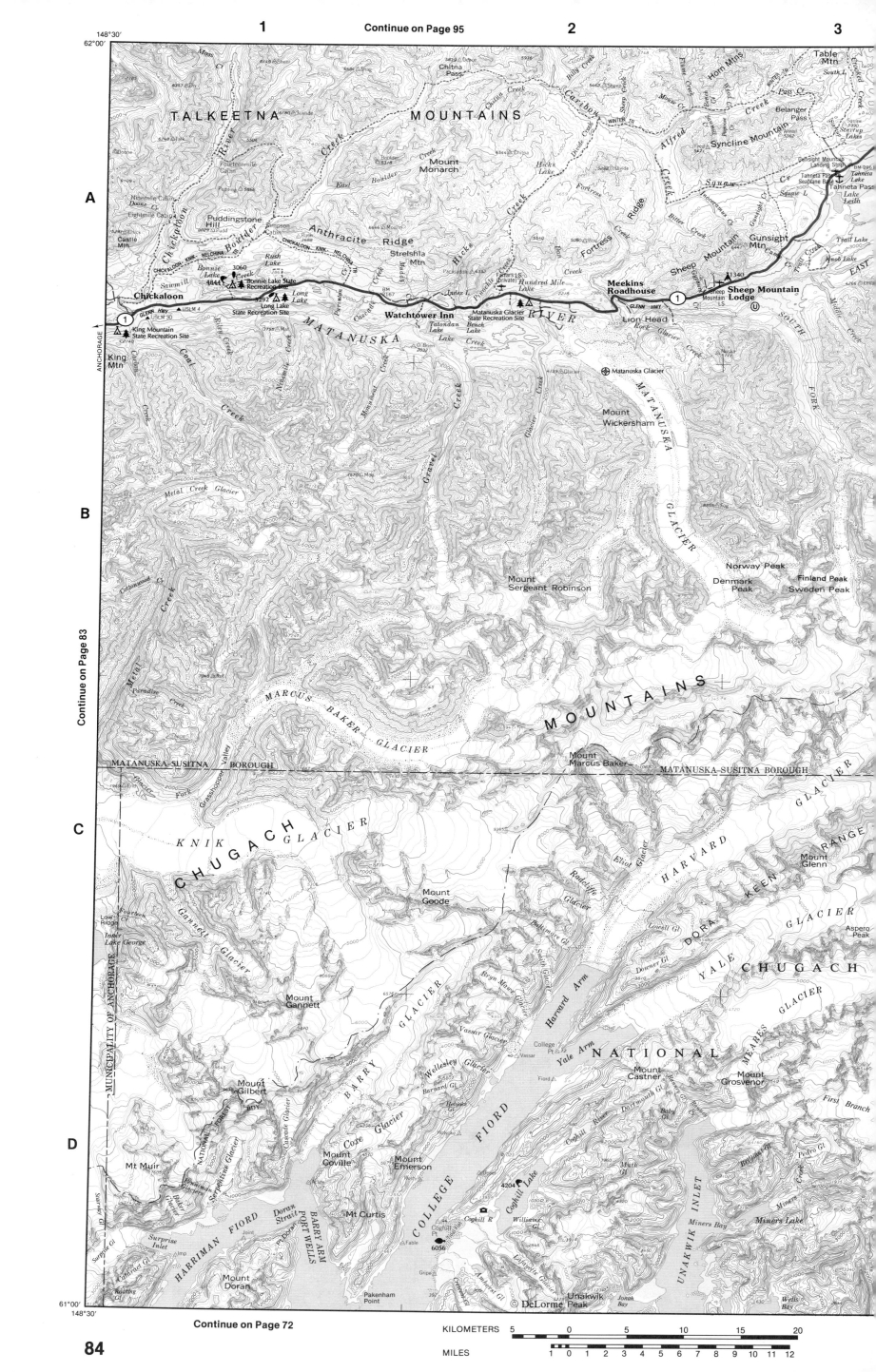

Continue on Page 95

1   **2**   **3**

148°30'
62°00'

TALKEETNA   MOUNTAINS

A

Puddingstone
Hill

Anthracite   Ridge

Strelshla
Mtn

Chickaloon

Bonnie
Lake

Mount
Monarch

Chitna
Pass

Billy Creek

Syncline Mountain

Horn Mtns

Table
Mtn

Belanger
Pass

Meekins
Roadhouse

Sheep Mountain
Lodge

Watchtower Inn

Long Lake
State Recreation Site

King Mountain
State Recreation Site

King
Mtn

ANCHORAGE

Lion Head

Mount
Wickersham

MATANUSKA   RIVER

Matanuska Glacier

B

Metal Creek Glacier

MATANUSKA

Mount
Sergeant Robinson

Norway Peak

Denmark
Peak

Finland Peak
Sweden Peak

GLACIER

Continue on Page 83

MARCUS   BAKER   GLACIER

M   O   U   N   T   A   I   N   S

Mount
Marcus Baker

MATANUSKA–SUSITNA BOROUGH

MATANUSKA–SUSITNA BOROUGH

C

KNIK   CHUGACH   GLACIER

CHUGACH

Mount
Goode

Radcliffe
Glacier

HARVARD

GLACIER

Mount
Glenn

KEEN   RANGE

DORA

Aspero
Peak

CHUGACH

Gannett
Glacier

Mount
Gannett

GLACIER

Vassar Glacier

Wellesley Glacier

Barnard Gl

College
Pt

Harvard Arm

YALE

GLACIER

MEARES

Mount
Gilbert

Coxe
Glacier

Barry
Glacier

N A T I O N A L

Mount
Castner

Mount
Grosvenor

MUNICIPALITY OF ANCHORAGE

D

Mt Muir

NATIONAL   FOREST

Mount
Coville

Mount
Emerson

Mt Curtis

4204

Coghill Lake

F I O R D

COLLEGE

Coghill
Pt

6056

UNAKWIK   INLET

Miners Bay

Miners Lake

HARRIMAN   FIORD

Doran
Strait

Mount
Doran

BARRY ARM
PORT WELLS

Surprise Inlet

Pakenham
Point

Unakwik
Bay

Jonah
Bay

Wells
Bay

© DeLorme
Peak

61°00'
148°30'

KILOMETERS   5   0   5   10   15   20

MILES   1 0 1 2 3 4 5 6 7 8 9 10 11 12

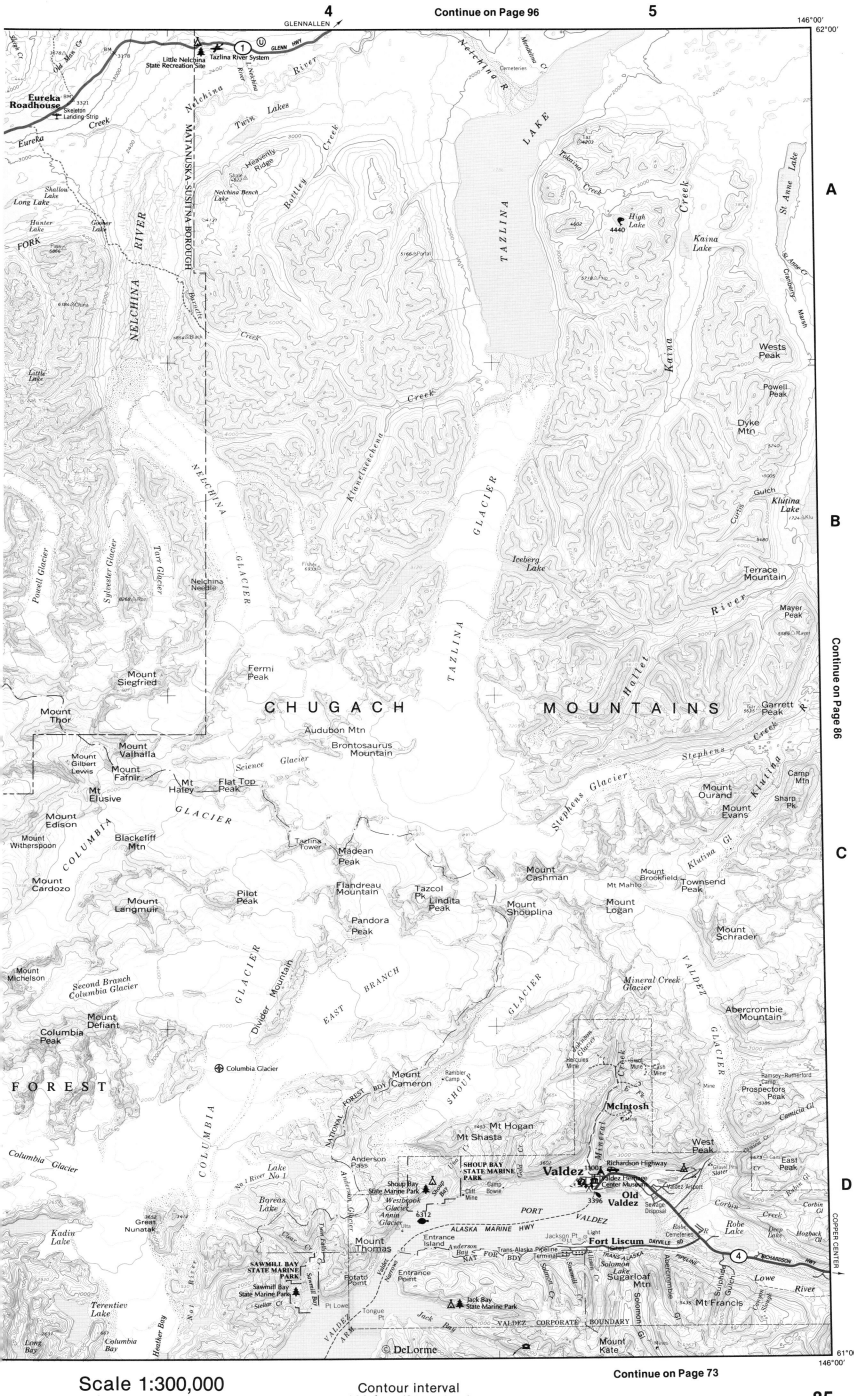

Continue on Page 86

Continue on Page 73

Scale 1:300,000
1 inch represents 4.8 miles

Contour interval
200 feet (61 meters)

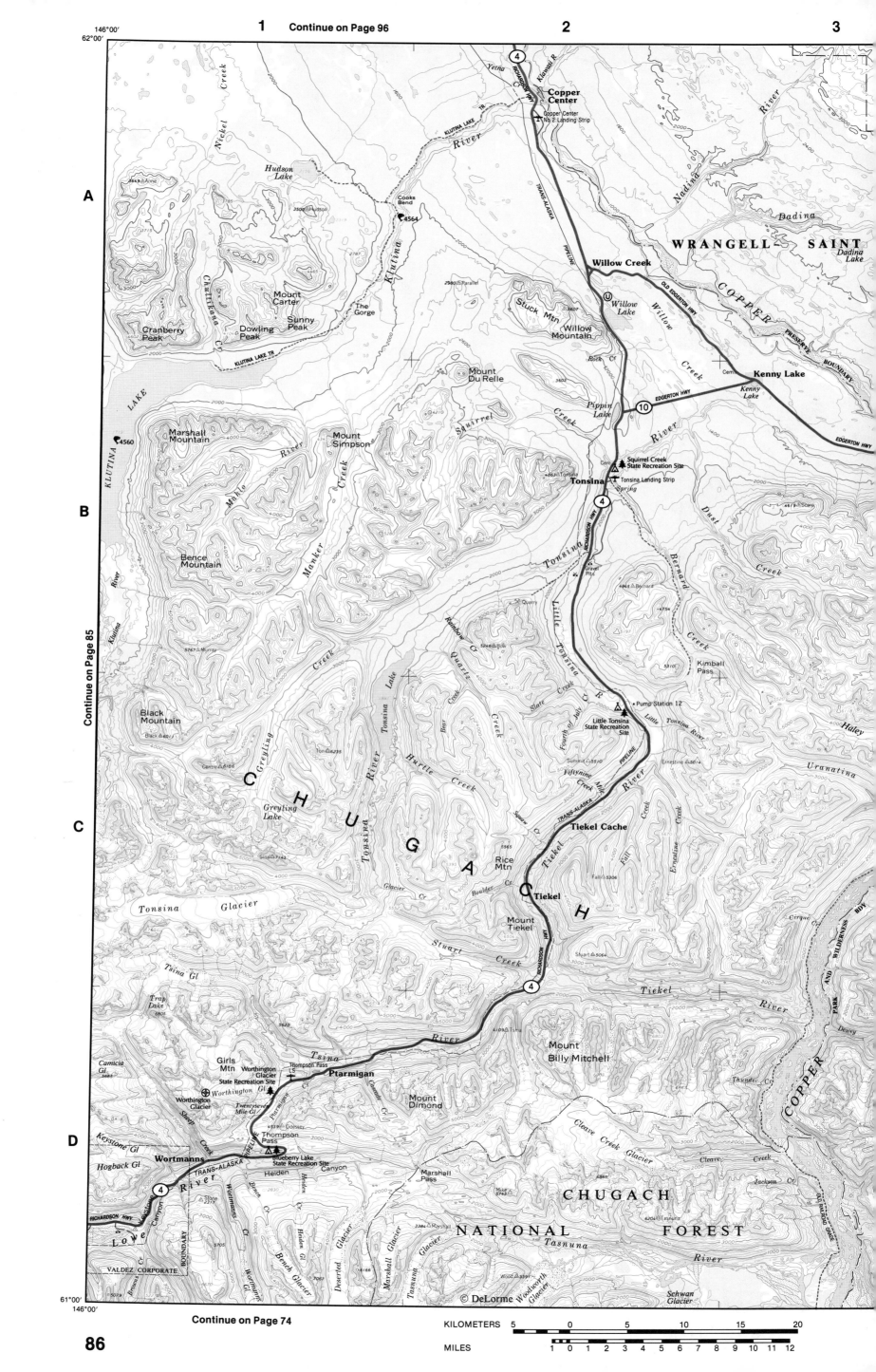

146°00'
62°00'

A

B

Continue on Page 85

C

D

61°00'
146°00'

© DeLorme Woodworth

KILOMETERS   5   0   5   10   15   20

MILES   1 0 1 2 3 4 5 6 7 8 9 10 11 12

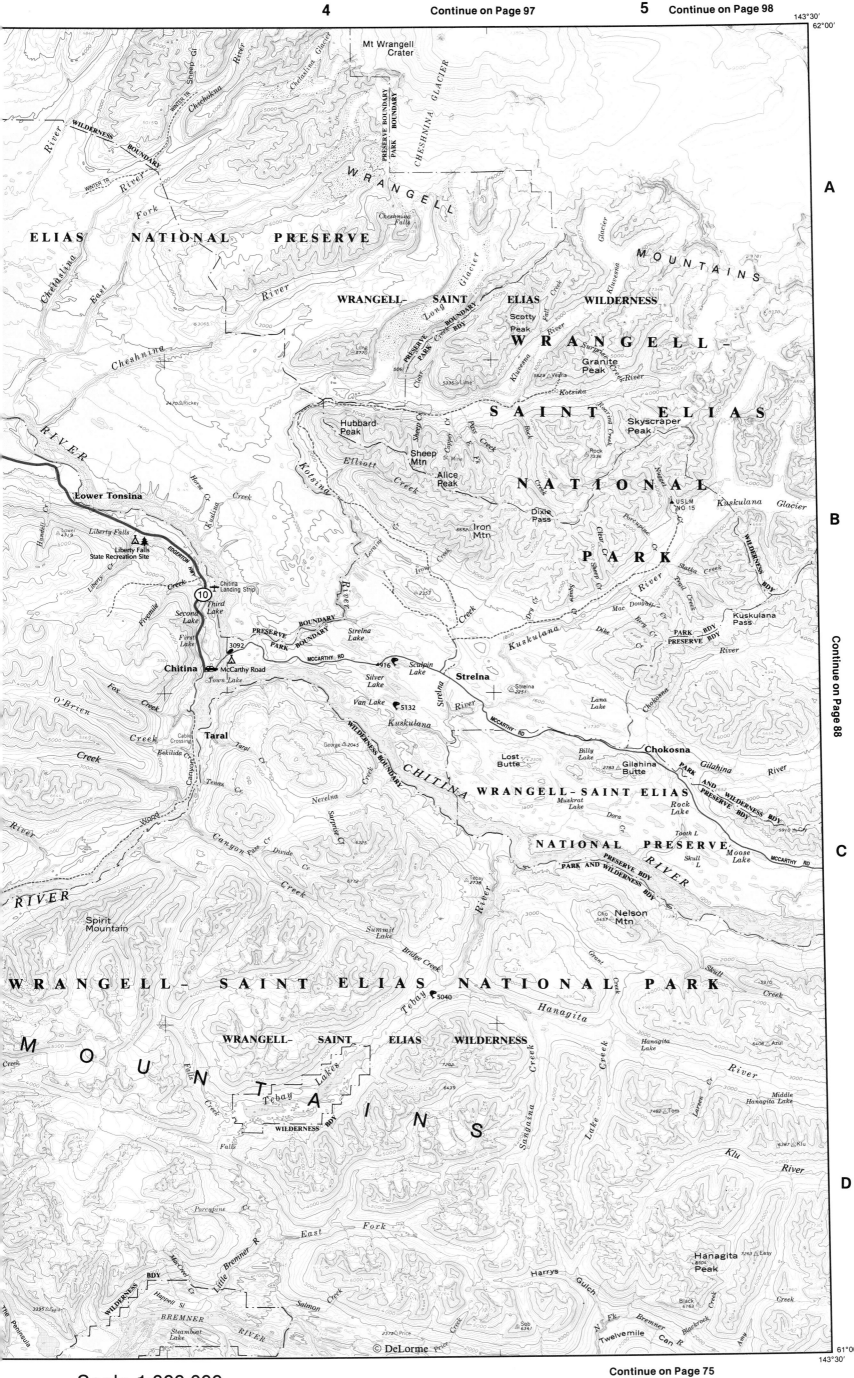

Continue on Page 88

Continue on Page 75

Scale 1:300,000
1 inch represents 4.8 miles

Contour interval
200 feet (61 meters)

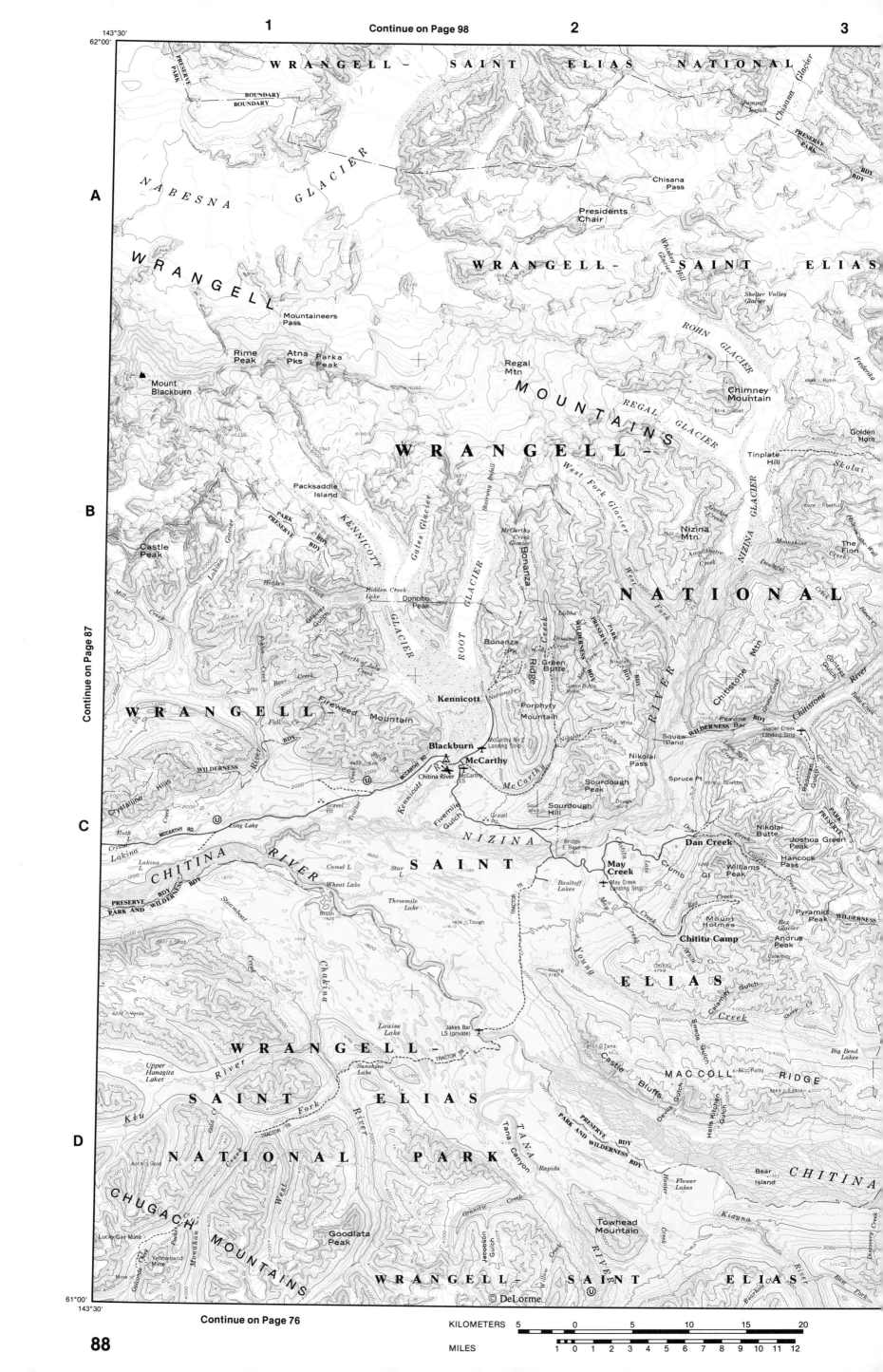

Continue on Page 87

KILOMETERS 5   0   5   10   15   20

MILES   1 0 1 2 3 4 5 6 7 8 9 10 11 12

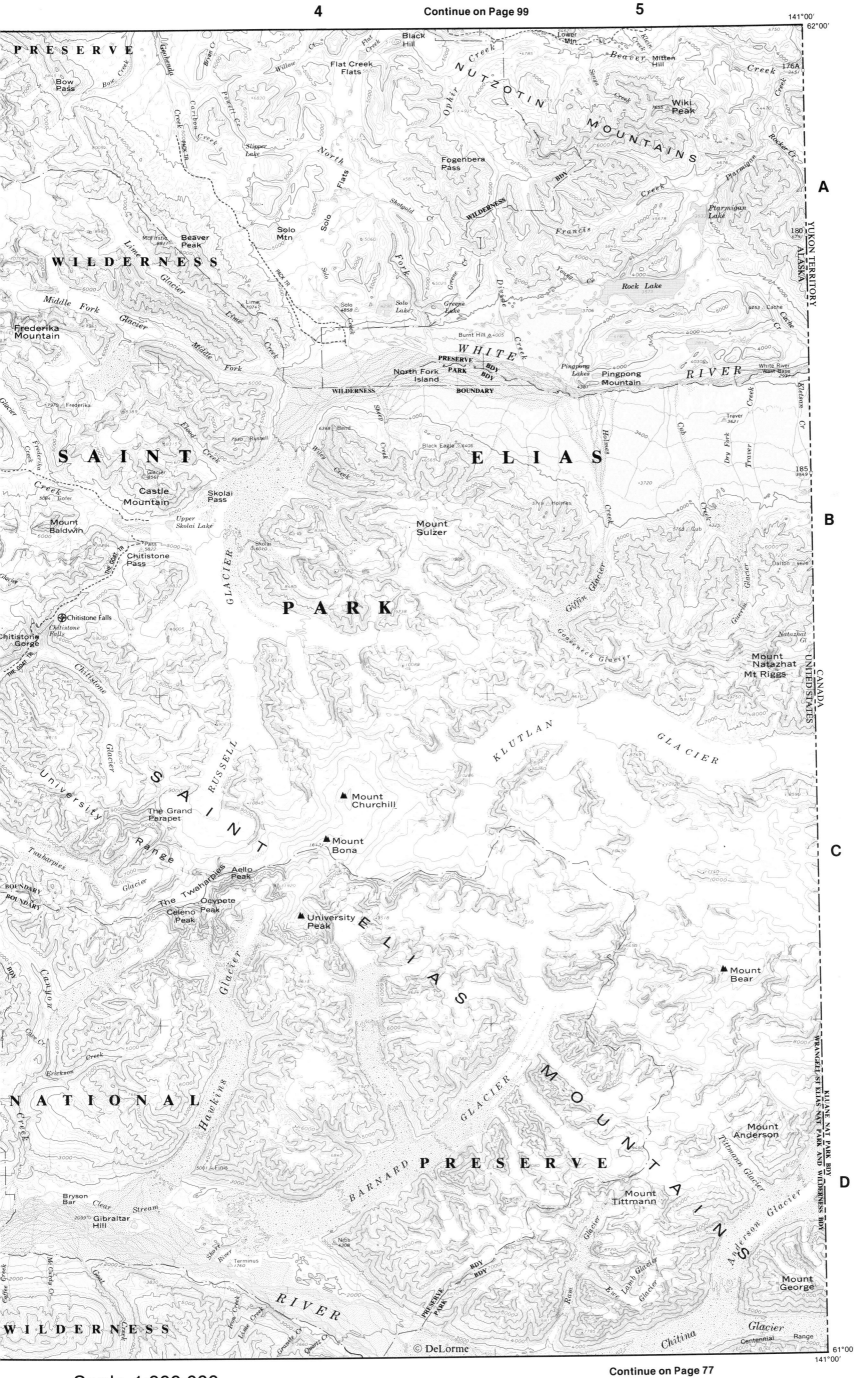

141°00'
62°00'

PRESERVE

Bow
Pass

WILDERNESS

Beaver
Peak

Middle Fork

Frederika
Mountain

SAINT

Castle
Mountain

Mount
Baldwin

Chitistone
Pass

Chitistone Falls

Chitistone
Gorge

NUTZOTIN

Black
Hill

Flat Creek
Flats

Lower
Mtn

Beaver

Mitten
Hill

Wiki
Peak

MOUNTAINS

176A

Fogenbera
Pass

WILDERNESS

Ptarmigan
Lake

Solo
Mtn

Solo
Flats

Francis

Rock Lake

YUKON TERRITORY
ALASKA

180

A

Solo
Lake

Greene
Lake

Burnt Hill

Pingpong
Lakes

Pingpong
Mountain

WHITE

RIVER

White River
West Base

North Fork
Island

PRESERVE
PARK
BDY
BDY

WILDERNESS   **BOUNDARY**

185

Russell

Bend

Black Eagle

ELIAS

Holmes

Traver

Dry Fork

Skolai
Pass

Upper
Skolai Lake

Skolai

Mount
Sulzer

B

GLACIER

PARK

Giffin Glacier

Gooseneck Glacier

Mount
Natazhat
Mt Riggs

SAINT

University

Range

The Grand
Parapet

Twaharpies

Mount
Churchill

Mount
Bona

KLUTLAN

GLACIER

CANADA
UNITED STATES

C

Aello
Peak

The Twaharpies
Ocypete
Peak
Celeno
Peak

University
Peak

ELIAS

Mount
Bear

BOUNDARY
BOUNDARY

Russell Glacier

Hawkins

NATIONAL

Canyon

MOUNTAINS

Mount
Anderson

KLUANE NAT PARK BDY
WRANGELL-ST ELIAS NAT PARK AND WILDERNESS BDY

D

Bryson
Bar

Gibraltar
Hill

BARNARD   **PRESERVE**

Mount
Tittman

Terminus

RIVER

WILDERNESS

BDY
BDY

PRESERVE
PARK

© DeLorme

Chitina

Anderson Glacier

Mount
George

Glacier

Range

61°00'
141°00'

Scale 1:300,000
1 inch represents 4.8 miles

Contour interval
200 feet (61 meters)

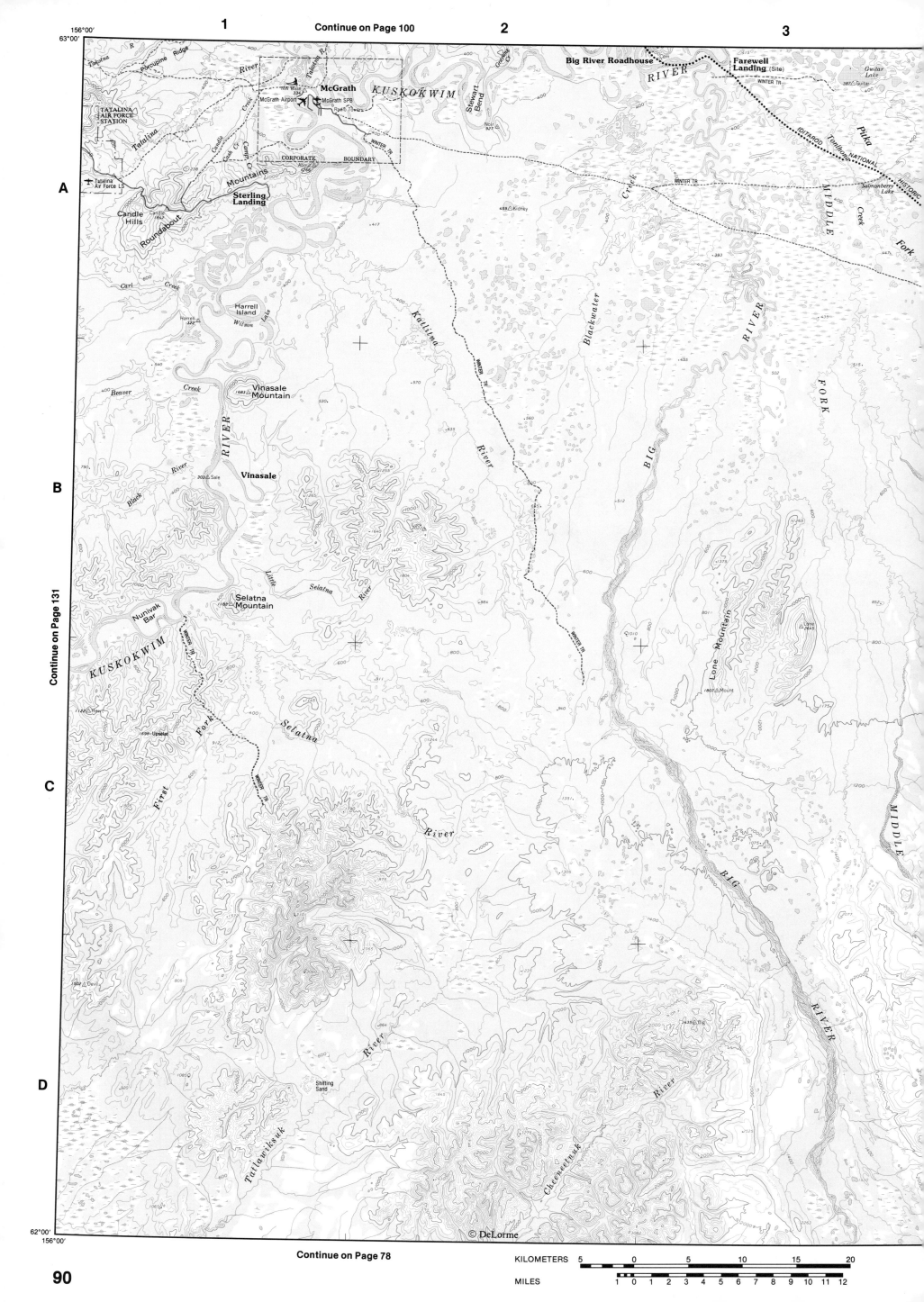

156°00'
63°00'

R
Tatalna
Porcupine Ridge
River
Tagount R.
Big River Roadhouse
RIVER
Farewell
Landing (Site)
Guitar
Lake
Guitar
Goodnews Cr
NW Base 334
McGrath
Tatalna
KUSKOKWIM
WINTER TR
McGrath Airport
McGrath SPB
Stewart
Bend
IDITAROD
NATIONAL
Tonzona
Pitka
TATALINA
AIR FORCE
STATION
Candle
Creek
Gold Cr
Camp
Radio Tower
Noir
927
HISTORIC
Salmonberry
Lake
MIDDLE
WINTER TR
238
CORPORATE   BOUNDARY
About
1266
WINTER TR
459△Kidney
WINTER TR
Creek

A

Tatalina
Air Force LS
Mountains
Sterling
Landing
Candle
Creek 1642
417
Blackwater
393
Creek
447
Candle
Hills
Roundabout

Carl
Creek
600
Beaver
Creek
Katlitna
Harrell Island
Lake
459
455
Harrell
322
Wilson
570
560
502
515

B

540
400
RIVER
Vinasale
Mountain
1683
530
635
RIVER
BIG
600
512
790
River
300△Sale
Vinasale
1265
645
852
Black
1230
1400
800
FORK
1375

Nunivak
Bar
Little
Selatna
River
1264
801
1807△Mount
Lone
Mount

C

KUSKOKWIM
Selatna
Mountain
1182
1640
1807
911
800
940
1175
1010
1200

First
Fork
1122△Heart
1698 Upsini
Selatna
912
1351
800
800
1205
1075
1200

D

1502△Devil
1876
River
265
1235
1400
Big
2000
Shifting
Sand
845
Tatlawiksuk
River
Cheeneetnuk
2000

62°00'
156°00'

© DeLorme

KILOMETERS   5   0   5   10   15   20

MILES   1 0 1 2 3 4 5 6 7 8 9 10 11 12

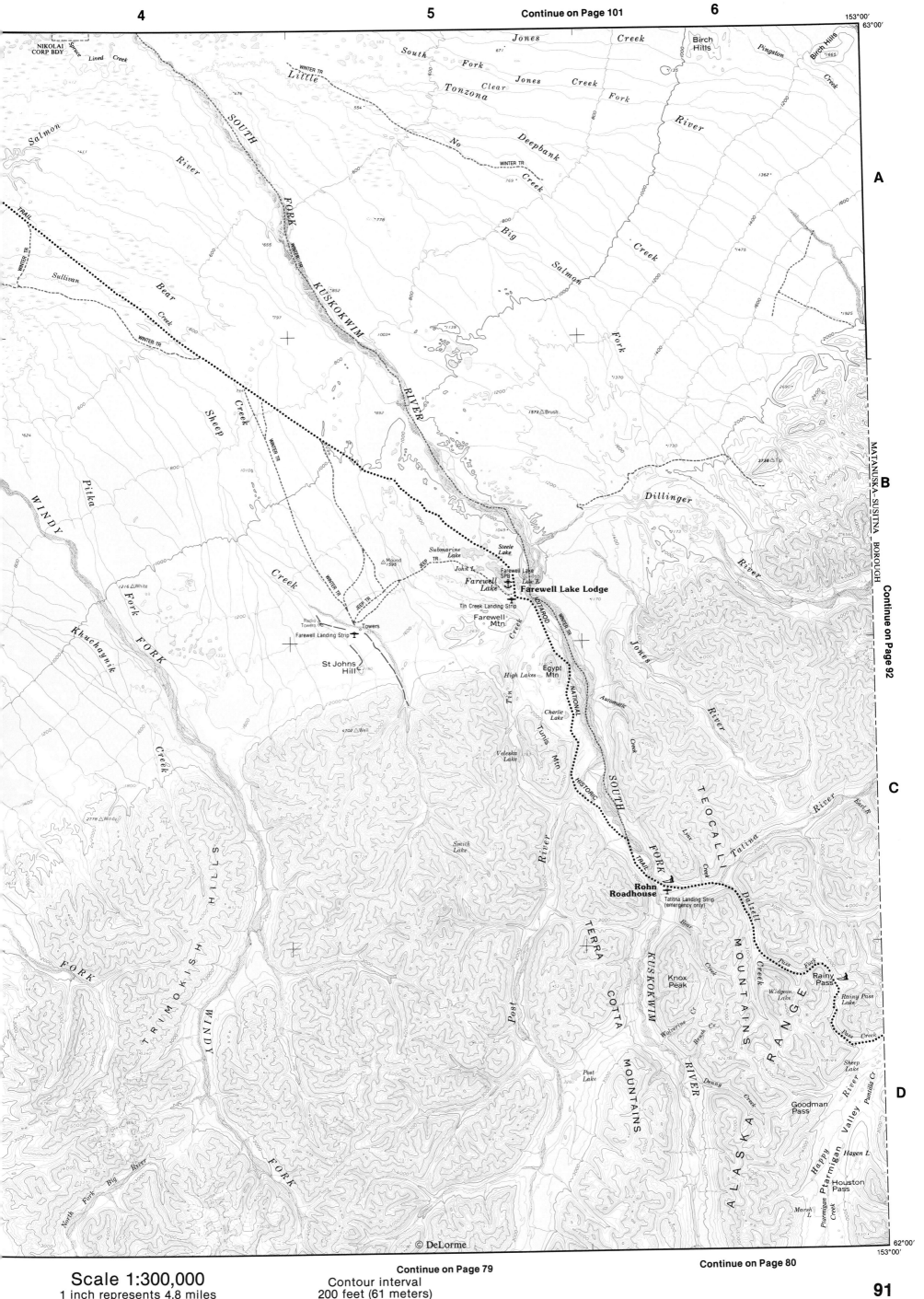

153°00'
63°00'

NIKOLAI CORP BDY

Spruce

Lined Creek

SOUTH

Salmon

River

FORK

Jones

Creek

Birch Hills

Pingston

Birch Hills
'1665

Little

South

Fork

Jones

Creek

Clear

Tonzona

Deepbank

No

Creek

Fork

River

'1362

A

WINTER TR.

KUSKOKWIM

Sullivan

Bear

Creek

WINTER TR

Sheep

Creek

WINTER TR

RIVER

Big

Salmon

Creek

Fork

'1475

'925

'370

'1573 △ Brush

'1730

B

MATANUSKA-SUSITNA BOROUGH

Continue on Page 92

WINDY

Pitka

Fork

WINTER TR

Creek

Submarine Lake

Steele Lake

Dillinger

River

3738 △ Tip

'2690

Khuchapnik

FORK

White

Mound

JEEP TR

John L

Farewell Lake

Farewell Lake Lodge

Radio Towers

Farewell Landing Strip

Towers

Tin Creek Landing Strip

Farewell Mtn

Jones

Creek

Automatic

Creek

St Johns Hill

High Lakes

Egypt Mtn

Charlie Lake

NATIONAL

HISTORIC

TEOCALLI

River

TRIMOKISH HILLS

Windy

Creek

Well

Veleska Lake

Tunis Mtn

SOUTH

Lyn

Creek

Tatina

River

East R

C

Windy

Smith Lake

River

FORK

Trail

Rohn Roadhouse

Tatina Landing Strip (emergency only)

Bear

MOUNTAINS

DALZELL

FORK

WINDY

FORK

Post

TERRA

COTTA

Knox Peak

Widgeon Lake

KUSKOKWIM

Creek

Park

Pass

RANGE

Rainy Pass

Rainy Pass Lake

North Fork Big River

Post Lake

MOUNTAINS

Wolverine

Brush Cr

RIVER

Denny

Creek

Pass Creek

ALASKA

Goodman Pass

Sheep Lake

Happy

Ptarmigan Valley

Pontilla Ct

Hagen L

D

Ptarmigan Creek

Marsh L

Houston Pass

62°00'
153°00'

Scale 1:300,000
1 inch represents 4.8 miles

Contour interval
200 feet (61 meters)

© DeLorme

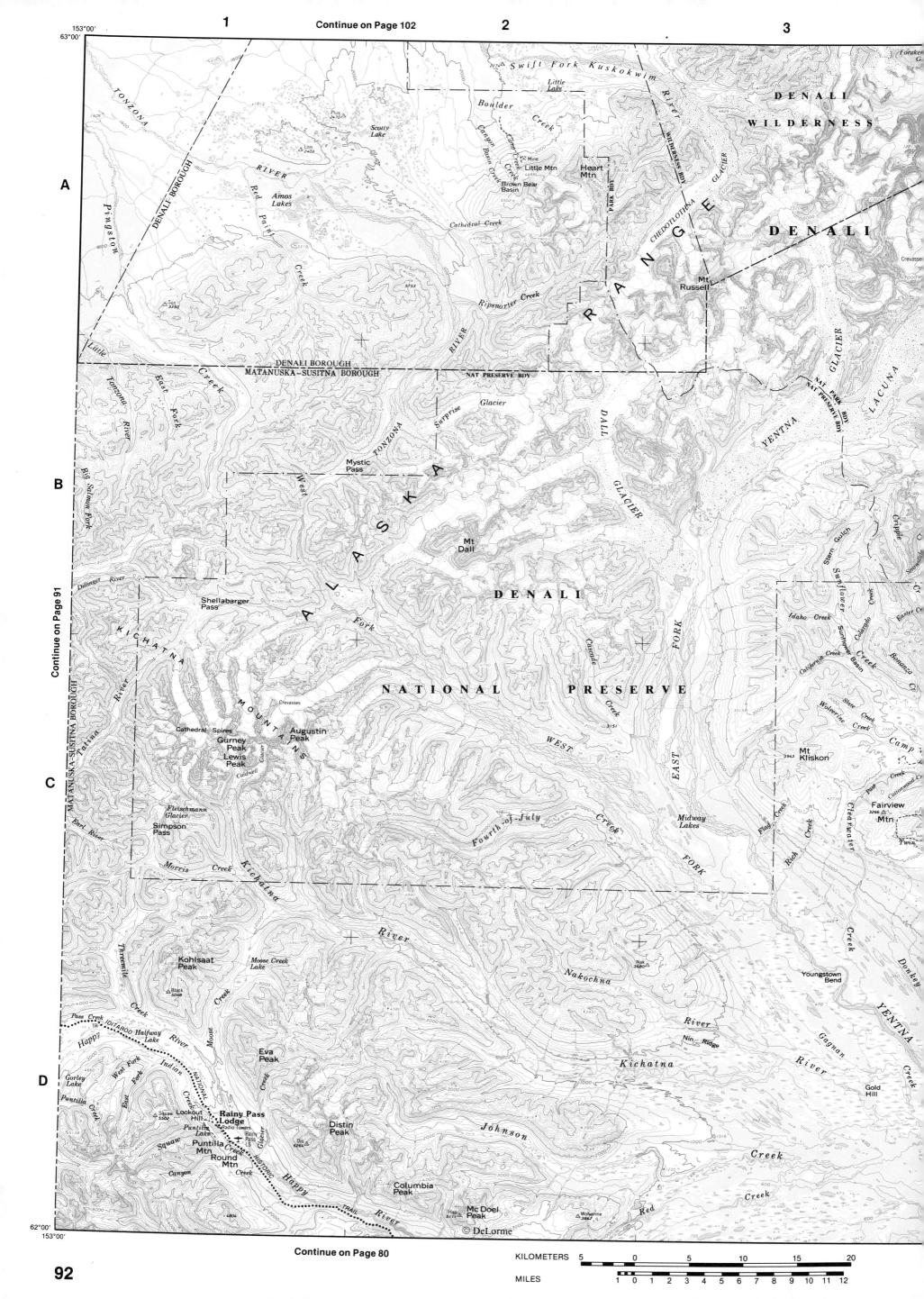

153°00'
63°00'

1 **2** **3**

A

Continue on Page 91

B

MATANUSKA–SUSITNA BOROUGH

C

D

62°00'
153°00'

92

DENALI
WILDERNESS

DENALI

TONZONA

RIVER

Pingston

Swift Fork Kuskokwim

River

Little
Lake

Boulder Creek

Scotty
Lake

Amos
Lakes

Red Paint Creek

DENALI BOROUGH

Little Mtn

Heart
Mtn

Brown Bear
Basin

Cathedral Creek

PARK BDY

WILDERNESS BDY

CHEDOTLOTHNA

GLACIER

Mt.
Russell

RANGE

Ripsnorter Creek

RIVER

DENALI BOROUGH
MATANUSKA–SUSITNA BOROUGH

NAT PRESERVE BDY

Surprise Glacier

Mystic
Pass

TONZONA

ALASKA

West Fork

Big Salmon Fork

East Fork

Tonzona River

Dillinger River

Shellabarger
Pass

Mt
Dall

DALL GLACIER

DENALI

YENTNA

NAT PARK BDY
NAT PRESERVE BDY

LACUNA

GLACIER

Stern Gulch

Cripple

KICHATNA

River

MOUNTAINS

Cathedral Spires
Gurney
Peak
Lewis
Peak

Augustin
Peak

Crevasses

Caldwell Glacier

NATIONAL

PRESERVE

Fork

WEST

Cascade Creek

EAST

FORK

FORK

Idaho Creek

California Creek

Sunflower Basin

Colorado Creek

Slate Creek

Wolverine Creek

Bonanza Cr

Easter Cr

Mt
Kliskon

Camp

Fleischmann
Glacier

Simpson
Pass

Earl River

Morris Creek

Kichatna

Fourth-of-July

Creek

Midway
Lakes

Flag Creek

Rich Creek

Pish Creek

Cled Faucter

Cottonwood Cr

Fairview
Mtn

Twin

Threemile

Kohlsaat
Peak

Black

Moose Creek
Lake

River

Moose Creek

Nak

Nakochna

Youngstown
Bend

YENTNA

Gold
Hill

Pass Creek
Happy

IDITAROD

Halfway
Lake

West Fork

Indian Creek

Gorley
Lake

Puntilla Creek

East Fork

Squaw

Lookout
Hill

Puntilla Lake

NATIONAL

Eva
Peak

Moose Creek

River

Distin
Peak

Johnson

River

Nin Ridge

Kichatna

Gagnan

River

Red Creek

Donkey Creek

Creek

Rainy Pass
Lodge
Radio Towers

Puntilla
Mtn
Round
Mtn

Squaw

Canyon

Columbia
Peak

Mc Doel
Peak

HISTORIC

Happy River

TRAIL

Wolverine

© DeLorme

KILOMETERS 5   0   5   10   15   20

MILES   1 0 1 2 3 4 5 6 7 8 9 10 11 12

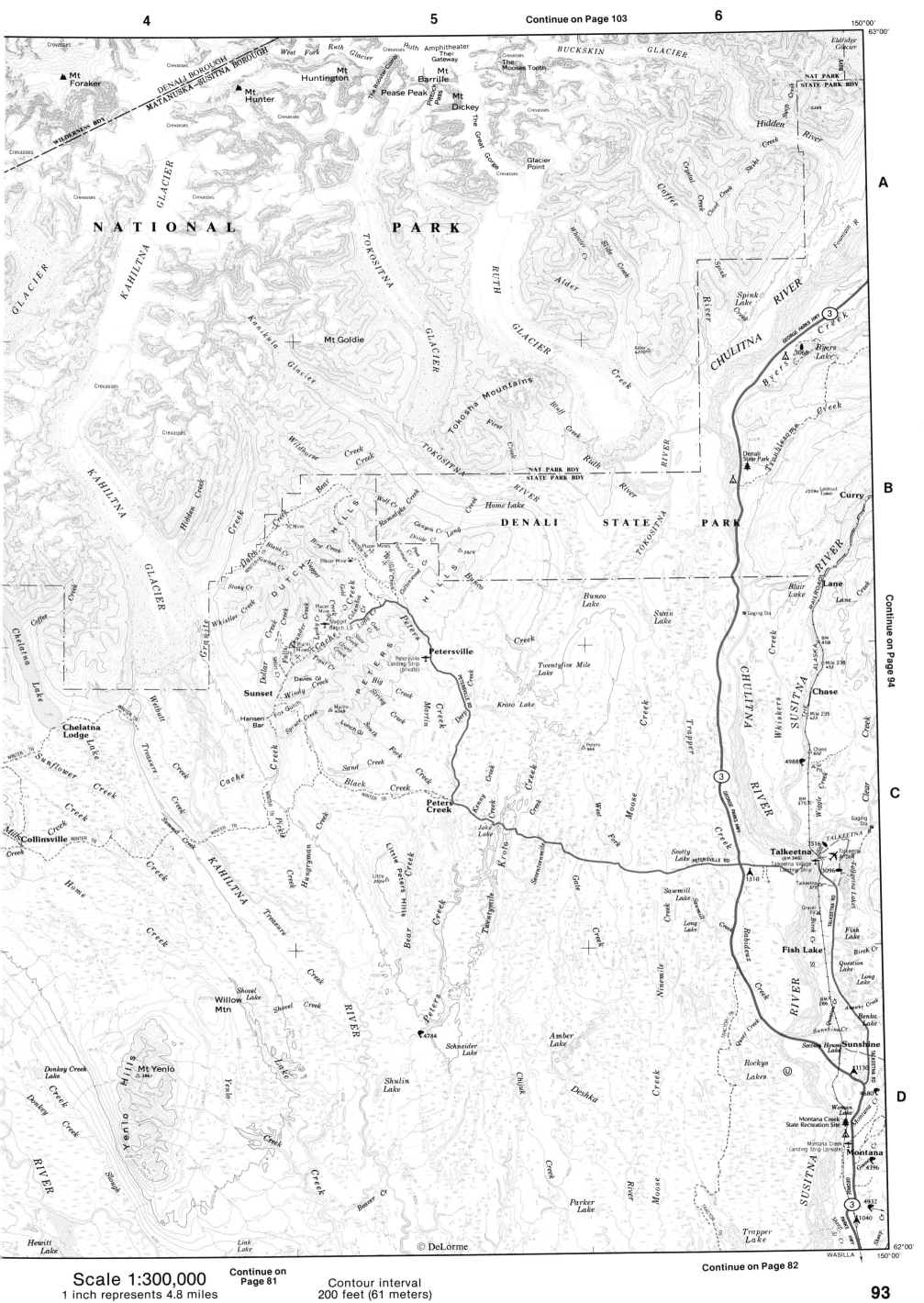

Continue on Page 103

Continue on Page 94

Continue on
Page 81

Continue on Page 82

Scale 1:300,000
1 inch represents 4.8 miles

Contour interval
200 feet (61 meters)

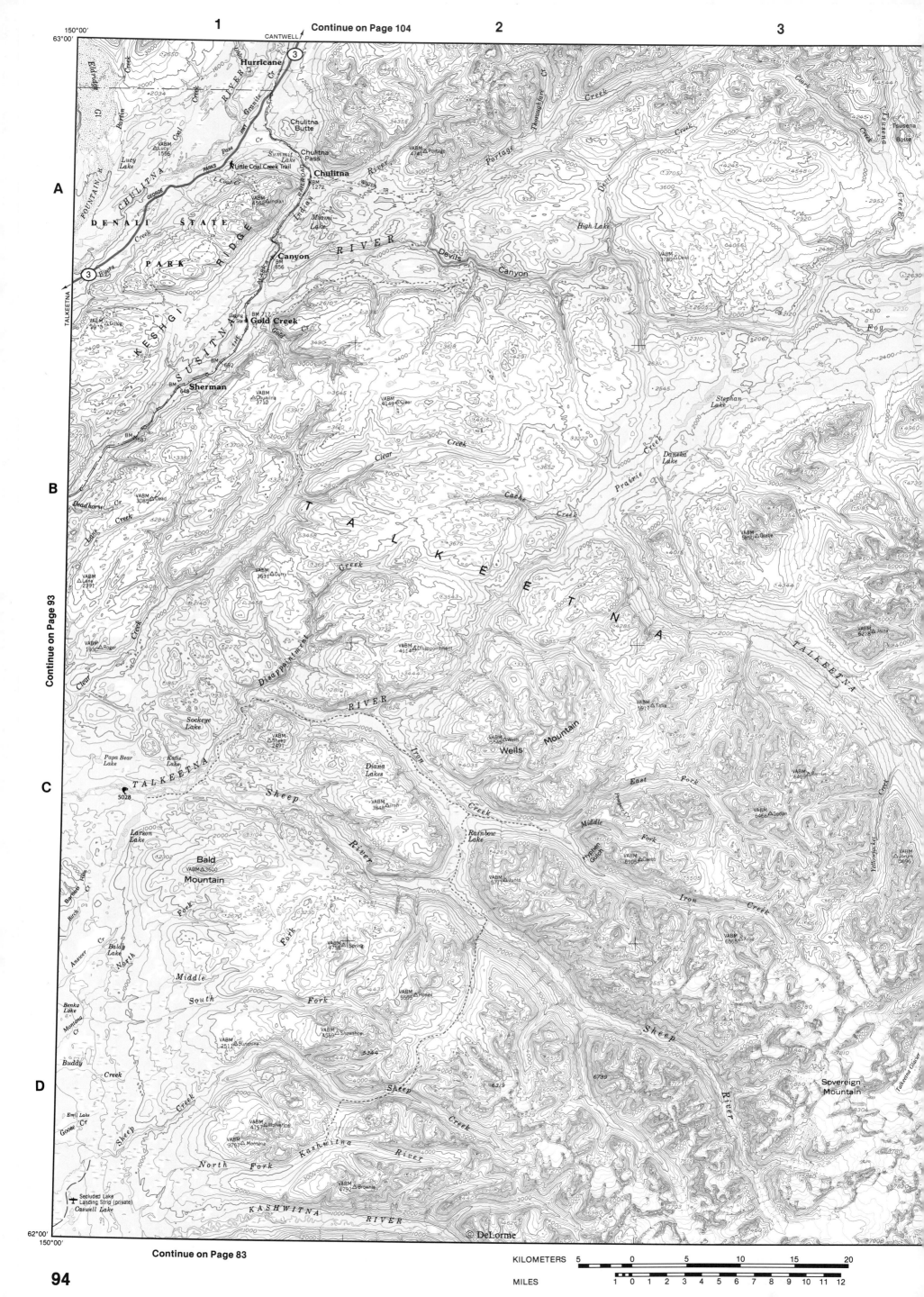

Continue on Page 93

KILOMETERS

MILES

© DeLorme

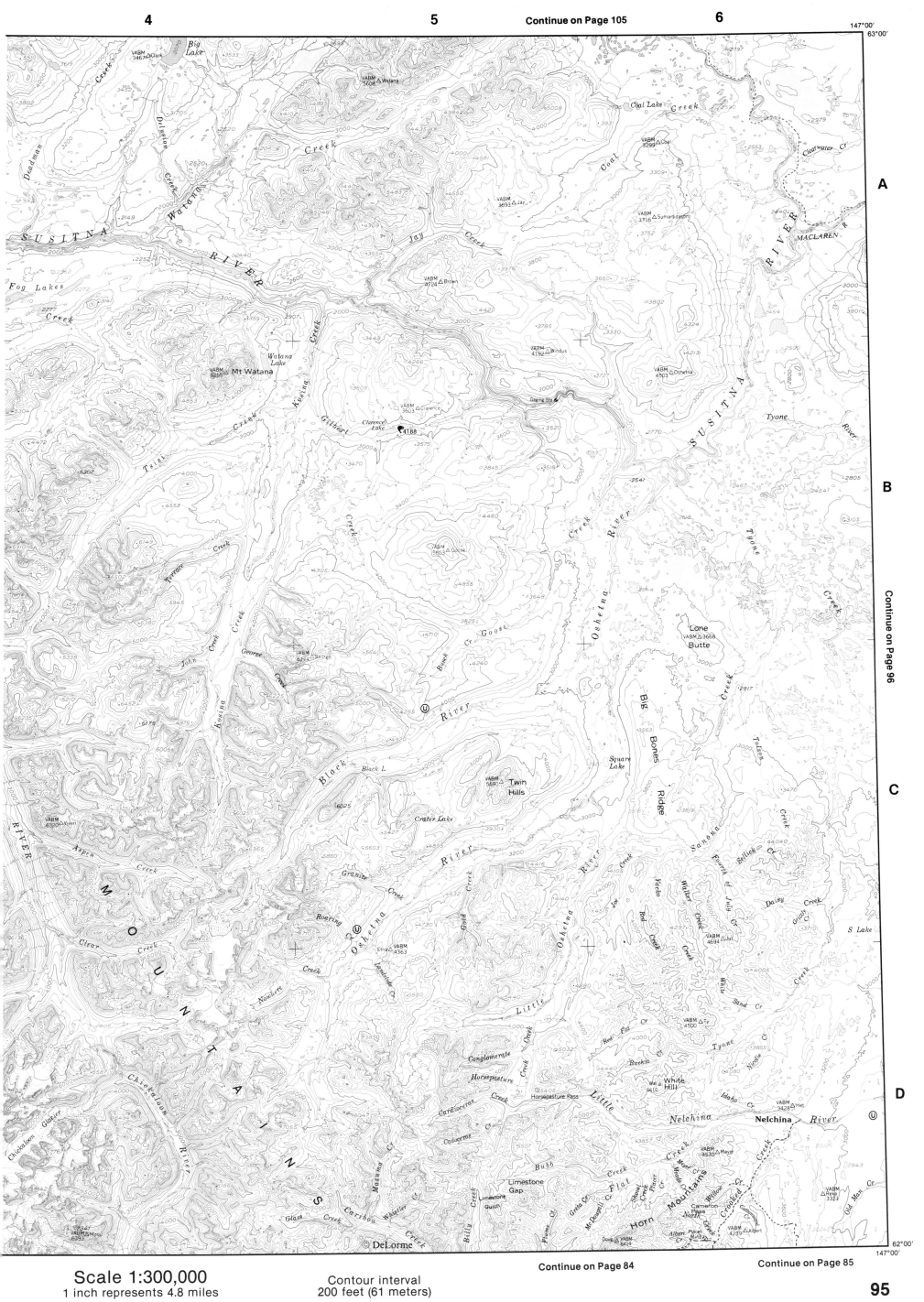

Continue on Page 96

Scale 1:300,000
1 inch represents 4.8 miles

Contour interval
200 feet (61 meters)

© DeLorme

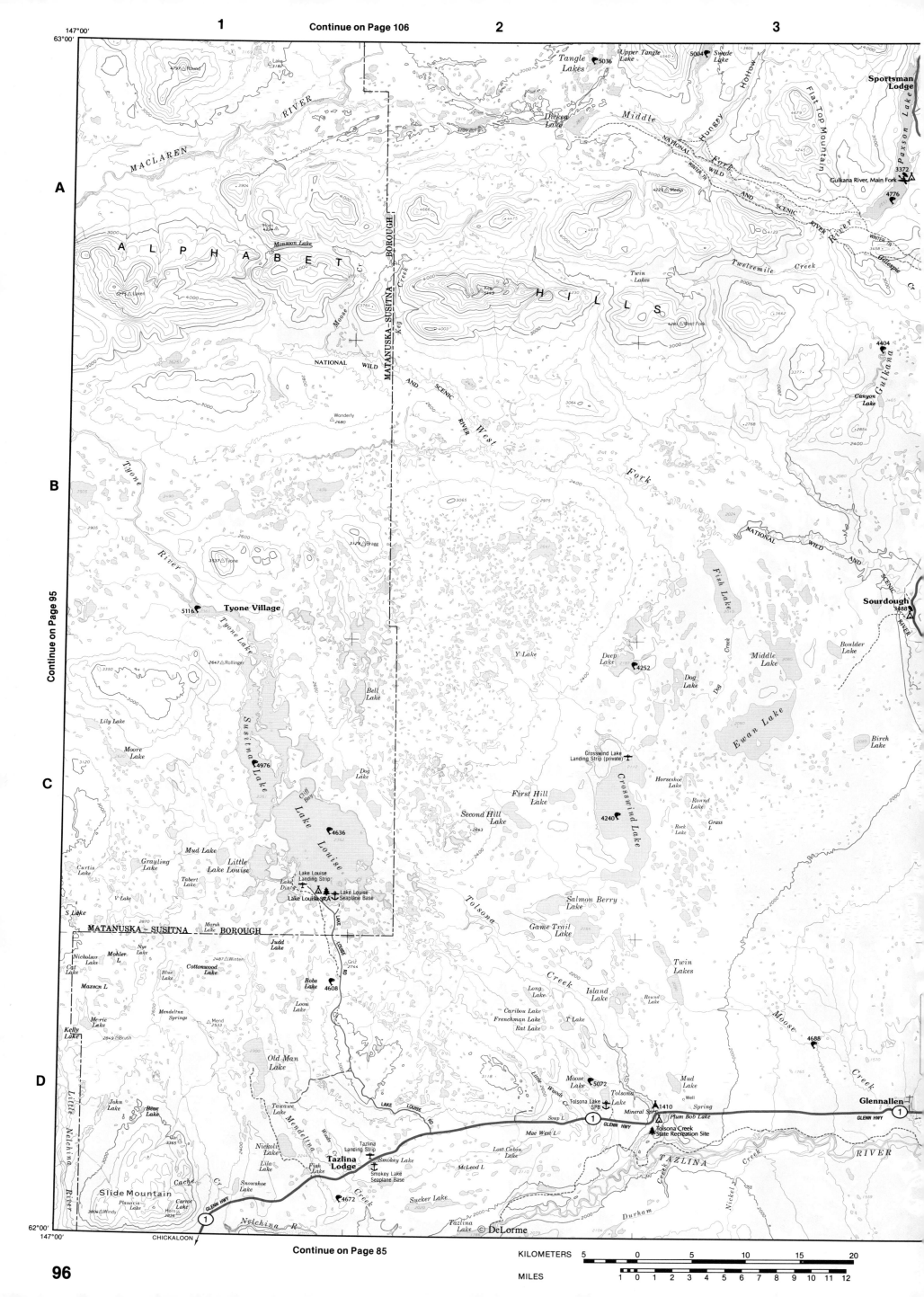

Continue on Page 95

Continue on Page 85

KILOMETERS 5   0   5   10   15   20

MILES   1 0 1 2 3 4 5 6 7 8 9 10 11 12

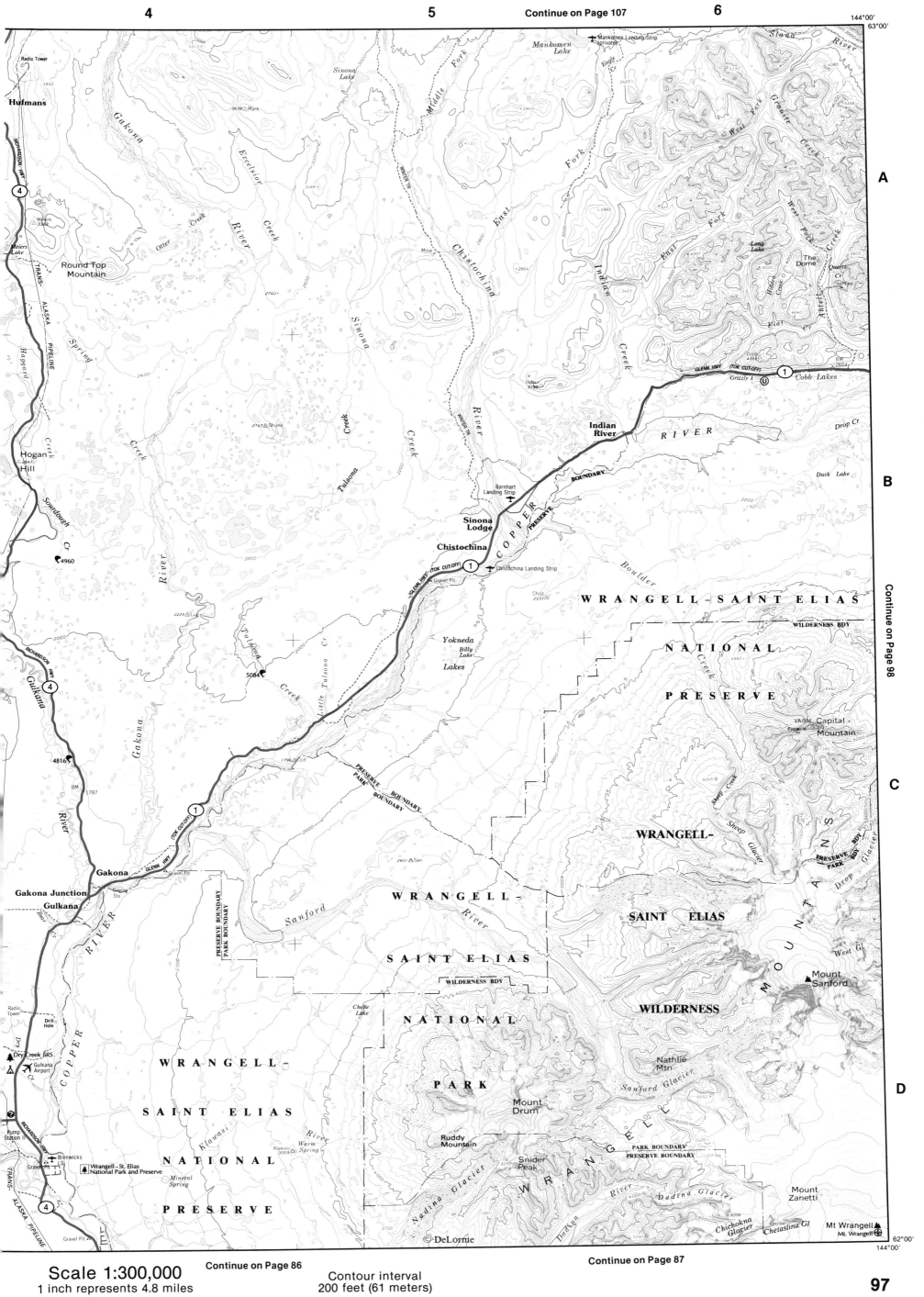

144°00'
63°00'

A

B

Continue on Page 98

C

D

144°00'
62°00'

© DeLorme

WRANGELL-SAINT ELIAS

NATIONAL

PRESERVE

WRANGELL-

SAINT ELIAS

WILDERNESS

WRANGELL-

SAINT ELIAS

NATIONAL

PARK

PRESERVE

Hufmans

Round Top Mountain

Hogan Hill

Gakona

Gakona Junction
Gulkana

Sinona Lodge

Chistochina

Indian River

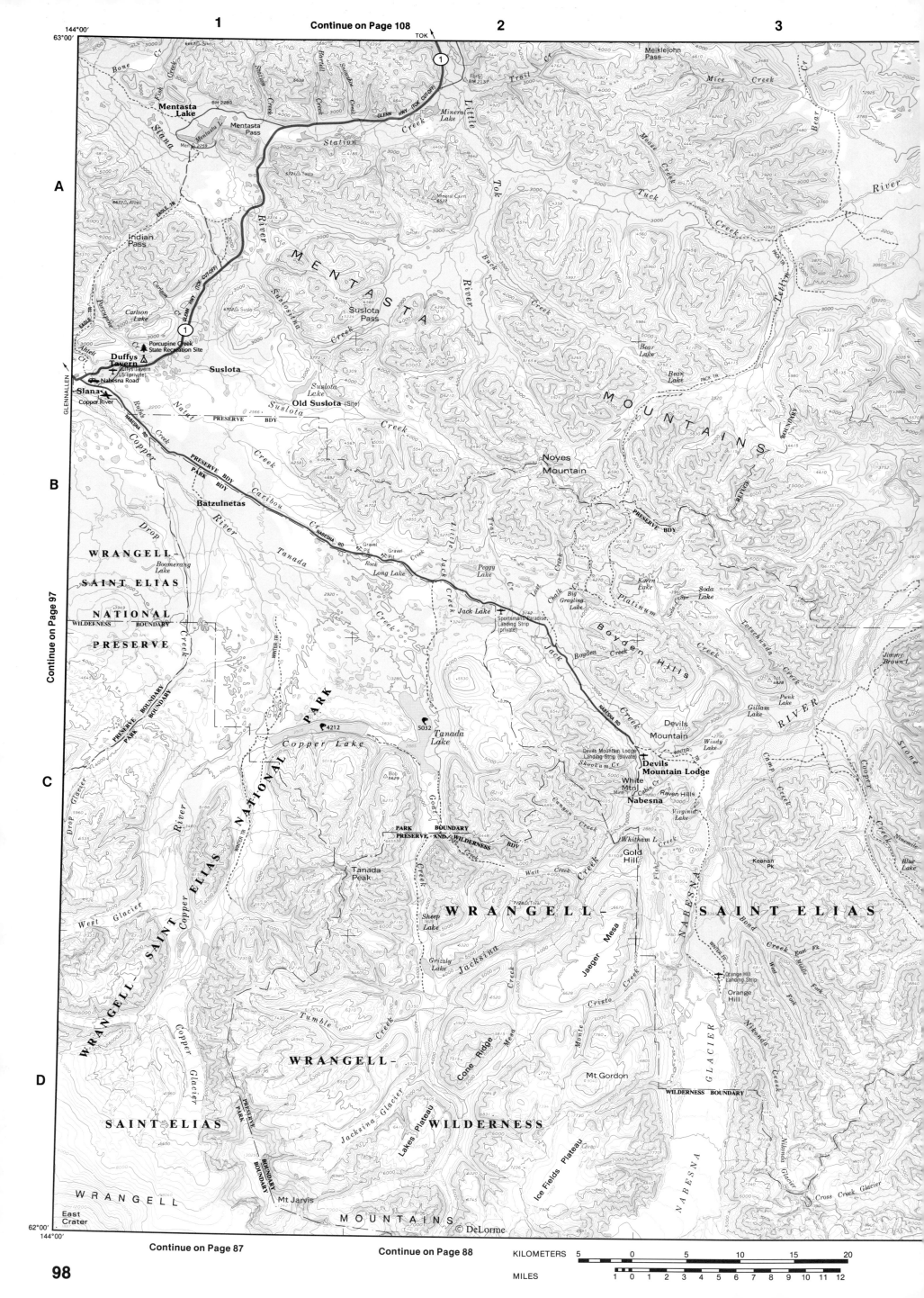

144°00'
63°00'

A

B

Continue on Page 97

C

D

62°00'
144°00'

© DeLorme

Continue on Page 87   Continue on Page 88

KILOMETERS 5   0   5   10   15   20

MILES   1 0 1 2 3 4 5 6 7 8 9 10 11 12

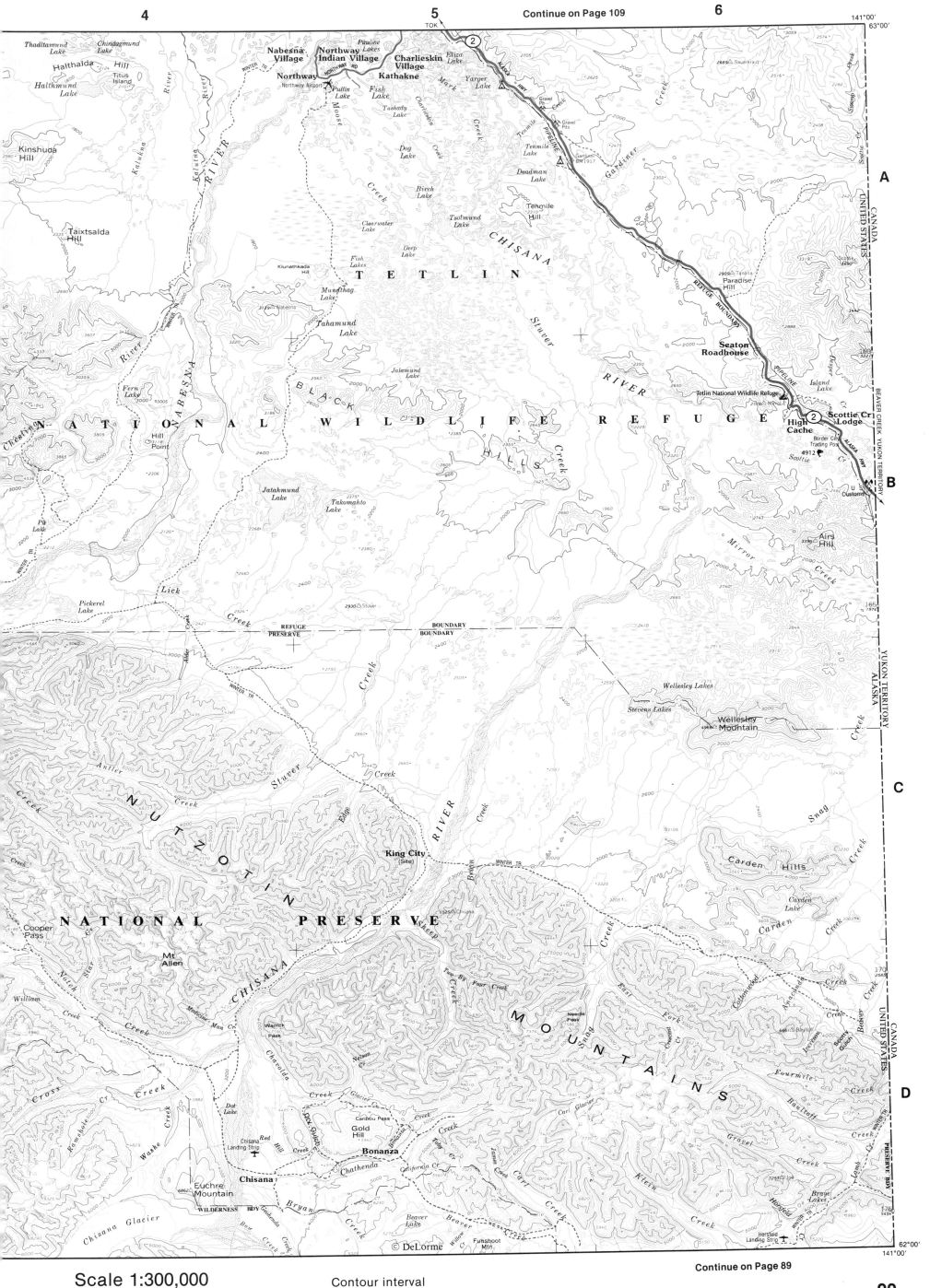

Scale 1:300,000
1 inch represents 4.8 miles

Contour interval
200 feet (61 meters)

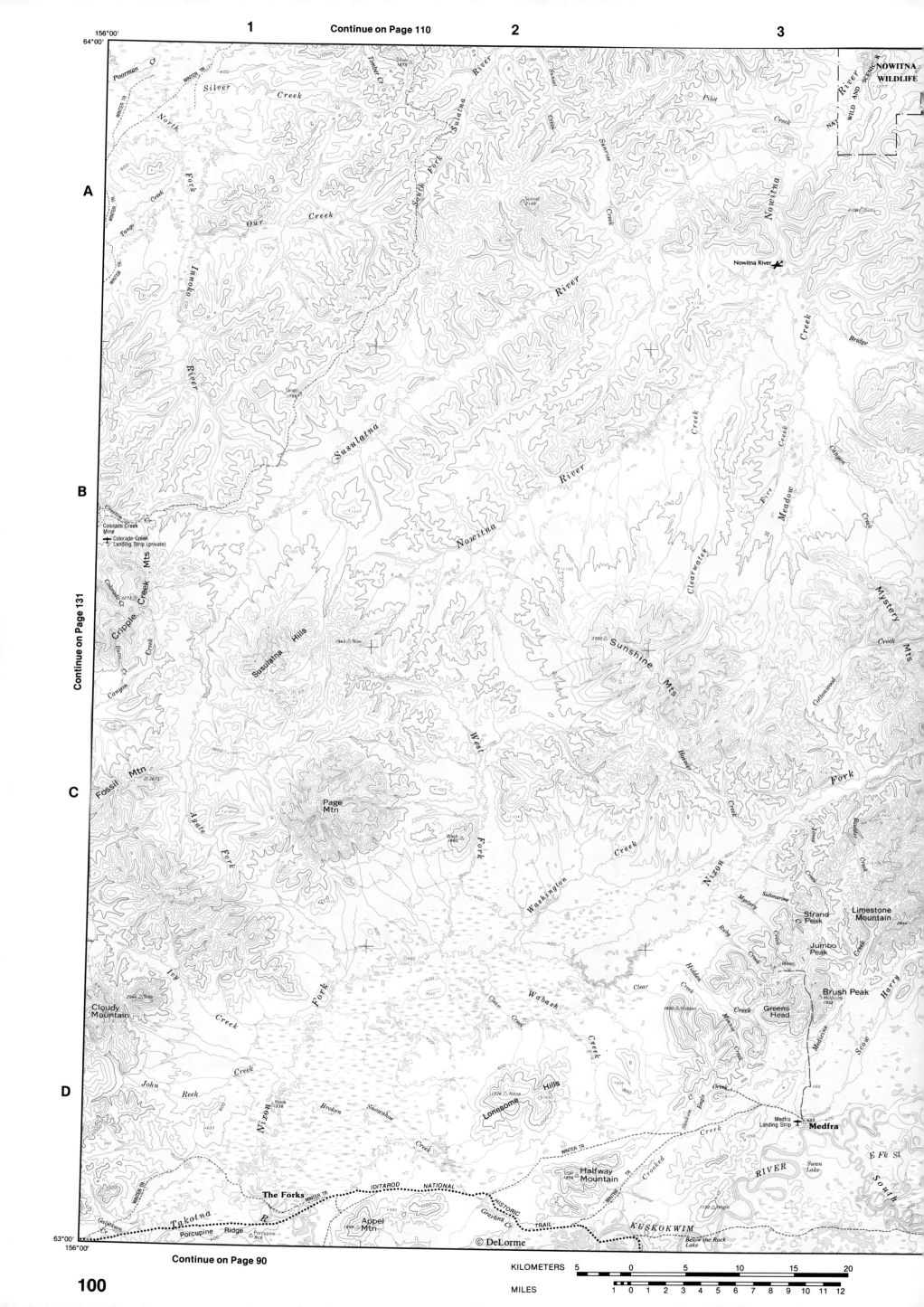

156°00'
64°00'

NAT   NOWITNA
WILD AND SCENIC   WILDLIFE

A

Continue on Page 131

B

Colorado Creek
Mine
Colorado Creek
Landing Strip (private)

Nowitna River

C

Fossil Mtn

Page
Mtn

Susulatna Hills

Sunshine
Mts

Mystery
Mts

Strand
Peak

Limestone
Mountain

Jumbo
Peak

Brush Peak

Cloudy
Mountain

Greens
Head

D

John   Creek

Lonesome   Hills

Medfra
Landing Strip   **Medfra**

Halfway
Mountain

The Forks

IDITAROD   NATIONAL

HISTORIC

Appel
Mtn

Grayling Cr   TRAIL

KUSKOKWIM

RIVER   Swan
Lake

E Fk Sl

South

Below the Rock
Lake

© DeLorme

63°00'
156°00'

KILOMETERS   5   0   5   10   15   20

MILES   1 0 1 2 3 4 5 6 7 8 9 10 11 12

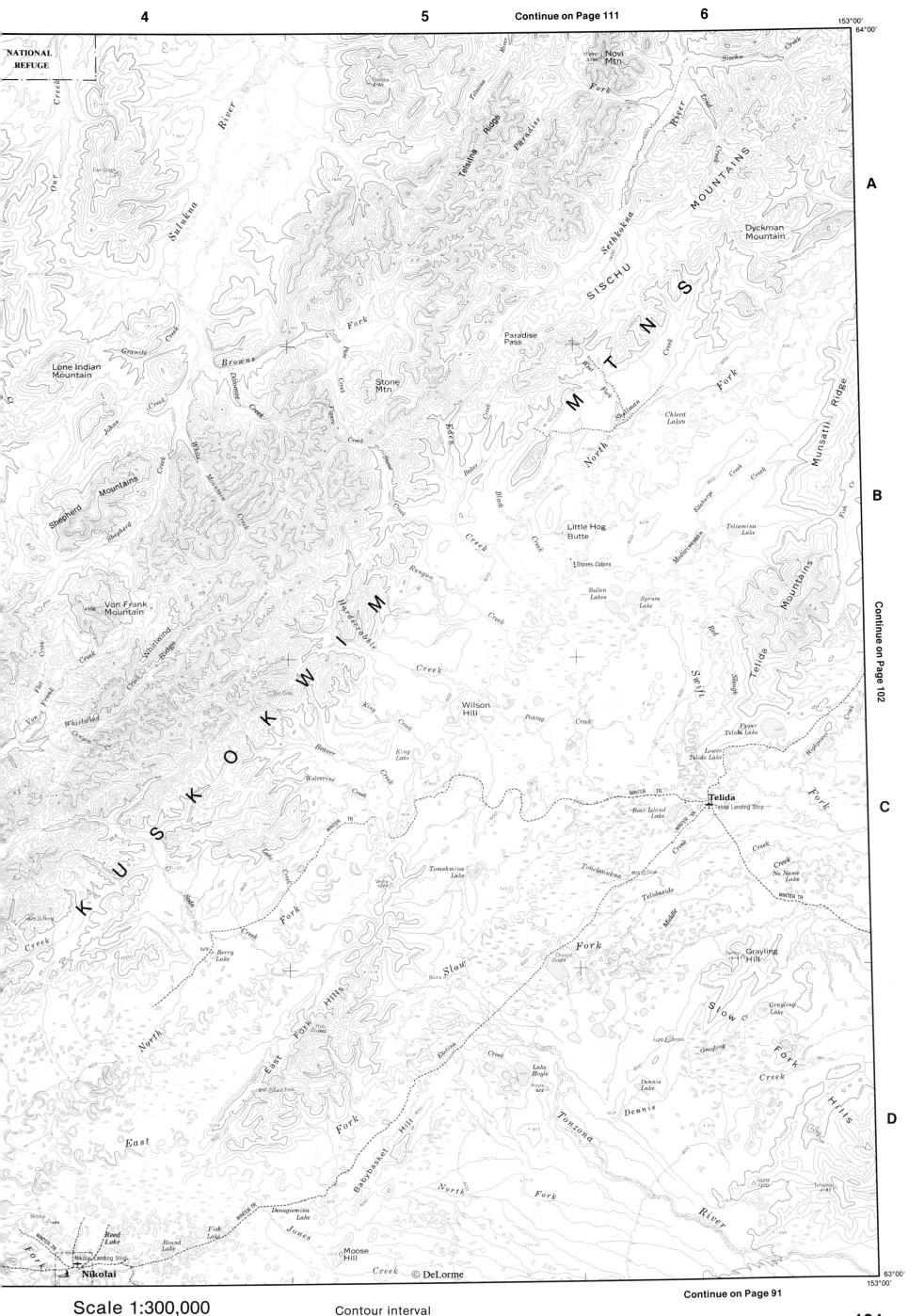

Continue on Page 102

Continue on Page 91

Scale 1:300,000
1 inch represents 4.8 miles

Contour interval
200 feet (61 meters)

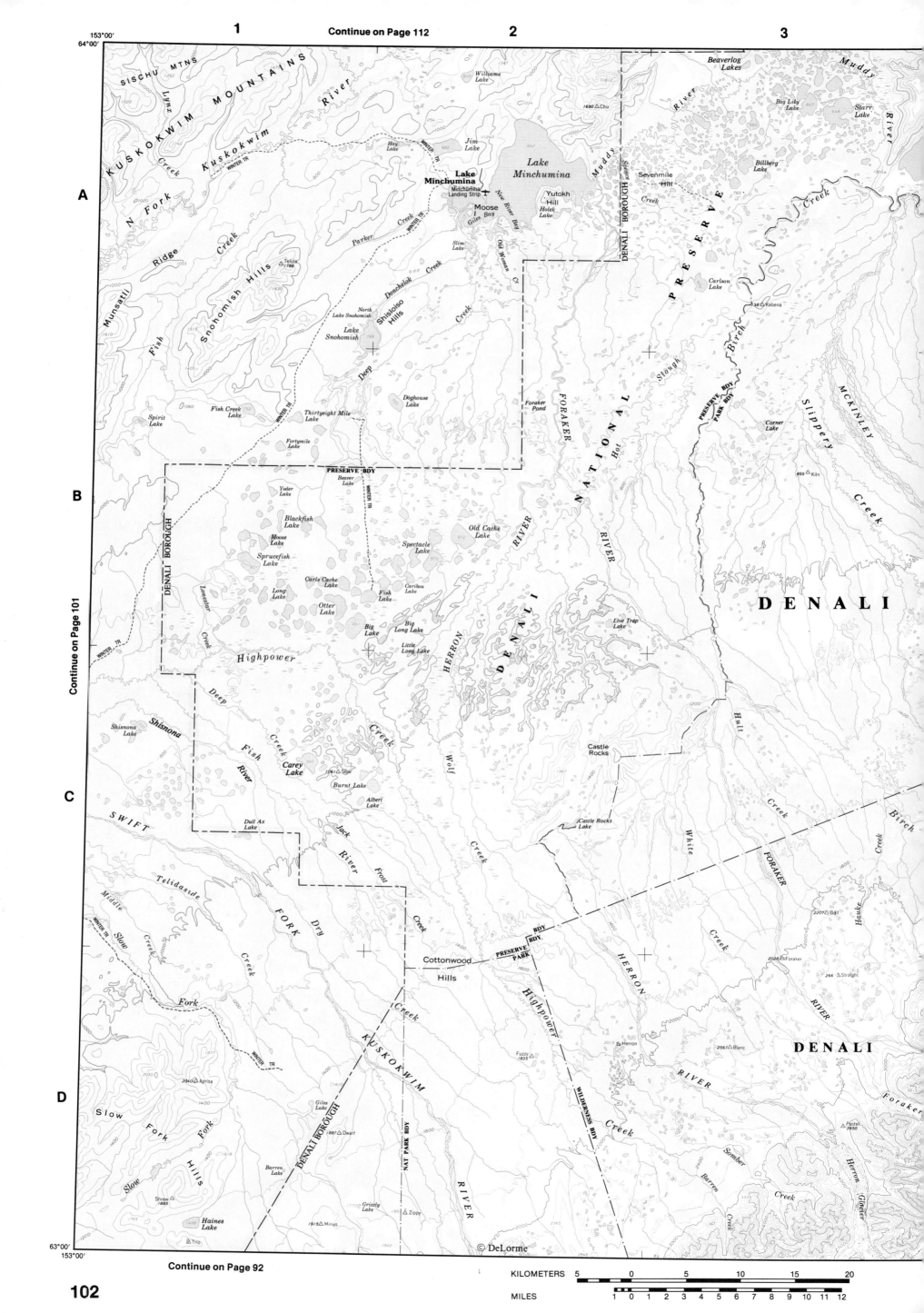

153°00'
64°00'

A

B

C

D

63°00'
153°00'

Continue on Page 101

Continue on Page 92

KILOMETERS   5   0   5   10   15   20

MILES   1 0 1 2 3 4 5 6 7 8 9 10 11 12

SISCHU MTNS

KUSKOKWIM MOUNTAINS

Lynx

Creek

N Fork

Kuskokwim

Creek

River

Kuskokwim

Ridge

Creek

Munsatli

Fish

Snohomish Hills

Telida
1786

North
Lake Snohomish

Shisloiso
Hills

Lake
Snohomish

Deep

Fish Creek
Lake

Spirit
Lake

Thirtyeight Mile
Lake

Fortymile
Lake

WINTER TR

Williams
Lake

Chu
1690

Jim
Lake

Lake
Minchumina

**Lake
Minchumina**

Minchumina
Landing Strip

Moose
Bay

Giles

Slim
Lake

Parker

Creek

Donchelok

Creek

Creek

Old Woman Cr

New River Bay

Yutokh
Hill

Holek
Lake

Muddy

Beaverlog
Lakes

River

Big Lily
Lake

Starr
Lake

Billberg
Lake

Sevenmile
Hill

DENALI BOROUGH

Carlson
Lake

Kabena

Creek

NATIONAL

PRESERVE

Birch

Creek

Muddy

River

Doghouse
Lake

Foraker
Pond

FORAKER

Hot

RIVER

Slough

PRESERVE
BDY
PARK BDY

Corner
Lake

Kiln
855

Slippery

MCKINLEY

Creek

PRESERVE BDY

WINTER TR

DENALI BOROUGH

Beaver
Lake

Yoder
Lake

Blackfish
Lake

Moose
Lake

Sprucefish
Lake

Long
Lake

Otter
Lake

Carls Cache
Lake

Fish
Lake

Big
Lake

Spectacle
Lake

Caribou
Lake

Big Long Lake

Little
Long Lake

Old Cache
Lake

RIVER

RIVER

DENALI

Live Trap
Lake

Lonestar

Creek

Highpower

Deep

Creek

HERRON

Wolf

Creek

Hall

Creek

Birch

Shisnona

Shisnona
Lake

Fish

River

Carey
Lake

Burnt Lake

Slow
1061

Alberi
Lake

Dull Ax
Lake

SWIFT

Creek

Jack

River

Frost

Creek

Dry

FORK

Creek

Castle
Rocks

Castle Rocks
Lake

1367

FORAKER

White

Creek

Gail
2207

2026 Foraker

Straight
266

Telidaside

Middle

Slow

Fork

WINTER TR

Creek

Cottonwood

Hills

Cottonwood

PRESERVE
PARK

BDY
BDY

Highpower

HERRON

Creek

RIVER

Fuzzy
1835

Herron
2015

Blanc
256

DENALI

Slow
Fork

Hills

Fork

Aprisa
2040

Giles
Lake

Dwarf
1887

DENALI BOROUGH

NAT PARK BDY

Creek

KUSKOKWIM

Slow

Barren
Lake

Shrew
1885

Haines
Lake

Trio

1418

Grizzly
Lake

Minus
1915

Zippy

RIVER

WILDERNESS BDY

Foraker

Somber

Creek

Barren

Creek

Pistol
3650

Herron

Glacier

© DeLorme

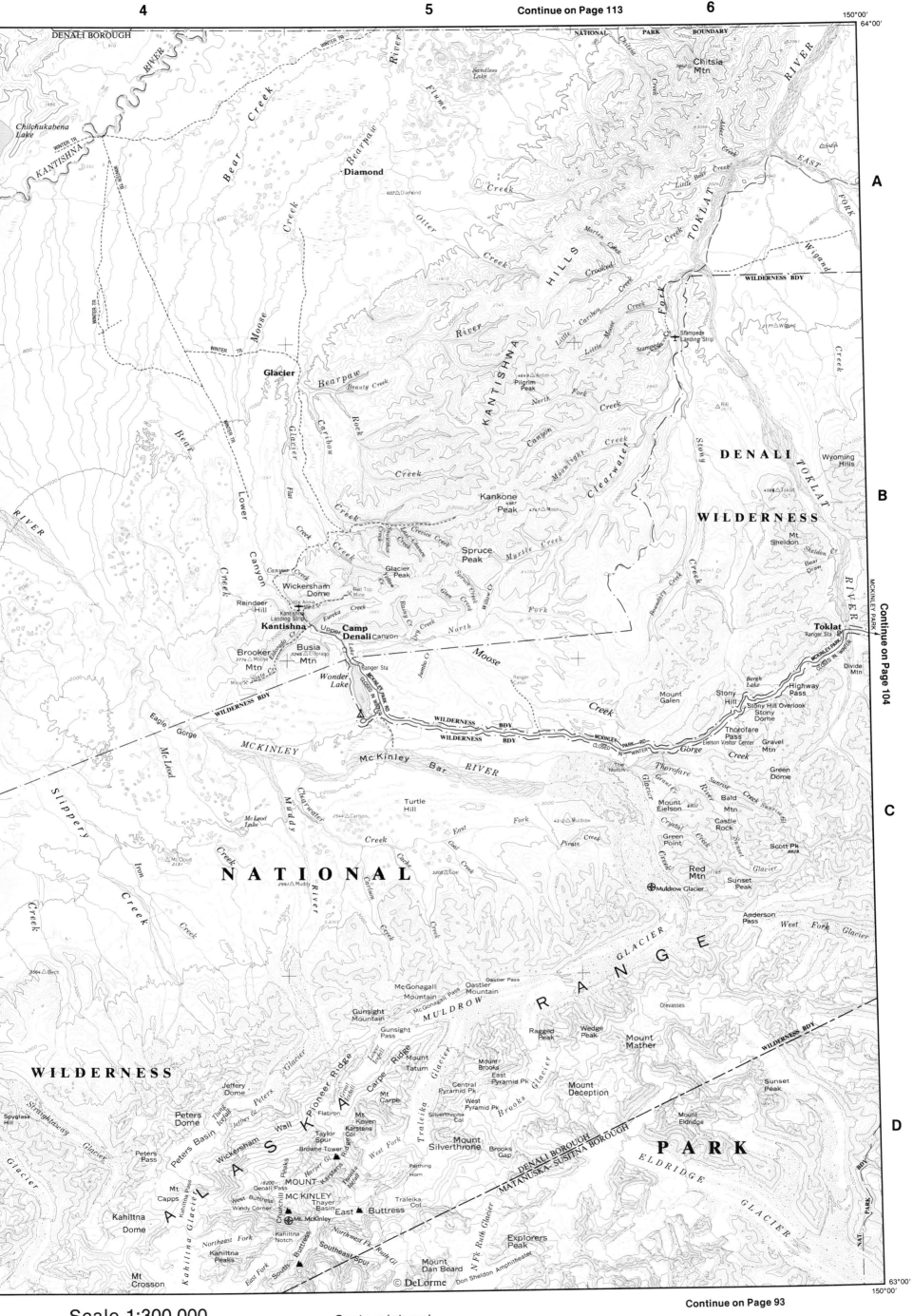

Continue on Page 104

Continue on Page 113

Continue on Page 93

Scale 1:300,000
1 inch represents 4.8 miles

Contour interval
200 feet (61 meters)

© DeLorme

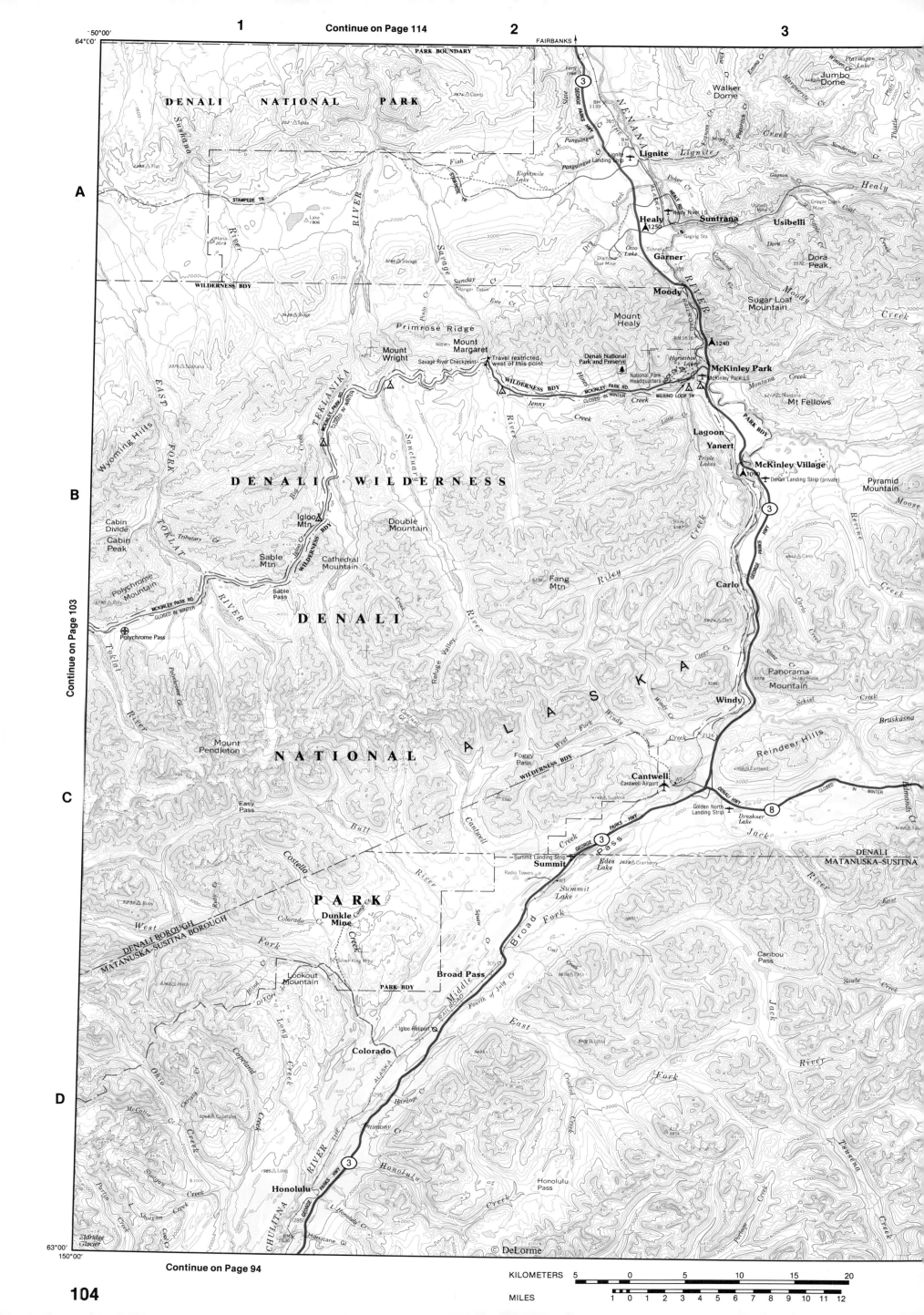

50°00'
64°00'
FAIRBANKS

DENALI NATIONAL PARK

PARK BOUNDARY

Walker
Dome

Jumbo
Dome

Lignite

STAMPEDE TR

STAMPEDE TR

Healy

Suntrana

Usibelli

Garner

Dora
Peak

WILDERNESS BDY

Moody

Sugar Loaf
Mountain

Mount
Healy

Primrose Ridge

Mount
Margaret

Mount
Wright

Savage River Checkpoint

Travel restricted
west of this point

Denali National
Park and Preserve

McKinley Park

WILDERNESS BDY

National Park
Headquarters

CLOSED IN WINTER

MERINO LOOP TR

Mt Fellows

Igloo
Mtn

DENALI WILDERNESS

Double
Mountain

Lagoon

Yanert

McKinley Village

Denali Landing Strip (private)

Pyramid
Mountain

Cabin
Divide

Cabin
Peak

Sable
Mtn

Cathedral
Mountain

WILDERNESS BDY

Carlo

Polychrome
Mountain

Sable
Pass

DENALI

Fang
Mtn

Panorama
Mountain

MCKINLEY PARK RD
CLOSED IN WINTER

Polychrome Pass

Mount
Pendleton

NATIONAL

ALASKA

Windy

Reindeer Hills

Easy
Pass

Foggy
Pass

WILDERNESS BDY

Cantwell

Cantwell Airport

Golden North
Landing Strip

Drashner
Lake

DENALI
MATANUSKA-SUSITNA

Summit Landing Strip

Radio Towers

Summit

PARK

Edes
Lake

Dunkle
Mine

Summit
Lake

Silver King Mtn

Lookout
Mountain

DENALI BOROUGH
MATANUSKA-SUSITNA BOROUGH

PARK BDY

Broad Pass

Caribou
Pass

Igloo Heliport

Colorado

Honolulu

Honolulu
Pass

Honolulu

Continue on Page 103

63°00'
150°00'

© DeLorme

KILOMETERS   5   0   5   10   15   20

MILES   1 0 1 2 3 4 5 6 7 8 9 10 11 12

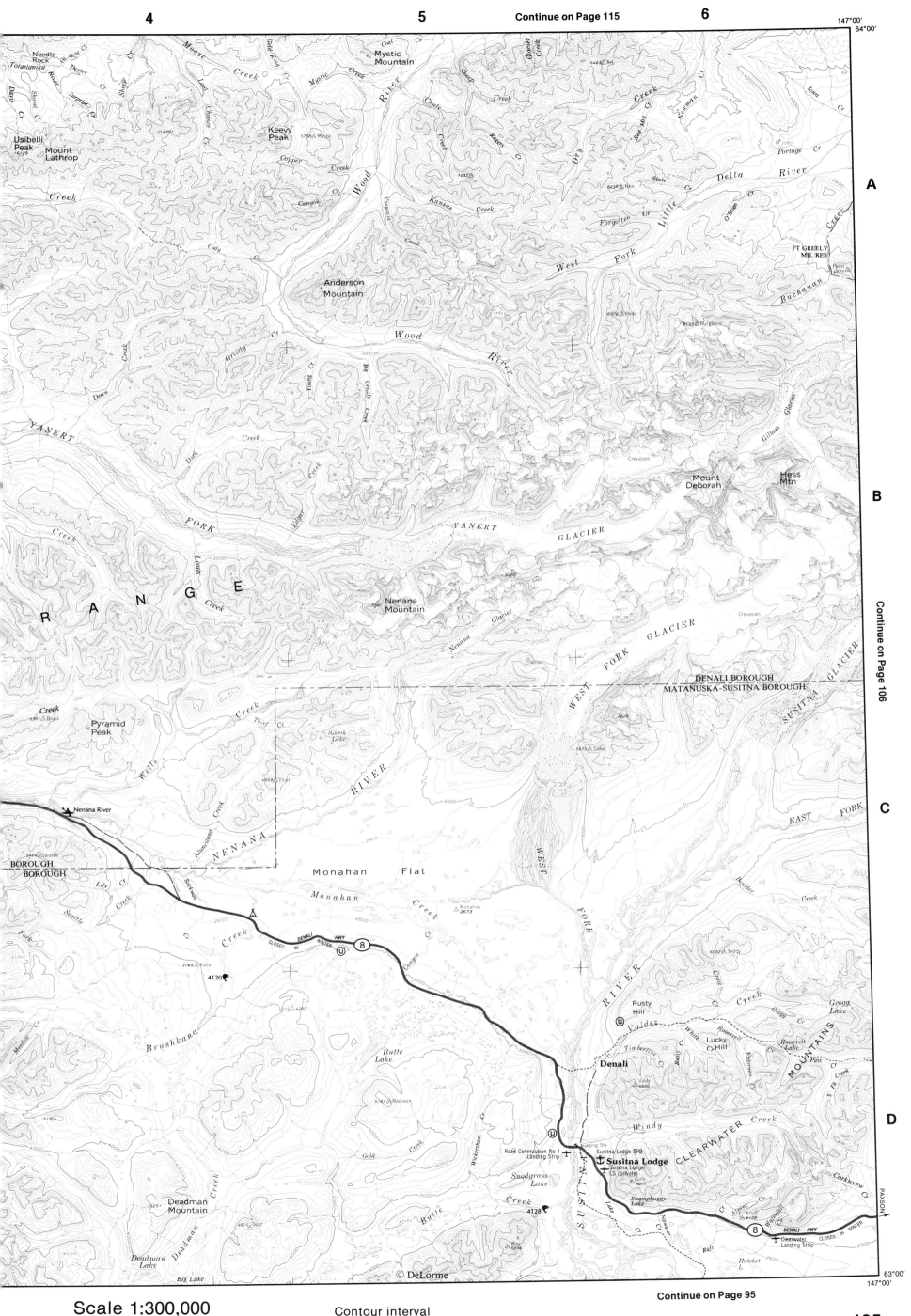

Continue on Page 106

Continue on Page 95

Scale 1:300,000
1 inch represents 4.8 miles

Contour interval
200 feet (61 meters)

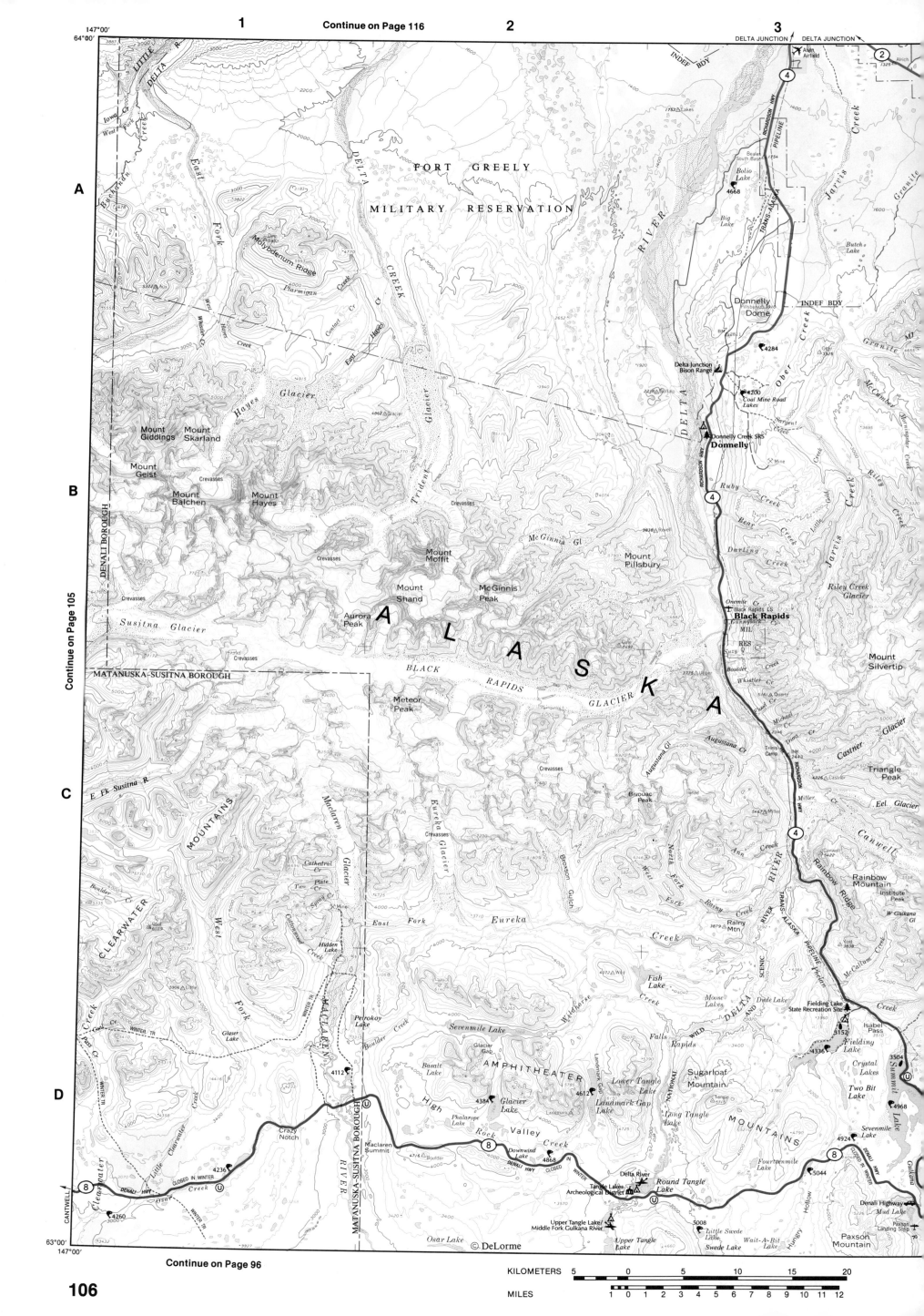

Continue on Page 105

Continue on Page 96

© DeLorme

106

KILOMETERS 5   0   5   10   15   20

MILES   1 0 1 2 3 4 5 6 7 8 9 10 11 12

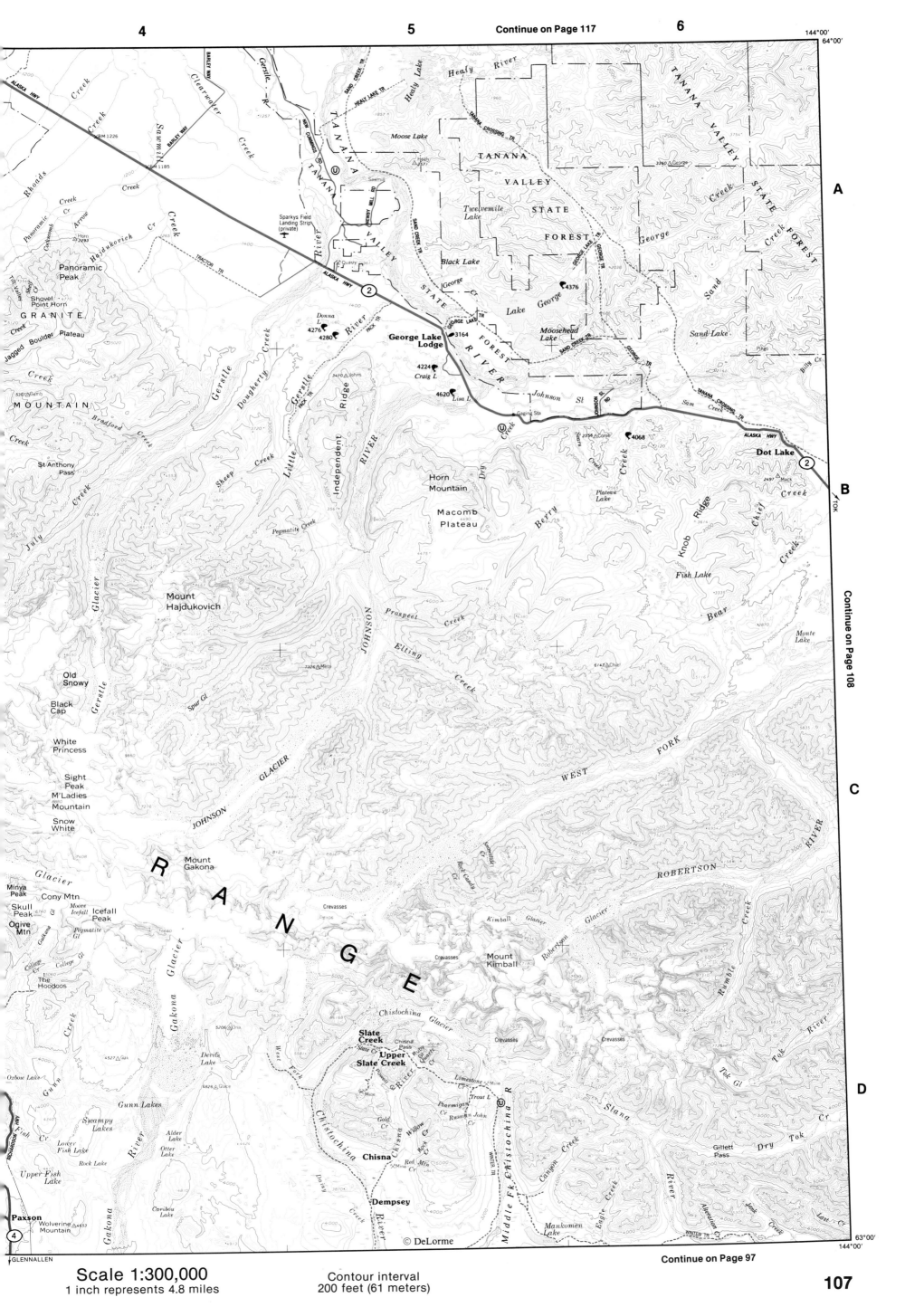

144°00'
64°00'

A

B

Continue on Page 108

C

D

63°00'
144°00'

Continue on Page 97

Scale 1:300,000
1 inch represents 4.8 miles

Contour interval
200 feet (61 meters)

© DeLorme

TANANA VALLEY STATE FOREST

TANANA VALLEY STATE FOREST

R A N G E

ALASKA RANGE

George Lake Lodge

Dot Lake

ALASKA HWY

Paxson

GLENNALLEN

Chisna

Dempsey

Slate Creek
Upper Slate Creek

Mount Kimball

Mount Gakona

Mount Hajdukovich

Horn Mountain

Macomb Plateau

Panoramic Peak

GRANITE MOUNTAIN

Old Snowy
Black Cap
White Princess
Sight Peak
M'Ladies Mountain
Snow White

Minya Peak
Cony Mtn
Skull Peak
Ogive Mtn
The Hoodoos

Icefall Peak

ROBERTSON

WEST FORK

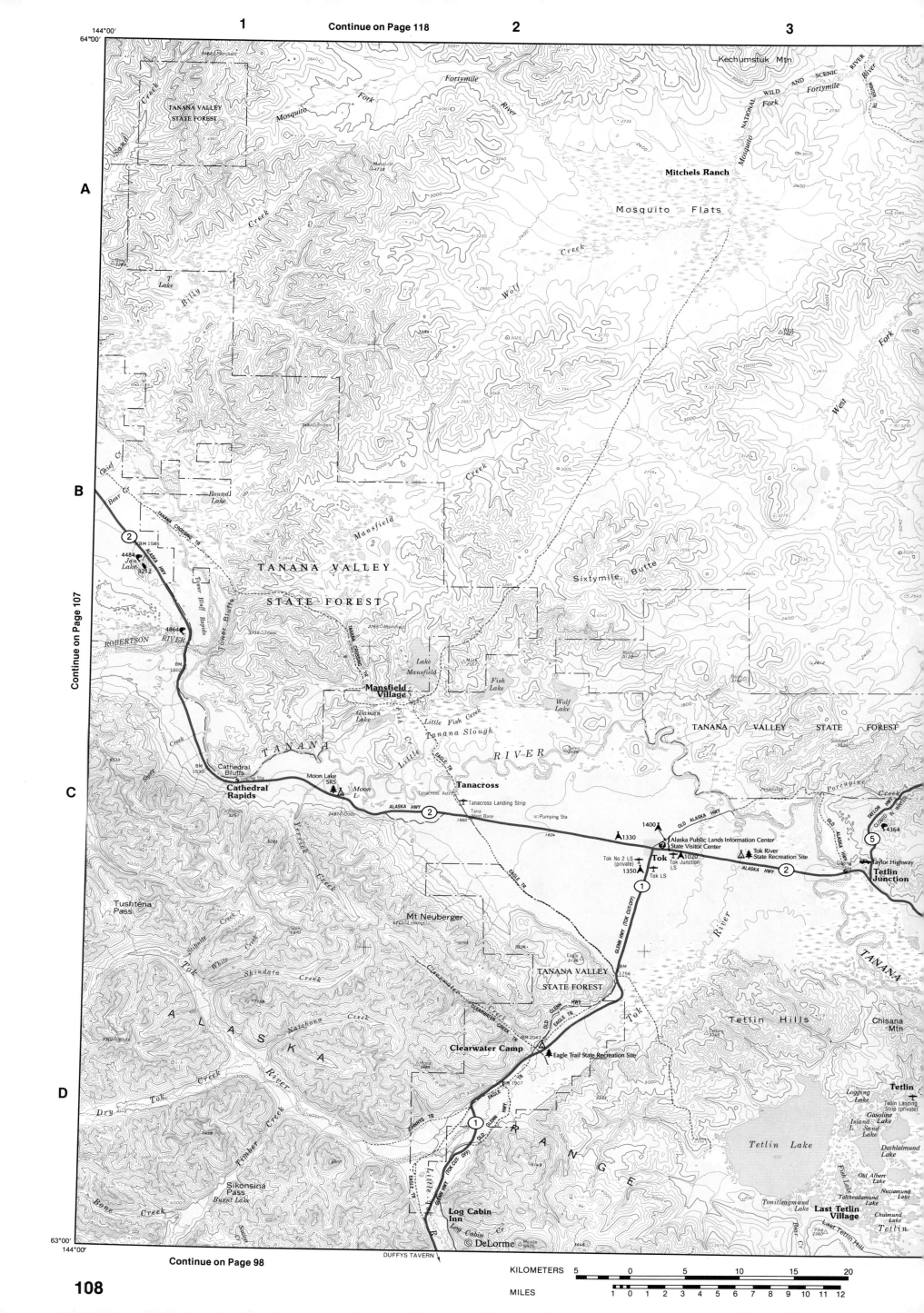

144°00'
64°00'

A

B

Continue on Page 107

C

D

63°00'
144°00'

Kechumstuk Mtn

Fortymile

Mitchels Ranch

Mosquito Flats

TANANA VALLEY
STATE FOREST

T
Lake

TANANA VALLEY
STATE FOREST

Round
Lake

Mansfield

Sixtymile Butte

Jan
Lake

Tower Bluffs

ROBERTSON RIVER

TANANA VALLEY
STATE FOREST

Lake
Mansfield

Fish
Lake

Mansfield
Village

Wolf
Lake

Glaman
Lake

Little Fish Creek

Tanana Slough

RIVER

TANANA VALLEY
STATE FOREST

Cathedral
Bluffs

Moon Lake
SRS

Moon
L.

Tanacross

Tanacross Landing Strip

Pumping Sta

Cathedral
Rapids

ALASKA HWY

OLD ALASKA HWY

1400

Alaska Public Lands Information Center
State Visitor Center

TAYLOR HWY

4364

Tok River
State Recreation Site

5

1330

Tok No 2 LS
(private)

1020

Tok

1350

Tok Junction
LS

Tok LS

ALASKA HWY

2

Taylor Highway

Tetlin
Junction

Tushtena
Pass

EAGLE TR

Mt Neuberger

Eagle

TANANA VALLEY
STATE FOREST

GLENN HWY (TOK CUTOFF)

1

Tok

TANANA

Tetlin Hills

Chisana
Mtn

Shindata Creek

ALASKA

Clearwater Camp

Eagle Trail State Recreation Site

RANGE

Tetlin

Logging
Lake

Tetlin Landing
Strip (private)

Gasoline
Island
Lake

Sand
Lake

Dry

Sikonsina
Pass

Burnt Lake

Little

Log Cabin
Inn

© DeLorme

Tetlin Lake

Dathlamund
Lake

Nuziamund
Lake

Old Albert
Lake

Taltheadamund
Lake

Chuimund
Lake

Last Tetlin
Village

Tetlin

KILOMETERS   5   0   5   10   15   20

MILES   1 0 1 2 3 4 5 6 7 8 9 10 11 12

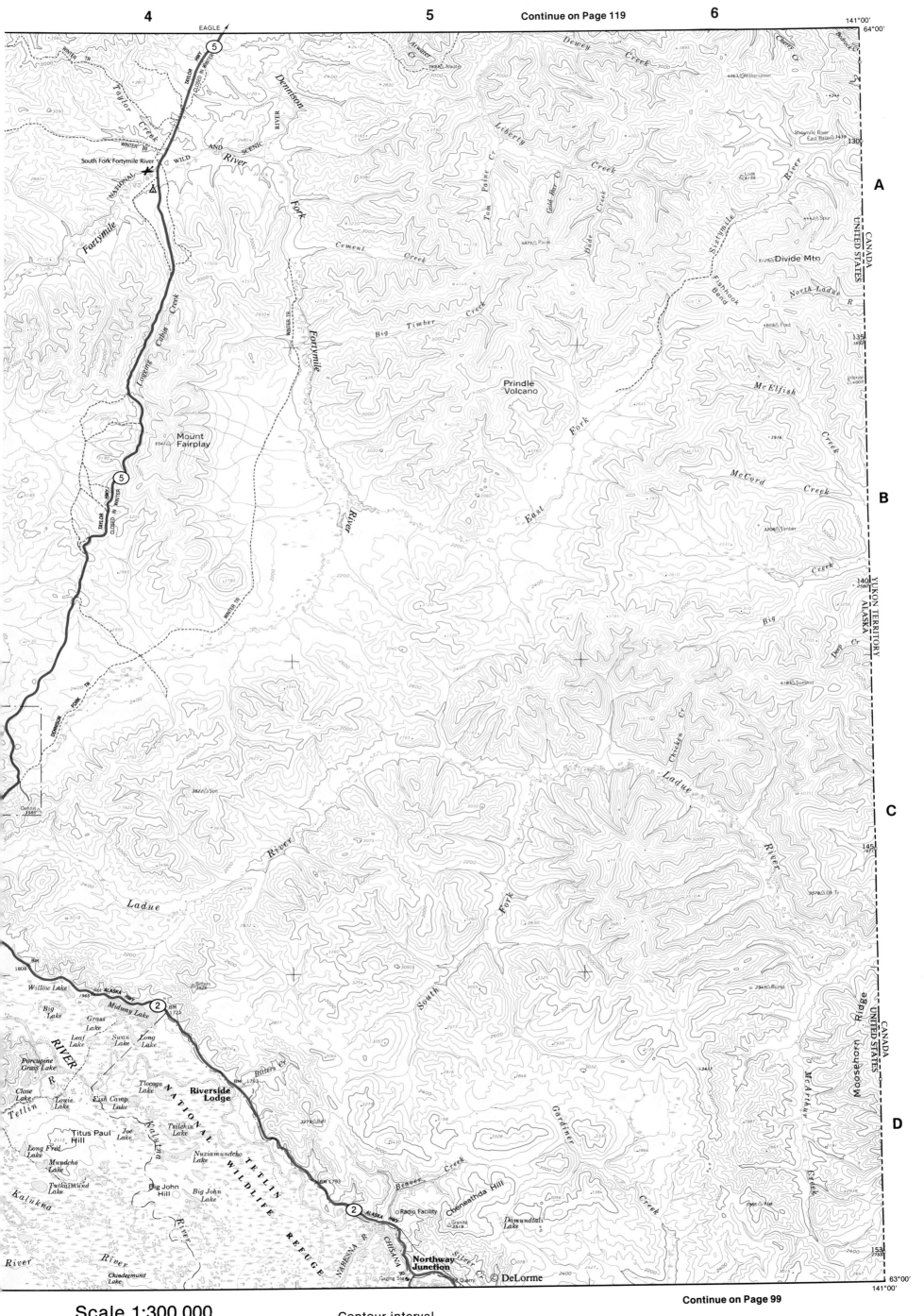

EAGLE

South Fork Fortymile River

Mount Fairplay

Prindle Volcano

Divide Mtn

McElfish

McCord Creek

Big Timber Creek

Cement Creek

Dewey Creek

Liberty Creek

Tom Point Cr.

Gold-Bar Cr.

Fishhook Bend

North Ladue R.

East Fork

Chicken Cr.

Ladue River

South Fork

Ladue River

CANADA
UNITED STATES

YUKON TERRITORY
ALASKA

A

B

C

D

Willow Lake

Big Lake

Grass Lake

Leaf Lake

Swan Lake

Long Lake

Midway Lake

Porcupine Grass Lake

Close Lake

Lonie Lake

Fish Camp Lake

Tlocogn Lake

Riverside Lodge

Titus Paul Hill

Joe Lake

Tsilehin Lake

Long Fred Lake

Mundcho Lake

Nuziamundcho Lake

Putkaimund Lake

Big John Hill

Big John Lake

Chindagmund Lake

NATIONAL TETLIN WILDLIFE REFUGE

Bitters Cr.

Beaver Creek

Gardiner Creek

Chenesthda Hill

Damundtali Lake

Radio Facility

Granite

McArthur Ridge

Moosehorn Ridge

CANADA
UNITED STATES

Nabesna R.

Chisana R.

Northway Junction

© DeLorme

© DeLorme

Scenic River

National Wild

Taylor Creek

Dennison River

Fortymile River

Logging Cabin Creek

Dennison Fork

Kalukna River

Tetlin R.

Kalukna River

RIVER

141°00'
64°00'

130

135

140

145

153

63°00'
141°00'

Scale 1:300,000
1 inch represents 4.8 miles

Contour interval
200 feet (61 meters)

Continue on Page 99

109

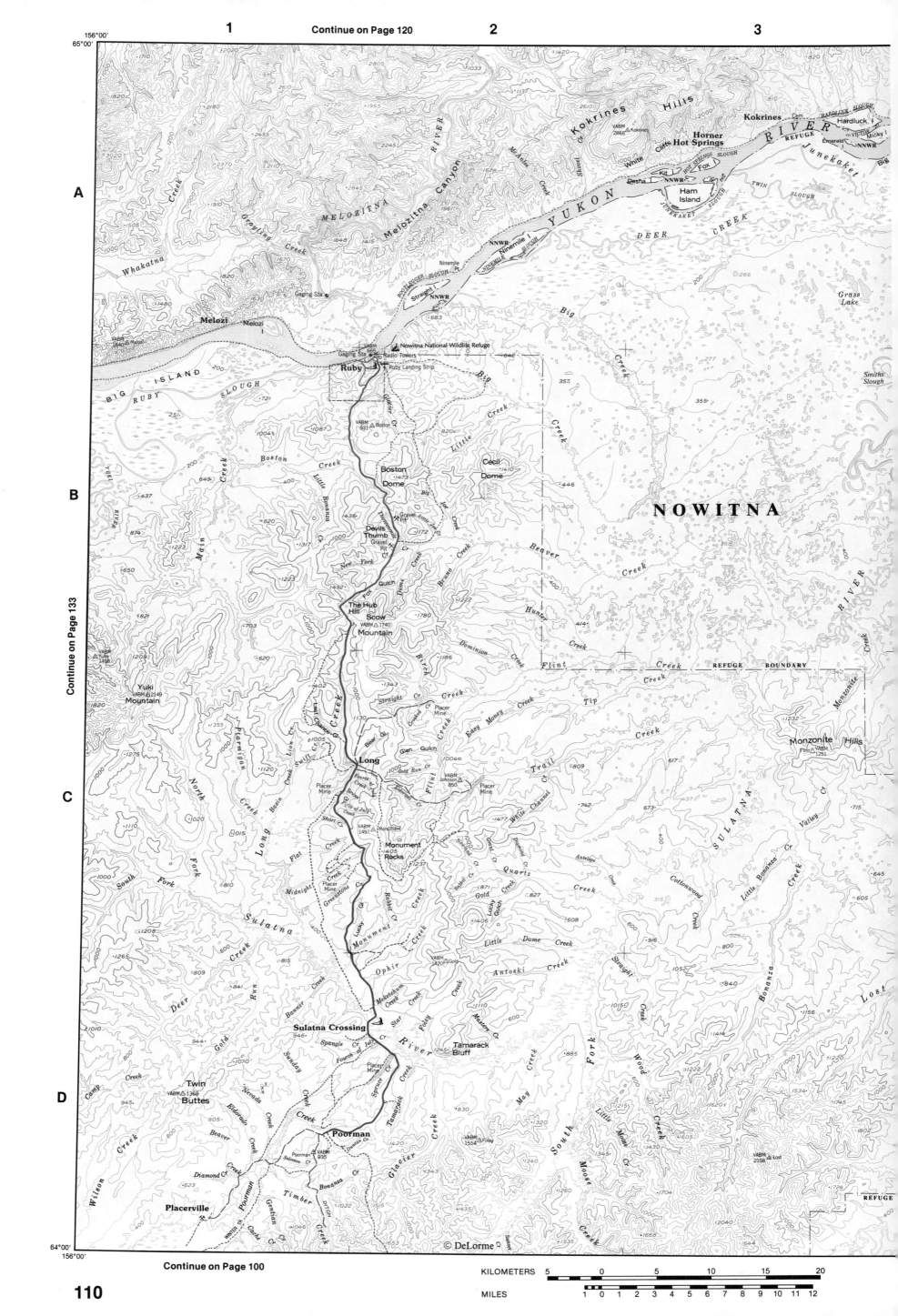

Continue on Page 133

KILOMETERS 5 0 5 10 15 20

MILES 1 0 1 2 3 4 5 6 7 8 9 10 11 12

© DeLorme

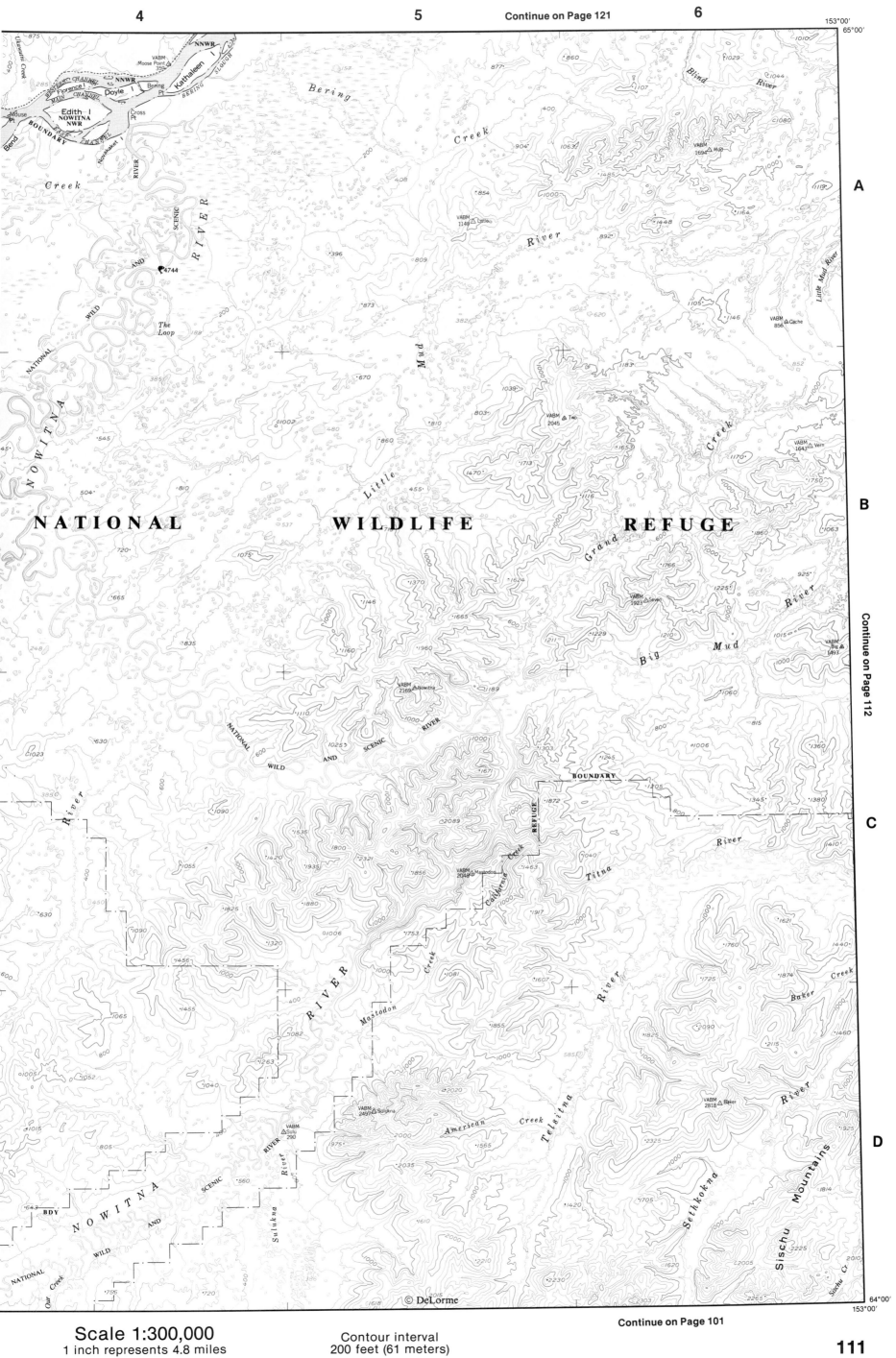

153°00'
65°00'

A

B

Continue on Page 112

C

D

64°00'
153°00'

© DeLorme

Scale 1:300,000
1 inch represents 4.8 miles

Contour interval
200 feet (61 meters)

111

NOWITNA NATIONAL WILDLIFE REFUGE

NATIONAL WILDLIFE REFUGE

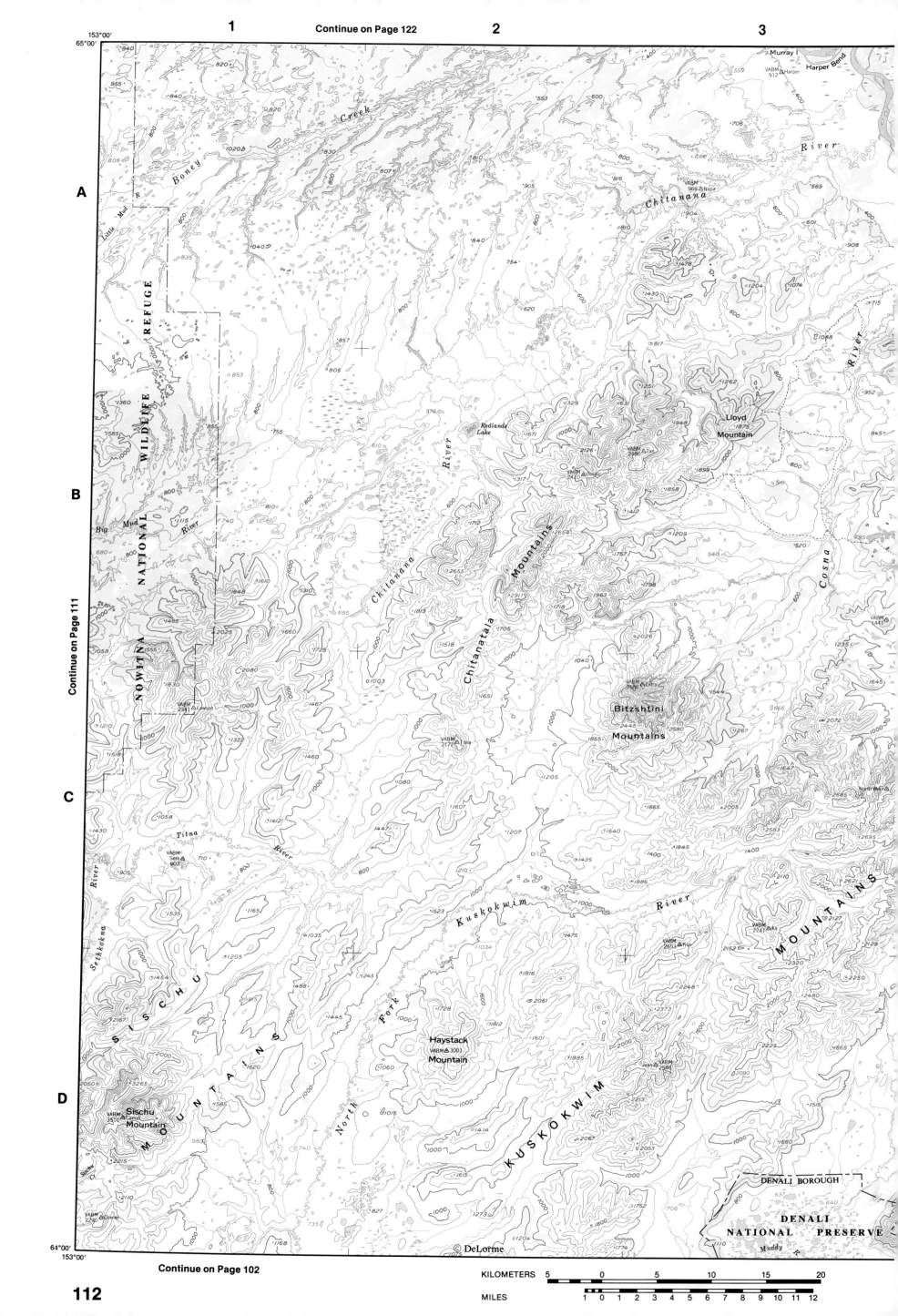

153°00'
65°00'

A

B

Continue on Page 111

C

D

WILDLIFE   REFUGE

NOWITNA   NATIONAL

Big   Mud   River

Little   Mud   R

Boney   Creek   River

Chitanana

Redlands
Lake

Lloyd
Mountain

Chitanana   River

Chitanatala   Mountains

Chitanatala   Mountains

Bitzshtini
Mountains

Cosna   River

MOUNTAINS

SISCHU   MOUNTAINS

Titna   River

Titna   River

Sethkokna   River

Haystack
Mountain

North   Fork

Kuskokwim   River

KUSKOKWIM

Sischu
Mountain

Sischu   Cr

KUSKOKWIM   MOUNTAINS

Murray I
Harper Bend
Harper

Napa

DENALI BOROUGH

DENALI
NATIONAL   PRESERVE

Muddy   R

© DeLorme

Continue on Page 102

64°00'
153°00'

KILOMETERS   5   0   5   10   15   20

MILES   1 0 1 2 3 4 5 6 7 8 9 10 11 12

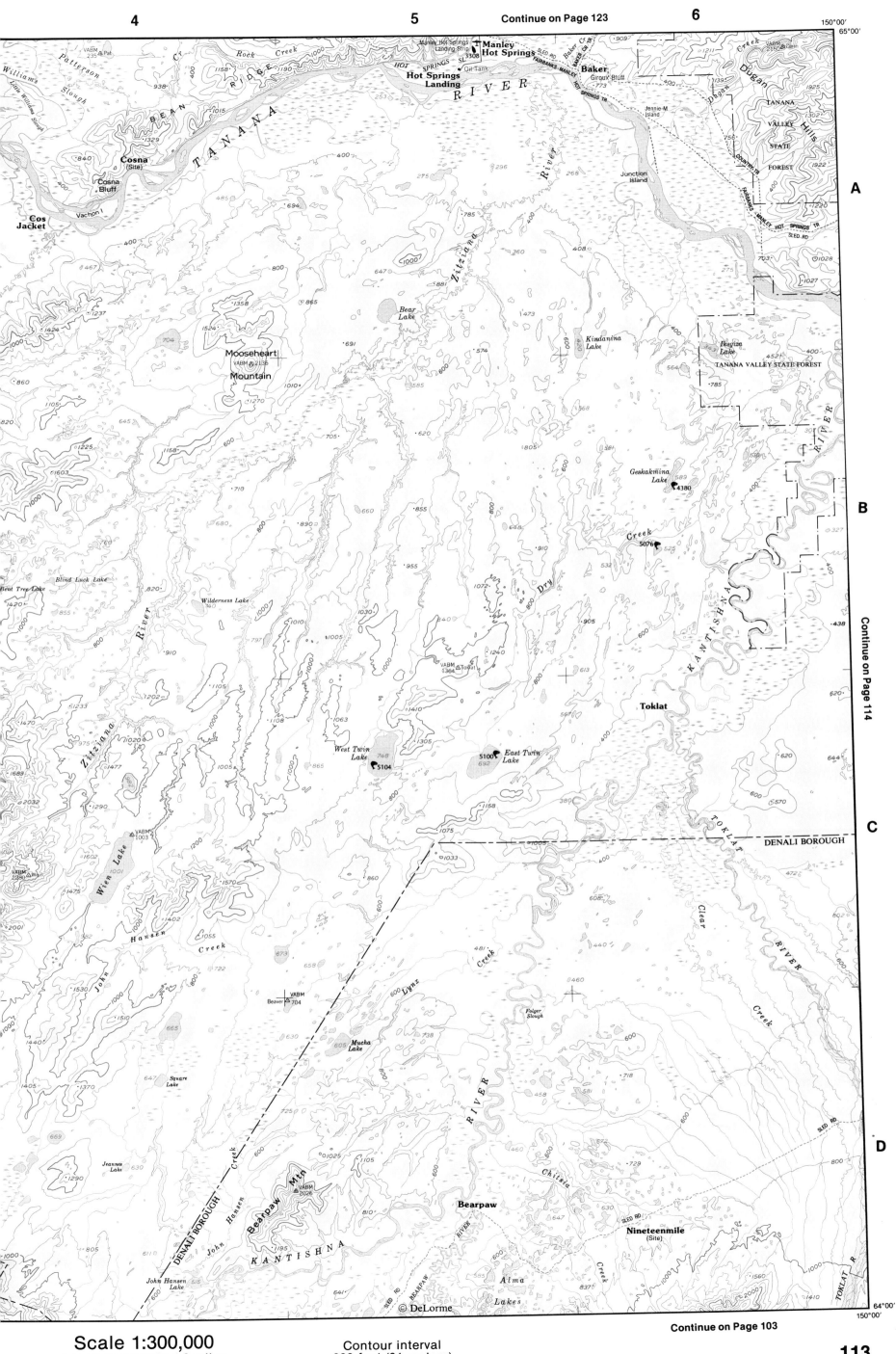

Continue on Page 114

Continue on Page 103

© DeLorme

Scale 1:300,000
1 inch represents 4.8 miles

Contour interval
200 feet (61 meters)

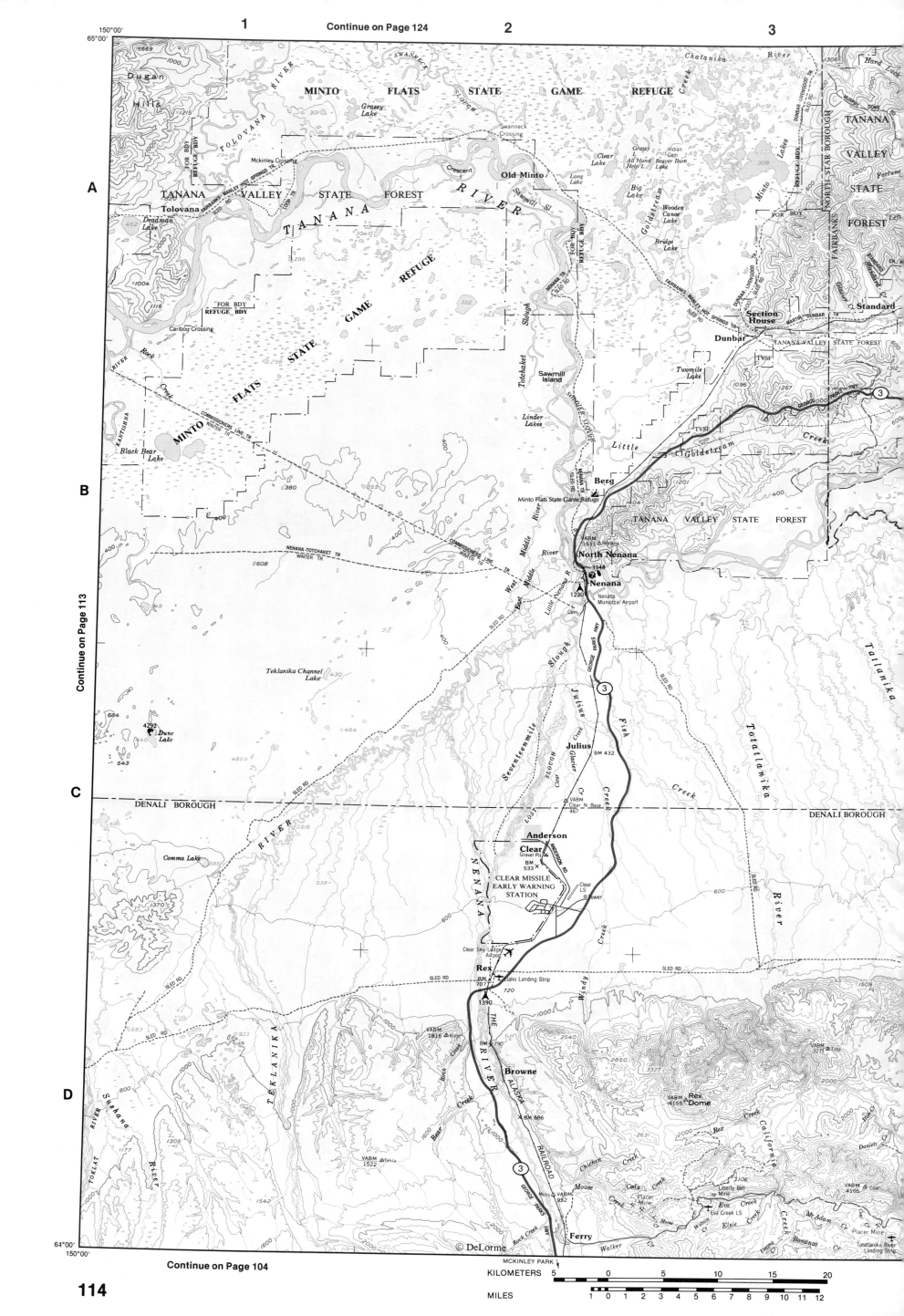

150°00'
65°00'

A

B

Continue on Page 113

C

D

64°00'
150°00'

Continue on Page 104

© DeLorme

114

KILOMETERS   5   0   5   10   15   20

MILES   1 0   1   2   3   4   5   6   7   8   9   10   11   12

MCKINLEY PARK

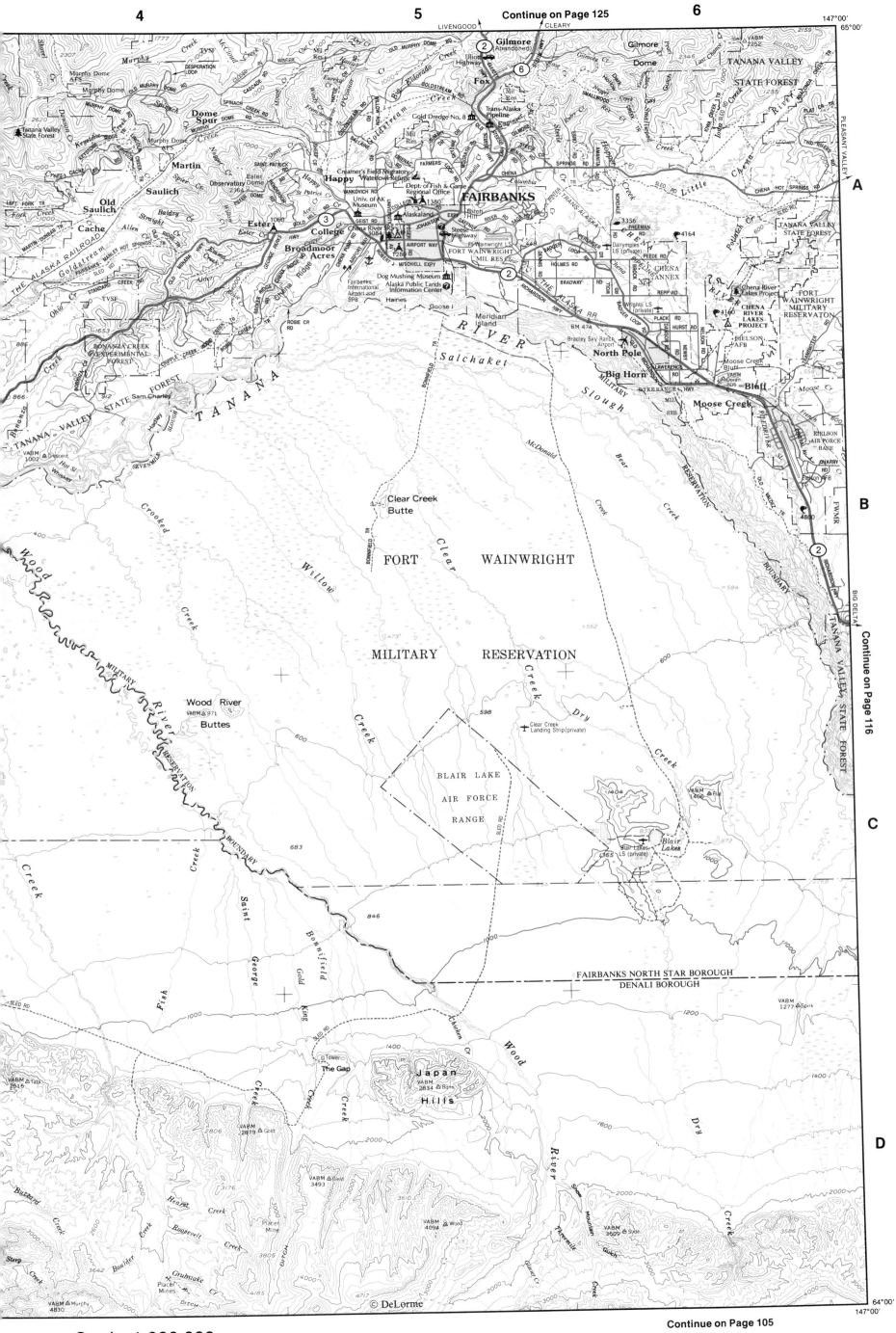

147°00'
65°00'

LIVENGOOD   CLEARY

Gilmore
(Abandoned)

Gilmore
Dome

TANANA VALLEY
STATE FOREST

Fox

Trans-Alaska
Pipeline

Gold Dredge No. 8

A

FAIRBANKS

Creamer's Field Migratory
Waterfowl Refuge

Happy

Martin

Saulich

Old
Saulich
Cache

Ester

College

Broadmoor
Acres

TANANA VALLEY
STATE FOREST

CHENA
ANNEX

FORT
WAINWRIGHT
RESERVATION

CHENA RIVER
LAKES
PROJECT

FT. WAINWRIGHT
MIL RES

Dog Mushing Museum
Alaska Public Lands
Information Center

North Pole

Big Horn

Bluff

Moose Creek

EIELSON
AIR FORCE
BASE

B

RIVER

Salchaket

Clear Creek
Butte

FORT   WAINWRIGHT

FWMR

Continue on Page 116

MILITARY   RESERVATION

Wood River
Buttes

Clear Creek
Landing Strip (private)

C

BLAIR LAKE

AIR FORCE

RANGE

Blair
Lakes

Blair Lakes
LS (private)

BOUNDARY

FAIRBANKS NORTH STAR BOROUGH
DENALI BOROUGH

The Gap

Japan
Hills

D

64°00'
147°00'

© DeLorme

Scale 1:300,000
1 inch represents 4.8 miles

Contour interval
200 feet (61 meters)

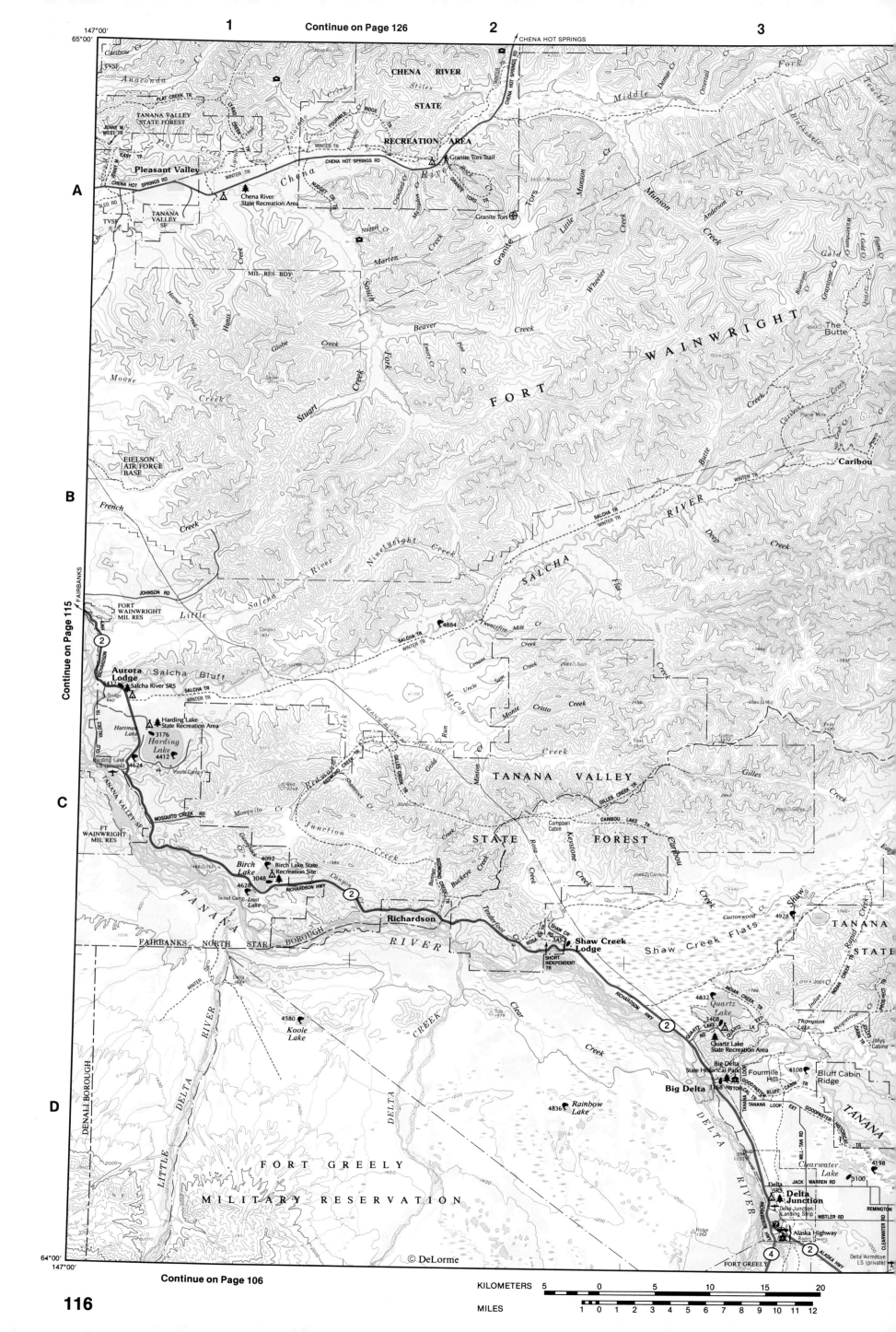

147°00'
65°00'

CHENA HOT SPRINGS

CHENA   RIVER

STATE

RECREATION   AREA

Granite Tors Trail

Pleasant Valley

A

Chena River
State Recreation Area

TANANA VALLEY STATE FOREST

JENNY M WEST TR

TVSF

SLED RD

TANANA VALLEY SF

Granite Tors

FORT   WAINWRIGHT

EIELSON
AIR FORCE
BASE

The Butte

Caribou

B

Continue on Page 115

FAIRBANKS

FORT
WAINWRIGHT
MIL RES

2

SALCHA

RIVER

4884

Aurora
Lodge

Salcha River SRS

Harding Lake
State Recreation Area

3176
Harding
Lake
4412

4624

TANANA   VALLEY

C

MOSQUITO CREEK RD

FT
WAINWRIGHT
MIL RES

Mosquito   Cr

4092

Birch
Lake
3048

4628

Birch Lake State
Recreation Site

Scout Camp–Loost
Lake

RICHARDSON HWY

2

STATE   FOREST

Campbell
Cabin

Richardson

RIVER

Shaw Creek
Lodge

3452

Shaw Creek Flats

4928

TANANA

STATE

FAIRBANKS   NORTH   STAR   BOROUGH

Delta
Lake

4580

Koole
Lake

CREEK

Top
2579

Clear

RICHARDSON HWY

2

4832

Quartz
Lake

1406

Quartz Lake
State Recreation Area

Thompson
Lake

Jollys
Cabin

4108

Bluff Cabin
Ridge

D

DENALI BOROUGH

LITTLE   DELTA   RIVER

4836
Rainbow
Lake

FORT   GREELY

MILITARY   RESERVATION

DELTA

RIVER

Big Delta
State Historical Park

3768

Big Delta

Fourmile
Hill

HISTORICAL

TANANA LOOP

Clearwater
Lake

4198

3100

Delta
SRS

Delta
Junction

Delta Junction
Landing Strip

Alaska Highway
Radio Towers

4

2

FORT GREELY

Delta Airmotive
LS (private)

© DeLorme

64°00'
147°00'

Continue on Page 106

KILOMETERS   5   0   5   10   15   20

MILES   1 0 1 2 3 4 5 6 7 8 9 10 11 12

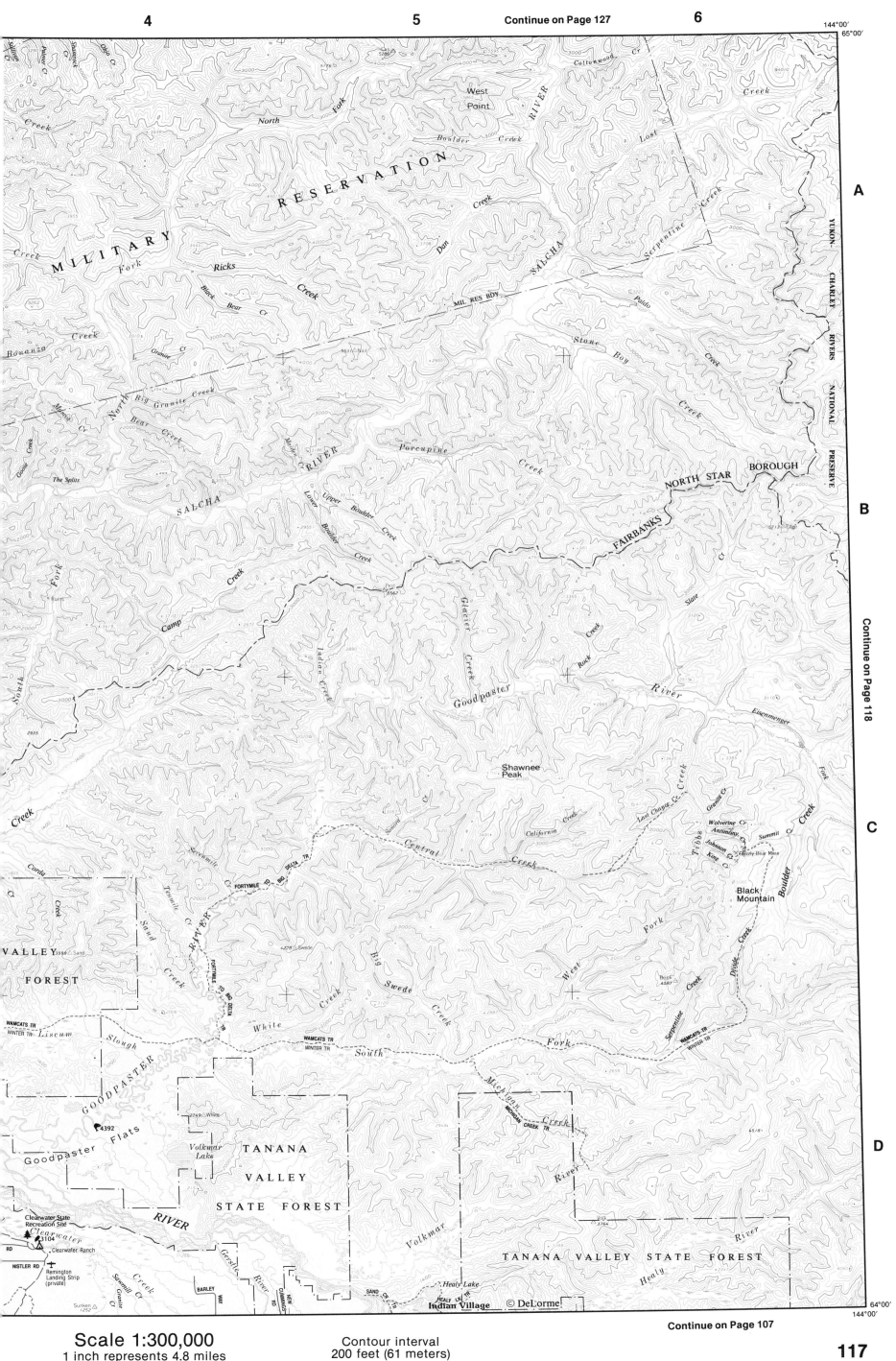

144°00'
65°00'

A

B

Continue on Page 118

C

D

64°00'
144°00'

Continue on Page 107

Scale 1:300,000
1 inch represents 4.8 miles

Contour interval
200 feet (61 meters)

© DeLorme

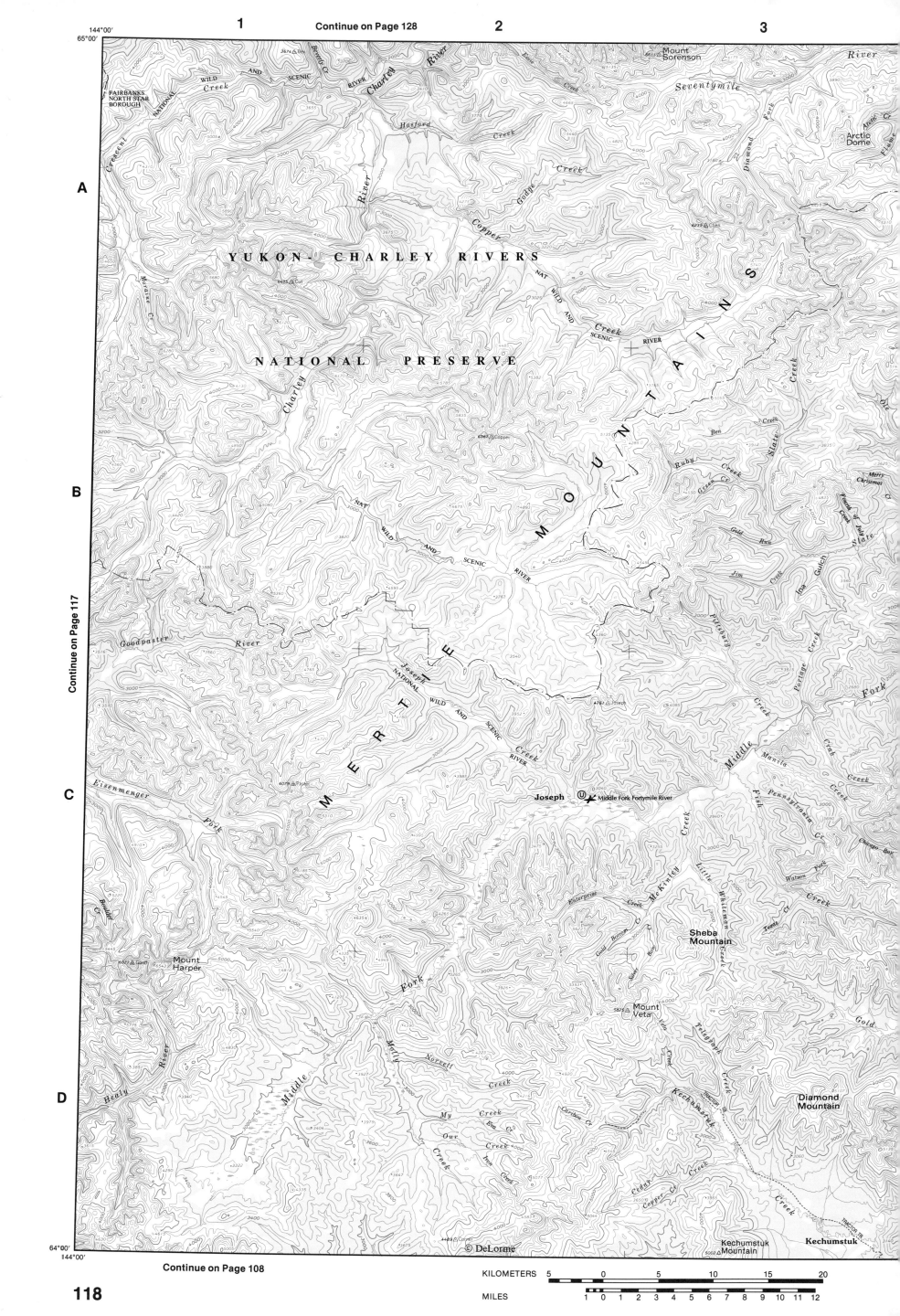

144°00'
65°00'

FAIRBANKS
NORTH STAR
BOROUGH

A

YUKON · CHARLEY RIVERS

NATIONAL   PRESERVE

MOUNTAINS

Mount
Sorenson

Seventymile

Arctic
Dome

Continue on Page 117

B

Goodpaster

River

Joseph

NATIONAL

WILD

AND

SCENIC

RIVER

Eisenmenger

Fork

C

Joseph   Middle Fork Fortymile River

Sheba
Mountain

Mount
Harper

Mount
Veta

D

Healy

Middle

Fork

Norrell

Creek

Diamond
Mountain

Kechumstuk
Mountain

Kechumstuk

© DeLorme

64°00'
144°00'

Continue on Page 108

KILOMETERS   5   0   5   10   15   20

MILES   1   0   1   2   3   4   5   6   7   8   9   10   11   12

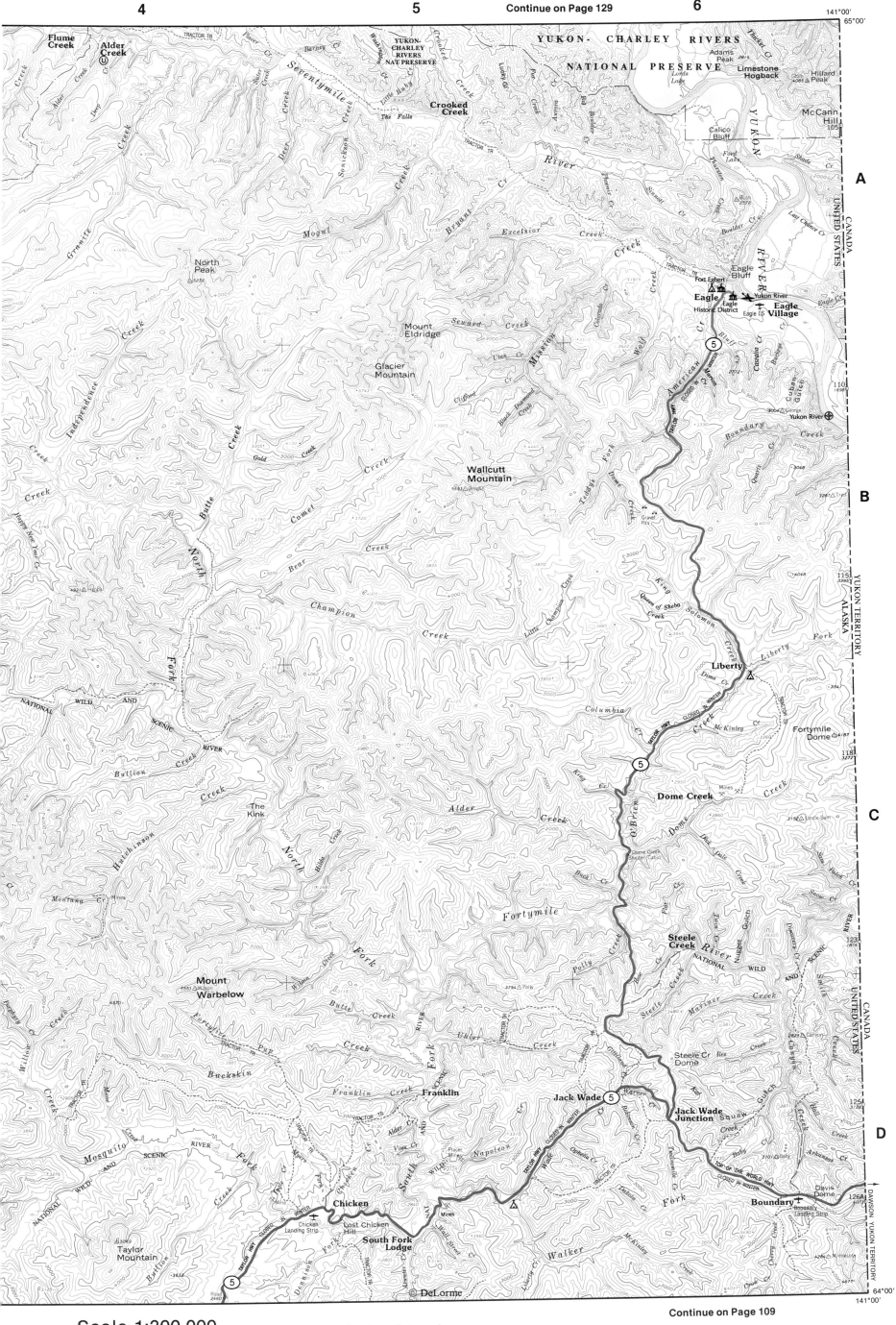

Continue on Page 109

Scale 1:300,000
1 inch represents 4.8 miles

Contour interval
200 feet (61 meters)

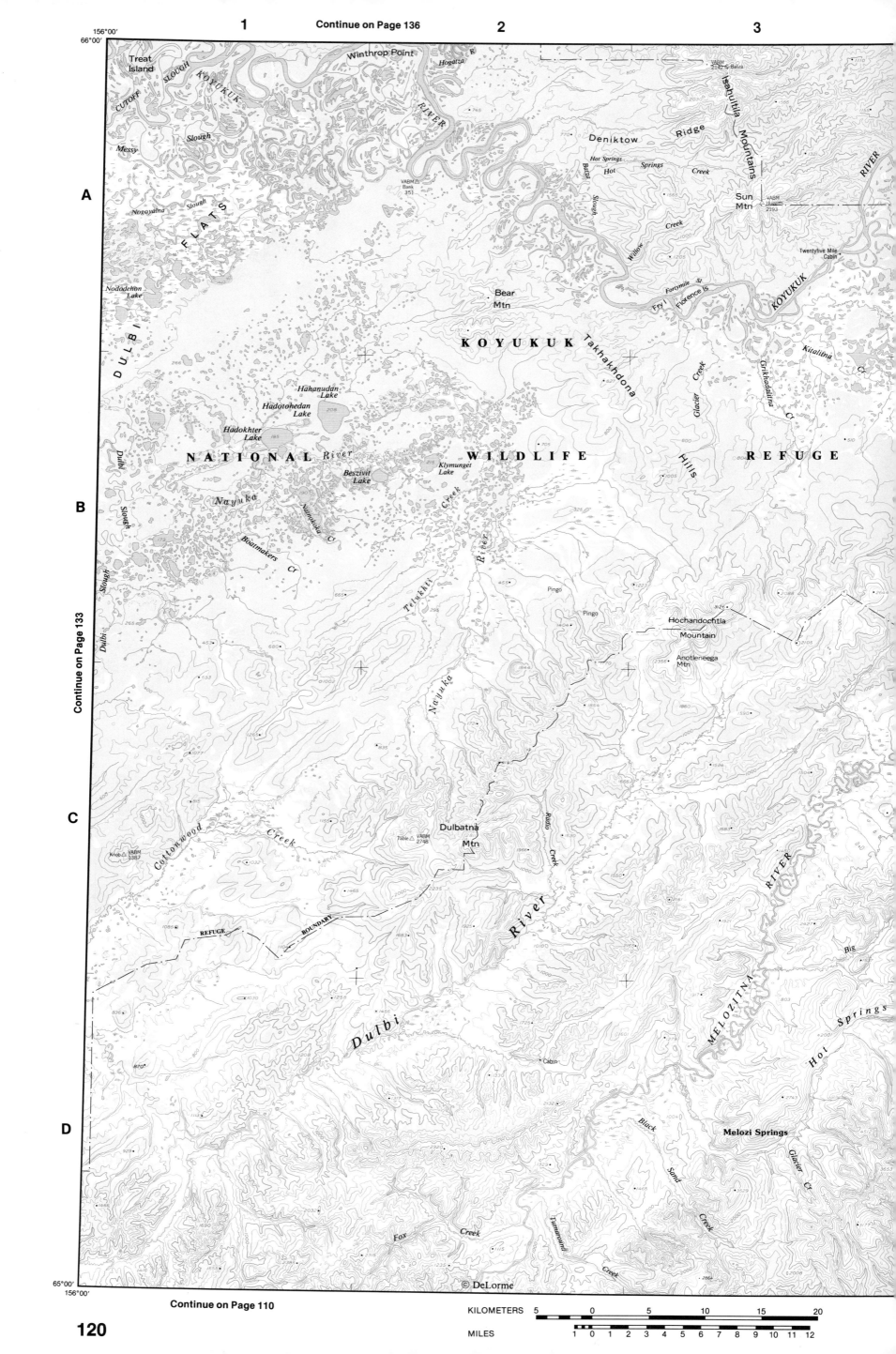

156°00'
66°00'

Treat
Island

CUTOFF SLOUGH

KOYUKUK

Winthrop Point

Hogatza R

Hogatza

RIVER

Isahuttila Mountains

RIVER

Messy
Slough

Deniktow

Ridge

Hot Springs
Hot Springs Creek
Batza
Slough

Sun
Mtn

VABM
Hughes
2193

A

Nogoyalna Slough

F L A T S

DULBI

Nododehon
Lake

Bear
Mtn

K O Y U K U K

Takhakhdona

Willow Creek

Fry I
Fortymile Sl
Florence Is

KOYUKUK

Twentyfive Mile
Cabin

Kitalitna

Cr

Hahanudan
Lake

Hadotohedan
Lake

Glacier Creek

Grikhadaltna Cr

Hadokhter
Lake

N A T I O N A L River **W I L D L I F E** **R E F U G E**

Hills

Klymunget
Lake

B

Nayuka

Beszivit
Lake

Namokoia Cr

Creek

Hochandochtla
Mountain

Boatmakers
Cr

Telukhit

River

Pingo

Pingo

Anotleneega
Mtn

Continue on Page 133

Nayuka

Dulbi Slough

Slough

Dulbatna
Mtn

Table VABM
2748

Radio Creek

C

Knob VABM
1387

Cottonwood Creek

RIVER

MELOZITNA

River

RIVER

REFUGE

BOUNDARY

River

Big

Dulbi

Springs

Hot

D

Black

Melozi Springs

Sand

Creek

Glacier Cr

Fox Creek

Tumanonti
Creek

© DeLorme

65°00'
156°00'

KILOMETERS   5   0   5   10   15   20

MILES   1 0 1 2 3 4 5 6 7 8 9 10 11 12

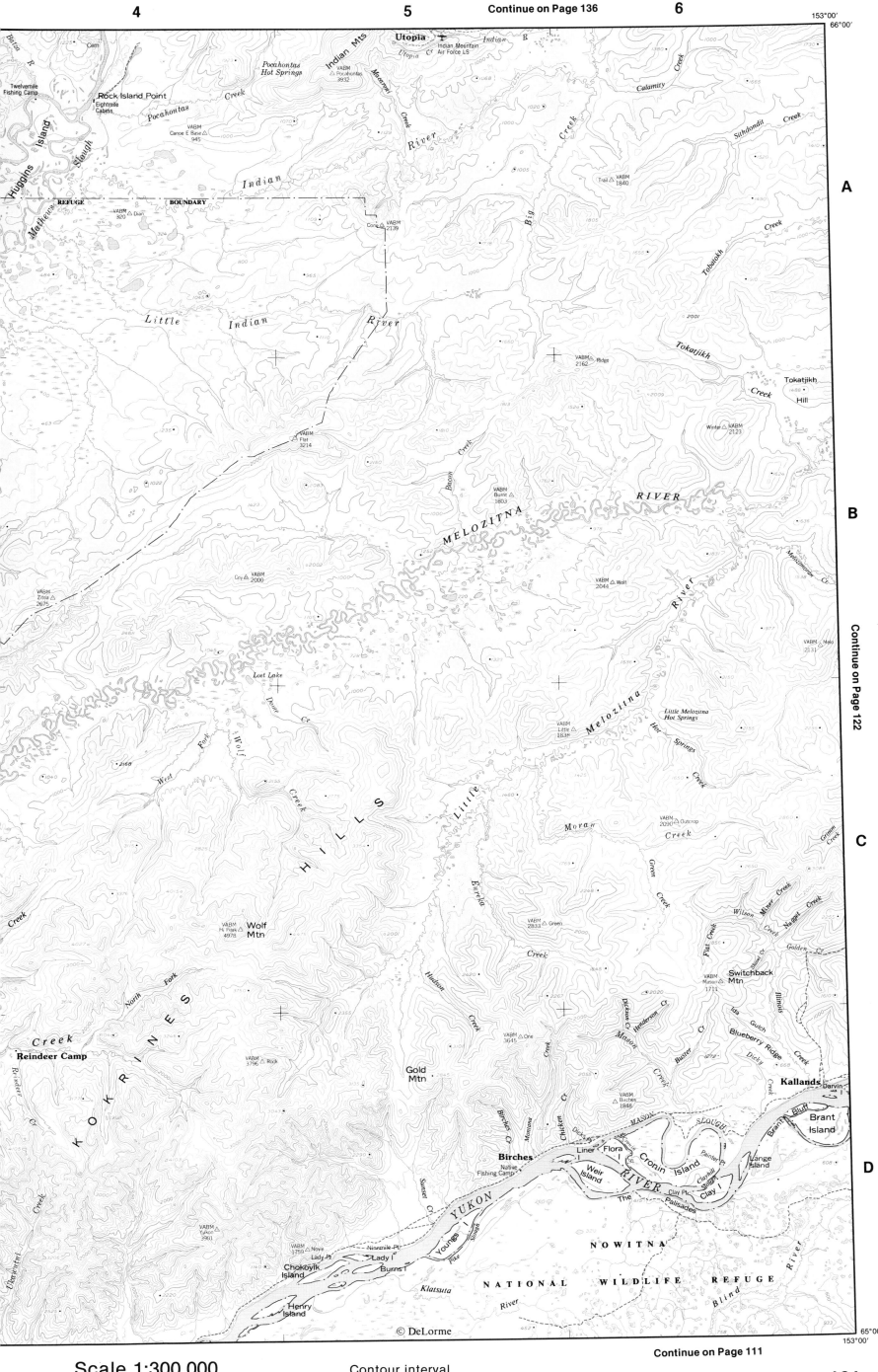

Continue on Page 122

Continue on Page 111

Scale 1:300,000
1 inch represents 4.8 miles

Contour interval
200 feet (61 meters)

121

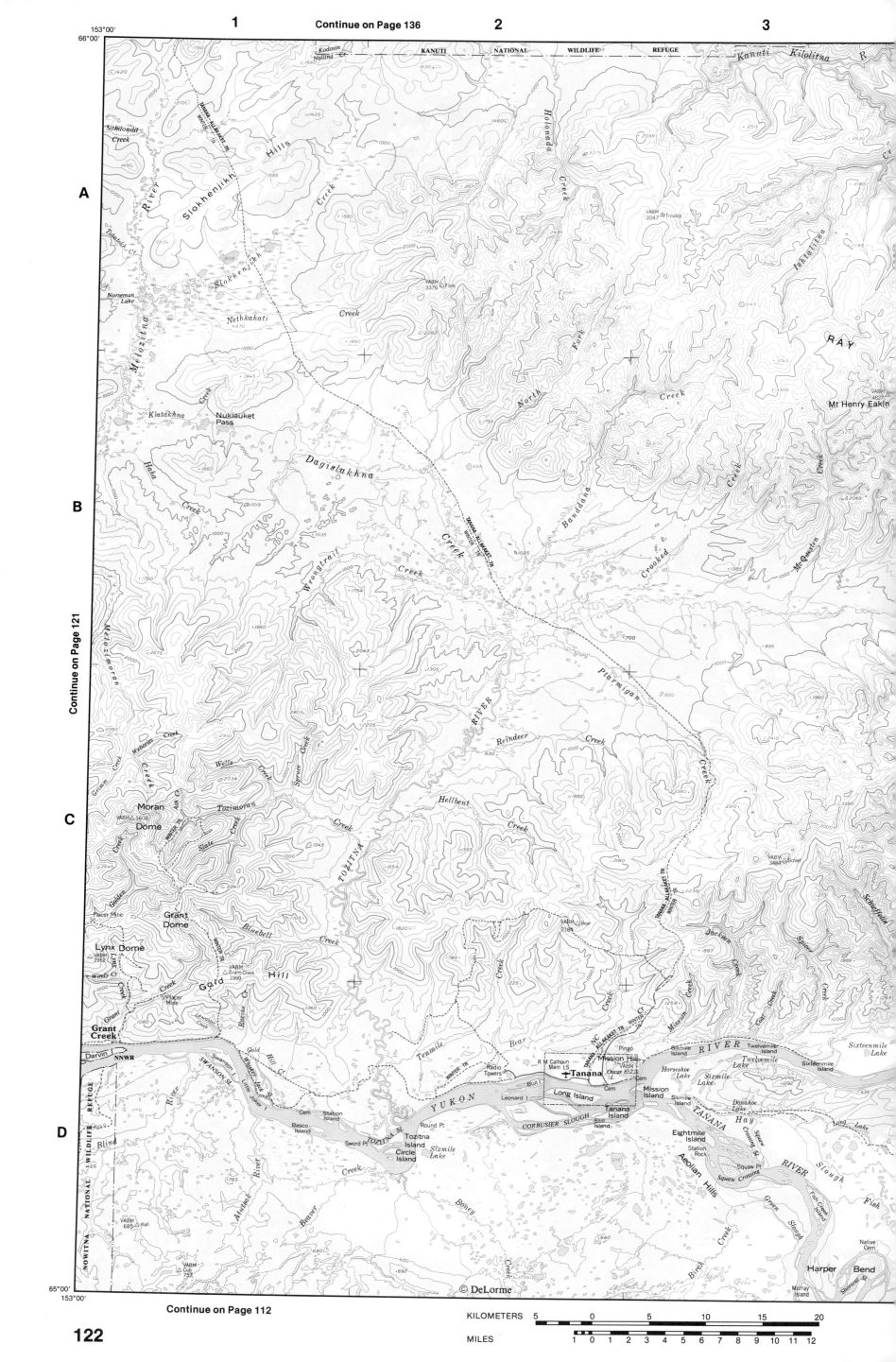

KANUTI   NATIONAL   WILDLIFE   REFUGE   *Kanuti* *Kilolitna* *R*

Kodosin
Nolitna *Cr*

Sithdonatt
Creek

Slokhenjikh *Hills*

A

Holonada
Creek

VABM
3047 *Trouble*

RAY

Melozitna
River

Tukatoka *Cr*

Norseman
Lake

Slokhenjikh

Nethkahati

VABM
3376 *Fork*

North *Fork*

Mt Henry Eakin

Klatakhna

Nuklauket
Pass

Dagislakhna

Creek

Banddana

Crooked

Mt Question

Haha
Creek

B

Creek
Creek

Wrangtraft

Creek

Continue on Page 121

Melozimoran

Creek

Ptarmigan

Creek

Weborias *Creek*

Wells *Creek*

RIVER

Reindeer   *Creek*

Graham *Creek*

Creek

Spruce *Creek*

Hellbent

Creek

Moran
Dome
VABM 3608

Tozimoran

C

Slate *Creek*

Ash *Cr*

TOZITNA

Creek

VABM
3484 *Schiefel*

Golden *Creek*

Grant
Dome

Bluebell

Creek

TANANA-ALLAKAKET TR
WINTER TR

Jackara
Creek

Schiefhill

Lynx *Dome*
VABM
1952

Gard   *O*   *Hill*

VABM
1959 *Grant Creek*

VABM
2184 *Bear*

Mission *Creek*

Windy Cr

Placer
Mine

Creek

Racine *Cr*

Squaw *Creek*

Grant
Creek

Creek

Bear

Pingo

Sixmile
Island

RIVER

Twelvemile
Island

Sixteenmile
Lake

Darvin
NNWR

SWANSON SL

River

Whisker Slough

Gold Hill Cr

Tenmile

Radio
Towers

R M Calhoun
Mem LS

Bull I

Tanana
VABM
Oscar 852

Cem

Mission Hill

Cem

Horseshoe
Lake

Sixmile
Lake

Twelvemile
Lake

Sixteenmile
Island

D

NOWITNA   NATIONAL   WILDLIFE   REFUGE

Blind

Altakdok *River*

Little Tozitna SL

Cem

Station
Island

Basco
Island

YUKON

Leonard I

Round Pt

Long Island

Mission
Island

Tanana
Island

CORBUSIER SLOUGH

Sixmile
Island

TANANA

Donahoe
Lake

Bay

Sword Pt

TOZITNA SL

Tozitna
Island

Circle
Island

Sixmile
Lake

Still
Island

Eightmile
Island

Aeolian
Hills

Station
Rock

Squaw Crossing SL

RIVER

Lewis
Slough

Beaver *Creek*

Boney *Creek*

Creek

Squaw Pt
Squaw Crossing

Birch *Creek*

Fan Green
Island

Fish
Slough

VABM
685 *Kall*

Harper   Bend

VABM
Cub 752

Native
Cem

Murray
Island

© DeLorme

Continue on Page 112

KILOMETERS   5   0   5   10   15   20

MILES   1 0 1 2 3 4 5 6 7 8 9 10 11 12

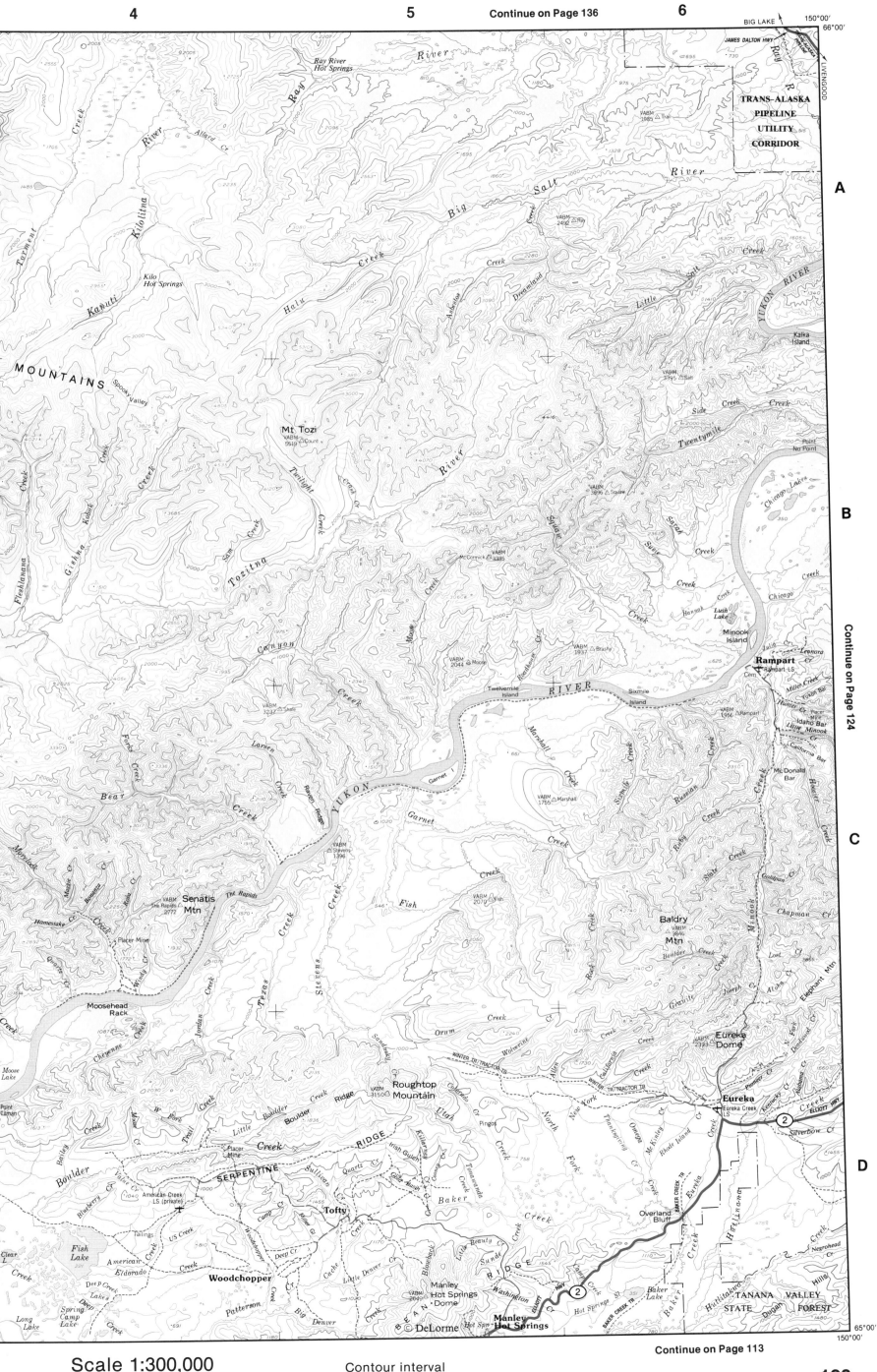

TRANS–ALASKA
PIPELINE
UTILITY
CORRIDOR

Continue on Page 124

© DeLorme

Continue on Page 113

Scale 1:300,000
1 inch represents 4.8 miles

Contour interval
200 feet (61 meters)

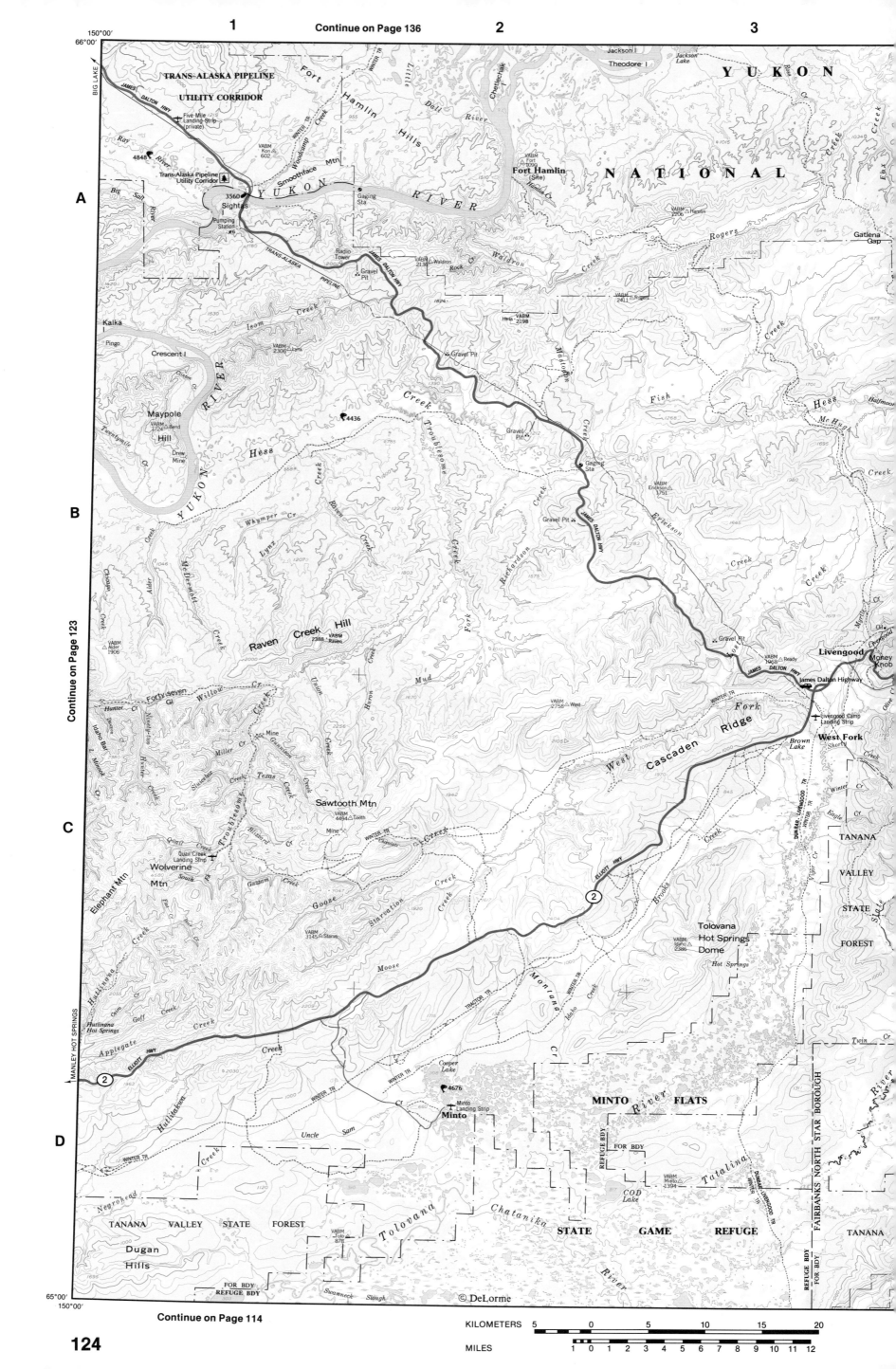

150°00'
66°00'

BIG LAKE

TRANS-ALASKA PIPELINE
UTILITY CORRIDOR

Fort Hamlin Hills

Y U K O N

N A T I O N A L

Fort Hamlin
(Site)

Gatlena Gap

A

Sightas
3560
Pumping Station

Smoothface Mtn

Y U K O N   R I V E R

Gaging Sta

Radio Tower

Gravel Pit

JAMES DALTON HWY

TRANS-ALASKA PIPELINE

Kalka

Crescent I

Maypole
Hill

Y U K O N   R I V E R

Hess

Gravel Pit

Gravel Pit

Gaging Sta

Fish

Hess

B

Raven Creek
Hill

Richardson Creek

JAMES DALTON HWY

Livengood

Money Knob

Continue on Page 123

Sawtooth Mtn

Mine

C

Wolverine
Mtn

Elephant Mtn

Quail Creek
Landing Strip

West Cascaden Ridge

Livengood Camp
Landing Strip

West Fork

Brown Lake

ELLIOTT HWY

(2)

TANANA

VALLEY

STATE

FOREST

Tolovana
Hot Springs
Dome

Hot Springs

D

MANLEY HOT SPRINGS

Hutlinana
Hot Springs

Applegate

ELLIOTT HWY

(2)

Cooper
Lake

4676

Minto
Landing Strip

Minto

MINTO   River   **FLATS**

REFUGE BDY

FOR BDY

Dugan
Hills

TANANA   VALLEY   STATE   FOREST

Tolovana

Chatanika

STATE   **GAME**   **REFUGE**

FAIRBANKS NORTH STAR BOROUGH

TANANA

FOR BDY
REFUGE BDY

© DeLorme

Continue on Page 114

124

KILOMETERS   5   0   5   10   15   20

MILES   1 0 1 2 3 4 5 6 7 8 9 10 11 12

65°00'
150°00'

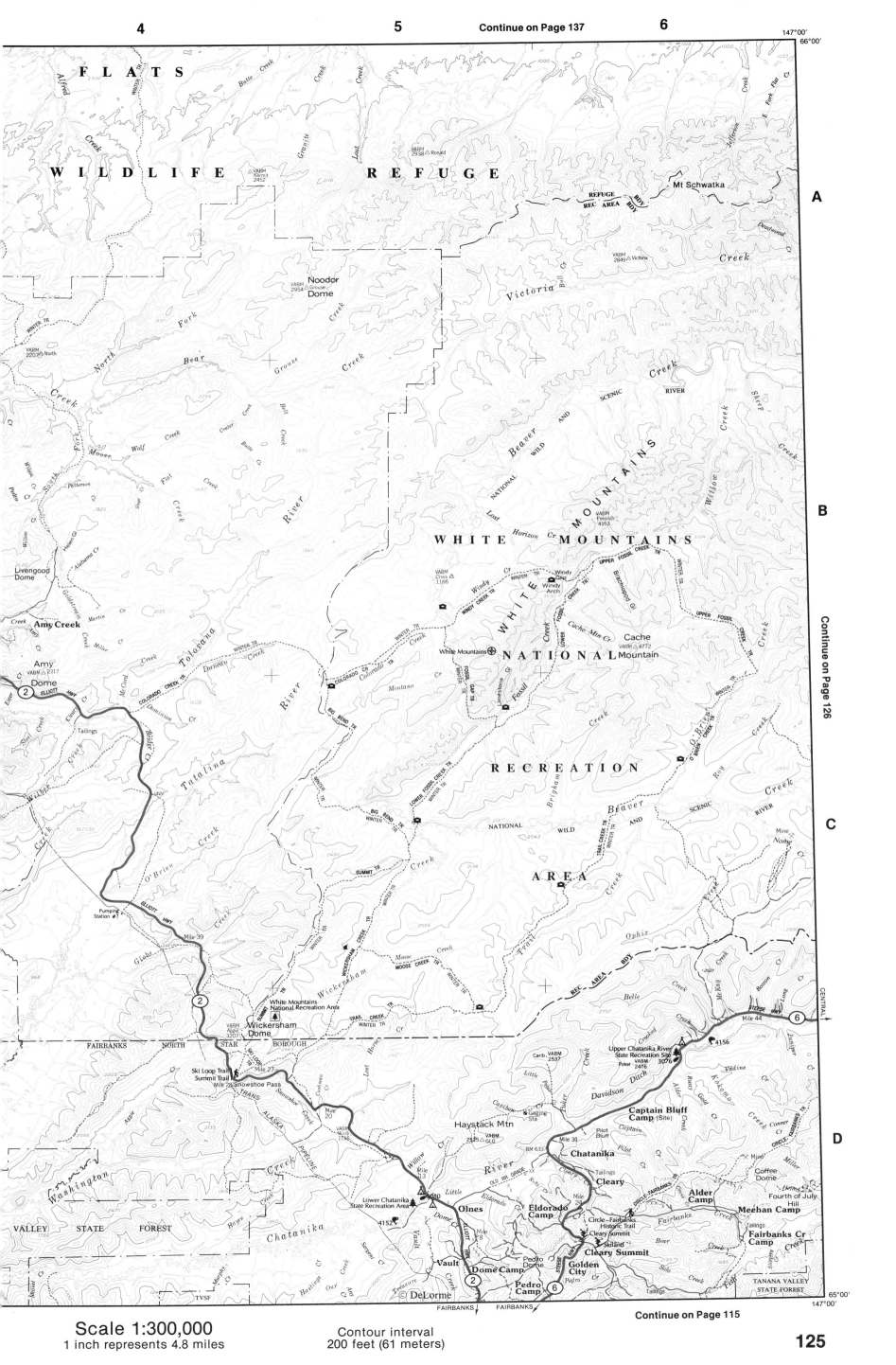

147°00'
66°00'

F L A T S

W I L D L I F E   R E F U G E

Mt Schwatka

A

REFUGE BDY
REC AREA BDY

VABM 2938 △ Ronald

VABM Kermit 2452

VABM 2954 △ Grouse
Noodor Dome

VABM 2849 △ Victoria

Deadwood

Continue on Page 126

VABM 2202 North

North Fork

Bear Creek

Grouse Creek

Victoria

Creek

Creek

SCENIC
RIVER

Creek

Sheep

B

Livengood Dome

Amy Creek

Amy Dome
VABM △ 2317

② ELLIOTT HWY

W H I T E   M O U N T A I N S

W H I T E   M O U N T A I N S

WINTER TR

BEAVER

AND

WILD

NATIONAL

VABM Fossil △ 4153

UPPER FOSSIL CREEK TR

WINTER TR

VABM Creek △ 1166

Windy Gap
Windy Arch

WINDY CREEK TR

FOSSIL CREEK TR

Brachiopod Gl

UPPER FOSSIL CREEK TR

White Mountains ✛

Cache Mtn Cr

Cache Mountain
VABM 4772

COLORADO CREEK TR

WINTER TR

Tolovana

Duncan Creek

COLORADO CR TR

Colorado Creek

Montana

N A T I O N A L

FOSSIL GAP TR

WINTER TR

Limestone

Fossil Creek

WINTER TR

C

Tailings

Bridge Cr

ELLIOTT HWY

Pumping Station #7

Tatalina

River

BIG BEND TR

SUMMIT TR

WINTER TR

LOWER FOSSIL CREEK TR

WINTER TR

BIG BEND WINTER TR

R E C R E A T I O N

NATIONAL

WILD

Brigham Creek

A R E A

Beaver

AND

SCENIC

RIVER

O'Brien Creek

O'Brien Creek

Roy Creek

Mine Nome

② Mile 39

WICKERSHAM CREEK TR

Moose Creek

MOOSE CREEK TR

WINTER TR

TRAIL CREEK TR
WINTER TR

Ophir

②

FAIRBANKS   NORTH   STAR   BOROUGH

White Mountains National Recreation Area

VABM Alder △ 3207

Wickersham Dome

SUMMIT TR

WINTER TR

SKI LOOP

TRAIL CREEK TR
WINTER TR

WINTER TR

REC AREA BDY

STEESE HWY

Mile 44

⑥

CENTRAL

Belle Creek

VABM 2707

McKay Creek

Boston Cr

Lone Creek

Juniper Cr

D

Ski Loop Trail
Summit Trail
Mile 27

Mile 28 Snowshoe Pass

TRANS ALASKA PIPELINE

Snowshoe Creek

Mile 20

Mile 18 VABM 1156

Haystack Mtn

VABM 2525 △ GLO

Pilot Bluff

Carib VABM 2537

Little

Caribou Cr

Gaging Sta

Mile 30

Davidson Ditch

Poker Creek

VABM 2476

Upper Chatanika River
State Recreation Site
VABM 3076

△ 4156

Vadine

Kokomo Creek

Rusty Gold Cr

Captain Bluff
Camp (Site)

Captain Cr

BM 633

Chatanika

Pilot

CIRCLE–FAIRBANKS TR

Cleary

Tailings

Coffee Dome

Miller

Mixed

Fourth of July Hill

WASHINGTON

VALLEY

STATE

FOREST

Willow Creek

Mile 13

△ 4080

Lower Chatanika
State Recreation Area

4152

Olnes

Dome Creek

Little Eldorado

ELLIOTT HWY

Vault Creek

River

OLD RR GRADE

CLEARY

Eldorado Camp

Mile 16

Circle–Fairbanks
Historic Trail
Cleary Summit

Cleary Summit

Golden City

Skiland

Bear Creek

Eldorado Camp

Alder Camp

Meehan Camp

Fairbanks Cr
Camp

Fish

Gilmore

Chatanika

Vault

②

Dome Camp

Pedro Dome

Pedro
Camp

⑥

65°00'
147°00'

TANANA VALLEY
STATE FOREST

© DeLorme

TVSF

FAIRBANKS   FAIRBANKS

Continue on Page 115

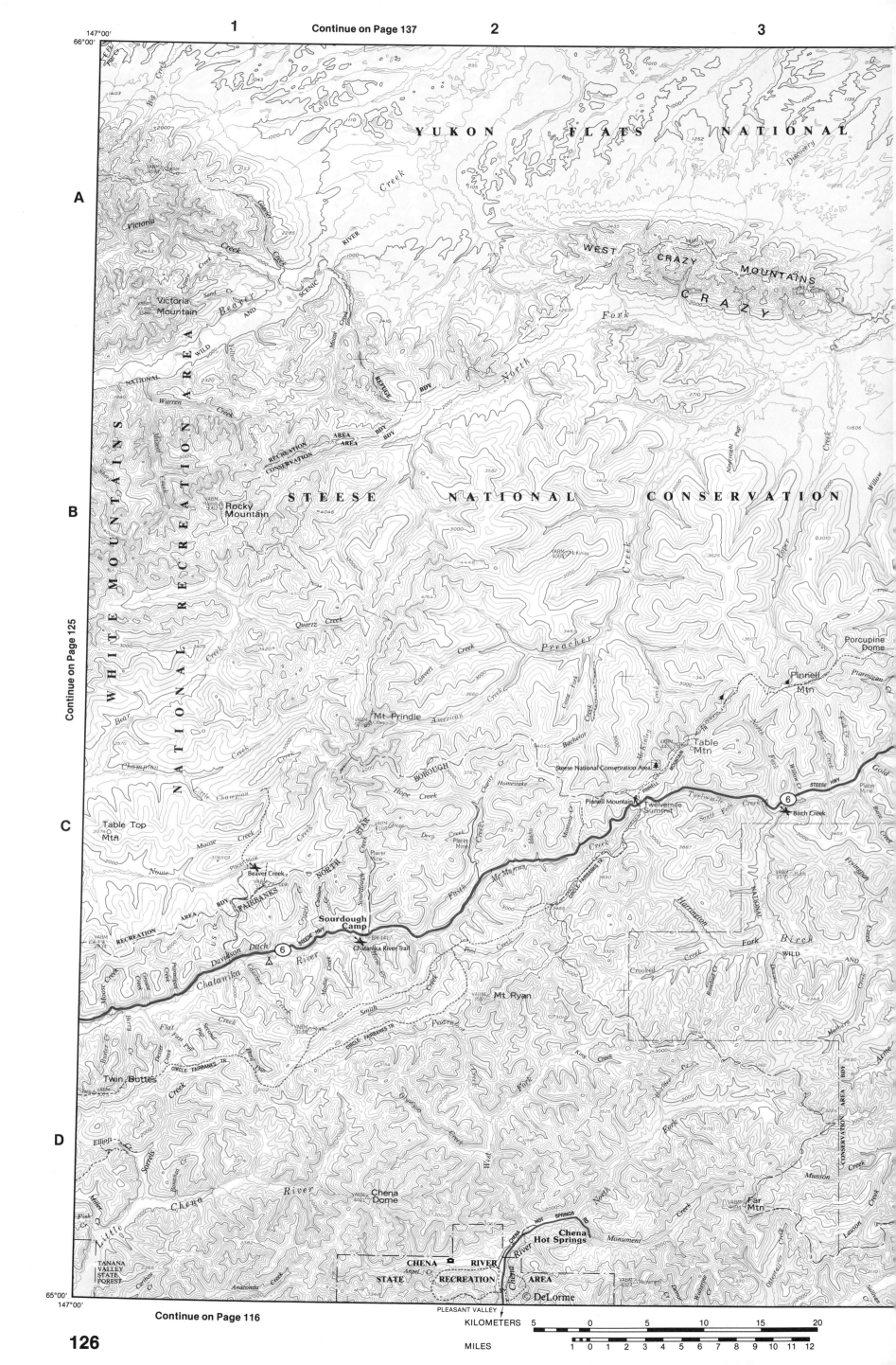

147°00'
66°00'

A

B

C

D

65°00'
147°00'

Continue on Page 125

YUKON FLATS NATIONAL

WEST CRAZY MOUNTAINS
CRAZY

STEESE NATIONAL CONSERVATION

Victoria
Mountain

Rocky
Mountain

Mt Prindle

Porcupine
Dome

Pinnell
Mtn

Table
Mtn

Table Top
Mtn

Pinnell Mountain
Twelvemile
Summit

Beaver Creek

Sourdough
Camp

Chatanika River Trail

Mt Ryan

Chena
Dome

Twin Buttes

Chena
Hot Springs

CHENA RIVER
STATE RECREATION AREA

© DeLorme

PLEASANT VALLEY

KILOMETERS 5 0 5 10 15 20

MILES 1 0 1 2 3 4 5 6 7 8 9 10 11 12

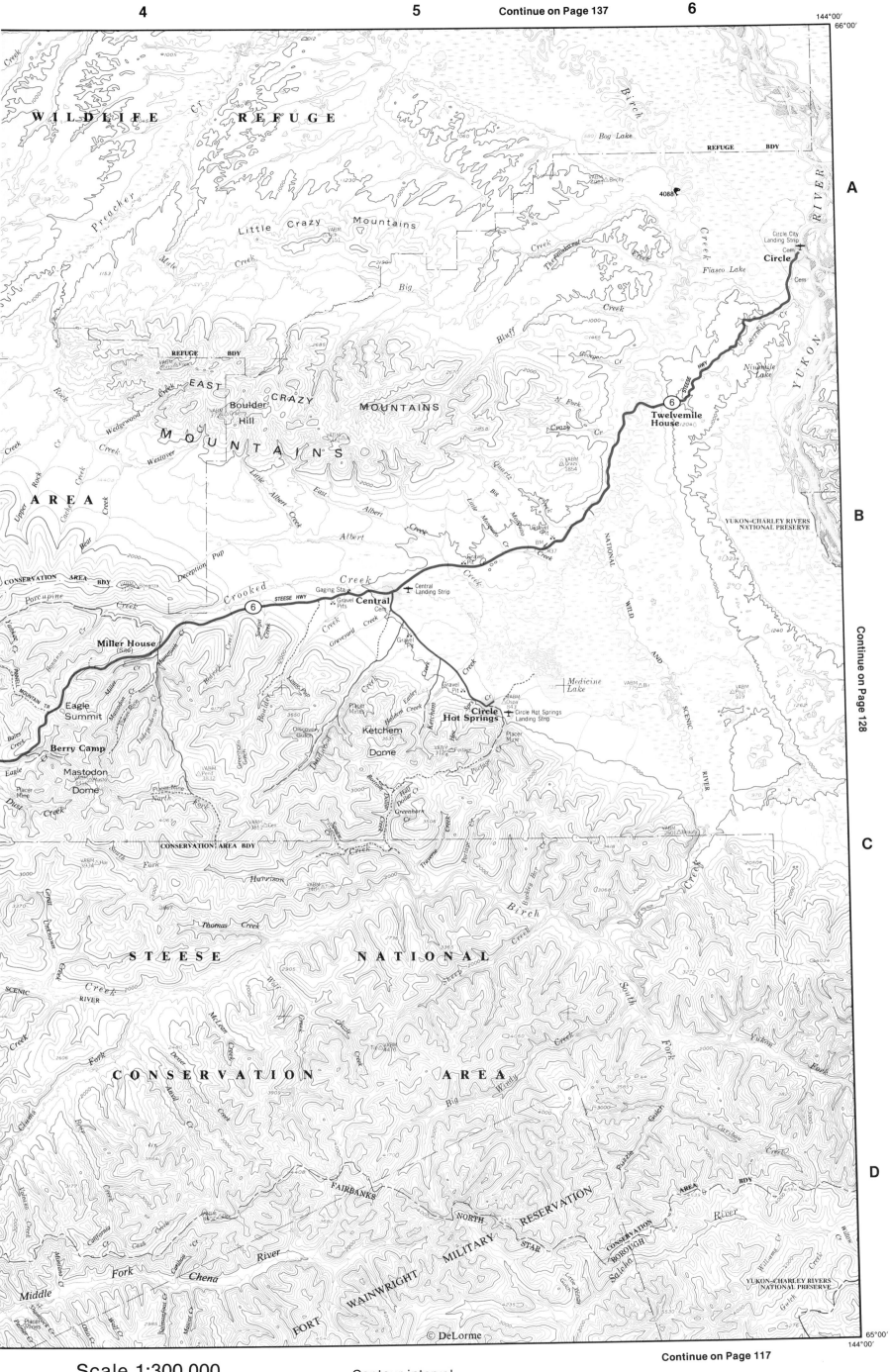

Continue on Page 128

Continue on Page 117

Scale 1:300,000
1 inch represents 4.8 miles

Contour interval
200 feet (61 meters)

© DeLorme

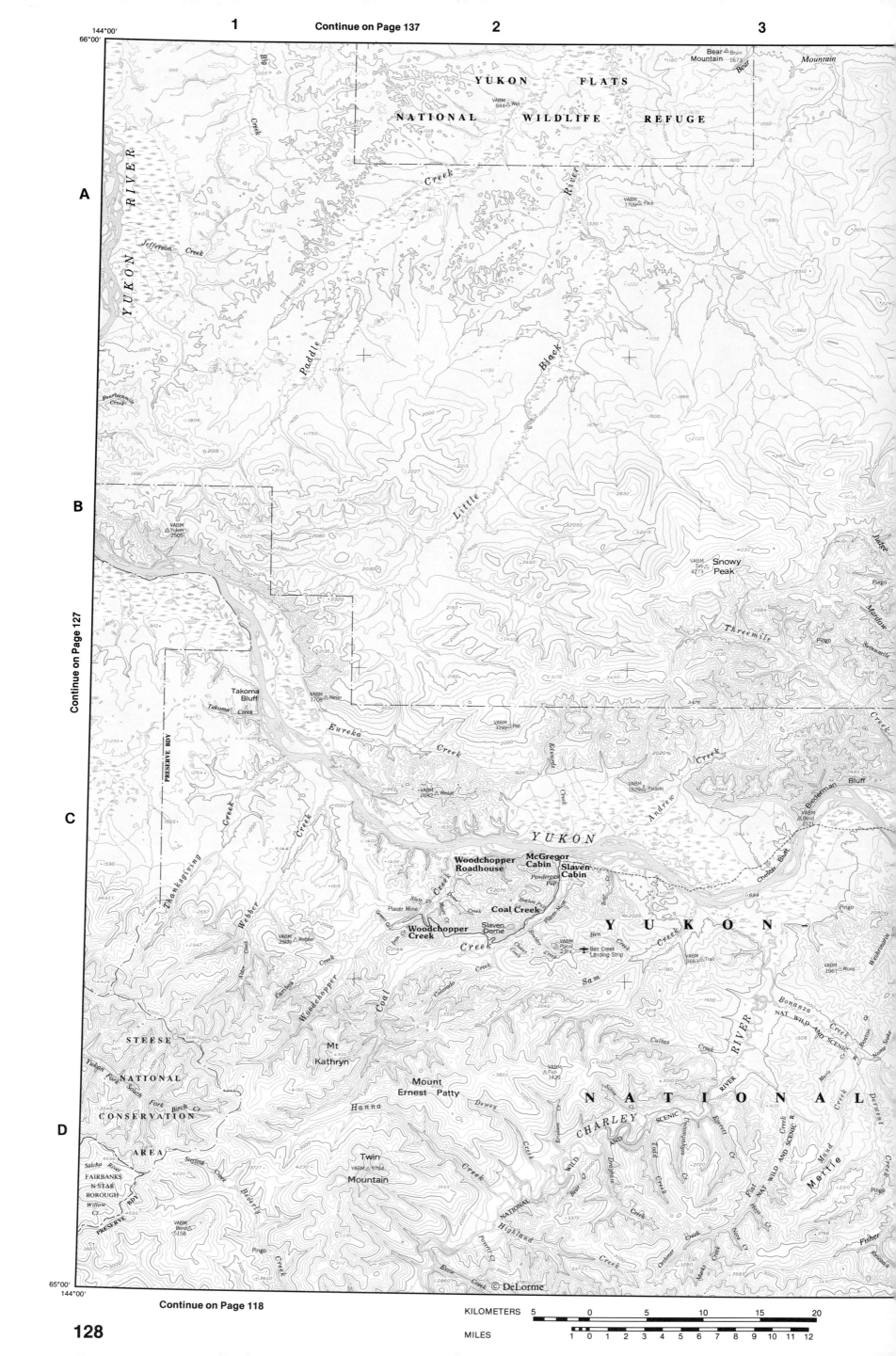

144°00'
66°00'

A

B

C

D

65°00'
144°00'

Continue on Page 127

YUKON RIVER

Jefferson Creek

Fourteenmile Creek

YUKON FLATS

NATIONAL WILDLIFE REFUGE

Bear Mountain

Bruin 1673

Mountain

VABM 844 Wet

VABM 1709 Pack

Big Creek

Paddle Creek

Black

Little

River

VABM Yukon 2505

VABM Takoma 4773

Snowy Peak

Threemile

Pingo

Pingo

Murdon

Judge

Sevenmile

PRESERVE BDY

Takoma Bluff

Takoma Creek

Eureka Creek

VABM 1708 Neler

VABM 3191 Pob

VABM 2642 Wedge

Edward

Creek

VABM 1309 Psodoso

Andrew

Creek

Biederman Bluff

VABM 2121 Bend

Bluff

Thanksgiving Creek

Weber Creek

Woodchopper Roadhouse

McGregor Cabin

Slaven Cabin

Pendergast Pup

YUKON

Chester Bluff

Pingo

Pingo

Placer Mine

Slate Cr

Coal Creek

Buton Pup

Placer Mine

VABM 2909 Webber

Woodchopper Creek

Slaven Dome

Creek

VABM 2374 Place

Ben Creek Landing Strip

Ben Creek

Sam Creek

YUKON-

VABM 1663 Trail

VABM 1961 Wood

Washington

Alan Cr

Caribou Cr

Woodchopper Creek

Coal Creek

Colorado Creek

Sam Creek

Cultas Creek

Bonanza Creek

NAT. WILD. AND SCENIC R.

RIVER

STEESE

Mt Kathryn

VABM Fish 3426

Dewey Creek

NATIONAL

CONSERVATION

Birch Cr

South Fork

Mount Ernest Patty

Hanna Creek

Erickson Creek

CHARLEY

AND SCENIC R.

WILD

NAT. WILD. AND SCENIC R.

Derwent

Mertie

AREA

FAIRBANKS N STAR BOROUGH

Salcha River

Willow Cr

Sterling Creek

Twin Mountain

VABM 5784

Bear Cr

NATIONAL

Dragman Creek

Tadd Cr

Flat Cr

Maud Cr

Fisher

PRESERVE

VABM Bend 5158

Pingo

Creek

Birch Cr

Beaver Creek

Powers Cr

HIGHLAND

Creek

Crescent Creek

Nora Cr

Orthmer Creek

Marle Cr

Mask Cr

©DeLorme

KILOMETERS   5   0   5   10   15   20

MILES   1 0 1 2 3 4 5 6 7 8 9 10 11 12

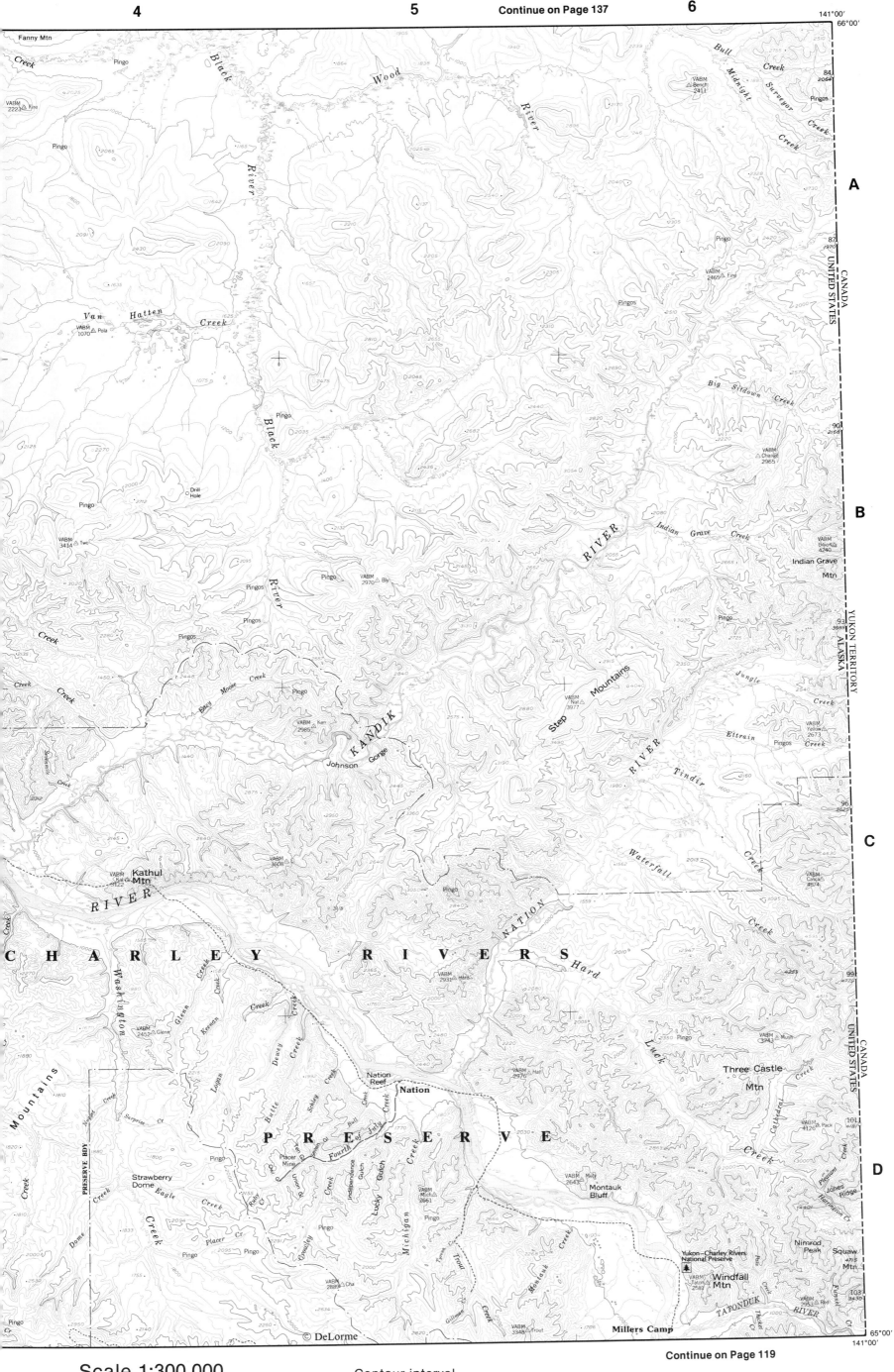

141°00'
66°00'

Fanny Mtn

A

CANADA
UNITED STATES

B

YUKON TERRITORY
ALASKA

KANDIK

Johnson Gorge

Step Mountains

C

Kathul
Mtn

RIVER

C H A R L E Y   R I V E R S

N A T I O N

Washington

Mountains

Nation
Reef
Nation

P R E S E R V E

Strawberry
Dome

Three Castle
Mtn

Montauk
Bluff

Nimrod
Peak

Squaw
Mtn

Yukon-Charley Rivers
National Preserve

Windfall
Mtn

CANADA
UNITED STATES

D

Millers Camp

TATONDUK RIVER

65°00'
141°00'

© DeLorme

Continue on Page 119

Scale 1:300,000
1 inch represents 4.8 miles

Contour interval
200 feet (61 meters)

129

Continue on Page 132

1

2

3

Continue on Page 138, Inset 1

168°00'
64°00'

A

B

C

D

NORTON   SOUND

BERING   SEA

Stuart I
STUART MTN   St Michael
480   LS and SPB
Hunting Pt
Stebbins
Stebbins LS
St Michael

Pikmiktalik
Pt Romanof
AMNWR
Pastol Bay
225!

Kothlik I
Kwikpak
Nunaktuk I
Nokogamiut I   Nokogamiut   Kotlik   YUKON
AMNWR   Kotlik LS   Pastolik
Agcklekak   DELTA
Emangak   Bill Moores
Naguchik
Emmonak   Kwiguk   Hamilton   WILDERNESS
Kaluchagun   Akumsuk   Kravaksarak   4040
Alakanuk   Lamont   New   NORTH
Agcklarok   Alakanuk LS   Hamilton   1755 PK
Sheldon Point LS   Trogshak   Kwikpuk
and SPB   Kwiklokchun   Tukukapak   1187
Waklarok   Sheldon Point   Fish Village
Eleutak   Arovirchagk

Black
Kwikak   .520
Bimiut   INGRICHUAK HILL
Knockhock   611   Mountain Village   Pilot
New Knockhock   Mtn Village LS   St Marys LS   Village
.2190   Pitkas Pt   St Marys   Takshak
Utukakarvik   Mukialik   Pilot Station   794!
Krekatok I   Pilot Station LS   Marshall
Neragon I   Scammon Bay   WINTER TR   Hills I
Scammon Bay   Owl Village   Kanapak
Cape Romanzof   Scammon Bay LS and SPB   Kwigorlak   The Landing
Aniktun I   TOWAK   Chakaktolik
Cape Romanzof Air Force LS   MTN   ASKINUK MTNS
Paimiut   KOCHILAGOK
Kokechik Bay   HILL   YUKON   DELTA
Hooper Bay
Nuok Spit   Hooper Bay LS
Chevak   .32
Chevak LS
364
Punoarat Pt   .620
Angyoyaravak Bay   NATIONAL   WILDLIFE
ALASKA   9.
MARITIME   Chakwaktolik
NWR   .33

Newtok   Nunapitchuk   20
Nunivachak I   Newtok LS   Nanvarnarluk   LS and SPB
Kigigak I   Newtok SPB   Kasigluk
Kasigluk LS   Akolmiut
Ukak   Paingakmeut
1485   Nelson   417   Napakiak
Tununak LS   Island   Napakiak LS
Cape Vancouver   Tununak   and SPB
Umkumiut   Toksook Bay
Nightmute   Toksook Bay LS   .53   Tuntutuliak
Mekoryuk   Nightmute LS   Tuntutuliak LS   .29
Mekoryuk LS   Cape Etolin   and SPB
Cape   Kikmiktalikamiut   Gufmut
Mohican   Nash Harbor   Cape   Akulurak
SEEMALIK BUTTE   Manning
866   Nash Harbor   ALASKA   Eek I
YUKON DELTA   TERN MTN.   Apokak
NWR   443
Nunivak Island   Chefornak   40
1675 ROBERTS MTN   Chefornak LS   Kulvagavik
1040   Karon L   and SPB   Kongiganak LS
Atahgo Pt   MARITIME   Kipnuk   Kwigillingok LS
Cape Corwin   NWR   Kipnuk LS   Kongiganak
Duchikthluk Bay   Kikegtek I   Anogok   Kwigillingok SPB   Kwigillingok
Cape Mendenhall   Pingurbek I

130   © DeLorme   Kwigluk I   KUSKOKWIM BAY

59°41'15"   59°41'15"
168°00'   162°11'14"

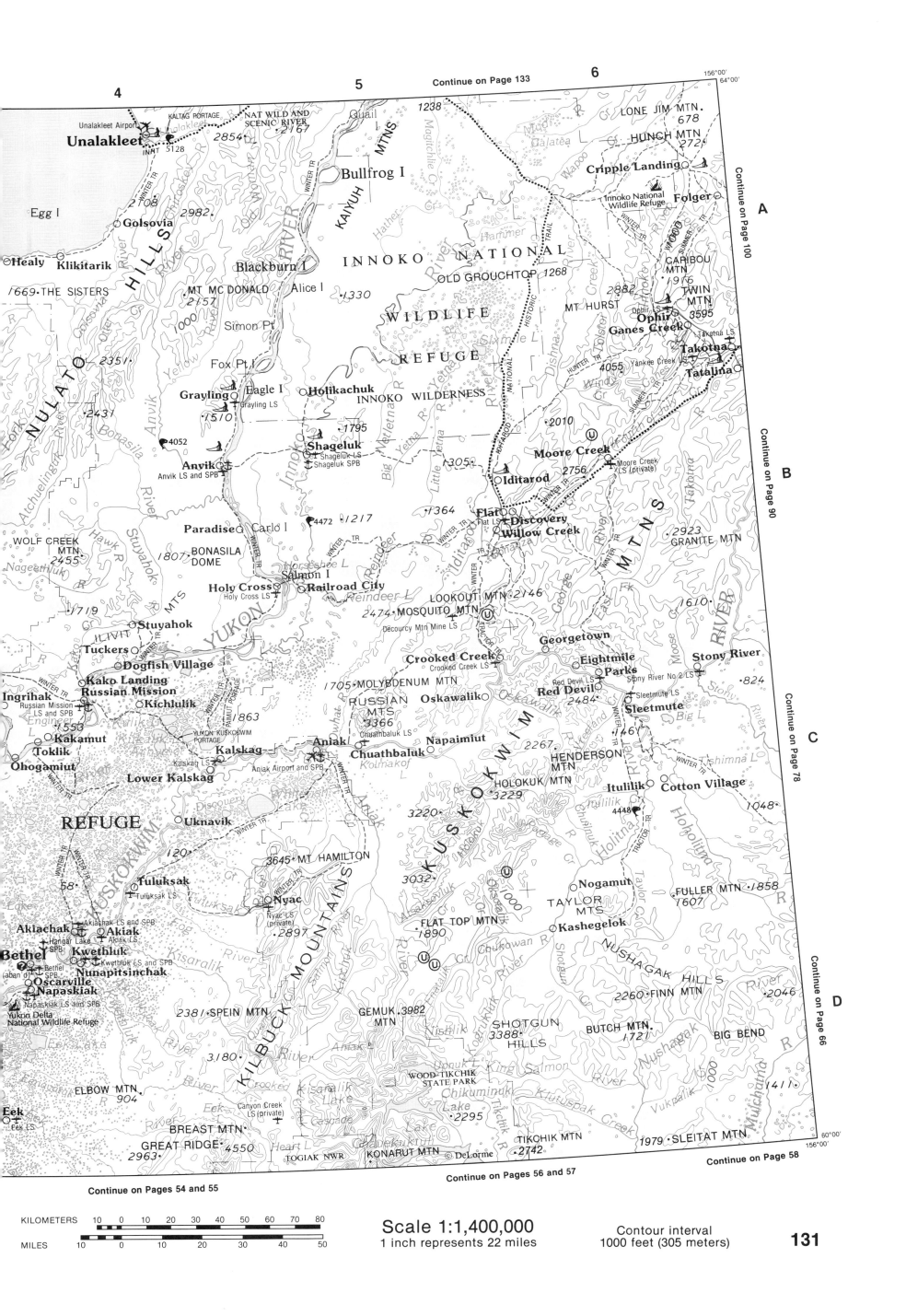

Continue on Page 133
Continue on Page 100
Continue on Page 90
Continue on Page 78
Continue on Page 66
Continue on Page 58
Continue on Pages 56 and 57
Continue on Pages 54 and 55

KILOMETERS 10 0 10 20 30 40 50 60 70 80
MILES 10 0 10 20 30 40 50

Scale 1:1,400,000
1 inch represents 22 miles

Contour interval
1000 feet (305 meters)

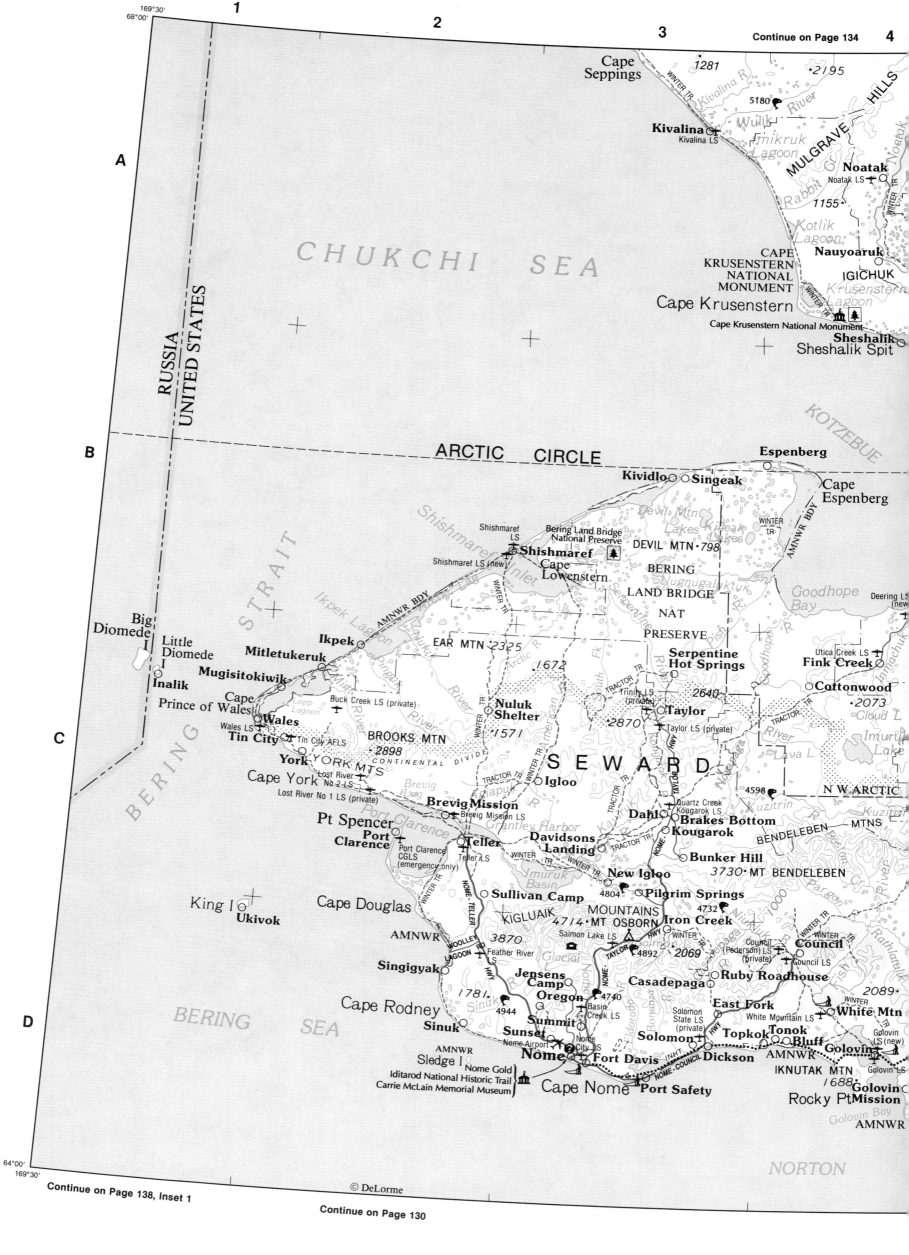

CHUKCHI SEA

BERING STRAIT

BERING SEA

NORTON

ARCTIC CIRCLE

RUSSIA
UNITED STATES

Cape Seppings
1281
•2195
5180
Kivalina
Kivalina LS
Wulik River
MULGRAVE HILLS
Imikruk Lagoon
Rabbit
Noatak
Noatak LS
1155
Kotlik Lagoon

CAPE KRUSENSTERN NATIONAL MONUMENT
Cape Krusenstern
Cape Krusenstern National Monument
Nauyoaruk
IGICHUK
Krusenstern Lagoon
Sheshalik
Sheshalik Spit

KOTZEBUE

Espenberg
Kividlo Singeak
Cape Espenberg
Devil Mtn Lakes Kitluk Lakes
WINTER TR
AMNWR BDY
BERING LAND BRIDGE NAT PRESERVE
DEVIL MTN •798
Goodhope Bay
Deering LS (new)

Shishmaref LS
Bering Land Bridge National Preserve
Shishmaref
Shishmaref LS (new)
Cape Lowenstern
Nugnugaliktuk
Serpentine Hot Springs
Utica Creek LS
Fink Creek

Big Diomede I
Little Diomede I
Inalik
Cape Prince of Wales
Wales
Wales LS
Tin City
Tin City AFLS
York
YORK MTS
Cape York
Lost River No 2 LS
Lost River No 1 LS (private)
Ikpek
Mitletukeruk
Mugisitokiwik
Ikpek Lagoon
AMNWR BDY
Lopp Lagoon
Buck Creek LS (private)
EAR MTN •2325
1672
Nuluk Shelter
1571
BROOKS MTN •2898
CONTINENTAL DIVIDE
2640
Trinity LS (private)
2870
Taylor
Taylor LS (private)
Cottonwood
•2073
Cloud L
Imuruk Lake
Lava L
Kuzitrin River
4598
N W ARCTIC

SEWARD
Igloo
Brevig Mission
Brevig Mission LS
Grantley Harbor
Pt Spencer
Port Clarence
Port Clarence CGLS (emergency only)
Teller
Teller LS
Davidsons Landing
Quartz Creek
Kougarok LS
Dahl
Brakes Bottom
Kougarok
BENDELEBEN MTNS
New Igloo
Bunker Hill
3730 •MT BENDELEBEN

King I
Ukivok
Cape Douglas
Sullivan Camp
4804
Pilgrim Springs
4732
Iron Creek
Council
Council LS
KIGLUAIK MOUNTAINS 4714 •MT OSBORN
3870
Salmon Lake LS
4892
2069
Council (Pederson) LS (private)
Council LS

AMNWR
Singigyak
Feather River
Glacial
Jensens Camp
Oregon
4740
Casadepaga
Ruby Roadhouse
2089
East Fork
White Mtn

Cape Rodney
1781
4944
Summit
Sunset
Basin Creek LS
Solomon State LS (private)
White Mountain LS
Solomon
Topkok
Tonok
Golovin LS (new)
Golovin

Sinuk
Sinuk
AMNWR
Sledge I
Nome Airport
Nome City LS
Nome
Fort Davis
Dickson
Bluff
IKNUTAK MTN 1688
Golovin Mission
Rocky Pt
AMNWR
Golovin Bay

Nome Gold
Iditarod National Historic Trail
Carrie McLain Memorial Museum
Cape Nome
Port Safety
INHT
NOME-COUNCIL HWY
AMNWR

NOME-TELLER HWY
WOOLLEY LAGOON RD
TAYLOR HWY
TRACTOR TR
WINTER TR

Continue on Page 138, Inset 1

© DeLorme

Continue on Page 130

132

| KILOMETERS | 10 | 0 | 10 | 20 | 30 | 40 | 50 | 60 | 70 | 80 |
| MILES | 10 | 0 | 10 | 20 | 30 | 40 | 50 | | | |

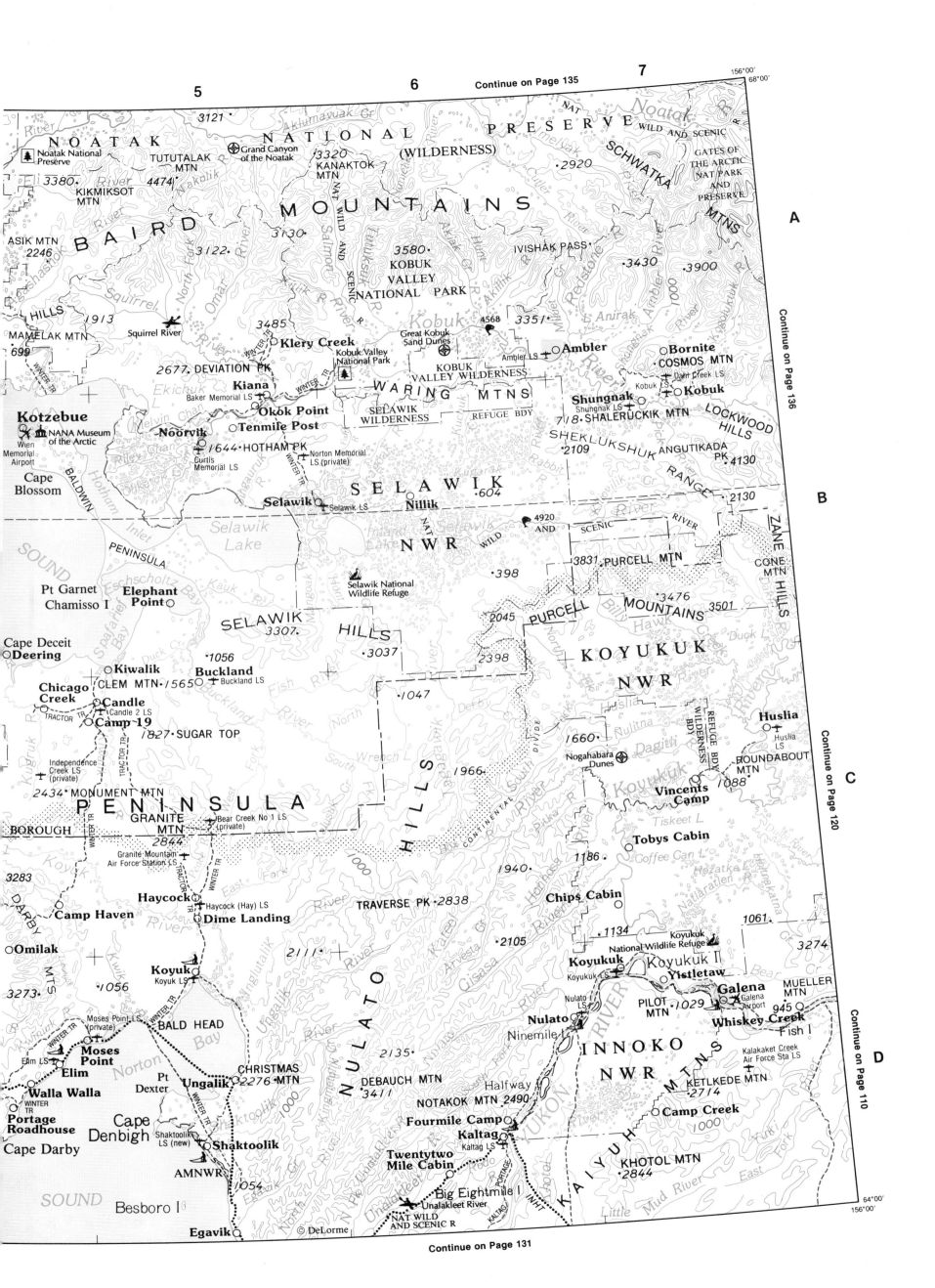

Continue on Page 135

5   6   7

68°00'
156°00'

A

Noatak *National*
Preserve
▲ Noatak National
Preserve

N O A T A K   N A T I O N A L   P R E S E R V E
Noatak WILD AND SCENIC

Grand Canyon
of the Noatak   3121·

3320
KANAKTOK
MTN

·2920
SCHWATKA
MTNS

GATES OF
THE ARCTIC
NAT PARK
AND
PRESERVE

TUTUTALAK
MTN

4474·   3380·
KIKMIKSOT
MTN

M O U N T A I N S

3130

3122·   3580·
KOBUK
VALLEY
NATIONAL PARK

IVISHAK PASS
·3430   ·3900

ASIK MTN
2246

B A I R D

3485

·4568   3351·

·699
MAMELAK MTN

HILLS   1913

Squirrel River

2677· DEVIATION PK

Klery Creek
Kobuk Valley
National Park

Great Kobuk
Sand Dunes

Ambler LS   Ambler

Bornite
COSMOS MTN
Dahl Creek LS

B

Kotzebue
▲ NANA Museum
of the Arctic
Wien
Memorial
Airport

Cape
Blossom

Kiana
Baker Memorial LS
Okok Point
Noorvik
Tenmile Post
·1644·HOTHAM PK
Curtis
Memorial LS

KOBUK
VALLEY WILDERNESS

W A R I N G   M T N S

SELAWIK
WILDERNESS

REFUGE BDY

Shungnak
Shungnak LS

Kobuk

7/8·SHALERUCKIK MTN

LOCKWOOD
HILLS

Selawik
Selawik LS

Norton Memorial
LS (private)

Nillik

S E L A W I K
·604

SHEKLUKSHUK
·2109   ANGUTIKADA
PK·4130

RANGE

·2130

Pt Garnet
Chamisso I

Elephant
Point

N W R

·398

4920
AND

·3831·PURCELL MTN

WILD

SCENIC

RIVER

ZANE HILLS

CONE
MTN

Selawik National
Wildlife Refuge

SELAWIK
3307·

HILLS
·3037

2045   PURCELL   MOUNTAINS   ·3476   3501

·2398

K O Y U K U K

C

Cape Deceit
Deering

SOUND

Kiwalik
CLEM MTN· 1565
Chicago
Creek
Candle
Candle 2 LS
Camp 19
TRACTOR TR

·1056

Buckland
Buckland LS

·1047

N W R

·1660·

1088

Huslia
Huslia
LS

ROUNDABOUT
MTN

1827·SUGAR TOP

1966·

Nogahabara
Dunes

Vincents
Camp

2434·MONUMENT MTN

P E N I N S U L A

BOROUGH

GRANITE
MTN
2844

Bear Creek No 1 LS
(private)

Granite Mountain
Air Force Station LS

Tobys Cabin

1186·

Independence
Creek LS
(private)

1940·

3283

Haycock
Haycock (Hay) LS
Dime Landing

TRAVERSE PK ·2838

Chips Cabin

·2105

·1134

1061

3274

DARBY

Camp Haven

2111·

·1186

Koyukuk
National Wildlife Refuge

Omilak

3273·

·1056

Koyuk
Koyuk LS

Koyukuk
Koyukuk LS

Koyukuk II
Yistletaw

MUELLER
MTN

MTS

N U L A T O

Nulato
LS

PILOT
MTN ·1029

Galena
Galena
Airport
945

D

Moses Point LS
(private)

BALD HEAD

Nulato

Whiskey Creek
Fish I

Moses
Point
Elim LS
Elim

Pt
Dexter

CHRISTMAS
·2276 MTN

2135·

I N N O K O

Ninemile I

Kalakaket Creek
Air Force Sta LS

Walla Walla

Ungalik

DEBAUCH MTN
·3411

Halfway

N W R

KETLKEDE MTN
·2714

Portage
Roadhouse

Cape
Denbigh

Shaktoolik
LS (new)
Shaktoolik

NOTAKOK MTN 2490

Fourmile Camp

Camp Creek

Cape Darby

AMNWR

·1054

Kaltag
Kaltag LS

KHOTOL MTN
·2844

Besboro I

Twentytwo
Mile Cabin

Egavik

Big Eightmile I
Unalakleet River
NAT WILD
AND SCENIC R

© DeLorme

HILLS

64°00'
156°00'

Continue on Page 136
Continue on Page 120
Continue on Page 110
Continue on Page 131

Scale 1:1,400,000
1 inch represents 22 miles

Contour interval
1000 feet (305 meters)

133

ARCTIC OCEAN

Pt Franklin
Pt Belcher
Peard

Wainwright LS · TR
·110·
Wainwright
Wainwright Air Force Station LS · +
WINTER · AMNWR

Kugrua Bay Lake

Pingorarok Pass

Kuk

Icy Cape
Icy Cape Air Force Station LS
·107·

Akoliakatat Pass

NATIONAL

Sikolik Lake
Tunalik

Solivik I
Utukok Pass
WINTER · TR

Kaseqaluk Lagoon

ALASKA MARITIME
NWR

Avak

Utu River

·220·

WINTER · TR

Avalik

Ketik

Akunik Pass

Point Lay
Point Lay Air Force LS

Kokolik

Kukpowruk Pass

Kokolik River

Chikmukusuk R

WINTER TR

RESERVE IN

SHANINGAROK
·610·

Pugutak L.
Tunusiktok L

Epizetka

Mumik L.
Kuvirok L.

Naokak

Avingak Cr
·4061·

River

TRACTOR

OMICRON HILL
·1160·

River

·1000·

River

LOOKOUT
·2344·

HILLS
·1487·

Cape Beaufort

Cape Sabine
NOONURLOOK

AMATUSUK
Cape Sabine LS

Turbid

Tupikchak

Utukok

·2367·

Colville

·2920·

(U)   MEAT MTN
·2900·

WINTER TR

·2080·

Cape
Lisburne
Cape Lisburne
Air Force LS
ALASKA
MARITIME
NWR

Wevok
MT HAMLET
·2034·

MTN
·2675·

Pitmegea

·3243·
IGLOO MTN

Noluok

Nuka

Cape Lewis
Cape Dyer

Alaska Maritime
National Wildlife Refuge
Chukchi Sea Unit

River

Windy L.

LISBURNE PENINSULA

·1462·

River

MT KELLY
·3152·

BROOKS

SPHINX ·3571·
MTN

BLACK MTN
·4915·

NAT

RESERVE

Point Hope
LS

Marryat
Inlet

·1331·

·1000·

M O U N T A I N S

Point
Hope

LISBURNE HILLS

Ipewik

Aiauta
Lagoon

Kukpuk

SAKLOLIK MTN
·701·

·3325·SHEEP MTN

NOATAK

Cape
Thompson
ALASKA MARITIME
NWR

Chariot

D E L O N G

·4180·

·4230·
MISHEGUK MTN

·3208·

N   SLOPE
NW ARCTIC

Kivalina River

·1000·

Red Dog LS (private)

DEADLOCK MTN
·2995·

© DeLorme

NAT

NAT
WILD AND
SCENIC
RIVER

PRESERVE

·4736·

Continue on Page 132

Continue on Page 133

KILOMETERS 10 0 10 20 30 40 50 60 70 80

MILES 10 0 10 20 30 40 50

167°00'
72°00'

68°00'
167°00'

1   2   3   4

A

B

C

D

Scale 1:1,400,000
1 inch represents 22 miles

Contour interval
1000 feet (305 meters)

Continue on Page 136
Continue on Page 136
Continue above right
Continue on inset below
Continue on Pages 136 and 137

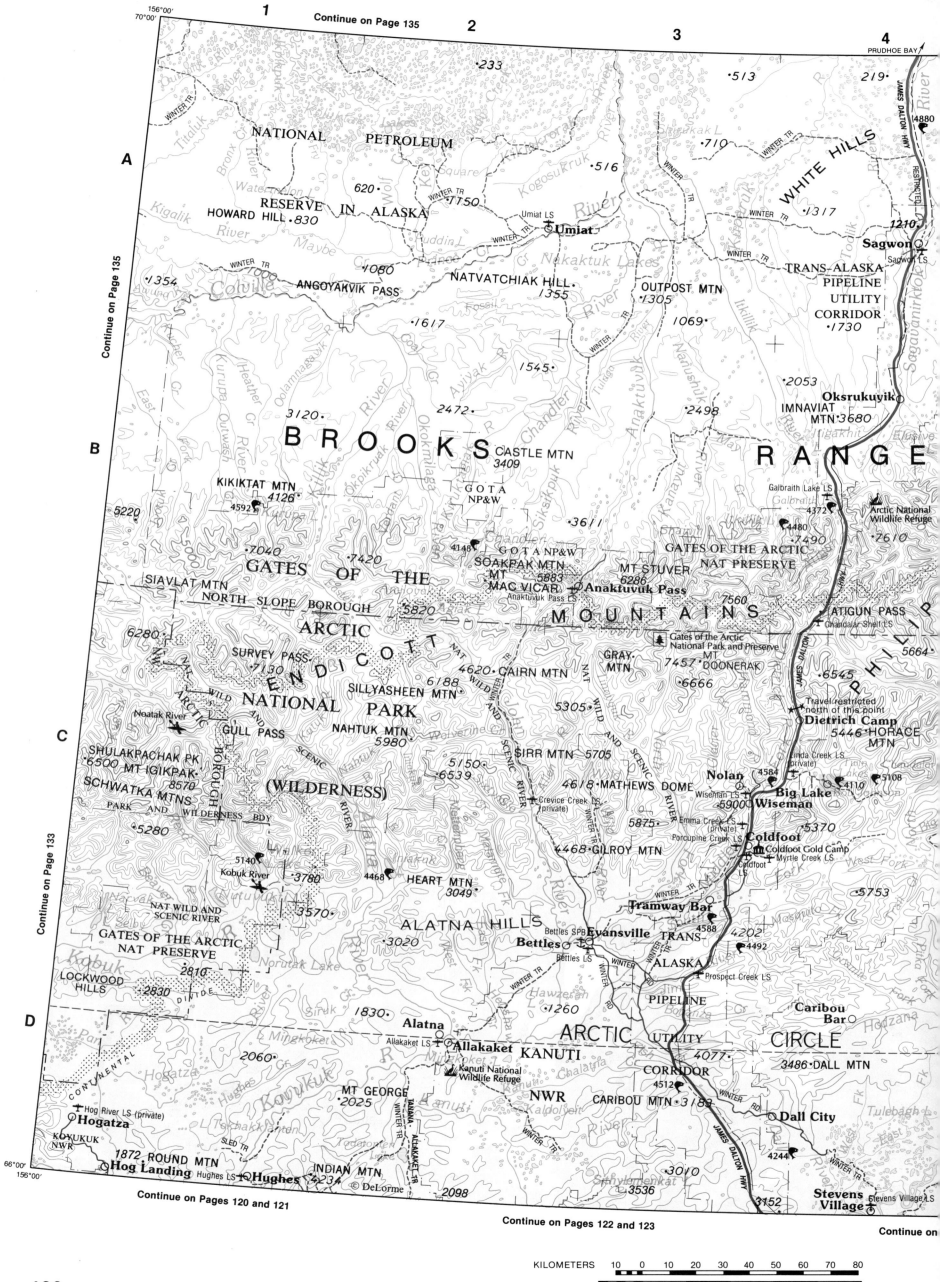

Continue on Page 135

Continue on Page 135

Continue on Page 133

Continue on Pages 120 and 121

Continue on Pages 122 and 123

Continue on

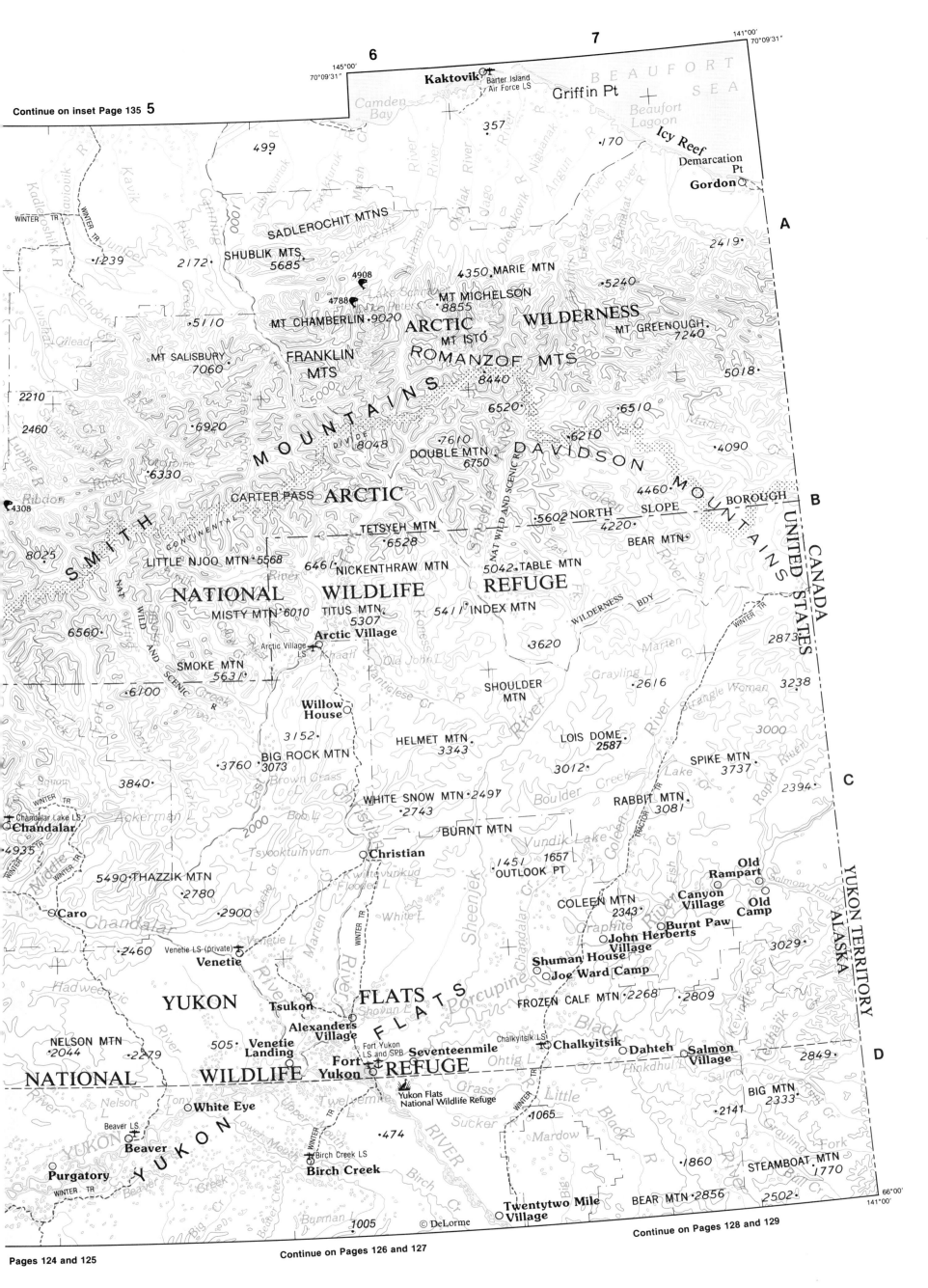

Continue on inset Page 135

6

7

Kaktovik
Barter Island
Air Force LS
Griffin Pt

B E A U F O R T   S E A

Camden Bay

Beaufort Lagoon

357

·170

Icy Reef

·499

Demarcation Pt

Gordon

A

·1239   SADLEROCHIT MTNS

SHUBLIK MTS 5685

2172·

·5110

4908

4788

·5240

2419·

4350·MARIE MTN

MT MICHELSON 8855·

MT CHAMBERLIN ·9020

ARCTIC   WILDERNESS

MT ISTO

MT GREENOUGH· 7240

·5018

MT SALISBURY 7060·

FRANKLIN MTS

ROMANZOF MTS

·8440

·6920

2210

2460

·6510

M O U N T A I N S

DIVIDE 8048

·7610

6520·

·6210

·4090

·6330

DOUBLE MTN 6750

D A V I D S O N

·4460

M O U N T A I N S

BOROUGH

B

·4308

Ribdon

S M I T H

CARTER PASS **ARCTIC**

TETSYEH MTN ·6528

·5602 NORTH   SLOPE

4220·

BEAR MTN·

8025·

CONTINENTAL

LITTLE NJOO MTN·5568

646· NICKENTHRAW MTN

5042·TABLE MTN

WILDERNESS BDY

2873·

NATIONAL   WILDLIFE   REFUGE

6560·

MISTY MTN·6010

TITUS MTN 5307

5411·INDEX MTN

·3620

·2616

3238

SMOKE MTN 5631·

Arctic Village
Arctic Village LS

·3000

·6100

SHOULDER MTN

LOIS DOME 2587

SPIKE MTN 3737

2394·

Willow House

3152·

HELMET MTN 3343

3012·

C

·3760 3073

BIG ROCK MTN

RABBIT MTN 3081

3840·

WHITE SNOW MTN·2497

·2743

BURNT MTN

Boulder Creek

4935·

Chandalar Lake LS
Chandalar

Christian

1451· 1657 OUTLOOK PT

Old **Rampart**

5490·THAZZIK MTN

·2780

COLEEN MTN 2343·

Canyon Village

Old Camp

3029·

Caro

·2900

·2460 Venetie LS (private)
Venetie

Burnt Paw

John Herberts Village

Shuman House

Joe Ward Camp

YUKON   FLATS   FLATS

FROZEN CALF MTN·2268

·2809

Tsukon

Alexanders Village

NELSON MTN ·2044

·2279 505· **Venetie Landing**

Fort Yukon LS and SPB
Fort Yukon

Chalkyitsik LSI
Chalkyitsik

Dahteh

Salmon Village

2849·

D

NATIONAL   WILDLIFE   REFUGE
Seventeenmile

Yukon Flats National Wildlife Refuge

BIG MTN 2333

White Eye

·1065

·2141

Beaver LS
Beaver

·474

·1860

STEAMBOAT MTN 1770

Purgatory

Birch Creek LS
Birch Creek

BEAR MTN·2856

2502·

66°00'
141°00'

© DeLorme

Twentytwo Mile Village

Continue on Pages 128 and 129

Pages 124 and 125

Continue on Pages 126 and 127

Scale 1:1,400,000
1 inch represents 22 miles

Contour interval
1000 feet (305 meters)

137

CANADA UNITED STATES

YUKON TERRITORY

ALASKA

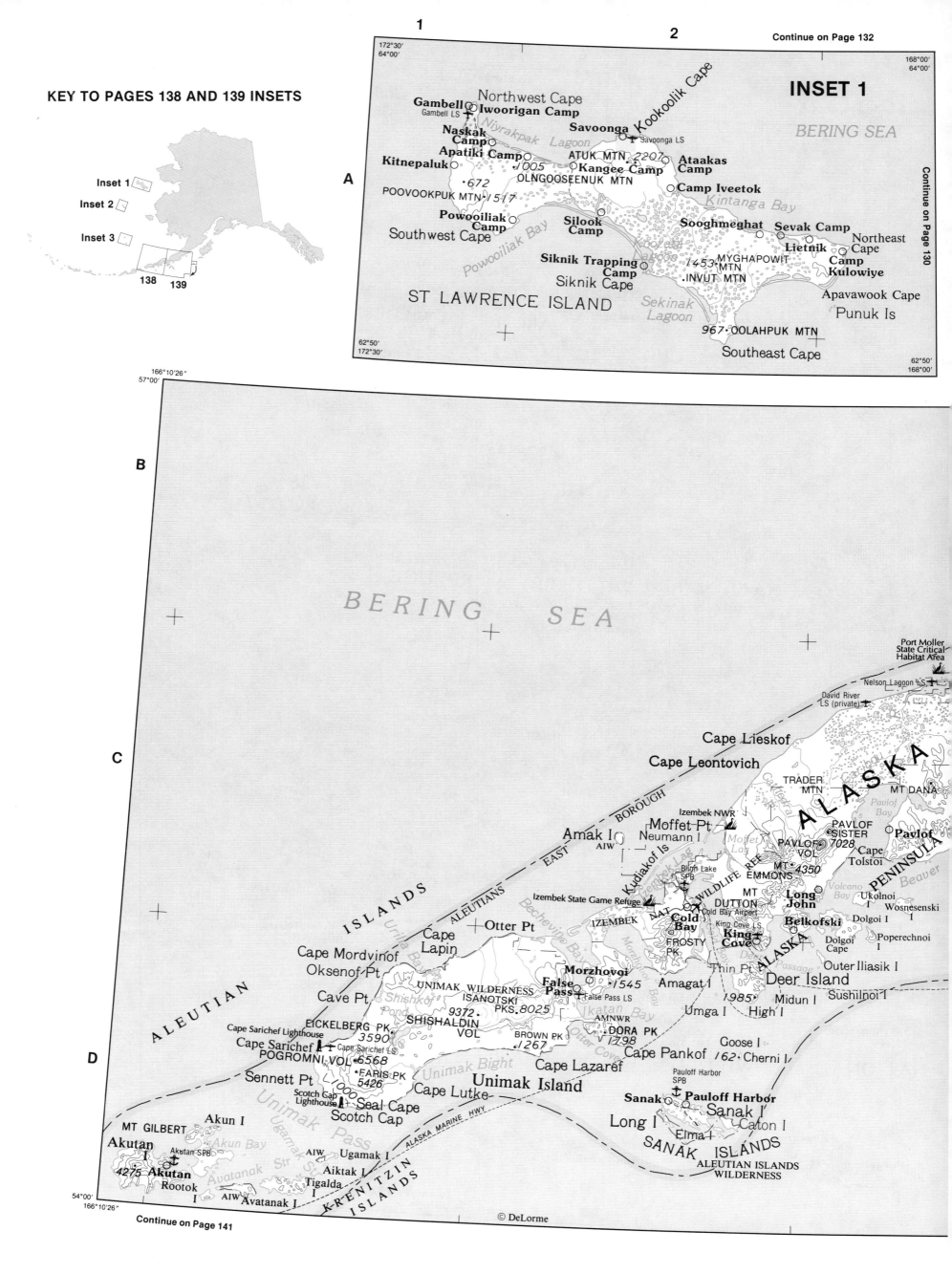

KEY TO PAGES 138 AND 139 INSETS

Inset 1
Inset 2
Inset 3

138   139

172°30'
64°00'

INSET 1

BERING SEA

Continue on Page 130

Gambell
Gambell LS   Iwoorigan Camp   Northwest Cape   Kookoolik Cape

Naskak Camp   Savoonga   Savoonga LS

Apatiki Camp   ATUK MTN ·2207   Ataakas Camp

Kitnepaluk   ·1005   Kangee Camp   Camp Iveetok

·672   OLNGOOSEENUK MTN

POOVOOKPUK MTN ·1517

Powooiliak Camp   Silook Camp   Sooghmeghat   Sevak Camp

Lietnik   Northeast Cape

Siknik Trapping Camp   ·1453 MYGHAPOWIT MTN   Camp Kulowiye

Siknik Cape   ·INVUT MTN

Kintanga Bay

Sekinak Lagoon   Apavawook Cape   Punuk Is

ST LAWRENCE ISLAND

967 ·OOLAHPUK MTN

Southeast Cape

62°50'
172°30'

62°50'
168°00'

168°00'
64°00'

B

BERING   SEA

Port Moller State Critical Habitat Area

Nelson Lagoon LS

David River LS (private)

Cape Lieskof

C

Cape Leontovich

ALASKA

TRADER MTN   MT DANA

Izembek NWR   PAVLOF SISTER 7028   Pavlof

Moffet Pt.   PAVLOF VOL   Cape Tolstoi

Amak I   Neumann I   Pavlof Bay

AIW

Kudiakof Is   Blini Lake   MT· 4350   Long John   Ukolnoi

EMMONS   Wosnesenski

Izembek State Game Refuge   WILDLIFE REF   MT DUTTON   Belkofski   Dolgoi I

Otter Pt   Cape Lapin   NAT   Cold Bay Airport   Dolgoi I   Poperechnoi

AMNWR   Cold Bay   King Cove LS   Dolgoi Cape

Cape Mordvinof   IZEMBEK   King Cove   Outer Iliasik I

Oksenof Pt   FROSTY PK   Thin Pt   Deer Island   Midun I   Sushilnoi I

Cave Pt   UNIMAK WILDERNESS   Morzhovoi   ALASKA   ·1985

ISANOTSKI   ·1545   Amagat I   Umga I   High I

PKS ·8025   False Pass   False Pass LS

EICKELBERG PK 3590   9372   SHISHALDIN VOL   BROWN PK   DORA PK   Cape Pankof ·162 ·Cherni I

Cape Sarichef Lighthouse   ·1267   AMNWR   ·1798   Goose I

Cape Sarichef   Cape Sarichef LS   Cape Lazaref   Pauloff Harbor SPB

POGROMNI VOL ·6568   Sanak   Pauloff Harbor

Sennett Pt   ·FARIS PK 5426   Cape Lutke   Unimak Island   Long I   Sanak I   Caton I

·1000   Scotch Cap Lighthouse   Seal Cape   Elma I

MT GILBERT   Akun I   Scotch Cap   SANAK ISLANDS

Akutan   Ugamak I   ALASKA MARINE HWY   ALEUTIAN ISLANDS WILDERNESS

AIW   Aiktak I

4275 ·Akutan   Tigalda I

Rootok I   AIW ·Avatanak I   KRENITZIN ISLANDS

ALEUTIAN   ISLANDS   EAST   BOROUGH   ALEUTIANS

Becherevin Bay   Urilia Bay   Unimak Bight

Avatanak Str   Ugamak Str   Unimak Pass

Akun Bay

166°10'26"
57°00'

54°00'
166°10'26"

© DeLorme

Continue on Page 141

KILOMETERS   10   0   10   20   30   40   50   60   70   80

MILES   10   0   10   20   30   40   50

3

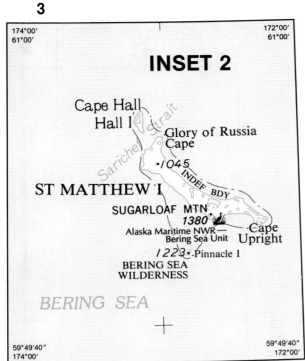

174°00' 172°00'
61°00'   61°00'

INSET 2

Cape Hall
Hall I
Glory of Russia
Cape
•1045
Saricheff Strait
INDEF BDY

ST MATTHEW I

SUGARLOAF MTN
•1380
Alaska Maritime NWR —
Bering Sea Unit
Cape
Upright
1223• •Pinnacle I
BERING SEA
WILDERNESS

BERING SEA

59°49'40'   59°49'40'
174°00'   172°00'

4   **5**

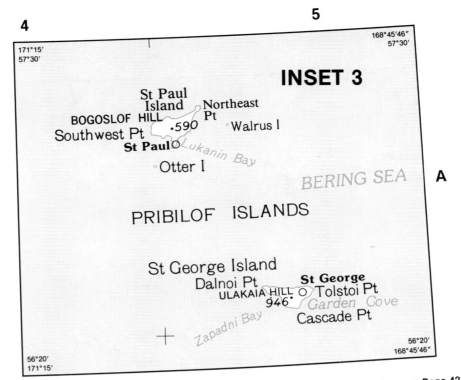

171°15'   168°45'46"
57°30'   57°30'

St Paul
Island   Northeast
BOGOSLOF HILL   Pt
Southwest Pt   •590   •Walrus I
St Paul○

Lukanin Bay   *BERING SEA*   **A**

•Otter I

PRIBILOF ISLANDS

St George Island
Dalnoi Pt   **St George**
ULAKAIA HILL ○ •Tolstoi Pt
946•   *Garden Cove*
Zapadni Bay   Cascade Pt

56°20'   56°20'
171°15'   168°45'46"

Continue on Pages 40 and 41   Continue on Page 42

156°00'
57°00'

Cape
Providence
Chiginagak Bay

Port Heiden
Airport   Aniakchak River
Strogonof Pt ✈ Aniakchak Caldera THE
Port Heiden   ANIAKCHAK   TWINS
CRATER   •3271
ANIAKCHAK   *Nakalilok Bay*
NAT PRESERVE
Port Heiden   ANIAKCHAK PINNACLE   Ugaiushak I
State Critical Habitat Area   NM   MTN ✠
Meshik River   *Yantarni Bay*   ALASKA MARINE HWY   **B**
Seal Is   Aniakchak National
Monument and
Preserve   Cape
Kujulik Bay Kumlik Kumlik Sutwik I
Ilnik○   •964 Foggy
Cape Kumliun   AMNWR   Cape
Cape Seniavin   *Wildman L*   BLACK PK   Unavikshak I
WEASEL MTN•
Chignik
Fisheries LS Anguvik I   •Nakchamik I
Cape Kutuzof REFUGE   •2965 ✈ Chignik Atkulik I
Chignik Lagoon✈ LS and SPB   Kak I
Chignik   •Castle Cape
Lake LS **Chignik**   Chankliut I   SEMIDI ISLANDS
Bear River○   **Chignik**   Alaska
Lake   Peninsula   Aghiyuk I •Aghik I
Kudobin   MT   NWR   •1024
Islands **Port**   VENIAMINOF   Anowik I
Moller   Kateekuk I Kiliktagik I
Cape   Johnsons   3294• *Warner Bay*   Suklik I
Rozhnof   Landing LS   SEMIDI 679• Chowiet I
Port Moller   Seal Cape   WILDERNESS South I Aliksemit I
Air Force LS
emergency only   WILDLIFE   *Mitrofania Bay*
Herendeen LS 2761•   Perryville LS
Herendeen 2963 Perryville ✈
Bay •3895   **Perryville** Ivanof   Mitrofania I   PENINSULA
NATIONAL MT STEPO   Bay SPB
•2963   *Sospee Bay*   AND
AMNWR Chiachi I   **LAKE**
Bluff •1594   Paul I Spitz I
Balboa Bay Pt   Jacob I   **C**
Guillemot I   Kupreanof Pt
Karpa I ALASKA MARINE HWY
Pirate   Korovin I
Cove
Sand Andronica   PACIFIC OCEAN
Unga **Point** I   Castle Rock
I Sand Point LS   Popof I Cape Thompson
•2030
Squaw Big Koniuji I
Harbor
Acheredin   **Unga**   1837•   •848
Pt   **Unga**   Atkins I
Cape   Nagai I   Turner I Little Koniuji I
John I   Twins   Simeonof I
Near I Murie Islets   •1436
E Nagai Str   1130•   SIMEONOF WILDERNESS   ✠
Mountain   •1609
SHUMAGIN Pt   Bird I •Chernabura I
Pt Farewell
ISLANDS

156°00'   *Continue on inset below*

54°28'17"   **D**
156°00'

© DeLorme   54°00'
157°09'42"

156°00' KODIAK *Pacific* 155°00'
56°00' ISLAND *Ocean* 56°00'
BOROUGH

West Chirikof I
Point South
Cape
55°38'34" 55°38'34"
156°00' 155°00'

Scale 1:1,400,000
1 inch represents 22 miles

Contour interval
1000 feet (305 meters)

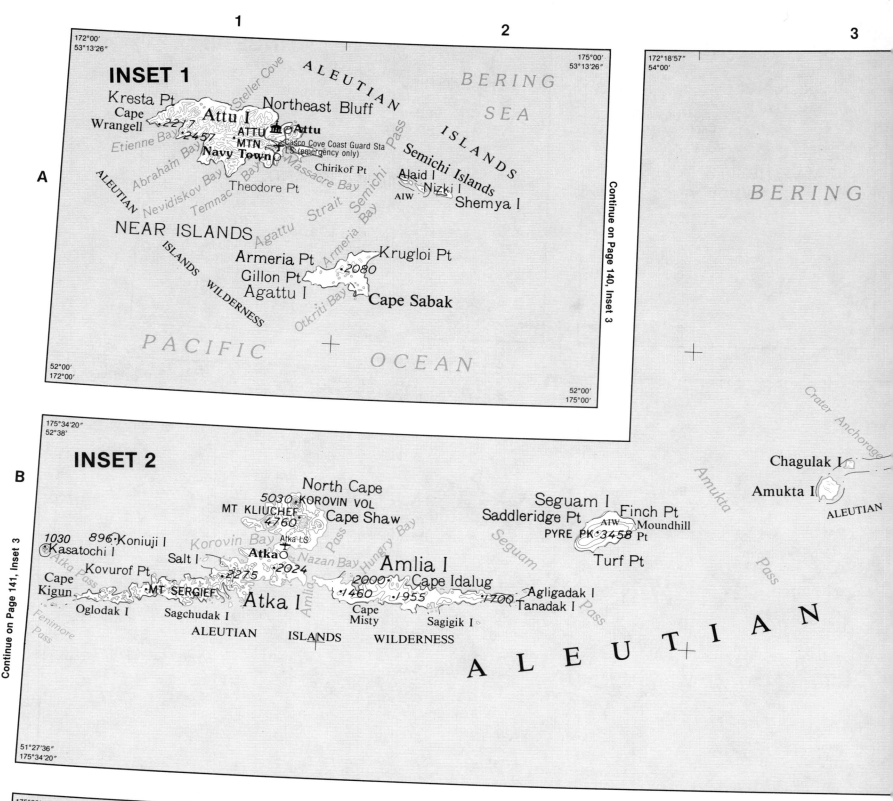

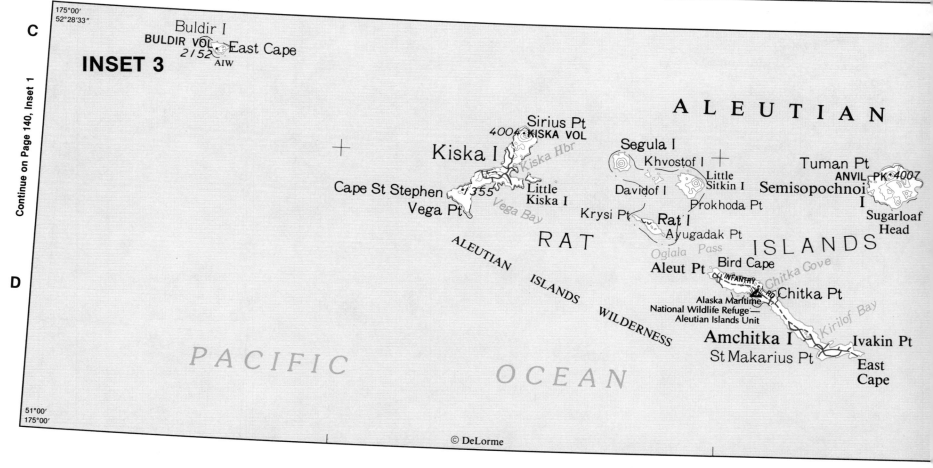

© DeLorme

KILOMETERS 10 0 10 20 30 40 50 60 70 80

MILES 10 0 10 20 30 40 50

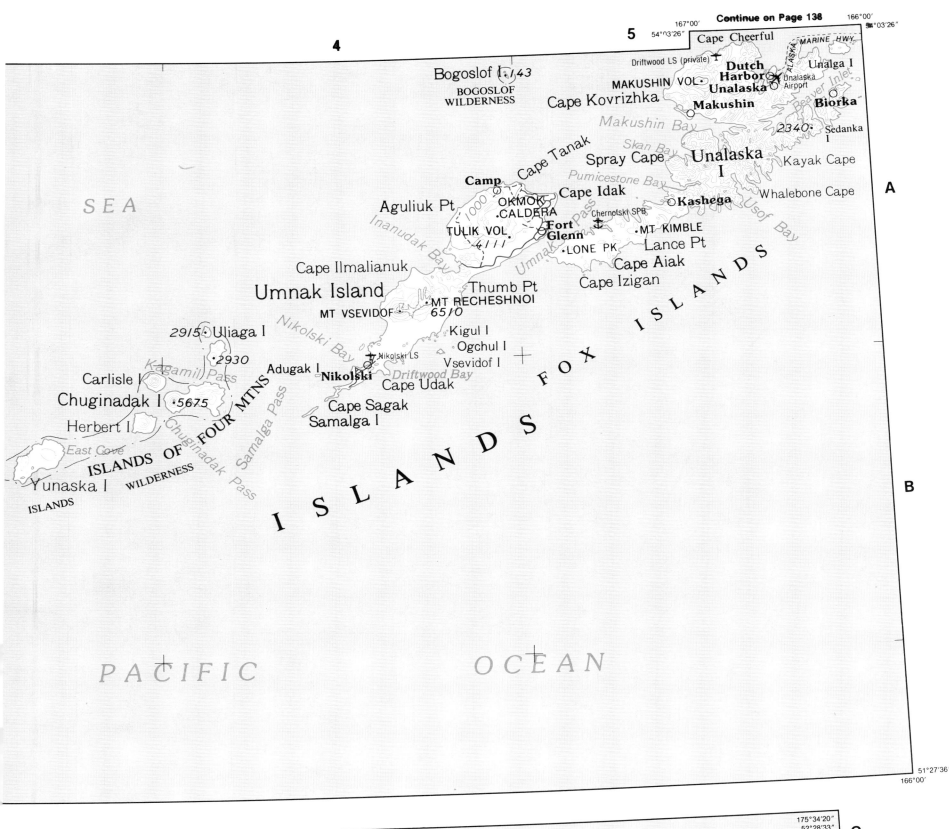

4

5

Continue on Page 140, above left

A

B

C

D

167°00'

166°00'

54°03'26"

166°00'

51°27'36"

175°34'20"

52°28'33"

51°00'

175°34'20"

Cape Cheerful

Driftwood LS (private)

ALASKA MARINE HWY

Unalga I

MAKUSHIN VOL.

Dutch Harbor

Unalaska

Unalaska Airport

Makushin

Biorka

Cape Kovrizhka

Bogoslof I. 43

BOGOSLOF WILDERNESS

Makushin Bay

Skan Bay

Beaver Inlet

2340

Sedanka I

Spray Cape

Cape Tanak

Pumicestone Bay

Unalaska I

Kayak Cape

Camp

Cape Idak

Whalebone Cape

Aguliuk Pt

OKMOK CALDERA

Kashega

Chernofski SPB

Usof Bay

Fort Glenn

TULIK VOL. 4111

MT KIMBLE

LONE PK

Lance Pt

Cape Aiak

Cape Ilmalianuk

Cape Izigan

Umnak Island

Thumb Pt

MT VSEVIDOF

MT RECHESHNOI 6510

2915 Uliaga I

Kigul I

Ogchul I

2930

Vsevidof I

Adugak I

Nikolski LS

Nikolski

Carlisle I

Kagamil Pass

Cape Udak

Driftwood Bay

Chuginadak I 5675

Cape Sagak

Herbert I

Samalga I

East Cove

Nikolski Bay

ISLANDS OF FOUR MTNS

Samalga Pass

Yunaska I

WILDERNESS

Chuginadak Pass

ISLANDS

ISLANDS

FOX ISLANDS

SEA

PACIFIC

OCEAN

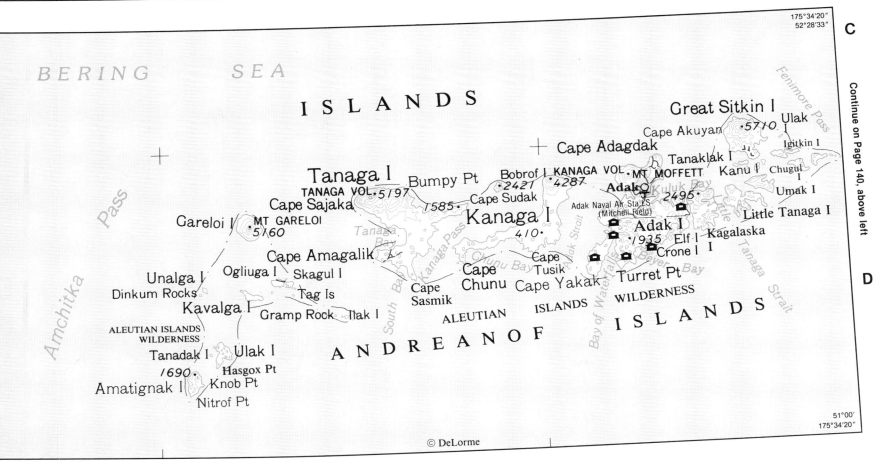

BERING SEA

ISLANDS

Great Sitkin I

Cape Akuyan

5710

Ulak

Fenimore Pass

Cape Adagdak

Igitkin I

Tanaklak I

Kanu I

Chugul

Tanaga I

Bumpy Pt

Bobrof I

KANAGA VOL.

MT MOFFETT

Umak I

TANAGA VOL. 5197

2421

4287

Adak

2495

Cape Sajaka

1585

Cape Sudak

Adak Naval Air Sta. LS (Mitchell Field)

Little Tanaga I

Gareloi I

MT GARELOI 5160

Kanaga I

410

Adak I 1935

Elf I

Kagalaska

Cape Amagalik

Crone I

Tanaga Bay

Kuluk Bay

Unalga I

Ogliuga I

Skagul I

Kanaga Pass

Little Tanaga Strait

Dinkum Rocks

Cape Chunu

Cape Tusik

Turret Pt

Kavalga I

Tag Is

Cape Yakak

WILDERNESS

Gramp Rock

Ilak I

Cape Sasmik

Bay of Waterfalls

Beaver Bay

ALEUTIAN ISLANDS WILDERNESS

South Bay

Chunu Bay

ALEUTIAN ISLANDS

ISLANDS

Tanadak I

Ulak I

1690

Hasgox Pt

A N D R E A N O F

Amchitka Pass

Knob Pt

Amatignak I

Nitrof Pt

© DeLorme

Scale 1:1,400,000
1 inch represents 22 miles

Contour interval
1000 feet (305 meters)

141

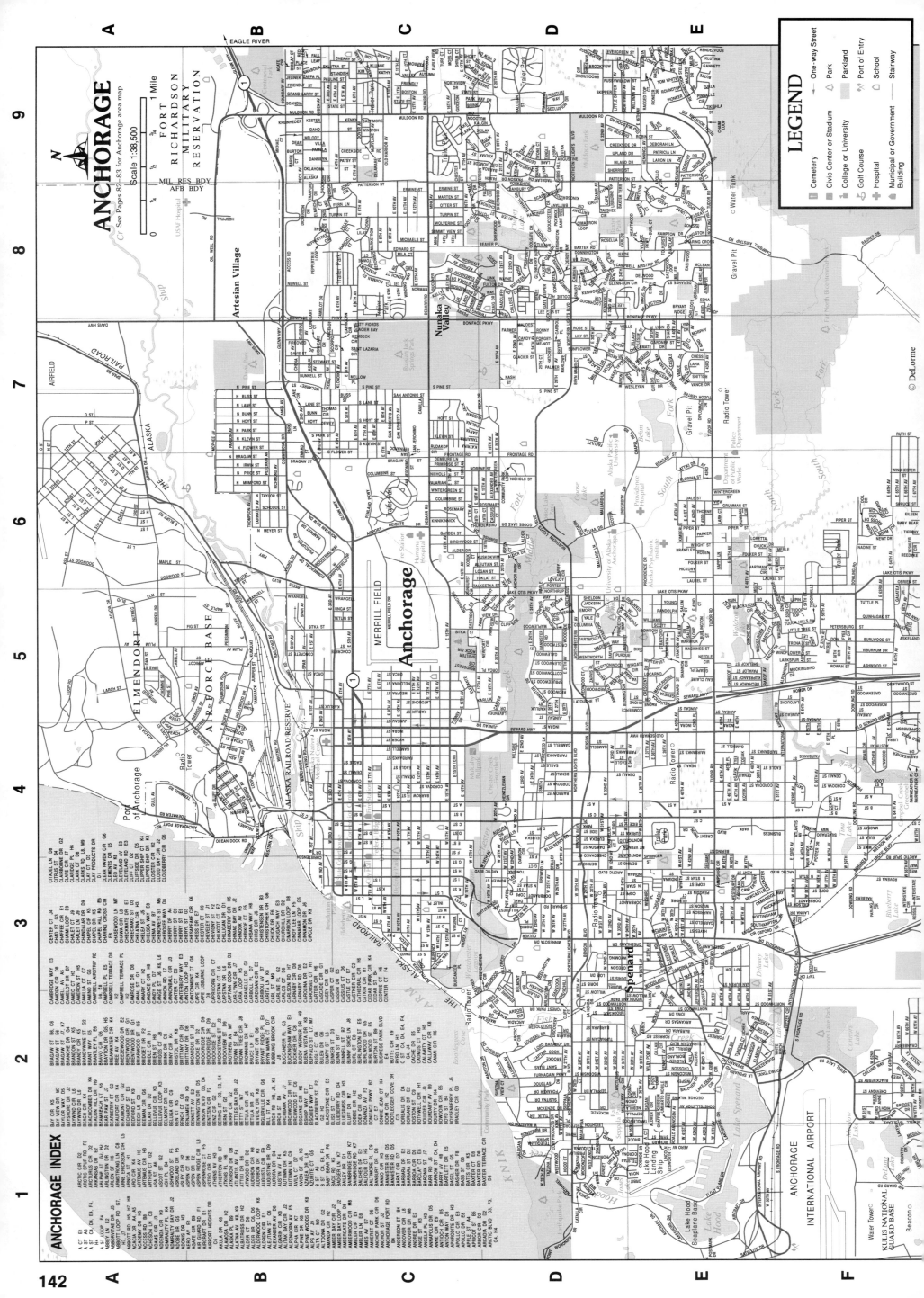

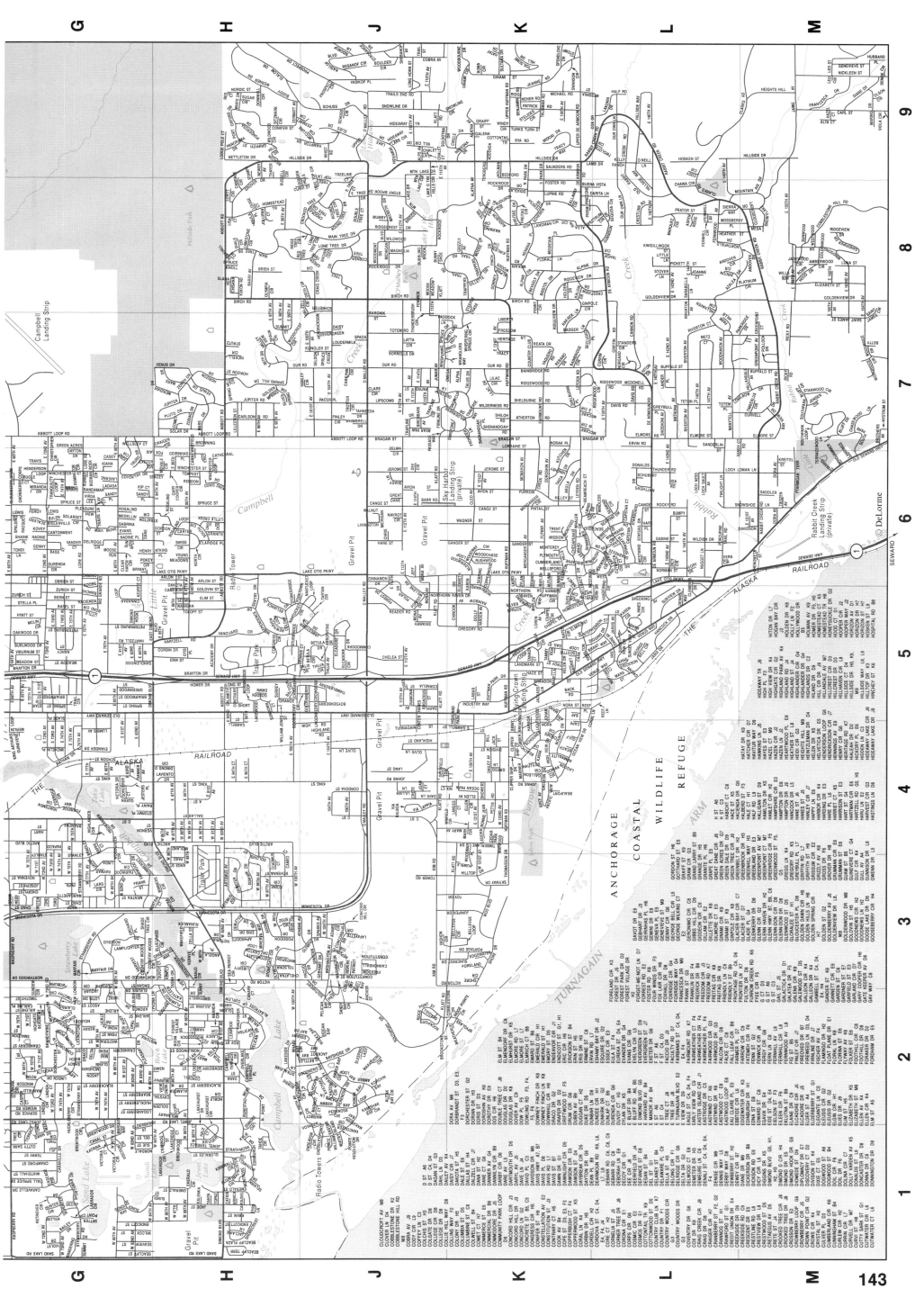

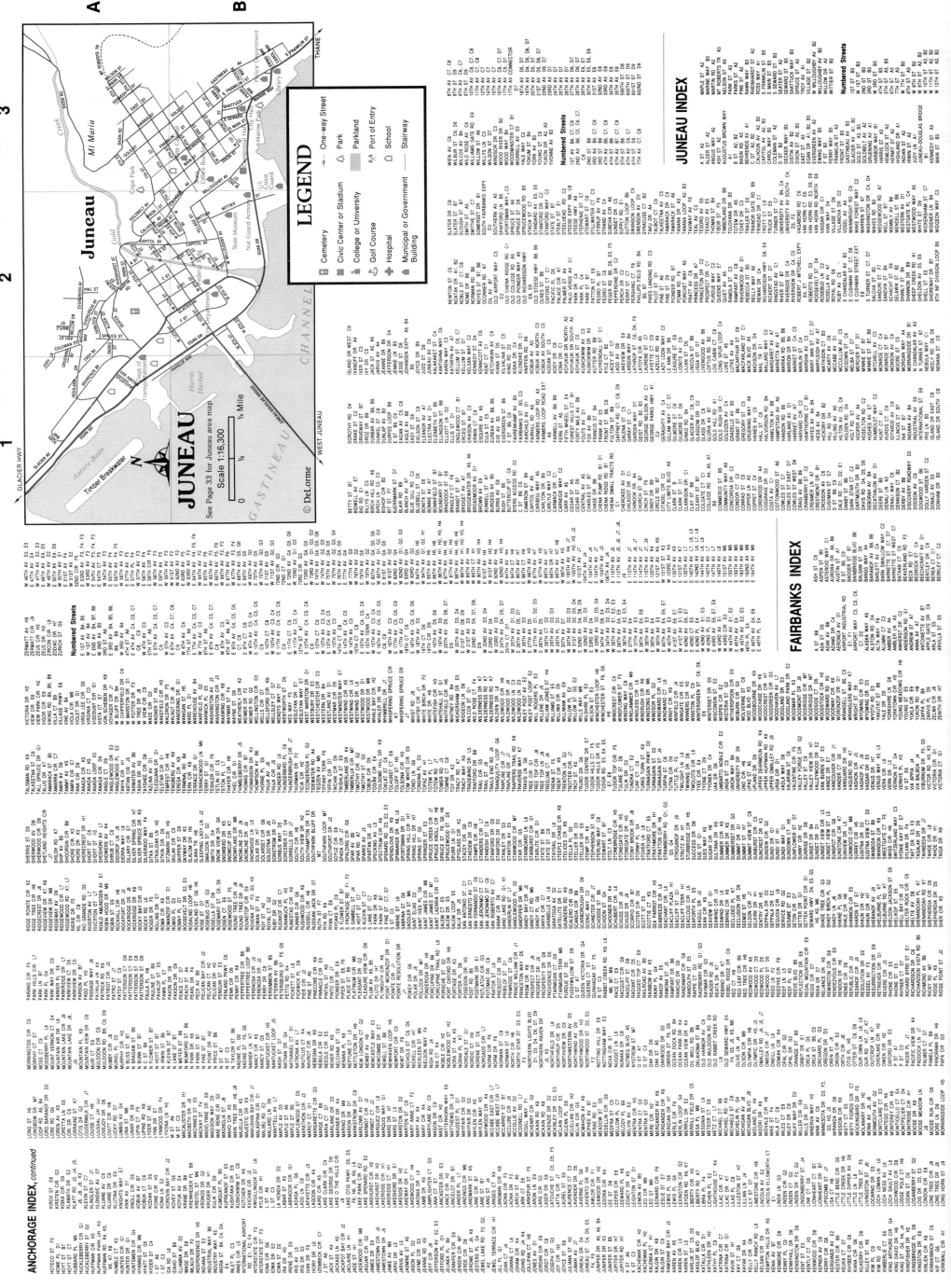

JUNEAU

See Page 33 for Juneau area map.

Scale 1:16,300

© DeLorme

LEGEND

- Cemetery
- Civic Center or Stadium
- College or University
- Golf Course
- Hospital
- Municipal or Government Building
- One-way Street
- Park
- Parkland
- Port of Entry
- School
- Stairway

ANCHORAGE INDEX, *continued*

FAIRBANKS INDEX

JUNEAU INDEX

Numbered Streets

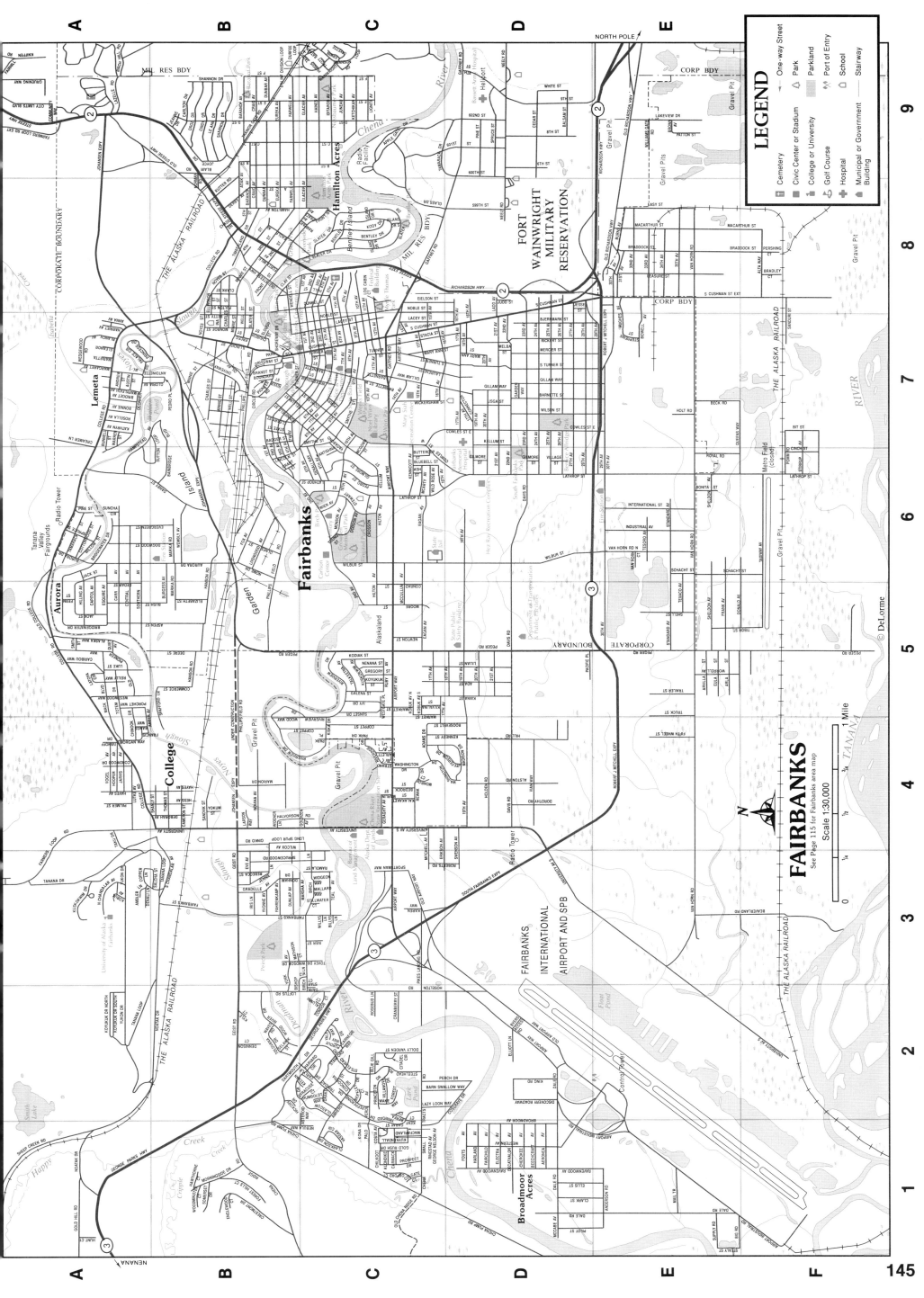

FAIRBANKS

See Page 115 for Fairbanks area map

Scale 1:30,000

0 ¼ ½ ¾ 1 Mile

© DeLorme

145

Index of Placenames and Physical Features

ABOUT THE INDEX

This index contains more than 16,000 features shown on the maps on pages 16–141. Names are listed alphabetically, followed by their respective map page('s) and grid coordinates to help locate them.

Guidelines for using this index:

- **boldface** type is used for placenames (cities, towns, crossroads etc.);
  example: **Fairbanks** 115 A5;
- *italic* type is used for drainage names (lakes, rivers, creeks, harbors, glaciers, icefields, fiords, canals, lagoons, springs, etc.);
  example: *Yukon River* 110 A2;
- roman type is used for all other features (mountains, islands, rocks, points, capes, peninsulas, parks, forests, wildlife refuges, lighthouses, major highways, airports, landing strips and seaplane bases, etc.);
  example: Admiralty Island 27 B4;
- different features having the same name are listed separately;
- grid coordinates are given for each occurrence of a feature name;
- names beginning with Cape, Lake, Mount, Point, Port and The have been indexed by the primary part of the name;
  example: McKinley, Mount 103 D4;
- rivers and creeks are listed by the main tributary name, followed by the fork where applicable;
  example: *Blue River, West Fork* 25 C4;
- features found in Canada are followed by asterisks;
  example: Bennett* 38 A3.

Abbreviations used in the index:

AF–Air Force   CG–Coast Guard   LS–Landing Strip   SPB–Seaplane Base

A

A B Mountain 38 B2
Aaron Creek 25 B3
Aaron Island 32 C3
Aats Bay 18 A1
Aats Point 18 A1
Abalone Island 17 A3
Abbe, Mount 31 A3
Abbess Island 19 B3
Abdallah, Mount 31 A4
Abercrombie Gulch 85 D5
Abercrombie Mountain 85 C5
Abernathy Creek 70 B3
Abraham Bay 140 C1
Abraham Islands 24 D1
Abyss Lake 31 B4
Ac Point 60 B2
Ace Creek 115 A5
Acheredin Point 13? C3
Ackerman Lake 137 C5
Acme Creek 76 D3
Acme Creek 54 B2
Acorn Peak 48 A2
Ada, Mount 22 B2
Adagdak, Cape 18 C2
Adair, Mount 71 C4
Adak 141 D5
Adak Island 141 D5
Adak Naval Air Station LS (Mitchell Field) 141 D5
Adak Strait 141 D5
Adam Mountains 21 B3
Adams Inlet 31 A5; 32 A1
Adams Peak 119 A6
Adams Point 19 B4
Adams Point 20 D1
Addington, Cape 18 C2
Addison Glacier 63 A5
Admiralty Bay '35 B6
Admiralty Cove 33 D3
Admiralty Forest 33 D3
Admiralty Island 27 B4; 28 A1; 33 D3
Admiralty Island National Monument–Kootznoowoo Wilderness 27 B4
Adolph Knopf, Mount 33 B3
Adolphus, Point 32 C1
Adugak Island 141 B4
Aello Peak 89 C4
Aeolian Hills 122 D3
Aeolus Mountain 47 A3
Afanasa Creek 70 B3
Affleck Canal 23 D3
Afognak 53 D4
Afognak Bay 53 D4
Afognak Island 45 A4; 53 D4
Afognak Lake 53 D4
Afognak Mountain 53 D4
Afognak Point '45 A4
Afognak River 53 D4
Afognak Strait 45 A4
Afonasi Creek 70 B3
Agashashok River 133 A4
Agassiz Glacier 36 A1
Agassiz Lakes 36 A1; 77 D5
Agassiz Mountain 20 D2
Agassiz Peak 29 D4
Agattu Island 140 A1
Agattu Strait 140 A1
Agcklarok 130 B2
Agekelak 130 B2
Agenuk Mountain 56 A3
Aggie Creek 125 D4
Aghik Island 139 A5
Aghiyuk Island 139 35
Agiak Lake 136 B2
Agiapuk River 132 C2
Agligadak Island 140 B2
Agnes Cove 63 A5
Agripina Bay 42 D2
Agripina River 42 D2
Aguchik Island 52 C1
Aguirre Bay 18 B3
Aguirre, Point 18 B3
Aguliak Islands 72 C2
Aguligik Island 52 C1
Agulukpak Lake 69 B5
Agulukpak River 56 B2
Ahduck Bay 35 B3
Ahklun Mountains 54 D2
Aho Lake 81 B4
Ahrnklin River 29 D4
Ahtell Creek 97 A6
Ahtell Creek 98 B1
Ahtell Creek, West Fork 97 A6
Aiak, Cape 141 A5
Aiaktalik Cove 52 C3
Aiaktalik Island 64 C3
Aialik Bay 63 A5
Aialik Cape 63 B5
Aialik Glacier 63 A5
Aialik Peninsula 63 A5

Aiautak Lagoon 134 D1
Aichilik River 137 A7
Aiken Cove 20 D1
Aiken Creek 20 D1
Aiken Lake 20 D1
Aiktak Island 138 D1
Airs Hill 99 B6
Ajax Reef 20 D2
Akalura Creek 44 D1
Akalura Lake 44 D1
Akamunuk Creek 55 A4
Akeku Point 17 C3
Akhiok 52 C2
Akhiok Bay 64 B2
Akhiok Island 64 B2
Akhiok LS 64 B2
Akhiok Reef 64 B2
Akiachak 131 D4
Akiachak LS 131 D4
Akiachak SPB 131 D4
Akiak 131 D4
Akiak Creek 133 A6
Akiak LS 131 D4
Akillik River 133 A6
Akjemguiga Cove 60 D1
Aklek, Cape 43 B3
Aklumayuak Creek 133 A5
Akoliakatat Pass 134 B2
Akolmiut 130 D3
Akula Lake 69 B5
Akulikutak River 131 D4
Akuluktok Peak 56 B2
Akulurak 130 B2
Akumwarvik Bay 60 D1
Akun 138 D1
Akun Island 138 D1
Akunik Pass 134 D2
Akusha Island 28 C2
Akutan 138 D1
Akutan Island 138 D1
Akutan SPB 138 D1
Akuyan, Cape 141 B5
Akwe Lake 35 C5
Akwe River 35 C5
Alabama Creek 123 D6
Alabama Creek 125 B4
Alaganik 74 C2
Alaganik Slough 74 C2
Alagnak River 58 D1, D3
Alagogshak Creek 51 D4
Alai Creek 42 C1
Alai, Mount 42 C1
Alaid Island 140 A2
Alakanuk 130 B2
Alakanuk LS 130 B2
Alaktak 135 B6
Alaktak River 135 B6
Alargate Rocks 18 B3
Alaska Chilkat Bald Eagle Preserve 38 C1
Alaska Highway 99 A5, B6; 107 A4, A5, B6; 108 B1, C2, C3; 109 D4, D5; 116 D3
Alaska Maritime National Wildlife Refuge–Alaska Peninsula Unit 139 B5
Alaska Maritime National Wildlife Refuge– Aleutian Islands Unit 140 D1
Alaska Maritime National Wildlife Refuge–Bering Sea Unit 139 A4
Alaska Maritime National Wildlife Refuge– Chukchi Sea Unit 134 D1
Alaska Maritime National Wildlife Refuge– Gulf of Alaska Unit 53 D4
Alaska Peak 18 B3
Alaska Peninsula 42 C1; 49 C5; 50 C1; 52 B1; 138 D2; 139 C3
Alaska Peninsula National Wildlife Refuge 139 C3
Alaska Range 80 D1; 91 D6; 92 B1; 103 D4; 104 C2; 108 D2
Alatna 136 D2
Alatna Hills 136 D2
Alatna River 136 C2
Alava Bay 20 D2
Alava Ridge 20 C2
Alava, Point 20 D2
Albert Channel 49 A5
Albert Creek 60 D5
Albert Creek 95 D6
Albert Creek 127 B5
Albert Creek 137 D5
Albert Ridge 25 C4
Alberto Islands 19 B3
Alder Camp 125 D6
Alder Creek 44 C2
Alder Creek 71 A4
Alder Creek 81 B4
Alder Creek 93 A5
Alder Creek 103 A6
Alder Creek 115 A4
Alder Creek 119 A4
Alder Creek 119 C5

Alder Creek 119 D5
Alder Creek 124 B1
Alder Creek 125 D6
Alder Creek 128 D1
Alder Lake 107 D4
Alder Rock 31 C4
Alder Stream 34 B2
Alecks Creek 23 B3
Alecks Lake 23 B3
Aleknagik 56 C2
Aleknagik Mission LS (Private) 56 C2
Aleknagik SPB 56 C2
Aleknagik, Lake 56 C2
Aleut Point 140 C1
Aleut Village 53 D4
Aleutian Islands 138 D1; 140 A1, C1
Aleutian Range 60 C1; 67 D5; 68 C1
Aleutian Rock 44 C2
Aleutkina Bay 22 A1; 27 D3
Alexander 82 C1
Alexander Creek 82 B1
Alexander Glacier 35 A4
Alexander Island 53 D4
Alexander Lake 28 B1
Alexander, Mount 35 A4
Alexander, Point 24 B1
Alexander, Port 22 D2
Alexanders Village 137 D6
Alexcy Lake 59 A5
Alf Island 44 C2
Alfred Creek 84 A2
Alfred Creek 125 A4
Alger Peak 80 A2
Alice Island 131 A5
Alice Lake 28 C2
Alice Peak 24 D1
Alice Rock 18 A2
Alice, Mount 71 A4
Alice, Port 18 A2
Algo Point 63 B5
Aliksemit Island 139 C5
Alikula Bay 18 A1
Alinchak Bay 43 A4
Alitak Bay 64 C2
Alitak Lagoon 64 C3
Alitak Shoal 64 C2
Alitak SPB 64 B2
Alitak, Cape 64 C2
Aliulik Peninsula 65 B3
All Gold Creek 105 A6
All Hand Help Lake 114 A2
Allah Creek 56 C2
Allakaket 136 D2
Allakaket Chilkat Bald Eagle Preserve 38 C1
Allan Point 27 D3
Allard Creek 123 A4
Allen Airfield LS 114 A4
Allen Creek 115 A4
Allen Creek 130 B3
Allen River 75 A3
Allen River 136 C3
Allen, Mount 99 D4
Alligator Island 59 C2
Allison Creek 85 D5
Alma Lakes 115 B5
Aloha Creek 123 C6
Alpenglow, Mount 71 A4
Alphabet Hills 96 A1
Alpine Cove 44 D2
Alpine Creek 105 D6
Alpine Lake 70 C2
Alsek Glacier 36 D1
*Alsek Ranges** 36 B3
Alsek River 35 D5; 36 D1
Alsek River LS 36 D1
Alta Peak 18 B3
Alta Hills 136 D2
Alatna River 136 C2
Alava, Point 20 D2
Amakatatee Creek* 55 A4
Amakdedori (Site) 60 C1
Amakdedori Creek 60 C1
Amakdedulia Cove 60 D1
Amalik Bay 51 D4
Amalu Lake 56 D1
Amargura, Point 19 C3
Amarilla Point 18 C2
Amatignak Island 141 D3
Amatusuk Hills 134 C2
Amber Bay 43 B5
Amber Lake 93 B5
Ambler 133 A7
Ambler LS 133 A6
Ambler Peak 23 A4
Amber River 133 A7
Amchitka Island 140 D2
Amchitka Pass 141 D3
Amee Bay 45 D3
Amee Island 45 D3
Amelia, Point 26 D2

Amelius Island 23 D4
Amelius, Point 23 D4
American Bay 17 A3
American Creek 51 A3
American Creek 70 B3
American Creek 111 B5
American Creek 119 B6
American Creek 126 C2
American Creek LS 123 D4
American River 132 C3
Amherst Glacier 84 D2
Amherst Peak 33 B4
Amik Island 84 D2
Amiloyak Lake 136 B2
Amilia Pass 140 B1
Amook Bay 44 B2
Amook Bay SPB 44 C2
Amook Island 44 B2
Amos Lakes 92 A1
Amphitheater Knob 34 A3
Amphitheater Mountains 106 D2
Amphitheatre Creek 88 B2
Amukta Island 140 B3
Amukta Pass 140 B3
Amy Creek 75 A5; 87 D5
Amy Creek 125 B4
Amy Dome 125 B4
Anaconda Creek 96 D6
Anaconda Creek 116 A1; 126 D1
Anakruak 135 B7
Anaktuvuk Pass 136 B3
Anaktuvuk Pass LS 136 B2
Anaktuvuk River 136 B3
Anan Bay 25 D3
Anan Creek 25 D3
Anan Creek, East Fork 25 D3
Anan Creek, East Fork 25 D3
Anan Lake 25 D3
Anchor Cove 44 D1
Anchor Cove 64 A1
Anchor Island 17 A4
Anchor Pass 20 A2
Anchor Point 47 A4
Anchor Point 62 A1
Anchor Point 62 A1
Anchor River and Fritz Creek State Critical Habitat Area 62 B1
Anchor River State Recreation Area 62 A1
Anchor River State Recreation Site 62 B1
Anchorage 83 D3
Anchorage Coastal Wildlife Refuge 82 D3
Anchorage International Airport 82 D3
Anchorage Point 38 C1
Ancon Rock 32 C1
Ancon, Point 24 C1
Andersen Creek 19 B4
Anderson 114 C2
Anderson Bay 73 C4
Anderson Creek 82 B1
Anderson Creek 118 A1
Anderson Glacier 85 D4
Anderson Glacier 89 D5
Anderson Mountain 105 A5
Anderson Pass 103 C6
Anderson Peak 71 B4
Anderson Point 20 C1
Anderson, Mount 33 C4
Anderson, Mount 89 D5
Andreafsky River 130 B3
Andreafsky River, East Fork 130 B3
Andreafsky River, West Fork 130 B3
Andreanof Islands 141 D4
Andrew Creek 24 B2
Andrew Creek 41 B5
Andrew Creek, South Fork 24 B2
Andrew Island 24 B2
Andrew Slough 24 B2
Andrew, Mount 19 B4
Andronica Island 139 B4
Andrus Peak 88 C3
Andy Simons Mountain 71 C4
Aneskett Point 23 D4
Angel Creek 126 D2
Angel Lake 19 B4
Angel, The 79 B4
Angle Creek 50 D3
Angoon 27 B4
Angoon SPB 27 B4

Angoyakik Pass 136 A1
*Ashmun, Mount** 37 B5
Asigukpak Spit 46 B2
Asik Mountain 133 A4
Askinuk Mountains 130 C2
Aspen Creek 95 C4
Aspen Lake 70 A2
Aspero Peak 84 C3
Aspid Cape 22 B1
Astley, Point 28 B2
Aston Island 17 A3
Astrolabe Bay 31 C4
Astrolabe Point 31 C4
Astrolabe Rocks 31 C4
Astronomical Point 21 D4
Asumcion, Port 22 C2
Ata-ai-ach Mountain 55 A4
Atahpo Point 130 D2
Atakas Camp 131 C4
Ataku Island 22 A1
Atatayk Mountain 55 A5
Atchuelinguk River 131 B4
Atigaru Point 135 B7
Atigun Pass 136 B4
Atigun River 136 B4
Atka 140 B1
Atka Island 140 B1
Atka Pass 140 B1
Atkins Island 131 A5
Atkulik Island 139 B5
*Atlin Lake** 39 C5
Atmautluak LS 130 D3
Atmo Mountain 43 A4
Atmugiak Creek 55 A4
Atna Peaks 88 A1
Atna Mountain 62 A1
Atna Mountain 103 C6
Atqasuk LS 135 B5
Atrevida Glacier 34 A3; 37 B3
Atsaksovluk Creek 131 D5
Atshichlut Mountain 55 B5
Attu 140 A1
Attu Island 140 A1
Attu Mountain 140 A1
Atuk Mountain 138 A2
Atushagvik, Cape 52 D1
Atutsak River 122 D1
Atwater Creek 109 A5; 119 D5
Audrey, Port 72 C2
Audubon Mountain 85 C4
August Hill 68 D2
Augusta Glacier 36 A2
Augusta, Mount 36 A2
Augusta, Mount 37 B3
Augustana Creek 106 C3
Augustana Glacier 106 C3
Augustine Bay 60 C3
Augustine, Cape 16 A2
Auk Bay 72 D1
Auke Bay 33 C3
Auke Bay 33 C3
Auke Lake 33 C3
Auke Mountain 33 C3
Aurel, Lake 45 B4
Aurora Creek 119 A5
Aurora Glacier 31 B4
Aurora Lagoon 62 B2
Aurora Lodge 116 C1
Aurora Peak 106 B3
Aurora, Point 17 B3
Aurora Spit 62 B2
Automatic Creek 91 C6
Avak River 134 A3
Avalanche Canyon 33 A4
Avalanche Mountain 83 D3
Avalik River 134 B4
Avalitkok Creek 138 A4
Avatanak Island 138 D1
Avatanak Strait 138 D1
Avery River 72 A2
Aviugak Cove 18 C3
Aquadaice Creek 35 A3
Avmulu Creek 44 D2
Avon Island 19 A4
Avoss Lake 22 B1
Awalik Creek 54 D5
Awayak Creek 55 C3
Awayak Lake 55 B3
Awuna River 135 C5; 136 C1
Axel Lind Island 72 A2
Ayakulik 43 D6
Ayakulik River 43 C5; 44 C1
Ayiyak River 136 B2
Aylesworth, Mount 35 A5
Ayugadak Point 140 C2
Azimuth Point 21 C4
Azimuth Point 45 A5
Azun Point 45 C5

B

Babbler Point 24 C4
Babe Island 20 D1
Babel River 79 B3
Babel Tower 79 B4
Baby Basket Hill 101 D5
Baby Glacier 84 D2
Babybasket Hill 101 D5
Bachatna Creek 69 A3
Bachatna Creek, West Fork 69 A4
Bachatna Flats 69 A3
Back Bay 53 D4
Back Island 20 B1
Back Range 60 B1
Backbone Mountain 21 D3
Bacon Creek 23 B5
Bacon Glacier 31 B5
Bactrian Point 21 D3
Badger Hill 62 D1
Badger Lake 21 C3
Bagley Icefield 76 B2
Bagot, Mount 38 C2
Bahovec Peak 23 A4
Baht Harbor 24 C1
Bailey Bay 20 A1
Bailey Creek 123 D4
Bailey Rock 20 C1
Bates Creek 81 A5

Bainbridge Glacier 72 D1
Bainbridge Island 72 D1
Bainbridge Passage 72 D1
Bainbridge Point 72 D1
Bainbridge, Port 62 A3; 72 D1
Bains Cove 24 B1
Baird Canyon 75 B3
Baird Glacier 29 D4
Baird Inlet 130 D2
Baird Island 36 B1
Baird Peak 83 B4
Baird Peak 19 A4
Baird Mountains 133 A6
Baird River 131 A4
Baj Creek 24 D2
Bay Lake 69 C5
Bay of Islands 51 B3
Bay of Isles 72 C2
Bay of Isles, Short Arm 72 C2
Bay of Isles, South Arm 72 C2
Bay of Pillars 23 B3
Bay of Waterfalls 141 D5
Bay Point 28 D3
Bay Point Knoll 28 D3
Bayard, Mount 35 B4
Bazan, Point 17 A3
Bazil, Point 65 A4
Balchen, Mount 106 B3
Bald Head 133 D5
Bald Head Chris Island 72 A2
Bald Hill 61 B3
Bald Ridge 20 D1
Baldry Creek 115 A4
Baldwin Mountain 133 B5
Baldwin Peninsula 133 B4
Baldwin, Mount 89 B3
Baldy Bay 19 D4
Baldy Lake 94 D1
Baldy Mountain 77 A3
Baleful Peak 83 C5
Balika Basin 45 A5
Ballena Islands 19 C3
Baltimore Glacier 84 C2
Ban Island 53 C4
Band Cove 23 A3
Banded Mountain 25 B4
Banks, Point 53 B3
Banks, Port 22 B1
Bar Creek 68 D1
Barabara Cove 45 A4
Barabara Creek 62 C1
Barabara Lake 70 A2
Barabara Point 62 B1
Baranof 27 C3
Baranof Island 22 A2; 27 C3
Baranof Lagoon 27 D3
Baranof River 27 D3
Barbara Point 44 C1
Barbara, Lake 83 C4
Barber, Point 73 A4
Bard Peak 71 B3
Barkley Lake 76 B2
Barkley Ridge 76 C2
Barling Bay 44 D3
Barlow Cove 32 C3
Barlow Islands 32 C3
Barlow Point 32 C3
Barnabas Rock 45 D4
Barnacle Rock 24 D1
Barnard Glacier 84 D2
Barnard, Mount 37 B4
Barnes Creek 72 C2
Barnes Lake 23 B3
Barnes, Mount 26 A1
Barnette Creek 85 A4
Barney Creek 119 A5
Barnhart LS 97 B5
Barnum 54 C2
Barnum Creek 54 C2
Baranof Island 22 A2; 27 C3
Baranof Lake 27 D3
Barren Cove 102 D3
Barren Island 16 D2
Barren Islands 45 A5
Barren Lake 102 B1
Barren Mountain 19 C4
Barren Mountain 68 C3
Barrett Creek 75 D4
Barrie Lake 71 B4
Barrier Creek 21 A3
Barrier Glacier 80 D3
Barrier Islands 17 A4
Barrier Islands 23 D4
Barrier Range 51 D5
Barrille, Mount 93 A5
Barrow 135 A5
Barrow, Point 135 A4
Barry Glacier 71 B3
Barry Lagoon 45 C5
Bart Lake 33 D4
Bartell Creek 98 A1
Barter Island AF LS 137 A7
Bartholf Creek 83 A4
Bartholomew Creek 21 C3
Bartlett Cove 32 C1
Bartlett Cove SPB 32 C1
Bartlett Hills 94 C4
Bartlett Point 27 D4
Bartlett River 32 B1
Bartolome, Cape 18 B2
Barwell Island 64 A1
Basalt Lake 106 D2
Basargin, Mount 24 B2
Basco Creek 122 D3
Bashful Rock 45 D4
Basin Creek 75 C4
Basin Creek 101 C1
Basin Creek LS 132 D3
Basin Lake 20 C2
Basin, The 85 D4
Basket Bay 27 A4
Basket Bay 27 B4
Basket Lake 27 B4
Bass Harbor 72 B3
Bass Lake 20 A1
Bassie, Mount 27 D3
Bat Point 20 B2
Bates Creek 81 A5*

Bates Creek 127 C4
Battery Islets 24 B1
Battle Point 38 D2
Battle Glacier 33 B3
Battle Lake 59 D5
Baturin Lake 22 C2
Batza River 121 A4
Batza Slough 120 A3
Batzulnetas 98 B1
Berry Island 23 A4
Baird Mountain 51 C4
Bautista Peak 19 C3
Bay Creek 71 A3
Bay Lake 69 C5*

Baker 113 A6
Baker Creek 111 D6
Baker Creek 123 D6, D6
Baker Creek, North Fork 123 D5
Baker Glacier 84 D1
Baker Island 18 C2
Baker Lake 123 D6
Baker Lake 18 D2
Baker Memorial LS 133 B5
Baker Point 19 B4
Baker, Mount 26 A1
Bakewell Arm 21 C3
Bakewell Lake 21 D3
Balandra Island 19 C3
Balboa Bay 139 C3
Balchen, Mount 106 B3*

Batzulnetas 98 B1
Berry Camp 127 C4
Berry Creek 105 D5
Berry Island 19 B4
Berry Lake 70 A1
Berry Lake 101 C4
Bert Millar Cutoff 17 B4
Bertha Bay 26 A1
Bertha Creek 71 A4
Bertha Glacier 39 D3
Bertha, Mount 31 B3
Besboro Island 133 D5
Beshta Bay 81 D5
Bess, Lake 84 B3
Bessie Creek 54 B1
Bessie Peak 24 C4
Besivit Lake 120 B1
Beth, Lake 82 C3
Bethel 131 D4
Bethel SPB 131 D4
Bettles 136 D2
Bettles Bay 71 A4
Bettles Bay State Marine Park 72 A1
Bettles Glacier 72 A1
Bettles Icefield 72 D2
Bettles Lake 45 A4
Bettles SPB 136 D3
Betton Head 20 B1
Betton Island 20 B1
Betton Point 20 B1
Betty Lake 22 C2
Beverley, Lake 56 B2
Beverley, Lake—Silver Horn 56 B2
Beverly Creek 118 A1; 128 D1*

Biali Rock 19 C3
Bidarka Point 17 A4
Biederman Bluff 128 C3
Bieli Rocks 27 C2
Big Alinchak Bay 43 A4
Big Alinchak Creek 43 A4
Big Bay 22 A1
Big Bay 53 B4
Big Bay 70 D1
Big Bear/Baby Bear Bays State Marine Park 27 B2
Big Bend 110 A3
Big Bend 111 A4
Big Bend Lakes 88 D3
Big Boulder Creek 87 B5
Big Boulder Creek 119 A6
Big Branch Bay 22 C2
Big Castle Island 24 B1
Big Chief Mountain 26 A1
Big Chutes 60 A1
Big Creek 19 D4
Big Creek 23 C4; 28 D2
Big Creek 23 C4
Big Creek 42 B2
Big Creek 49 C5
Big Creek 104 B1
Big Creek 110 A2, B2
Big Creek 109 A6
Big Creek 127 B6
Big Creek 125 A1; 137 D6
Big Creek 127 A5
Big Creek 135 D6
Big Creek 137 D1
Big Creek 121 A5
Big Creek 121 A5
Big Creek 125 A4
Big Creek 125 D6
Big Creek 127 B4
Big Creek 127 C4
Big Creek 125 A4
Big Creek 127 C4
Big Creek 128 D2
Big Creek 128 D2
Big Creek 132 D3
Big Creek No 1 LS 133
Big Delta 116 D3
Big Delta State Historical Park 116 D3
Big Denver Creek 123 D5
Big Diomede Island (Russia) 132 C1
Big Eldorado Creek 116 A5
Big Flat 49 B5
Big Fort Channel 53 C5
Big Fort Island 53 C5
Big Goat Lake 21 B3
Big Granite Creek 117 B4
Big Grayling Lake 88 B2
Big Grizzly Creek 105 B5
Big Hazy Inlet 18 D1
Big Hill 60 C1
Big Horn 115 B6
Big Indian Creek 70 A3
Big Island 26 C2
Big Island 52 B3
Big Island 110 B1
Big Joe Creek 110 B2
Big John Bay 23 A4
Big John Lake 109 D4
Big Kitoi Lake 53 D5
Big Koniugi Island 139 C4
Big Lake 19 A4
Big Lake 20 C2
Big Lake 82 B3
Big Lake 82 B3
Big Lake 95 A4; 105 D4
Big Lake 102 B1
Big Lake 105 D4
Big Lake 109 D4
Big Lake 114 A2
Big Lake 136 A1
Big Lake 136 B3
Big Lake North State Recreation Site 82 B3
Big Lake South State Recreation Site 82 B3
Big Lily Lake 102 A3
Big Long Lake 102 B2
Big Mosquito Creek 127 B5
Big Mountain 59 C4
Big Mountain 69 A4
Big Mountain LS (Private) 59 C4
Big Mud River 111 B6; 112 C1
Big Port Walter 22 C2
Big River 36 D1
Big River 52 B1, B2
Big River 59 A4; 90 B3, C3
Big River 79 A4
Big River, Lyman Fork 79 A4
Big River, North Fork 68 A3
Big River, North Fork 79 A3; 91 D4
Big River, South Fork 68 B3
Big River Roadhouse 90 A2
Big Rock 53 B4
Big Rock 60 B3

Index continues on next page

INDEX, cont'd

Index continues on next page

Index continues on next page

153

Index continues on next page

156